Time Out

VOLUME 1
LONDON
WALKS

30 WALKS BY
LONDON WRITERS

Time Out Guides Limited
Universal House
251 Tottenham Court Road
London W1T 7AB
Tel + 44 (0)20 7813 3000
Fax + 44 (0)20 7813 6001
Email guides@timeout.com
www.timeout.com

Senior Designer Oliver Knight
Junior Designer Chrissy Mouncey
Digital Imaging Dan Conway

Picture Desk
Picture Editor Jael Marschner
Deputy Picture Editor Tracey Kerrigan
Picture Researchers Monica Roche, Helen McFarland

Editorial
Editor Sarah Guy
Deputy Editors Adam Barnes, Simon Cropper
Listings Checker Cathy Limb
Researchers Helen Babbs, Adam Barnes, Catherine Blake,
Christopher Blake, Christina Dee, Jan Fuscoe, Tess
Goldenberg, Kate Lawrence, Amy Nelson, Rob Norman,
Holly Pick, Helen Scott, Alan Simeoni, Zoe Strimpel
Indexer Jonathan Cox

Editorial/Managing Director Peter Fiennes
Series Editor Sarah Guy
Deputy Series Editor Cath Phillips
Business Manager Gareth Garner
Guides Co-ordinator Holly Pick
Accountant Kemi Olufuwa

Design
Art Director Scott Moore
Art Editor Tracey Ridgewell

Marketing
Marketing Director Mandy Martinez
Marketing & Publicity Manager, US Rosella Albanese

Production
Production Director Mark Lamond

Time Out Group
Chairman Tony Elliott
Managing Director Mike Hardwick
Group Financial Director Richard Waterlow
Group Commercial Director Lesley Gill
Group Marketing Director John Luck
Group General Manager Nichola Coulthard
Group Circulation Director Jim Heinemann
Group Art Director John Oakey
Online Managing Director David Pepper
Group Production Director Steve Proctor
Group IT Director Simon Chappell

Maps JS Graphics (john@jsgraphics.co.uk).

Photography pages 3, 36, 44, 45, 49, 60, 72, 75, 81, 99, 111, 124, 157, 159, 247 Mockford & Bonetti; pages 4, 5, 20, 25, 26, 27, 43, 52, 74, 82, 88, 89, 90, 91, 93, 96, 97, 98, 120, 127, 131, 134, 140, 143, 150, 151, 172, 185, 186, 189, 192, 195, 196, 199, 202, 203, 204, 220, 221, 224, 225, 248, 251, 257, 258, 259, 275, 283 Jonathan Perugia; pages 10, 14 Paul Mattson; pages 13, 16, 77 Gordon Rainsford; pages 32, 53, 67, 70, 71, 85, 123, 125, 130, 132, 133, 146, 152, 162, 164, 189, 196, 218, 237, 241, 243, 278, 281, 292 Matt Carr; pages 35, 89 Sarah Blee; pages 37, 65, 105, 106, 114, 137, 141, 158, 161, 165, 259 Hadley Kincade; pages 38, 47, 184 Francesca Yorke; pages 55, 174, 238 Alys Tomlinson; pages 56, 101, 218, 236 Amanda C Edwards; page 67 James Winspear; pages 148/149 Georgie Scott; page 149 Britta Jaschinski; page 166 Heloise Bergman; pages 176, 177, 228 Dominic Dibbs; pages 178, 179, 226 Andrew Brackenbury; pages 211, 214, 217, 218, 219 Thomas Pakenham; page 235 Barry J Holmes; pages 253, 256 Fabienne Fossez; pages 260, 267, 268, 271 Lukas Birk; page 272 Camera Press; pages 285, 291 the Art Archives; page 292 Rob Greig.
The following image was provided by the featured establishment: page 63.

The Editor would like to thank Andrew White for editing the first two editions of the guide.

Published by Time Out Guides Ltd, a wholly owned subsidiary of Time Out Group Ltd.
Time Out and the Time Out logo are trademarks of Time Out Group Ltd.

© Time Out Group Ltd 2005
Previous editions 1998, 2002.

10 9 8 7 6 5 4 3 2 1

This edition first published in Great Britain in 2005 by Ebury
Ebury is a division of The Random House Group Ltd,
20 Vauxhall Bridge Road, London SW1V 2SA

Random House Australia Pty Limited, 20 Alfred Street, Milsons Point, Sydney, New South Wales 2061, Australia

Random House New Zealand Limited, 18 Poland Road, Glenfield, Auckland 10, New Zealand

Random House South Africa (Pty) Limited, Endulini, 5A Jubilee Road, Parktown 2193, South Africa

Random House UK Limited Reg. No. 954009

Distributed in USA by Publishers Group West
1700 Fourth Street, Berkeley, California 94710

Distributed in Canada by Penguin Canada Ltd
10 Alcorn Avenue, Toronto, Ontario, Canada M4V 3B2

For further distribution details, see www.timeout.com

ISBN 1-904978-86-X

A CIP catalogue record for this book is available from the British Library

Colour reprographics by Icon, Crowne House, 56-58 Southwark Street, London SE1 1UN

Printed and bound in Germany by Appl
Papers used by Ebury Press are natural, recyclable products made from wood grown in sustainable forests

Contents

Contents

About the guide

We strongly recommend that you read the entire text of any walk before setting out. Not only should this whet your appetite and give an overview of the journey ahead, it will also help you to plan stopping-off points according to opening times provided in the listings. Indeed, for the longer walks, it'll give you a chance to plan at which point you want to abandon the walk and stagger to the nearest pub.

In the interests of not interfering with the flow of the prose, we have avoided endless directions in the text. The text and the maps should be used alongside each other, so if one seems unclear, consult the other. That said, every one of the routes has been walked and scrupulously checked at least twice, so we hope you'll find it very hard to get lost…

Maps

The route is marked in red. Two thin red lines indicate that at some point you will be required to retrace your steps. Short diversions from the main route are also indicated. The dotted lines mark suggested routes to the start and from the finish of the walk (for public transport); the upright dashes are alternative routes suggested by the writer. Some, but not all, of the sites highlighted in the walk are marked on the maps.

Distance

The distances given are to the nearest half-mile or half-kilometre.

Time

The timing of the walks obviously depends on the speed of the walker, and the length and frequency of stops. The times given are therefore approximate, and assume that there are no lengthy stops en route (though of course these are highly recommended), and that a healthy pace is maintained.

Notes

These are largely self explanatory and merely aim to help the walker plan the timing of the walk, and forewarn them of any peculiar features.

Listings

All listings included are on the routes, whether they are mentioned in the text or not (the only exceptions are the pubs for the Hampstead Heath walks). We have included virtually every pub, restaurant, shop, museum, gallery, church, park and relevant organisation mentioned in the text that is open to the public, and occasionally some more besides. They are arranged by category and alphabetically, not following the chronology of the walk. The details were all accurate at time of writing.

For the eating and drinking sections, we have, where relevant, given a brief description of the type of food served. The fuller descriptions are for those venues that are also reviewed in Time Out's *Pubs & Bars* or *Eating & Drinking* guides. In some cases we have added venues that are on the route (but not mentioned in the text), and are also recommended by Time Out's guides. All the remaining listings are taken from the text, and are divided, sometimes somewhat crudely, into categories. The 'Other' and 'Information' categories list some organisations that readers might wish to contact should the walk inspire further investigation.

Disabled

Two of the walks (**Museum piece** and **Freewheeling**) are by William Forrester, a wheelchair user. **Freewheeling** outlines a route in one of the most wheelchair-friendly parts of London.

Further information can be found in *Access In London* by Gordon Couch, William Forrester and David McGaughey (Bloomsbury, 2003). Admirably comprehensive, it is written and researched by a team of able-bodied and disabled people and includes detailed maps of step-free routes and accessible tube stations. The guide is available at some bookshops, or free of charge (although a £10 donation is appreciated) from Access Project, 39 Bradley Gardens, W13 8HE (www.accessproject-phsp. org). Alternatively, contact William Forrester, 1 Belvedere Close, Guildford, Surrey GU2 6NP (01483 575401). London Transport also publishes a booklet, *Access to the Underground*, available from ticket offices or from LT's Unit for Disabled Passengers (172 Buckingham Palace Road, SW1 9TN; 7222 5600; www.tfl.gov.uk) and at LT Travel Information Centres.

Introduction

London remains one of the world's great cities; and the best way to get to know the whole sprawling mess – its vivid history and current vitality – is by walking the streets. In 1998 Time Out published the first edition of this collection of London walks; we are now publishing the third edition. All the walks have been fully revised and updated to take account of the changes that have swept the capital – all the routes have been walked again, the text rewritten where appropriate and the listings checked. And since in the meantime we have also published an entirely new Time Out collection of walks around the capital – *London Walks, Volume 2* (£11.99 in all good bookstores) – we have renamed this collection Volume 1.

Those of you familiar with the series will be aware that our idea of a walks book is different from most others'. We aren't just concerned with historic buildings and blue plaques – although they certainly have their place – we also want to capture the living city from a number of different perspectives. So we've collected together a group of novelists, historians, comedians, cartoonists and journalists who have devised their own walks through London, drawing on historical, architectural and personal observation. We not only learn about the city's past and present, but also what delights and irritates the writers.

John Vidal trudges 29 miles along the side of the Thames, giving a passionate critique of soulless developments and sensitive regeneration from the Thames Barrier to Hampton Court. Margaret Forster lets us in on her regular walk around Hampstead Heath; Kate Kellaway makes a nostalgic return to her childhood in Kentish Town and Hampstead; and Irma Kurtz rediscovers the monied pavements of Knightsbridge and Kensington.

Several of the walks carry a theme. Dr Ruth Richardson sets off on the trail of bodysnatchers, Dan Cruickshank passes an architectural eye over the City, Yvonne Roberts contrasts the class-conscious commons of Clapham and Wandsworth, Graham Norton takes us to the gay bars and clubs of Soho and Lucinda Lambton leaps from grave to grave in Kensal Green Cemetery.

In all, there are 30 walks, offering a mix of styles, outlooks and settings. From ancient woodland to modern skyscrapers, motorway underpasses to stately homes, most parts of the metropolis are subjected to the scrutiny of the writers. The end result is a book that can be read with pleasure at home, as a collection of writing about London, and (above all) used as a practical and thought-provoking guide to a series of walks through the capital.

And if, as I have, you retrace all the walks, clocking up over 150 miles in the process, you discover parts of the city you never even knew existed, and begin to understand how a city evolves and mutates from day to day. Your gaze wanders above the shop fronts, down alleys and through net curtains; modern monstrosities earn grudging admiration, anonymous patches of green reveal a colourful history; and the people no longer clog up the city, but enliven it.

Dr Johnson (who else) once remarked 'By seeing London, I have seen as much of life as the world can show.' Overstated, perhaps. But it's not a bad place to start.
Andrew White

Stepping out

Graham Norton

A stroll around gay Soho and Bloomsbury, taking in bars, clubs,
shops, a live sex show and a couple of churches, before climaxing
in the spawning grounds of Russell Square.

> **Start:** Piccadilly Circus tube
> **Finish:** Russell Square
> **Distance:** 2.5 miles/4km
> **Time:** 1.5 hours
> **Getting there:** Bakerloo or
> Piccadilly line to Piccadilly Circus
> **Getting back:** short walk to
> Russell Square tube (Piccadilly
> line). A lively night-time walk.
> Shops and cafés change regularly.

London isn't the most tolerant city on the planet. The proliferation of obvious gay and lesbian landmarks all around the capital is because so many gay men and lesbians have now made London their home that the bigots can't shout at us every time they see us in the street, or throw a brick through every gay bar window. They simply don't have the time. Instead I imagine them staying at home indulging in some armchair queer-bashing, leaving us to drink our lager and fancy coffees, to kiss and to cruise wherever we want. Any corner of London now has a gay bar or two, but the walk I've chosen centres on the heart of modern gay London, which is Soho, but also takes in some of the quieter, prettier streets and squares – they're historical as well, obviously, but we are a shallow people so pretty is best.

Piccadilly Circus is where high art and culture meet the street. The sophistication of Piccadilly and Regent Street meets the plastic pop world of Leicester Square. Out of the tube station take the Lower Regent Street/Eros exit (by subway 3). You'll

have plenty of time to find it because you'll be trapped behind a large group of Italian students. Above ground, the naked figure of Eros, with his arrow, stands over an area that (and I'm no size queen) is smaller than you expect it to be. Less Times Square, more Village Green. But few village greens will have seen the staggering number of prostitutes that have made this area notorious. Rent boys were plying their trade here long before the arrival of Eros. In the 18th century 'Mollies', as male prostitutes were known, were as common in this area as the 'Marjories' and 'Mary Annes', the male prostitutes of the early and late 19th century. Nowadays they don't seem as prevalent; or maybe it's just that I'm distracted by all those Italian students. The statue was supposed to be a Christian angel of charity, but the sculptor, Sir Alfred Gilbert, perhaps inspired by the location's reputation, went for the raunch fest instead.

Across the Circus is what's left of the London Pavilion, a theatre and music hall that was a notorious pick-up joint in the 1880s. Now it's home to a lot of shops that you see at airports and never really needed to see again. Behind you is the glittering world of the Criterion. The restaurant is overseen by the famous Marco Pierre White and therefore rather pricey, but you must check out the interior – a blaze of golden mosaic. The theatre also has a wonderful tiled interior and back in the 1960s was the West End home of Joe Orton's *Loot* and more recently had Kevin Elyot's wonderful gay play *My Night with Reg*, which was later filmed.

Other obvious sights before we move off are Lillywhite's, a large sports shop, which doesn't have any obvious appeal except that lesbians might want to loiter in the tennis and golf departments while the men might browse in swimwear.

Bidding farewell to the Italian boys, head towards Burger King and Boot's, which sounds like a seedy leather bar but you'll see what I mean. Take a right when you reach them and curve around into Shaftesbury Avenue. Ahead you'll see various theatre awnings, for this really is London's West End. Be very

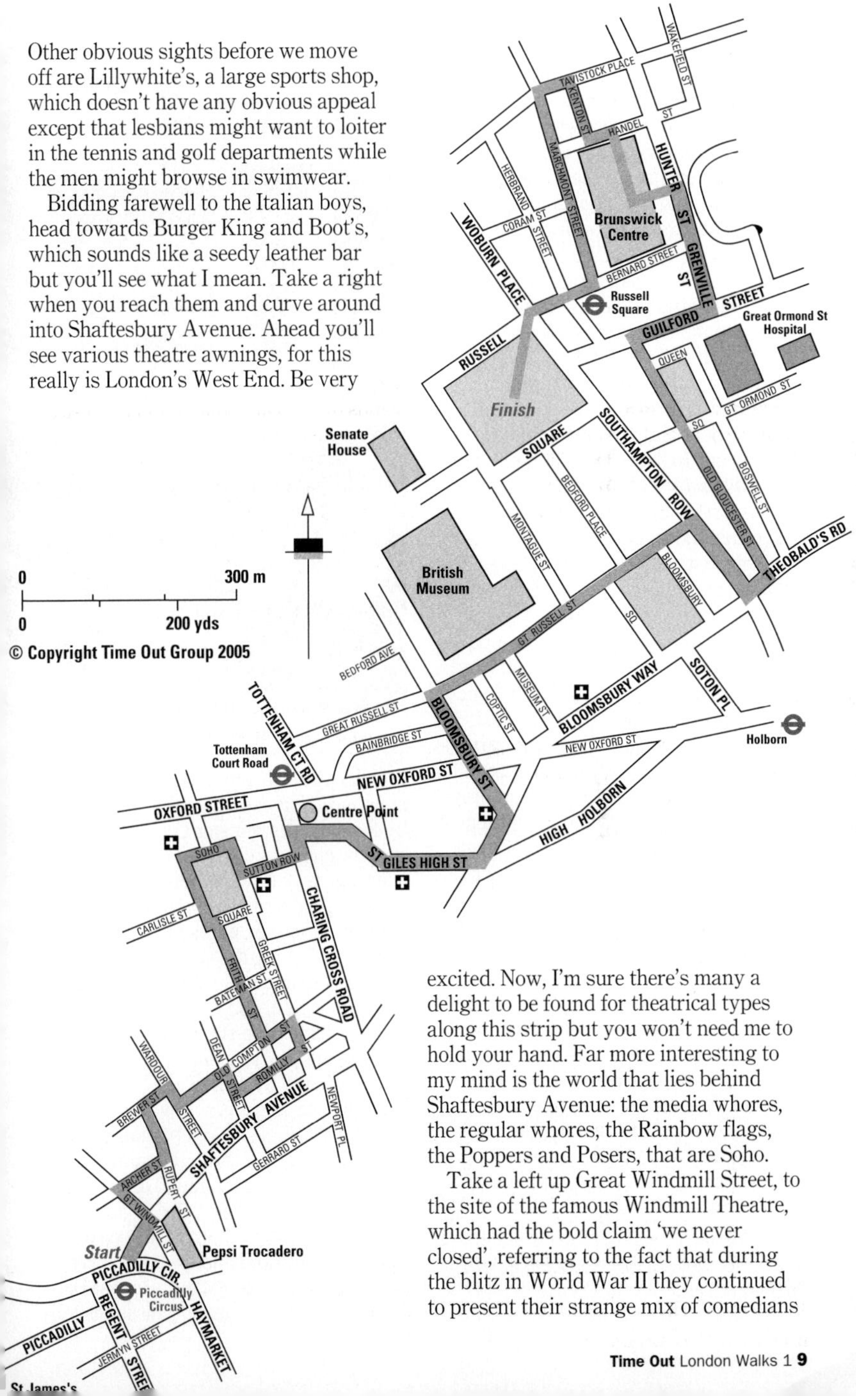

0   300 m

0   200 yds

© Copyright Time Out Group 2005

excited. Now, I'm sure there's many a delight to be found for theatrical types along this strip but you won't need me to hold your hand. Far more interesting to my mind is the world that lies behind Shaftesbury Avenue: the media whores, the regular whores, the Rainbow flags, the Poppers and Posers, that are Soho.

Take a left up Great Windmill Street, to the site of the famous Windmill Theatre, which had the bold claim 'we never closed', referring to the fact that during the blitz in World War II they continued to present their strange mix of comedians and naked women. Nowadays it's the modern equivalent, minus the comedy: a table-dancing club. On the right we pass the first of quite a few stage doors we'll see. This one belongs to the Lyric.

Take a right into Archer Street and oh look! Joy and jubilation, much clapping of hands: it's our first gay bar. This one is called Barcode and is one of the least daunting of the new breed of gay bars. The interior gives a nod to what passes for modern design but you can still tell the difference between one of the bar stools and a lighting fixture. Now tear your hand from the door and your eyes from the window and look around. Archer Street is like a *Reader's Digest* tour of Soho. So, one street has a gay bar and, on the corner, the stage door of the Apollo; but look, just near Barcode sits a sex shop. Happily, attempts to sanitise Soho haven't been completely successful.

A couple of doors have ads for models upstairs, which, for fear you think Kate Moss is having open house in her London pad, means that there are prostitutes available. A word here about the various signs you'll see advertising 'Live Sex Shows'. Don't go! After a couple of drinks – well, maybe more than that – a friend and I decided to go and see one of these shows. As a way of sobering up it was a great deal more effective than black coffee. First of all, the price of the drinks is roughly equivalent to the national debt of a small African republic, but this seemed almost reasonable compared to the show. A couple of women from Leeds who had been huddled around a gas fire drinking tea made their way to a single divan bed placed in the middle of the room. Only the lights making their nylon slips glisten a bit added a note of glamour and excitement. They lay down and some man was pushed from the back room. He had the air of a man who had lost a bet or pulled the shortest straw. He put his knee on the divan and that was the end of the show. This sounds unlikely but I

Berwick Street Market

promise that I've omitted no detail. An announcement explained that the strict by-laws of Westminster Council meant that the show couldn't be more explicit. In a strange way it was a relief, because both of us felt badly about exploiting the poor workers in the sex industry, when in fact they were having the last laugh. It's as if we were being punished for our low-rent lust – and rightly so.

If you have been standing in the street reading this story, a small crowd will have gathered by now. Keep moving.

At the end of Archer Street turn left into Rupert Street. You'll probably be winding your way through market stalls. These won't prove too much of a distraction, as they are piled high with cut-price junk and, though the idea of market traders and barrow boys is very erotic, the reality is usually a bit too Bob Hoskins-like for my taste. This is the tail end of Berwick Market where Marc Bolan used to help his mum on their family stall.

On your right, at the corner of Winnett Street, is another of the trendy new breed of gay bars. It's called Rupert Street because it's on Rupert Street and gay people are very imaginative. This place is designed within an inch of its life, and is so up-to-the-minute that it became dated before it even opened. However, it's always packed so what do I know? Nearly opposite and easy to miss is the entrance to the Yard at No.57. A little alley leads down to a courtyard with two bars. The one upstairs is the closest I've ever got to visiting a loft, while downstairs is best and busiest in the summer. Right at the top of the street where it meets Brewer Street is Prowler, our very own gay department store. Don't get too excited: I mean, how many departments can there be? Videos, magazines and skimpy T-shirts for the disco bunnies.

Across Brewer Street is the famous Madame Jo Jo's. This is essentially a drag bar that puts on shows in a faded velvet setting. I've never been a big fan, as, whenever I've been, it's always been full of businessmen with their secretaries/ mistresses, who've come to stare at the transvestite waitresses, in a sort of gay zoo way. I hear they filmed scenes here for *Eyes Wide Shut*, the Tom Cruise and Nicole Kidman movie. I'll let you decide for yourselves whether that should be a stop on a gay tour of Soho.

Next to Jo Jo's is Escape, another gay drinking hole that occasionally features live music. It's all right as these places go, but I loved it so much more as the Piano Bar. This was a late-night drinking hole where chorus boys, rent boys, waiters finishing their shifts, and older men working their way through all the others would sip warm beer and weak cocktails while watching a strange mixture of drag queens and people from West End musicals ritually slaughter classic songs. Bliss. Before heading on, fans of glam rock might be interested to know that

David Bowie had his first paid gig at a wedding reception at 10 Brewer Street.

Take a right along Brewer Street. You'll pass the back entrance (I'm saying nothing) of Village on your right. This was the first bar to really change the gay scene in London. There were clear glass windows, it was nicely decorated. This bar was assuming acceptance and tolerance in a way the normal bars – blacked-out windows and sticky carpets – weren't. It seems such a small thing now but it was a tremendous step forward to get away from the self-imposed shame of the old-style bars. Brewer Street hits Wardour Street and across the road to your left is the Freedom Bar. Part owned by Marc Almond, this is by far the closest thing to a fashion victim graveyard you'll ever see in daylight. Still, if that's your bag, there it is.

Cross Wardour Street veering slightly to the right and you'll end up in Old Compton Street. This is Soho's main street and despite not being very long manages to satisfy practically every gay need. There are quite a few gay bars, including: Comptons, which until the mid 1980s was the only gay bar in the area; Balans, a late night, reasonably priced gay café/bar; Outlet, a gay accommodation agency; Clone Zone, the gay sex shop; and on and on. Explore at will. The most famous gay bar on this strip is the Admiral Duncan, where a bomb exploded one Friday evening in 1999, killing two and injuring several. The solo perpetrator was conducting a vicious hate campaign against gays and ethnic minorities (bombs also went off in Brixton and Brick Lane), but also succeeded in killing whites and straight people. He obviously failed to understand that, happily, the various communities in London can and do mix. There is a memorial to the tragedy inside the pub.

The first cross street you come to is Dean Street. The corner here was the site of a failed venture – a gay peep show. Presumably it didn't work because we weren't willing to pay for something that's basically available for free in public toilets.

Across Dean Street to your left is the media mecca that is the Groucho Club. Turn right down Dean Street and then take a left into Romilly Street. On the corner is a pub called the Golden Lion. This is where the serial killer Dennis Nilson picked up several of his rent boy victims. Oddly it's not gay any more. I imagine that a customer killing the rest of your clientele can't be very good for business. Continue down Romilly Street across Frith Street until you see Kettners restaurant on your left. Nowadays this is a pizza place, but there are still hints of its former grandeur. In October 1892 Oscar Wilde hosted a dinner here for a group of young men who weren't quite rent boys but at the same time knew how to say thank you for dinner.

Take a left up Greek Street, past the coffee-and-cake haven of old-style Soho Maison Bertaux, and turn left into Old Compton Street. Opposite the Prince Edward Theatre looms large. Why mention that on a gay tour, you might ask. Well, because *Evita* premièred here and Madonna was in the movie. OK? Almost next to the theatre is the Old Compton Café. This seems to be open nearly 24 hours, and for each and every one of those hours the tables seem populated by men with designer bodies squeezed into designer clothes. My question is how? Don't they have jobs? When do they find the time to go to the gym? How did they get that tanned sitting on Old Compton Street? If there was a gay version of the *X Files*, this café would be an episode.

Turn right into Frith Street and head towards Soho Square. Along the way you'll pass the Bohemian nirvana that is Bar Italia. Like everything in this city that Londoners really enjoy, it reminds us of being abroad. Interestingly this building is also where John Logie Baird demonstrated television for the very first time in 1926. Forget all the jazz greats that must have appeared at the famous Ronnie Scott's jazz club just behind you, and give up a silent prayer of thanks for everything from *Here's Lucy* to *Absolutely Fabulous*.

Frith Street leads you into Soho Square. Now if you're wondering what's gay about this place, just come here during the summer and see all the bike messengers with their shirts off. It's like a Bruce Weber wet dream. However, be warned – with most bike messengers, it's a case of admiring their package, but don't expect them to deliver.

Walking around the square to the left you'll reach the Edge on the north side. This is another gay bar but spread over three floors and with a later licence – so they can serve after 11pm. Odd to see such wanton indulgence right next door to the Hari-Krishna Restaurant (Govinda's). Peering up Soho Street you can see Oxford Street. My advice is to avoid it. It's full of amateur shoppers and people with huge placards that have been advertising a golf sale since the beginning of time.

If you like history, you can take a little detour now. Number 19 Cleveland Street (which runs parallel to Tottenham Court Road) was the site of a notorious male brothel, where Queen Victoria's grandson and Heir Presumptive to the throne, Prince Eddie, along with quite a few other members of the aristocracy, got involved in a sex scandal in the 1880s. In one of those odd loops of history and walks, Prince Eddie's tomb was designed by Sir Alfred Gilbert, the man that made Eros of Piccadilly Circus.

If this detour doesn't appeal, simply continue around the square taking a left down Sutton Row as you reach the red-brick holiness of St Patrick's Church. On the corner of Sutton Row and Charing Cross Road is the London Astoria. This is home not just to straight music events, but also massive gay parties. Any of the gay bars that we've passed will have stacks of free gay papers and magazines to let you know what's going on. Charing Cross Road is still bookshop central and the bigger ones such as Foyles and Borders

Old Compton Street

OLD COMPTON STREET W1

CITY OF WESTMINSTER

have fairly good gay and lesbian sections. Directly opposite you is the Centre Point, still the tallest building in central London. It is not a gay thing. Over to your left you can see the imposing front of the Dominion Theatre. This is where David Cassidy took over from Cliff Richard in the superb musical *Time*. This, to my mind, is enough to get it mentioned on any gay walk.

Cross Charing Cross Road and head down Andrew Borde Street to the right of Centre Point. Follow this round to the right. On the corner is First Out. This gay coffee shop opened in the mid 1980s and was something of a revolution. It was somewhere to meet, chat, cruise and eat that appealed equally to lesbians and gay men. Since then it's really only the Freedom Bar on Wardour Street that has managed to emulate this achievement, but there, it seems to me, fashion is a greater bonding agent than sexuality. Wind around St Giles High Street until you see the Shaftesbury Theatre in front of you. When it was the temporary home for the Royal Opera House it appealed to

a certain sort of queen, but as the theatre that housed the West End productions of *M Butterfly*, *Follies*, *Kiss of the Spiderwoman* and *Carousel*, it appeals to another type. Directly across from the theatre is the Oasis Sports Centre. This is open to non-members and has an outdoor pool, which in the summer sees more tragedy and comedy than the Shaftesbury Theatre ever will.

Follow the bend to the left and walk up to New Oxford Street, just marvelling at the continuing existence of James Smith & Sons on the right, a beautiful old emporium of umbrellas and walking sticks. Cross over and continue up Bloomsbury Street until you reach Great Russell Street. You might be smelling large quantities of cheap cologne around here. Look to your left. See that large grey modern building? Well, that's the YMCA. A cliché with an address. If you fancy, you could keep going up Bloomsbury Street until it turns into Gower Street. Then along the right-hand side you'll find the Royal Academy of Dramatic

Art (RADA). So many stars have walked through the doors it's silly to start naming them, but with Joan Collins, Maggie Smith and Joe Orton among them, you can understand the appeal.

If you don't fancy the detour, just turn right down Great Russell Street. This street is all about the British Museum. Not to visit the museum seems perverse, given the amount of cool stuff we've managed to nick from the rest of the world – the problem is it's just too big. It's got everything from the dawn of man to the present day and sadly that's about how long it takes to see it all. My advice is to go in with a Christmas Eve shopping attitude. Move fast and only stop when something really catches your eye. The effect of the Great Court scheme is that the whole museum is now an exhibit in itself. Just one more thing you'll have to look at.

Great Russell Street leads into Bloomsbury Square. Number 20 is where Gertrude Stein spent a winter with her brother Leo in 1902, recovering from an unhappy lesbian *ménage à trois*. If you glance to your left down Bedford Place, you can understand why we make so many costume dramas in this country – the sets are so cheap. Keep walking, cross Southampton Row and take a right. At the traffic lights take a left down Theobald's Road, past Central St Martin's College of Art and Design (hang around for long enough and you're sure to see a few) and the Cochrane Theatre where Orton's *Loot* was produced in 1966. This was the production that later transferred to the Criterion.

Take a left up Old Gloucester Street: a quirky little street full of odd houses and little bits of green. At No.24 you'll find the peaceful and intriguing October Gallery. How your friends will snigger when they see the name of the square I've brought you to: Queen Square. Apart from the name there isn't really anything specifically gay about this place, but it's very pretty and has quite a few hospitals around it so the chances of bumping into

a nice male nurse must be quite high. And though I don't like stereotyping I'd be very surprised if Mary Ward House, home of a women studies group and a vegetarian café, doesn't have a few lesbians in attendance.

Walking straight up the left side of the square you pass St George the Martyr Church, which is wonderfully un-English-looking. Built in 1706 it became known as the Sweeps' Church, because they gave free Christmas lunches to the young sweeps. Similarly the little pub called the Queen's Larder has a very tenuous gay connection. It dates back to 1710 when the tavern was used by Queen Charlotte to store delicacies for her ill husband, King George III, who was staying with his doctor in Queen Square. In the movie *The Madness of King George*, the part of George was played by Nigel Hawthorne, an out actor. I warned you it was tenuous. At 3 Queen Square are the publishers Faber & Faber, and, rather like RADA, this door must have seen quite a bit of celebrity action over the years.

Taking either of the alley exits at the top of the square, you'll emerge into Guilford Street. Take a right. This pleasant tree-lined street is filled with lovely Georgian houses, which sadly are now a bit run down and split into flats. What's remarkable is the absence of blue plaques. I can't help but think that whoever occupied such homes must have been famous or achieved something.

At Grenville Street take a left. This comes out into Brunswick Square. Numbers 27 and 26 (no longer standing) were home to the queer novelist EM Forster for 15 years. He's probably most famous for creating *A Room with a View* and Helena Bonham Carter's career. These days the square is dominated by the Brunswick Centre, a huge local authority housing development. To get a real feel for it you need to go inside. Climb up the steps that go past the Renoir cinema. This is an arthouse cinema and the first clue that this is no normal housing estate. Trendy noodle bars sit next to classic greasy spoon cafés. Low rents and the fantastic central location mean that the people who live here are a real mixture. Wander through the main concourse – there are a couple of supermarkets if you need to stock up. Ahead you'll see the Territorial Army Centre. Go down the steps into Handel Street, ignoring all the attractive young men with short hair – they're probably from the army. Go left, then right along Kenton Street, left into Tavistock and left again almost immediately into Marchmont Street. This is a sweet community street, with a dry-cleaner, a post office, a hairdresser and, at No.66, London's best gay bookshop, Gay's the Word. The staff here are amazingly knowledgeable and despite the small space they stock a huge range of titles. At the bottom of Marchmont Street take a right into Bernard Street, walk past the tube and on to the last point of our walk, Russell Square.

This square is notorious as a gay cruising area, which comes alive at night after the pubs shut. Alan Hollinghurst, in his book *The Swimming Pool Library*, pays full homage to the area. As you might imagine, local residents aren't that thrilled and Camden Council has tried everything – lights, chopping down all the shrubbery, they are even planning to put up big gates.

Of course, what they fail to realise is that none of this will be effective. Gay men are like salmon – we must return to where we've spawned before. Maybe we're our own worst enemies; certainly, the very last point of interest concerns a man who was his own. Bedford Way leads out of the north of the square and it was at No.31, the former home of a Rev Stewart Hedlam, that Oscar Wilde spent his last few hours in England on 19 May 1897. It was from this house that he left for Victoria Station to catch the boat train for Dieppe. Sorry to finish on a rather depressing note, but perhaps it is fitting since Oscar Wilde's story reminds us just how much has changed for gay men and lesbians living in this city, while also reminding us how much still needs to change.

Eating & drinking

Admiral Duncan
54 Old Compton Street, W1D 4UD (7437 5300). **Open** noon-11pm Mon-Sat; noon-10.30pm Sun. Cheaper pints than in many gay bars, and a livelier, younger scene than before the homophobic attack.

Balans Café
34 Old Compton Street, W1D 4TS (7439 3309/ www.balans.co.uk). **Open** 24 hours daily. Breakfast around the clock and sandwiches galore.

Balans Restaurant
60 Old Compton Street, W1D 4UG (7437 5212/ www.balans.co.uk). **Meals served** 8am-5am Mon-Thur; 8am-6am Fri, Sat; 8am-2am Sun. A big, stylish bar/restaurant in three parts.

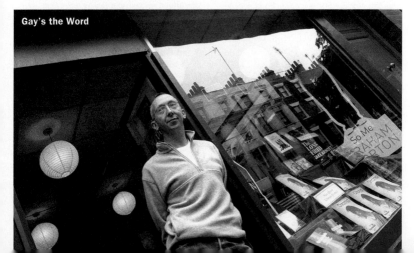

Gay's the Word

Barcode

3-4 Archer Street, W1D 7AP (7734 3342/www.bar-code.co.uk). **Open** 4pm-1am Mon-Sat; 4-10.30pm Sun. **Admission** £3 after 11pm Fri, Sat. One of the more rough-edged gay bars, but not unwelcoming.

Bar Italia

22 Frith Street, W1V 5PS (7437 4520/www.bar italiasoho.co.uk). **Open** 24hrs Mon-Sat; 7am-4am Sun. Mammoth paninis and Italian coffee, available all night long at *the* place for people-watching.

Comptons of Soho

51-53 Old Compton Street, W1D 6HJ (7479 7961/ www.comptons-of-soho.co.uk). **Open** noon-11pm Mon-Sat; noon-10.30pm Sun. Soho's oldest gay bar.

Criterion

224 Piccadilly, W1J 9HP (7930 0488/www.white starline.org.uk). **Lunch served** noon-2.30pm Mon-Sat. **Dinner served** 5.30-11.30pm Mon-Sat. Classy French restaurant.

Edge

11 Soho Square, W1D 3QE (7439 1313/www.edge. uk.com). **Open/food served** noon-1am Mon-Sat; noon-10.30pm Sun. A four-floored stalwart of the Soho gay scene, that attracts a mixed crowd and a fair few women.

Escape Dance Bar

8-10 Brewer Street, W1F 0SU (7734 2626/www. kudosgroup.com). **Open** 5pm-3am Mon-Sat. **Admission** £3 after 11pm.

First Out

52 St Giles High Street, WC2H 8LH (7240 8042/ www.firstoutcafebar.com). **Open** 10am-11pm Mon-Sat; 11am-10.30pm Sun. Mixed clientele, though mostly lesbian, not least on girls only 'Girl Friday'.

Freedom

66 Wardour Street, W1F 0TA (7734 0071). **Open** 5pm-3am Mon-Sat; 5-10.30pm Sun. **Food served** 5pm-2am Mon-Fri; 2pm-2am Sat; 2-9.30pm Sun. **Admission** £5-7 after 10.30pm Fri, Sat. Busy, mixed and a touch retro.

Govinda's

9 Soho Street, W1D 3DL (7437 4928/www.iskcon-london.org/govindas). **Open** noon-8pm Mon-Sat. Vegetarian restaurant

Kettners

29 Romilly Street, W1D 5HB (7734 6112/www. kettners.com). **Open** *Bar* noon-1am Mon-Sat; noon-10.30pm Sun. *Restaurant* noon-1am Mon-Sat; noon-midnight Sun. Pizzas and wonderful apple pie in the restaurant; the champagne bar is perfect for a date.

Maison Bertaux

28 Greek Street, W1V 5LL (7437 6007). **Open** 8.30am-8pm daily. Easy-going, delicious cakes and decidedly French.

Admiral Duncan

Queen's Larder

1 Queen Square, WC1N 3AR (7837 5627). **Open** 11am-11pm Mon-Fri; noon-11pm Sat; noon-10.30pm Sun. **Food served** noon-6pm daily. Tiny and cosy, downstairs and up. There are plenty of ales, and tables outdoors on Queen Square.

Rupert Street

50 Rupert Street, W1D 6DR (7292 7141). **Open** noon-11pm Mon-Sat; noon-10.30pm Sun. **Food** served noon-5pm Mon-Thur; noon-6pm Fri-Sun. One of Soho's trendiest, and therefore also busiest, hangouts.

Village Soho

81 Wardour Street, W1D 6QD (7434 2124). **Open/food served** 4pm-1am Mon-Sat; 4pm-midnight Sun. **Happy hour** 4-8pm daily. **Admission** £3 after 10pm Fri, Sat. A relaxed, bring-your-straight-mates gay bar.

Yard Bar

57 Rupert Street, W1V 7HN (7437 2652/www. yardbar.co.uk). **Open** 1-11pm Mon-Sat; 1-10.30pm Sun. A gay bar, but one where a genuine mix of all persuasions sit around chatting rather than simply cruising.

Churches

St George the Martyr

Queen Square, WC1N 3AH (7831 0588/www.sgtm. org). **Open** call for details.

St Patrick's Church

21A Soho Square, W1D 4NR (7437 2010/www.st patricks.uk.com). **Open** 8am-7pm daily.

Film

Renoir
Brunswick Centre, Brunswick Square, WC1N 1AW (7837 8402/www.artificial-eye.com/ cinemas.htm).

Leisure

Central YMCA
112 Great Russell, WC1V 3NQ (7343 1700/www. centralymca.org.uk). **Open** 6.30am-10pm Mon-Fri; 10am-8.30pm Sat; 10am-6.30pm Sun.

Oasis Sports Centre
32 Endell Street, WC2H 9AG (7831 1804/www. camden.gov.uk). **Open** 6.30am-9.30pm Mon-Fri; 9.30am-5.30pm Sat, Sun.

Literature & Film

Eyes Wide Shut (Stanley Kubrick, 1999, US/GB)
Evita (Tim Rice & Andrew Lloyd Webber, 1979)
Loot Joe Orton (1967)
The Madness of King George (Nicholas Hytner, 1994, GB/US)
My Night with Reg Kevin Elyot (1994)
M Butterfly (David Henry Hwang, 1988)
Follies (Stephen Sondheim, 1971)
Kiss of the Spiderwoman (John Kander & Fred Ebb, 1993)
Carousel (Richard Rodgers & Oscar Hammerstein II, 1945)
A Room with a View EM Forster (1908)
Swimming Pool Library Alan Hollinghurst (1988)
Time (Dave Clark, 1986)

Museums & art galleries

British Museum
Great Russell Street, WC1B 3DG (7636 1555/www. thebritishmuseum.ac.uk). **Open** *Galleries* 10am-5.30pm Mon-Wed, Sat, Sun; 10am-8.30pm Thur, Fri. *Great Court* 9am-6pm Mon-Wed, Sun; 9am-11pm Thur-Sat. *Highlights tours* (90mins) 10.30am, 1pm, 3pm daily. **Admission** free; donations appreciated. *Temporary exhibitions* prices vary. *Highlights tours* £8; £5 concessions.

October Gallery
24 Old Gloucester Street, WC1N 3AL (7242 7367/ www.octobergallery.co.uk). **Open** 12.30-5.30pm Tue-Sat.

Nightlife

London Astoria (LA1)
157 Charing Cross Road, WC2H 0EN (7434 9592/ www.meanfiddler.com). **Open** *Concerts* 7-10.30pm daily. *GAY club night* 11pm-4am Mon, Thur, Fri, Sat. Opening times may vary, phone for details. **Admission** varies.

Madame Jo Jo's
8-10 Brewer Street, W1F 0SE (7734 3040). **Open** 10pm-3am Wed, Fri, Sat; 9pm-3am Thur; 10pm-2am Sun.

Ronnie Scott's
47 Frith Street, W1D 4HT (7439 0747). **Open** 8.30pm-3am Mon-Sat; 7.30-11pm Sun.

Windmill
17-19 Great Windmill Street, W1D 7PH (7439 3558). **Open** 8pm-3.30am Mon-Sat.

Shopping

Borders
120 Charing Cross Road, WC2H 0JR (7379 8877). **Open** 8am-11pm Mon-Sat; noon-6pm Sun.

Clone Zone
54 Old Compton Street, W1D 4UQ (7287 3530). **Open** 11am-9pm Mon-Sat; noon-8pm Sun.

Foyles
113-119 Charing Cross Road, WC2H 0EB (7437 5660). **Open** 9.30am-9pm Mon-Sat; noon-6pm Sun.

Gay's the Word
66 Marchmont Street, WC1N 1AB (7278 7654). **Open** 10am-6.30pm Mon-Sat; 2-6pm Sun.

James Smith & Sons
53 New Oxford Street, WC1A 1BL (7836 4731). **Open** 9.30am-5.25pm Mon-Fri; 10am-5.25pm Sat.

Lillywhites
24-36 Lower Regent Street, SW1Y 4QF (7930 3181). **Open** 10am-9pm Mon-Sat; noon-6pm Sun.

Outlet
60-62 Old Compton Street, W1D 4TP (7287 4244). **Open** 10am-6pm Mon-Fri; noon-5pm Sat.

Prowler Soho
3-7 Brewer Street, W1R 3FN (7734 4031). **Open** 11am-10pm Mon-Sat; noon-8pm Sun.

Theatres

Apollo Shaftesbury
Shaftesbury Avenue, W1D 6AB (box office 7494 5070).

Cochrane Theatre
Southampton Row, WC1B 4AP (7269 1600).

Dominion Theatre
Tottenham Court Road, W1P 0AG (7413 1713).

Prince Edward Theatre
Old Compton Street, W1D 4HS (7447 5400).

Shaftesbury Theatre
Shaftesbury Avenue, WC2H 8DP (7379 5399).

The performance of power

Robin James

Enter the theatre of church and state through the streets of Westminster.

Start: Embankment tube
Finish: Sherlock Holmes pub,
10 Northumberland Street, WC2
Distance: 3.5 miles/5.5km
Time: 2 hours
Getting there: Bakerloo, Circle,
District or Northern lines to
Embankment
Getting back: 3-minute walk
to Embankment
Note: access to the House
of Commons usually requires
queuing, or securing tickets
in advance (ask your local MP),
though after 5pm the queues
are usually shorter.

History is written by the victors, and they tend to put up the biggest buildings, too. It's not surprising, then, that the dominant impression one gets from walking around Westminster is of Victorian and Edwardian grandiosity. Most of the buildings that catch the eye date from Britain's heyday as global superpower. But Westminster has been around a lot longer than that and the area has been through many changes. One feature has remained constant about the central core, running from Whitehall to the Houses of Parliament. For good or evil, this has been a place where power has been exercised. People have come here to influence power, or to challenge it.

Let's start with a building that isn't there any more. Leave Embankment tube and walk up Northumberland Avenue,
lined with gloomy office buildings. On your left as you approach Trafalgar Square, there is nothing to tell you that here stood an enormous Jacobean mansion, Northumberland House. It was built by the Earl of Northumberland in 1605-8 to give him handy access to the royal Court, a few hundred yards down Whitehall. Then as now, proximity to the top people was what counted. The great house survived long enough to be recorded by the camera, but was pulled down – an act of vandalism – in 1874.

A horseback statue of James I's son, the ill-fated King Charles I, now surveys Whitehall from a plinth on the south side of Trafalgar Square. He looks down towards the site of the palace from which he ruled, which was also where he was put to death. Picturing the now vanished Whitehall Palace takes quite an effort of imagination. Whitehall 400 years ago was not a processional avenue, but a narrow street jinking between Tudor gatehouses and a cluster of courtyards and royal apartments. Most of these burnt down in 1698. The only part of the palace that can still be seen is the Banqueting House, built by command of James I and finished in 1622. This was the first major building in England in a 'pure' classical style. Originally surrounded by rambling medieval architecture, it was a startlingly modern building, anticipating the later style of Georgian London. Even now it doesn't look ancient, despite being at least 150 years older than its neighbours.

The Banqueting House is a good place to think about the ironies that history

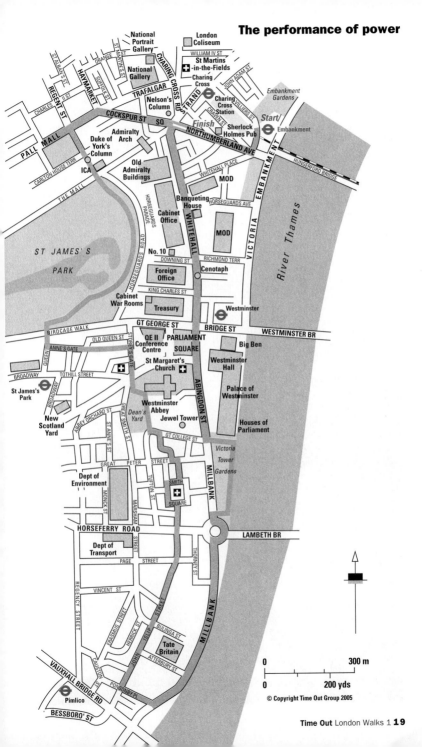

The performance of power

National Portrait Gallery

London Coliseum

St Alban's St

St Martin's St

ORANGE

CHARING CROSS RD

SUFFOLK ST

National Gallery

REGENT ST

CHARLES ST

HAYMARKET

COCKSPUR ST

PALL MALL

Duke of York's Column

THE MALL

CARLTON HOUSE TERR

ICA

ST JAMES'S PARK

WILLIAM IV ST

St Martins-in-the-Fields

TRAFALGAR

Charing Cross

Nelson's Column

Finish

TRAFALGAR SQ

Admiralty Arch

Old Admiralty Buildings

Cabinet Office

HORSEGUARDS PARADE

HORSEGUARDS ROAD

Banqueting House

WHITEHALL

No. 10

DOWNING ST

Foreign Office

KING CHARLES ST

Cabinet War Rooms

Treasury

BIRDCAGE WALK

OLD QUEEN ST

ANNE'S GATE

QUEEN

BROADWAY

St James's Park

TOTHILL STREET

New Scotland Yard

STOREY'S GATE

GT GEORGE ST

QE II Conference Centre

STRAND

JOHN ADAM ST

Charing Cross Station

Sherlock Holmes Pub

Start/

Embankment

Embankment Gardens

HUNGERFORD BRIDGE

River Thames

NORTHUMBERLAND AVE

WHITEHALL PLACE

MOD

HORSEGUARDS AVE

EMBANKMENT

VICTORIA

MOD

RICHMOND TERR

Cenotaph

BRIDGE ST

Westminster

WESTMINSTER BR

PARLIAMENT SQUARE

Big Ben

ABINGDON ST

St Margaret's Church

Westminster Hall

Westminster Abbey

Dean's Yard

Jewel Tower

Palace of Westminster

Houses of Parliament

GREAT SMITH ST

ABBEY ORCHARD ST

ST ANNE'S ST

GT COLLEGE ST

Victoria Tower Gardens

GREAT PETER STREET

Dept of Environment

MONCK ST

MARSHAM

TUFTON ST

SMITH SQUARE

HORSEFERRY ROAD

MILLBANK

LAMBETH BR

Dept of Transport

PAGE STREET

STREET

VINCENT ST

REGENCY STREET

ERASMUS STREET

HERRICK ST

JOHN

STREET

BULINGA ST

Tate Britain

ATTERBURY ST

PONSONBY PL

CAUSTON

VAUXHALL BRIDGE RD

Pimlico

BESSBORO' ST

0   300 m

0   200 yds

© Copyright Time Out Group 2005

Portcullis House and Big Ben.

throws up. It was built as a theatre of monarchy. Here the Stuart kings were presented to their subjects in court masques as figures of godlike majesty. The sumptuous ceiling painted by Rubens depicts James I as imperial monarch being received into heaven. Fourteen years after the painting was installed, Charles I was forced to walk beneath it on his way to execution at the hands of his subjects. He left the Banqueting House through a first-floor window and was beheaded on a temporary wooden stage outside. This regicide was also a kind of political theatre: in Andrew Marvell's words, 'Hence the royal actor borne, The tragic scaffold did adorn, While round the armèd bands, Did clap their bloody hands.' By this act of violence an English republic was created. Across the road nowadays, the Queen's Life Guards, cuirassed cavalrymen whose regiment traces its origins to Charles I's bodyguard, are a reminder that the republic did not last.

Modern Whitehall is a parade of ministries. Some are unobtrusive, like the Welsh Office in its modest Georgian house, or the former Ministry of Agriculture, now part of the Environment, Food and Rural Affairs super-ministry. Others are overbearing, like the Ministry of Defence, a great white hulk, out of scale with its neighbours. The Cabinet Office, the Foreign Office and the Treasury, lined in a row, offer variations on a classical scheme. Downing Street is tucked in the middle, now blocked to public access by big ironwork gates. They are pure 1880s in style, but were actually put up as a security measure in the 1980s. They did not prevent a serious terrorist attack in 1991: the IRA lobbed home-made mortars from a van parked in Whitehall, and only narrowly missed a room where the Cabinet was meeting.

Whitehall is also a street of statues, almost all depicting generals. Artistically the finest is the equestrian figure of Sir Douglas Haig. There are two views about Haig. He is remembered by some as the commander who won final victory in World War I, but by others as a bungler whose failed offensives on the Somme and at Passchendaele cost hundreds of thousands of lives. Outside the MoD are two recent statues of World War II generals, Slim and Alanbrooke. They are embarrassing reminders that the art of portrait sculpture in this country is not what it used to be.

Like a giant punctuation mark at the end of Whitehall stands the Cenotaph, designed by Sir Edwin Lutyens to commemorate the dead of World War I. In its simplicity, it seems more adequate to the grief and emotion that the war left in its wake than a more nakedly dramatic monument would have been.

Beyond the Cenotaph the architectural mood changes. The transition from Whitehall to Parliament Square is abrupt. Civil service classicism gives way to exuberant politicians' Gothic. The Palace of Westminster on the left dominates the scene. It is one of the world's great buildings, not least because of the endless vistas and combinations of spires and towers that open up as one walks around or through it. Over to the right, behind the church of St Margaret's, is Westminster Abbey. It is no coincidence that the two greatest buildings of the English church and state stand next to each other. They were founded together in the 1050s by King Edward the Confessor, on bleak Thorney Island, named after the briars that infested it. Two hundred years earlier a monk had called this *locus terribilis*, a fearful place. The island was formed by a little river, the Ty Burn, which here divided on its way to the Thames. The Ty Burn still flows in culverts beneath the road and buildings, discharging invisibly beneath the surface of the Thames.

Nothing remains from the Confessor's Palace, but the stone walls of the hall built in the 1090s by William Rufus still stand in the middle of the modern parliamentary complex. Surmounting them is the large roof that you can see to the right of Big

Ben (with a black turret, or flèche, halfway along). The timberwork of the roof, added by Richard II in the 1390s, is a triumph of medieval carpentry. This is Westminster Hall, which was intended both by Rufus and by Richard as a place of political theatre, where ceremonies glorifying their rule would take place. The Hall is dogged by the same ironies as the Banqueting House. The first state ceremony under Richard's new roof was his own deposition, a scene that Shakespeare later turned literally into theatre. In the Hall took place many of the great treason trials of alleged rebels against the Crown. The earliest was that of William Wallace, the 'Braveheart' of the 1995 film, who as a Scot denied that he owed any allegiance to the English Crown. He was sentenced to death here in 1305, as were Sir Thomas More in 1535, Guy Fawkes in 1606, the Jacobite lords in 1746 and many others. But here, too, the wearer of the crown, Charles I, was tried and sentenced by a revolutionary tribunal, as an enemy of his people.

Long before Charles's time, the Palace of Westminster had been handed over by the Crown for use by the law courts, which remained there till the 1880s, and as the first permanent home for Parliament, which still occupies the building. The old palace, a rabbit warren of decaying chambers and courtyards, burnt down in 1834. Only Westminster Hall (and parts of the crypt and cloisters) survived. Around these fragments, the architect Barry and the greatest of all interior designers, Pugin, erected the present Houses of Parliament. These, too, were built as a setting for political theatre, this time that of an emerging bourgeois democracy. It was now, as it remains, a People's Palace.

After about 5pm on days when Parliament is sitting, it's usually easy to get seats in the gallery of the Commons or the Lords, and on your way through you can snatch a glimpse of the magnificence of Westminster Hall. You also pass through St Stephen's Hall, built by Barry but reproducing the proportions of the old House of Commons Chamber that stood on this site until the fire. Brass studs on the floor mark where the Speaker's Chair and the Table of the House stood. The hall is lined with statues of eminent parliamentarians in pairs, facing each other as though across the Chamber, their gestures of debate frozen in marble. If you look closely at the fifth statue on the left, of Lord Falkland, you will see that the spur on one of his boots is broken. This happened before World War I, when a suffragette chained herself to the statue in protest against women being denied the vote. When she was removed, part of the statue came with her.

There's a fair amount to see even while remaining outside the building. The courtyard to the left of Westminster Hall, which you can see through the stone gates, now consists of a rather stunted little garden sitting on top of a five-storey car park for MPs. This is what remains of New Palace Yard, which used to be a much bigger space open to the public. Here mobs used to gather outside the main entrance to the King's palace. The modern fountain in the middle, built in the 1970s, is a successor to a medieval one that used to flow with wine on coronation days. Its remains were found when the car park was excavated.

Here, too, in the 17th and 18th centuries were coffee houses, frequented by politicians. Pepys's diary for early 1660 records his membership of a club of politically conscious Londoners who met in one of the coffee houses to hold intense discussions about the nature of an ideal constitution; the Restoration of Charles II put an end to that kind of free speculation, and the club disbanded.

Over to the left, beyond Bridge Street, stands Portcullis House, the new office block for MPs, completed in 2000 at a cost of some £250 million. Its black 'chimneys' (actually ventilation shafts) are a striking addition to the Westminster skyline. Below this building – and worth a detour –

is Westminster tube station, completely rebuilt by the same architect (Michael Hopkins), but in a very different style: three levels of escalators plunge downwards through a great concrete hall while massive circular columns rise beside them to support Portcullis House far above. The effect is industrial, Piranesian and grand.

Now return to Parliament Square and carry on beyond the gates to New Palace Yard. Here are more statues of men of the sword: Cromwell and Richard the Lionheart. Opposite is the east end of Westminster Abbey. The stonework was renewed in the early 1990s as part of a conservation programme supervised by an aptly named clerk of works, Donald Buttress. The details are worth looking at, especially the wonderful wriggly stone dragons twisting and turning around the pinnacles.

Carry on down the road alongside Parliament. On your left is the Victoria Tower, which marks the south end of the Palace of Westminster. This contains the parliamentary records, on 12 air-conditioned floors. To the right, on the other side of the road, is a much smaller building, the free-standing Jewel Tower, which was built 600 years ago to contain the Crown Jewels and now hosts an exhibition on the history of Parliament.

Beyond it is a patch of grass with a Henry Moore sculpture in the middle. This is College Green, where during the upheavals of the Major government politicians vied with each other to address TV cameras. For security reasons, they are no longer allowed to give interviews outdoors, but have retreated to the safety of No. 4 Millbank, just down the road on the right. The BBC, ITN and others base their political coverage here. You will have seen the staircase inside a hundred times without realising it, as interviews with MPs on TV news bulletins are often accompanied by shots of them arriving and climbing up the stairs. More often than not, a camera crew is waiting

outside, sharing the pavement with office workers enjoying a hasty cigarette.

Carry on down Millbank – for part of the way you can walk beside the river through Victoria Tower Gardens. At the entrance to the gardens is the statue of Emmeline Pankhurst, placed symbolically close to the doors of Parliament as a memorial to the suffragette struggle that she helped to lead. A little further on is another monument to non-violent political resistance, Rodin's *The Burghers of Calais*. This sculpture, a gift from the French, commemorates the leading citizens of Calais who in 1347 offered themselves as hostages to the English king Edward III in the hope that he would spare their besieged city. Edward sentenced them to die, but they were reprieved in response to the pleas of his queen, Philippa.

As you walk beside the river away from Parliament, the office buildings to the right are drab and oppressive, but the view of the river to your left is pleasant. Directly opposite is Lambeth Palace, a rural-looking Tudor survival that is the official home of the Archbishop of Canterbury. Further down, beyond Lambeth Bridge, is a solid wall of giant 1950s office blocks (although there is currently also a new residential block being built), vaguely reminiscent of Eastern Europe in the Krushchev era. Maybe thoughts of the Cold War are conjured up by unconscious association with the flamboyant cream and emerald building beyond them, which has been compared to a Babylonian ziggurat, and is actually the new home of MI6. It's an extraordinarily extrovert building for a secret intelligence agency.

One of the office buildings on the right, the tall 1960s glass-and-steel stump, is worth pausing briefly to inspect – not because of the architecture but because this is Millbank Tower, headquarters of the Labour Party and the place where the 1997 and 2001 General Election victories were planned. A minute's walk takes you on to Tate Britain, well worth several hours of anyone's time for its superb collections of British art.

The gallery stands on the site of the Millbank Penitentiary, a gigantic six-sided prison erected in the 1810s on the 'panopticon' principle, whereby corridors radiated from a central hub, enabling a small number of warders to see through strategically placed windows into all the cells and keep every prisoner under continuous surveillance. These days such an idea sounds creepy and Kafkaesque; back then it was held to be rational and enlightened. The prison was the biggest in London, and was used to hold convicts before they were transported to Australia. Cholera, scurvy and mental illness were rife. Nothing above ground remains to show that the building ever existed, but in the basement of the Morpeth Arms, 100 yards on down Millbank, there survives part of a tunnel through which convicts were escorted to barges in the river. The Morpeth Arms marks the halfway point of the walk and is a good place to stop for refreshment.

Leaving the pub, turn away from the river down Ponsonby Place, then right down John Islip Street. This part of Westminster, now dull and lifeless, used to be squalid and dangerous. Before the building of the Embankment in the 1860s, the marshiness of the ground made for an unhealthy environment. By the 18th century the Millbank district, originally uninhabited, had filled with houses, and was known for its poverty, prostitution and crime. Body-snatching was common from the burial grounds. The young Dickens prowled round here looking for material for his urban reportage. Elegant street names such as Great Peter Street are more recent: in the unsanitised past, the streets bore names like Black Dog Alley, Thieving Lane and Dirty Lane.

Pockets of respectability always existed. Inevitably, it's their architecture, rather than that of the slums, that has survived. Carry on down Dean Ryle Street and crowning the vista is the extraordinary baroque church of St John's, Smith Square – its four towers (leaning slightly askew, in testimony to the sogginess of the soil) bring to London a flavour of Borromini's Rome. Just before you get to the church, note Transport House on the right, which for many years was the Labour Party's headquarters, and No.32 on the left. This was Conservative Central Office for 45 years, the scene of televised election night jollifications, or (depending on the result of the ballot) dismal post-mortems.

On the far side of Smith Square, walk along Lord North Street (note the faded World War II signs on both sides of the road directing the public to bomb shelters beneath the pavements), Cowley Street and Barton Street. These are among the most perfect Georgian streets in London. In recent years houses here were much sought after by senior Conservative politicians. Winston Churchill, Brendan Bracken, Anthony Eden, Margaret Thatcher, Michael Portillo and Jonathan Aitken have all lived in this area. The Liberal Democrats have their headquarters in Cowley Street. The inhabitants of these streets were not always so grand. In the 18th and 19th centuries this was a tradesmen's neighbourhood, full of pubs, corner shops and lively street life.

Carry on to the end of Barton Street. To the right, down Great College Street, is the crumbling wall of the medieval Abbey precinct, leading left to Little College Street, where Oscar Wilde used to meet rent boys. Turn to the left, then at the end turn right through the gateway into Dean's Yard. This is the nearest Westminster Abbey gets to having a close. The yard is shared by three institutions: the Abbey itself, Church House (the headquarters of the Church of England) and Westminster School. One of the minor mysteries of London is the whereabouts of Westminster School: a major English public school manages to conceal itself so effectively among surrounding buildings that it is possible

St James's Park

to live and work in the area and never notice its presence. The entrance to the school is in fact through an unassuming archway halfway down the right-hand side of Dean's Yard – but large notices saying 'Strictly Private' do not encourage you to go any further.

Exit the Yard through the gatehouse in the far left corner. Westminster Abbey is on the right, its restored façade now a dazzling white. The Abbey itself is a treasure house of architecture and sculpture, but made almost unbearable by the multitudes of tourists shuffling through it. As this is a political walk, I shall only mention one or two aspects of the Abbey that have political connections.

600 years ago the House of Commons had no permanent home and used to take over the Chapter House for its sittings. The monuments that swarm across the Abbey's interior include many to political leaders, mostly from the Georgian and Victorian eras. My favourite, for its sheer effrontery, is the one to Pitt the Younger sited above the West Door. With an imperious gesture, Pitt's statue commands the nave, accompanied by sculpted figures representing History (recording his words) and Anarchy (in chains, grovelling before him).

Less bombastic but more moving are the recently installed statues of 20th-century Christian martyrs placed above

Cabinet War Rooms

the same door on the outside. They
represent people of different nations and
religions who fought against political
and religious oppression. They include
the civil rights leader Martin Luther King,
and Maximilian Kolbe, the Catholic priest
who died in Auschwitz.

The whole Abbey itself, as rebuilt
by Henry III in the 13th century, had a
political purpose. Like the Banqueting
House and Westminster Hall, it was
designed as a theatre for royal display.
The drama enacted here was that of
coronation. The church is centred upon
the Coronation Chair in Edward the
Confessor's shrine. Unusually wide
galleries run at first-floor level round
the nave and transepts; these allowed
thousands of people to assemble and

watch the rite of crowning from above.
The most recent royal drama to take place
in the Abbey was the funeral of Diana,
Princess of Wales. Millions rather than
thousands of people watched this, on
television sets around the world – but
in a sense the Abbey was continuing to
function just as Henry III had intended, as
a spectacular backdrop for royal pageantry.

I'll now break my rule about 'politics
only': go and see the Henry VII chapel,
at the far end, because it is stunning
and beautiful.

When leaving the Abbey, ignore the
dreary canyon of Victoria Street straight
ahead. Instead, cross the road to the large
modern building on the right. This is the
Queen Elizabeth II Centre, used by the
Government to host international

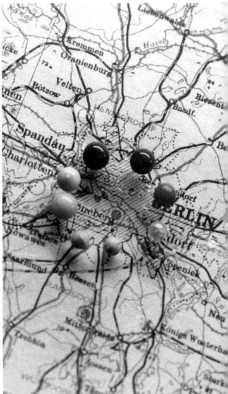

conferences. It is striking outside, but bog-standard 1980s office accommodation inside. Next door is the Methodist Central Hall, the venue for the first meeting of the United Nations in 1946. Over to its right is the Westminster Arms, a crowded but companionable pub. Go down the alley beyond, which ends with another pub, a sweet little place called the Two Chairmen. Straight ahead is Queen Anne's Gate, another street with well-preserved Georgian houses. A rash of blue plaques shows that various political bigwigs have lived here, including Palmerston and Lord Grey.

At the end of Queen Anne's Gate, to the left you can see the Home Office, a huge 1970s Brutalist building. The architectural effect is of a towering concrete fortress: one almost expects to

see battlements with black cannon poking through. In public relations terms, this is a curious choice of external appearance for the government department charged with the defence of civil liberties. It's architecture I feel I ought to dislike, but for some unaccountable reason, I've always been fond of it.

Anyway, don't turn left towards the Home Office, but right, which will take you into St James's Park. Follow the path to the right, skirting the lake and its famous pelicans (a feature here since Charles II's time). Senior civil servants and diplomats enjoy strolling through the park at lunchtime – they'll be the ones not wearing baseball caps and shorts. The road to the right runs along the back of Whitehall. At the near end, signposted, is the entrance to the Cabinet War Rooms, the bomb-proof underground chambers in which Churchill plotted the course of the war. They are now open to the public. Beyond Clive Steps (with a splendidly haughty statue of Clive of India) and the back of Downing Street is Horseguards Parade, where Trooping the Colour takes place in June each year.

Keep going north around the park to the Mall. Cross the road and climb York Steps, surmounted by the Grand Old Duke of York on a column. On the left, graced by a gilded statue of Athene, is the Athenaeum Club, traditionally a haunt of bishops and cabinet ministers. Like all the grander clubs, it doesn't bother to display its name at the entrance. Round the corner to the left in Pall Mall are other clubs, the Travellers' and the Reform. Members of the latter are required to sign an undertaking that they support the principles of the 1832 Reform Act; people who support rotten boroughs and the restriction of the franchise to the upper classes need not, therefore, apply.

One hundred years ago, much of the governance of Britain took place in these and similar West End clubs. Political grandees would dine and discuss politics at their clubs before walking back across the park to the House for wind-up speeches and votes at the end of the day's main debate. This is the world immortalised in Trollope's 'Palliser' novels.

Turn right and walk down Pall Mall into Trafalgar Square. To the right, on the corner of Whitehall, is Drummond's Bank, now a branch of the Royal Bank of Scotland, but for 200 years an independent bank. George III kept an account here. In a display case off the foyer are the excavated bones of elephants. These beasts died here some 120,000 years ago, at a time when the climate was semi-tropical and what is now Whitehall formed part of the muddy flood plain of the Thames.

Carry on back to Northumberland Street, dodging the traffic and the tourists across the site of the Jacobean earl's vanished mansion. Just before you reach Embankment tube station, a final refreshment stop can be made at the Sherlock Holmes pub. The concept of a Holmes pub sounds naff, but in fact this one is rather fun. On the ground floor there is a good collection of Sherlockiana. This includes the face-mask used for the Hound of the Baskervilles in the 1960s Hammer movie, complete with phosphorescent paint. Upstairs, behind glass, is a re-creation of Holmes's Baker Street study, originally made for exhibition at the 1947 Festival of Britain. Regular coachloads of tourists enter, take pictures of each other grinning happily and leave, sometimes without delaying to buy a drink. The pub has no political connection that I know of, but never mind – the beer is good.

Eating & drinking

The Atrium
4 Millbank, SW1P 3JA (7233 0032/www.simpsons ofmayfair.com). **Lunch served** noon-3pm, **dinner served** 6-9.45pm Mon-Fri. A fusion of Asian and Mediterranean dishes served to a mix of politicians and journalists.

Marquis of Granby
51-52 Chandos Place, WC2N 4HS (7836 7657). **Open** 11am-11pm Mon-Sat; noon-10.30pm Sun. **Food served** noon-9pm daily.

Morpeth Arms
58 Millbank, SW1P 4RW (7834 6442). **Open** 11am-11pm Mon-Sat; noon-10.30pm Sun. **Food served** noon-9pm Mon-Fri; 12.30-4pm Sat, Sun. Perfect for the Tate; good beers and food served.

Sherlock Holmes
10 Northumberland Street, WC2N 5DB (7930 2644). **Open** 11am-11pm Mon-Sat; noon-10.30pm Sun. **Food served** noon-10pm daily. Typical pub grub available in a cosy Victorian boozer brimming with Holmes memorabilia.

Tate Britain Restaurant
Tate Britain, Millbank, SW1P 4RG (7887 8825/ www.tate.org.uk). **Breakfast served** 10-11.30am, **lunch served** 11.30am-3pm, **afternoon tea** served 3-5pm daily. High-quality international food is served beneath Rex Whistler's memorable mural in this formal restaurant.

Two Chairmen
39 Dartmouth Street, SW1 0BP (7222 8694). **Open** 11am-11pm Mon-Fri. **Food served** noon-3.30pm, 5.30-8pm Mon-Fri. Reasonably priced, stately little pub with traditional and ambitious dishes available.

Westminster Arms
9 Storey's Gate, SW1P 3AT (7222 8520). **Open** 11am-11pm Mon-Fri; 11am-8pm Sat; noon-6pm Sun. **Food served** 11am-8pm Mon-Fri; noon-4pm Sat, Sun. The pub serves several real ales, a wide range of wines and cigars, and a healthy menu within a waddle of Parliament.

Churches

St John's, Smith Square
Smith Square, SW1P 3HA (7222 1061/www.sjss. org.uk). **Open** *box office* 10am-5pm Mon-Fri; until start of performance on concert nights.

St Margaret's Church
Parliament Square, SW1P 3PL (7222 5152/www. westminster-abbey.org). **Open** 9.30am-3.45pm Mon-Fri; 9.30am-1.45pm Sat; 3-5pm Sun (times change at short notice due to services). *Services* 11am Sun; phone to check for other days. **Admission** free; donations welcome.

Westminster Abbey
20 Dean's Yard, SW1P 3PA (7222 5152/www. westminster-abbey.org). **Open** *Chapterhouse, Nave & Royal Chapels* 9.30am-3.45pm Mon, Tue, Thur, Fri; 9.30am-7pm Wed; 9.30am-1.45pm Sat. *Abbey Museum* 10.30am-4pm Mon-Sat. *Cloisters* 8am-6pm Mon-Sat. *College Garden* Apr-Sept 10am-6pm Tue-Thur; Oct-Mar 10am-4pm Tue-Thur. Last entry 1hr before closing. **Admission** £8; £6 concessions; free under-11s with paying adult; £18 family.

Information

Conservative Party Central Office
25 Victoria Street, SW1H 0DL (7222 9000/ www.conservatives.com).

Drummond's Bank
49 Charing Cross Road, SW1A 2DX (7839 1200/ www.rbs.co.uk). **Open** 9.15am-4.45pm Mon, Tue, Thur, Fri; 10am-4.45pm Wed.

Labour Party
16 Old Queen Street, SW1H 9HP (7802 1000/ www.labour.org.uk).

Liberal Democrats
4 Cowley Street, SW1P 3NB (7222 7999/ www.libdems.org.uk).

Queen Elizabeth II Conference Centre
Broad Sanctuary, Westminster, SW1P 3EE (7222 5000/www.qeiicc.co.uk).

St James's Park
The Mall, SW1 (7930 1793/www.royalparks.org.uk). **Open** dawn-midnight daily.

Trooping the Colour
Horse Guards, Whitehall, SW1 (7414 2479 for tickets – apply in January and February for a mid March ballot).

Museums & galleries

Banqueting House
Whitehall, SW1A 2ER (7930 4179/www.hrp.org.uk). **Open** 10am-5pm Mon-Sat (sometimes shut at short notice; phone to check). **Admission** £4; £3 concessions; £2.60 5-15s; free under-5s.

Churchill Museum & Cabinet War Rooms
Clive Steps, King Charles Street, SW1A 2AQ (7930 6961/www.iwm.org.uk). **Open** 9.30am-6pm daily (last admission 1hr before closing). **Admission** £10; £4-£8 concessions; free under-15s.

Houses of Parliament
Parliament Square, SW1A 0AA (Commons information 7219 4272/Lords information 7219 3107/tours information 0870 906 3773/www. parliament.uk). **Open** *(when in session) House of Commons Visitors' Gallery* 2.30-10.30pm Mon; 11.30am-7.30pm Tue-Thur; 9.30am-3pm Fri. *House of Lords Visitors' Gallery* from 2.30pm Mon-Wed; from 11am Thur, Fri. Phone to check times. *Tours* summer recess only; phone for details. **Admission** Visitors' Gallery free. *Tours* £7; £5 concessions; free under-5s; £22 family.

ICA Gallery
The Mall, SW1Y 5AH (7930 3647/www.ica.org.uk). **Open** *Exhibitions* noon-7.30pm daily. **Admission** £1.50; £1 concessions Mon-Fri; £2.50, £1.50 concessions Sat, Sun.

Jewel Tower
Abingdon Street, SW1P 3JY (7222 2219/www. engligh-heritage.org.uk). **Open** *Apr-Oct* 10am-5pm daily. *Nov-Mar* 10am-4pm daily. **Admission** £2.60; £2 concessions; £1.30 5-16s; free under-5s.

Tate Britain
Millbank, SW1P 4RG (7887 8000/www.tate.org.uk). **Open** 10am-5.50pm daily. *Tours* 11am, noon, 2pm, 3pm Mon-Fri; noon, 3pm Sat, Sun. **Admission** free. *Special exhibitions* prices vary.

Movies, murder & the macabre

Kim Newman

A bloodstained trail of film murder sites through Soho.

Start: Russell Square tube
Finish: Piccadilly Circus tube
Distance: 2 miles/3km
Time: 1.5 hours
Getting there: Piccadilly line
Getting back: Piccadilly or Bakerloo lines
Note: best for film buffs, or those who enjoy exploring dark alleys.

It's hard to know whether to start this walk at Russell Square tube station or outside the British Museum. Both sites have equal validity, and are central to one of the great unknown London films, Gary Sherman's *Death Line* (1974). The opening scene of the movie takes place on the platform at Russell Square, as sleazy bowler-hatted dignitary James Cossins is abducted late at night by a troglodytic cannibal who has been haunting the Underground. The nugget of the film's plot is one of London's odder urban legends, going back to a tube station called British Museum that was abandoned during construction in the last century when a cave-in entombed a gang of navvies. *Death Line* assumes there were survivors, who bred a race of man-eating ghouls who prey to this day on stray commuters.

So alight at Russell Square – in *Death Line*, the cannibal can only communicate through three words, 'mind the doors' – then hurry down Southampton Row, turn into Bloomsbury Place and make your way along Great Russell Street to the museum. Here, the film associations begin to fall into place: there's the roof over which the villain is pursued in the finale of Hitchcock's first talkie, *Blackmail*, the reading room in which a ghostly force manifests itself in Jacques Tourneur's eerie *Night of the Demon*, and the Hall of Egyptian Antiquities where Charlton Heston revives an evil princess in Mike Newell's *The Awakening*. With its monolithic façade, associations with high culture, imperial looting, guilt-ridden Edwardian horror stories and extraordinary inventory, the British Museum is one of the foci of the city, at once a stop on the official tourist map and unmissable for those interested in the secret history, the psychogeography (to borrow from Iain Sinclair) of the capital.

From the museum, you should scurry down Great Russell Street, turn right into Tottenham Court Road, cross the road, then slip under a building into Stephen Street, curving to the right (via Gresse Street) into Rathbone Place, which leads into Rathbone Street. Here is where you find a byway as obscure as the British Museum is famous, and yet as crucial to this wander through the vanished fogs: Newman Passage. It's easy to miss, but find the Newman Arms pub at 23 Rathbone Street, and you'll chance upon the arched entry to Newman Passage. It angles downward sharply past a school of massage as a covered walkway, then kinks between a couple of ad-design places to feed out on to Newman Street.

Christopher Petit wrote an essay/story titled 'Newman Street' for the *Time Out Book of London Short Stories*. We're here for the same reason Petit was: it's the site of the murder that opens Michael Powell's 1960 masterpiece of London psycho-noir, *Peeping Tom*. Seen partially through the viewfinder of the murderer's cine-camera, the scene follows prostitute Dora (Brenda Bruce) – a rare, realistic, middle-aged tart – into the passage and up a stairway to the right, which should logically take her to the upper rooms of the pub, where she

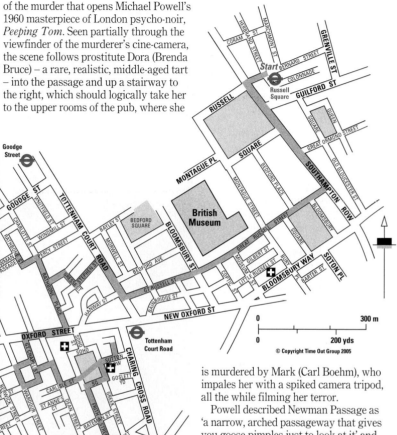

is murdered by Mark (Carl Boehm), who impales her with a spiked camera tripod, all the while filming her terror.

Powell described Newman Passage as 'a narrow, arched passageway that gives you goose-pimples just to look at it' and put about a rumour that it was associated with Jack the Ripper, though Petit says this is unlikely and counter-claims that the passage used to be known as Jekyll and Hyde Alley. Given that this walk will ramble in the direction of Hyde Park and that we shall more than once encounter RL Stevenson's doubled protagonist, this adds an extra frisson. Jack the Ripper's patch was, of course, Whitechapel in the East End, but the very real serial murderer has become a phantom often confused with Mr Hyde and also recurs in this macabre but evocative little amble. Explore Newman Passage, but don't pass through it. The second leg of the kink is a disappointment, airy rather than covered, ad-agency glass rather than tarts-and-killers cobbles.

Retrace your steps from Newman Passage to the newsagent's shop on the corner of Rathbone Place and Percy Street, which is also featured in *Peeping Tom*. In a typical bit of film fudging of London geography, a dissolve and a shot of Mark on a Vespa suggest that the newsagent's – a real location not a set (the Marquis of Granby pub can be glimpsed through the window) – is a longer trip away from the murder site than it actually is. All these years later, the newsagent's is still trading, though it presumably doesn't have the cosily seedy studio above the shop where Mark takes nudie photographs of Millie (1950s glamour model Pamela Green) that are sold to prurient elderly gentlemen typified by Miles Malleson. Towards the end of the picture, Mark murders Millie in the studio, further bloodying our trail.

Walk south on Rathbone Place, cross Oxford Street, then slip through the right angle of Great Chapel Street and you're on Wardour Street. This has been the administrative heart of the British film industry since the 1920s, but it's a curiously underfilmed thoroughfare. There are no studios here, just the offices of distributors, production companies, publicists and post-production facilities. Britain has produced few films about its film industry along the lines of Hollywood's *Sunset Boulevard* or *Singin' in the Rain*, so you have to make do with the glimpses of preview theatres and distributors' offices caught in Martin Campbell's *Eskimo Nell* (1974), a surprisingly apt insider's view of 1970s British porn filmmaking. The preview theatres that were in business when I was first working as a film critic all feature in *Eskimo Nell*, and it was a delight to see they hadn't changed – all coloured chunky glass and velvet wallpaper – in ten years. The decor was still there when they mostly closed down

Newman Passage, of *Peeping Tom* fame.

a few years ago, to be replaced by clubs, coffeeshops (not cafés) and head offices of part-works.

At 113 Wardour Street is Hammer House, once owned by Hammer Films, but now being refitted as a Toni & Guy. There's an in-joke in producer Herman Cohen's 1958 American movie *I Was a Teenage Frankenstein*, as Dr F (Whit Bissell) plans on dissecting his creation and posting him in bits to 113 Wardour Street. It's tempting to see this as a significant handing-on of the baton of horror, since *I Was a Teenage Frankenstein* was at least partly an attempt to cash in on Hammer's *The Curse of Frankenstein*, made a year earlier, and came at a moment when the Gothic flame was burning far brighter in Britain than at the American studios that had created the monster movie in the 1930s. Actually, no such reference was intended: many distributors worked out of 113, including Lippert – who were involved in the marketing of Cohen's film.

Nip back towards the top of Wardour Street and slip towards Dean Street via Sheraton Street, turn left and you'll find tiny Diadem Court. One of those places which is in italics in the London *A-Z* because it's so small it goes unnamed on the maps. Diadem Court is the address of yet another murdered prostitute, Champagne Ivy (Miriam Hopkins), mistress of Fredric March's brutal Mr Hyde in Rouben Mamoulian's 1932 *Dr Jekyll and Mr Hyde*. Unlike *Peeping Tom*, it was shot an ocean and a continent away in Hollywood; but it's unusual that an American film of the period would take such care as to give a real address – until the Clean Up Soho campaign, exactly the sort of milieu where a trollop like Ivy would lodge – for a throwaway character.

Crossing Dean Street and nipping along Carlisle Street, you find yourself in Soho Square, a patch of green frequented by cycle messengers waiting for the call, abusers of various substances and (in summer) lunching employees of the British Board of Film Classification, Bloomsbury Publishing and 20th Century Fox. Soho Square crops up very occasionally in fiction (my own *Organ Donors*, Ramsey Campbell's *Ancient Images* and Christopher Fowler's *Rune* have scenes set there), but is surprisingly rarely filmed, though it's a favourite spot for getting vox pop statements for local news items. If you cross the square and feint towards Charing Cross Road via Sutton Row, you find Falconberg Court (off Falconberg Mews), a right angle around the back of the Astoria that was the given address of the Alan Howard character in *The Cook, the Thief, His Wife and Her Lover*, the library where Howard and Helen Mirren conduct their adulterous affair and where Howard is stuffed full of pages torn out of his books. Peter Greenaway probably chose the address because it used to be the site of Mr Young's Preview Theatre (now moved to D'Arblay Street on the other side of Wardour Street), an especially prized Soho film facility. It's now home to gay club Ghetto.

Returning to Soho Square and trailing out via Frith Street, you will sadly fail to find the Café l'Egypte, described as a front for an opium den run by everyone's favourite oriental master villain in Sax Rohmer's *The Hand of Fu Manchu*. Walking towards Old Compton Street, the Soho you see gets more like the Soho you imagine: the name had enough associations in 1978 for someone to deem it worth making *Emmanuelle in Soho*, and it is well enough known internationally to crop up as a fantastical locale recreated on soundstages in Berlin or Budapest for *The Gorilla of Soho*, *The Hunchback of Soho* and *The Phantom of Soho*.

It is this imaginary Soho that is the haunt of the fused image of Jack the Ripper and Mr Hyde: an actor possessed by the role of the Ripper stalks through the German *The Monster of London Town*, set in some Teutonic version of these streets, while *Edge of Sanity*, made in Hungary, has Anthony Perkins as a Dr Jekyll who becomes 'Jack Hyde' under the influence of 19th-century crack and murders yet more of the doomed tarts who are so indelibly associated with the region in the popular imagination.

This never-never district was enshrined in the British imagination by *The Blue Café*, a 1933 play about drug-dealing that was turned down for filming by the censor of the day for its scandalousness but which nevertheless inspired a few picturesquely criminal quickies such as the 1939 *Murder in Soho*.

It's possible to identify the sites of your favourite movie sleaze moment. Old Compton Street is the site of the strip club run by thin-moustached Christopher Lee in the 1962 classic *Beat Girl*, outside which Adam Faith is beaten so badly that he throws his guitar into a waste bin with a significance roughly equal to that of Dirty Harry chucking away his badge; and it's also the address of the private club in *Mona Lisa* where Bob Hoskins asks a lady in leather (JoAnne Sellar, who used to manage the Scala Cinema and recently produced *Boogie Nights*) if there's any chance of a cup of tea and is told to piss off.

Soho clubs feature in a great many movies, but those that were actual places – like the ones featured in *The Krays* – are now as elusive and vanished as the imaginary sinkpots of iniquity explored in the forgotten *Noose* (in which Nigel Patrick incarnated that archetypal London layabout, the spiv) and the original, masterly *Night and the City*. The closest to the fantasised vision of a smoky collection of picturesque characters drinking late at night is probably Gerry's Club in Dean Street. We'll pass the Groucho Club (No.45) in silence, except to note that it might be much enlivened if the management was required to pay protection money to Herbert Lom (mastermind of *The Frightened City*) or be regularly smashed up by Sid James and Bernard Bresslaw.

On Old Compton Street, you can still find espresso cafés and Italian restaurants, though you'd be hard put to find the actual joints where Tony Hancock demands coffee 'with no froth' in *The Rebel*, Cliff Richard and Tommy Steele are 'discovered' in *Expresso Bongo* and *The Tommy Steele Story*, or a magic realist family saga plays itself out in *Queen of Hearts*. Bombed out in the War and the site of a decades-long struggle between the purveyors of caffeine and porn – as chronicled in the TV serial *Our Friends in the North* – Old Compton Street is, for me, the main thoroughfare of Soho, a genuine collision of the wonderfully imagined and the grubbily actual. It crosses Wardour Street and turns into the less appealing Brewer Street: this is the site of the jazz club in the minor Michael Caine vehicle *Blue Ice*, but the associations are wearing thin, unless you can be bothered to search out Ingestre Place and assume that it's named after the hero of that long-lasting melodrama *Sweeney Todd* – though the murderous barber's territory was well to the east in Fleet Street.

You might as well get off Brewer Street on to Shaftesbury Avenue via Great Windmill Street. The Windmill Theatre, known for its nude tableaux, was the subject of a fakey Hollywood biopic *Tonight and Every Night*, with Rita Hayworth standing up to the Blitz. But true connoisseurs of British tat much prefer *Murder at the Windmill*, a backstage whodunnit featuring Jon Pertwee and Jimmy Edwards doing their demob ENSA acts, and the undeservedly forgotten *Secrets of a Windmill Girl*, in which a very young Pauline Collins (who leaves it off her CV these days) suffers mightily for coming to the big city. The Raymond Revuebar (now closed) in nearby Walkers Court was no competition, though it did feature in *The Playbirds* and several other 1970s skinflicks. The Windmill boasts 'table-dancing', and its impressive

Soho Square – one of Soho's few green spaces.

upper storeys mark it out as different from some of the dirty neon, dirty mac joints in the vicinity.

Given London's international reputation as a theatre capital, Shaftesbury Avenue has been somewhat short-changed by the lack of any British equivalents to *The Lullaby of Broadway* or *42nd Street*. But Piccadilly has been commemorated in a few lowlife titles, notably the early serial killer drama *East of Piccadilly*, in which Niall MacGuinness is the strangler of (yet again) good-time girls.

Filmmakers have long complained that the London authorities are far less amenable to the staging of large-scale action sequences than those of many American cities, and so there are few equivalents to the breathless San Francisco, Los Angeles or New York car chases of *Bullitt*, *Speed* and *The French Connection*. But John Landis did stage the climax of *An American Werewolf in London* in the Circus, crashing a satisfying collection of vehicles and gunning down his lycanthrope in a handy alley.

Grubbily alluring **Old Compton Street** – all human life is here.

Before dying, Landis's American werewolf is cornered by ghosts in the Eros Cinema. So named because of the nearby statue, not its repertoire of porn movies (it was originally a 'news' cinema, specialising in newsreels), the Eros was still open when I first started working as a film critic and was the sort of place where films that didn't get press shows were shown to critics along with the cinema's genuine patrons. A few weeks later, the Eros closed down, driven out of business by video cassettes, and the building now hosts a Virgin Megastore.

We finish our traipse among the crowds by the statue. Though the werewolf died near here, this is one of the spots that is cinematic not through particular movies but because stock shots of Piccadilly Circus crop up in numberless films to establish a London locale, from *Night and the City* to *Brannigan*. How many times have you seen those same 1930s newsreel shots of boxy cars in black and white under pointillist illuminated signs hawking English products like Ovaltine rather than the American or Asian names now blazing out in red neon?

We've covered a lot of territory in such a short walk and it's time to blend in, to become an extra, to scurry off and let the stars get on with the story.

Eating & drinking

Dog & Duck
18 Bateman Street, W1D 3AJ (7494 0697). **Open** noon-11pm Mon-Sat; noon-10.30pm Sun. The oldest pub in Soho, with a glorious tiled interior.

Glass Bar & Solution
Marlborough Hotel, Bloomsbury Street, WC1B 3QD (7636 5601/www.radissonedwardian.com). **Open** *Solution* 10am-11pm daily. *Glass Bar* 10am-1am Mon-Fri; noon-11pm Sun. Two venues in different styles, both serving grand drinks and snacks at grand prices.

Newman Arms
23 Rathbone Street, W1T 1NG (7636 1127/www. newmanarms.co.uk). **Open** 11.30am-11pm Mon-Fri. *Pie Room* noon-3pm Mon-Fri. A fine pint of Bass and award-winning pies upstairs.

On Anon
1 Shaftesbury Avenue, W1V 1NG (7287 8008). **Open** noon-3am Mon-Sat; noon-midnight Sun. Eight distinct bars, all offering deep-fried snacks and bottled beers.

Toucan
19 Carlisle Street, W1B 5RJ (7437 4123). **Open** 11am-11pm Mon-Fri; 1-11pm Sat. Famed for its Guinness, Irish whisky and Irish sausages.

Films

An American Werewolf in London (John Landis, 1981, GB)
The Awakening (Mike Newell, 1980, GB)
Beat Girl (Edmond T Gréville, 1960, GB)
Blackmail (Alfred Hitchcock, 1929, GB)
Blue Ice (Russell Mulcahny, 1992, US)

Boogie Nights (Paul Thomas Anderson, 1997, US)

Brannigan (Douglas Hickox, 1975, GB)

Bullitt (Peter Yates, 1968, US)

The Cook, the Thief, His Wife and Her Lover (Peter Greenaway, 1989, GB/Fr)

The Curse of Frankenstein (Terence Fisher, 1957, GB)

Death Line (Gary Sherman, 1972, GB)

Secrets of a Windmill Girl (Arnold Louis Miller, 1965, GB)

Dr Jekyll and Mr Hyde (Rouben Mamoulian, 1932, US)

East of Piccadilly (Harold Huth, 1940, GB)

Edge of Sanity (Gerard Kikoine, 1988, US)

Emmanuelle in Soho (David Hughes, 1978, GB)

Eskimo Nell (Martin Campbell, 1975, GB)

Expresso Bongo (Val Guest, 1959, GB)

The French Connection (William Friedkin, 1971, US)

The Gorilla of Soho (Alfred Vohrer, 1968, W Germany)

The Hunchback of Soho (Siegfried Schaurenberg, 1966, W Germany)

I Was a Teenage Frankenstein (Herbert L Strock, 1957, US)

The Krays (Peter Medak, 1990, GB)

The Monster of London Town (Siegfried Schaurenberg, 1966, W Germany)

Mona Lisa (Neil Jordan, 1986, GB)

Murder at the Windmill (Val Guest, 1949, GB)

Murder in Soho (Norman Lee, 1939, GB)

Night and the City (Irwin Winkler, 1992, US)

Night of the Demon (Jacques Tourneur, 1957, GB)

Noose (Edmond T Gréville, 1948, GB)

Peeping Tom (Michael Powell, 1960, GB)

The Phantom of Soho (Franz Josef Gottlieb, 1964, W Germany)

The Playbirds (Willy Roe, 1978, GB)

Queen of Hearts (Jon Amiel, 1989, GB)

The Rebel (Robert Day, 1960, GB)

Sweeney Todd, the Demon Barber of Fleet Street (George King, 1936, GB)

The Tommy Steele Story (Gerard Bryant, 1957, GB)

Tonight and Every Night (Victor Saville, 1945, US)

Information

British Board of Film Classification

3 Soho Square, W1D 3HD (7440 1570/ www.bbfc.co.uk).

Hammer House

113-117 Wardour Street, W1F 0UN.

20th Century Fox

31-32 Soho Square, W1D 3AP (7437 7766/ www.fox.co.uk).

Museums

British Museum

Great Russell Street, WC1B 3DG (7636 1555/ recorded info 7323 8783/www.thebritish museum.ac.uk). **Open** *Galleries* 10am-5.30pm Mon-Wed, Sat, Sun; 10am-8.30pm Thur, Fri. *Great Court* 9am-6pm Mon-Wed, Sun; 9am-11pm Thur-Sat. **Admission** free.

Nightlife

Astoria (LA1)

157 Charing Cross Road, WC2H 8EN (7434 9592). **Open** 7.30-10.30pm Mon-Thur; 11pm-3am Fri; 10pm-6am Sat. Times vary, phone the venue for details.

Gerry's Club

52 Dean Street, W1D 5BJ (7437 4160). Private club for actors.

Groucho Club

45 Dean Street, W1D 4QP (7439 4685/www.the grouchoclub.com). Private drinking club.

Shopping

Virgin Megastore

1 Piccadilly, W1J 0TR (7439 2500/www.virgin megastores.co.uk). **Open** 9am-midnight Mon-Sat; noon-6pm Sun.

The British Museum

Anatomical London

Dr Ruth Richardson

Dissecting the heart of the city – definitely not for the squeamish.

Start: Marble Arch tube
Finish: London Bridge tube/rail or George Inn, 77 Borough High Street, SE1
Distance: 6.5 miles/11km
Time: 3.5 hours
Getting there: Central line to Marble Arch
Getting back: Jubilee or Northern line from London Bridge; short walk from George Inn to London Bridge tube/rail
Note: the Royal Academy Art School and Gordon Museum are not open to the public.

The study of human anatomy in London has a long history, from the time of Henry VIII right up to the present day. This walk will take you to some of the key sites in the story.

We start at Marble Arch, for centuries the site of the famous Tyburn gallows. It was here that bodies of hanged criminals were handed over to the surgeons for dissection after death, under a grant initiated by Henry VIII in 1540, continued by Charles II and extended by Parliament in 1752. The old site of the 'Tyburn Tree' gallows is marked with a metal plate in the roadway of Cumberland Gate as it swings north past Hyde Park towards the Bayswater Road – too dangerous for

Marble Arch

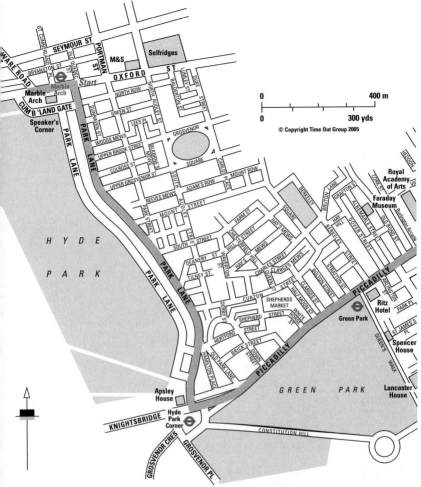

a pedestrian to locate. Standing at the corner of Bayswater Road and Hyde Park, facing towards Oxford Street, it lies to your right, towards Speakers' Corner.

The gallows was later moved to an open area on the northern side of Bayswater Road at the corner with the Edgware Road, as a plaque in the traffic island at the foot of the Edgware Road records.

Criminals would be brought here along with their coffins on a cart from Newgate (now Old Bailey) along High Holborn, St Giles' High Street and down the

Tyburn Road (now Oxford Street). So many were hanged here – often for paltry offences – that my mother used to say that the fountains ought to run red. On the journey to Tyburn in 1714, one prisoner flew into a rage and threatened to haunt a Holborn pawnbroker when he refused to return her best smock for her execution, as it was the custom to be hanged wearing white.

The surgeons who needed corpses to study anatomy were feared and hated by criminals and their friends. Dissection

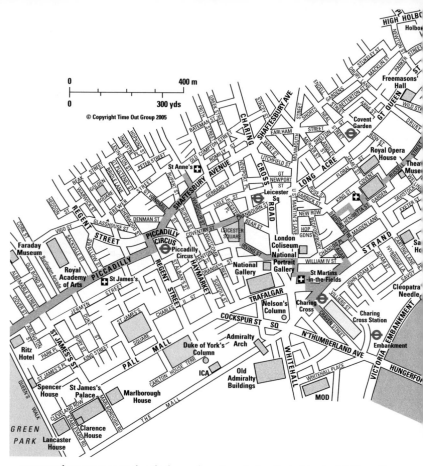

prevented attempts to revive the hanged (which, when tried, occasionally worked) and denied the dead person both a proper funeral and a decent burial. People still fostered notions of physical resurrection on Judgement Day, and found the idea of dismemberment utterly repugnant. The law, too, regarded dissection as a fate worse than death, and used it only for the worst murderers. Others were 'hanged in chains' after execution: covered in tar and caged suspended on a gibbet in a prominent place near the site of the crime, where in time the body would rot away in public view. Either way, murderers were denied a decent burial.

Dissection wasn't inflicted on the many others who were executed for lesser crimes, unless the surgeons got hold of them before their friends did. If you'd been standing hereabouts on a hanging day in the mid 18th century, you might have witnessed ferocious fights, which sometimes developed into riots, for custody of the dead. These battles, and the fact that Tyburnia was becoming built up with fashionable houses, were among the reasons the gallows was eventually removed from here in the 1780s to the 'new drop' at Newgate.

The desire for decent burial was shared throughout society. It explains the fierce hostility expressed both towards the surgeons during riots at the gallows, and towards the bodysnatchers who supplemented the doctors' legal supply by stealing the freshly buried dead from graveyards.

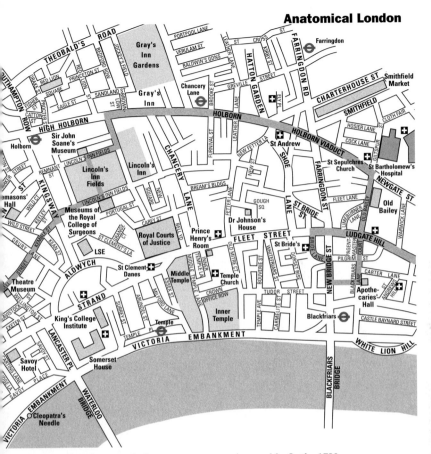

The Georgian age was the key era of anatomical discovery, and the bodysnatchers' heyday. Every burial ground in London and for miles around was subject to their depredations. They were highly efficient. Sir Astley Cooper, a famous anatomist in the Regency period, once told Members of Parliament investigating the matter: 'There is no person, let his situation in life be what it may, whom if I was disposed to dissect, I could not obtain. The law only enhances the price, it does not prevent the exhumation.'

Cooper's analysis was astute. Rich and poor were vulnerable to the bodysnatchers' shovels. While opposition and expedients to prevent bodysnatching (such as patent iron coffins) succeeded in causing shortages, they never prevented the trade. Prices

rose inexorably. In the 1790s, a gang caught after exhumations in a Lambeth graveyard was selling adult bodies for 'two guineas and a crown', while those of children sold for 'six shillings for the first foot, and ninepence per inch' thereafter. By the 1820s adult corpses raised between 10 and 20 guineas apiece. A good wage for a working man at the time was less than one guinea a week.

Look back along the north side of the Bayswater Road towards Bayswater. Past the Tyburn shrine and convent you will notice a break in the buildings and the trees on the site of the old graveyard belonging to St George's, Hanover Square. The old ground (between Albion Street and Stanhope Place), now cleared of its fine stones and of its dead, is inhabited by

an ugly apartment block. In the Georgian period, the ground was flanked with double walls, between which watchmen with dogs patrolled to protect the dead from bodysnatchers. Current residents assure me that parts of these walls survive even today.

Walk down the old Tyburn Lane (now Park Lane) or make your way through the park to Hyde Park Corner. Before you

The **Lanesborough Hotel**, giving no hint of its less glamorous past.

turn into Piccadilly, look across to the south-west at what was St George's Hospital (now the Lanesborough Hotel). The famous surgeon-anatomist John Hunter worked in an older building on this site, and died here during an argumentative board meeting in 1793. It was in the present building that Henry Gray, author of *Gray's Anatomy* – perhaps the most famous anatomical textbook of modern times – penned his first edition in 1858.

Walk along Piccadilly to the present home of the Royal Academy at Burlington House. The RA Art School, in the basement of this building, is home to two remarkable anatomical artefacts, which, although not on public display, you might nevertheless be interested to know about. Both are plaster casts of men executed at Tyburn, flayed (skinned) and put into poses while still warm, until rigor mortis set in. One, a smuggler, was set in the pose of a famous classical statue, the *Dying Gladiator*, and the cast is known as *Smugglerius*. The other, in order to assist devotional artists, was crucified.

Cross Piccadilly Circus, go up Shaftesbury Avenue and turn north into Great Windmill Street. On the right, by the stage door of the Lyric Theatre, is a blue plaque marking the site of William Hunter's school of anatomy. So famous (or infamous) was this school that a contemporary cartoonist pictured its galleried interior on Resurrection Day, with a number of limbless and dismembered individuals seeking their lost parts.

Returning to Shaftesbury Avenue, turn north into Wardour Street to glance at the churchyard of St Anne's, Soho. Notice how enclosed the churchyard is and how high above street level. The walls and gates protect a small area in which over a hundred thousand bodies have been laid. Joseph Rogers, a remarkable local doctor commemorated by a blue plaque on 33 Dean Street (just around the corner), campaigned to get this graveyard closed in the 1840s. Caring for a patient whose leg ulcers refused to heal, Rogers decided to investigate a foul-smelling fluid oozing into her room, and found that it came from the decaying corpses heaped up in the soil

Somerset House

on the other side of her wall. Sexton Fox of St Anne's was well known among his brethren for being adept at getting many bodies into a small space. No one knows how many were snatched from here.

Turn south on Wardour Street, cross Shaftesbury Avenue and walk down towards Leicester Square. We pass Gerrard Street, where there was an anatomy school in the 18th century, and enter Leicester Square. In the south-east corner stands a bust of John Hunter, whose anatomical school and museum were on the east side of the square. Sir Joshua Reynolds lived opposite.

Walk down Irving Street, cross Charing Cross Road to St Martin-in-the-Fields churchyard and cut down behind the church to cross the Strand to Craven Street. In the 18th century No.36 was the home of the American scientist and statesman Benjamin Franklin and of his friend William Hewson, who had an anatomy school on the lower floors here in the 1780s. Building work in the basement recently unearthed human bones, almost certainly from snatched bodies, showing signs of having been cut for anatomical demonstration. Their future is still undecided.

Walk east along the Strand and up Agar Street (passing the old Charing Cross Hospital, now a police station), right into Chandos Place (the Hospital Medical School was on the north side) and up Bedford Street to the great gates at the back of the churchyard of St Paul's, Covent Garden. Notice the watchman's sentry box near the church's west door, facing the churchyard. Go round to the east end of the church (there are gated alleys to both north and south), and cut through the centre of the market buildings to Russell Street, then Kemble Street, crossing Kingsway, and pass along Sardinia Street to Lincoln's Inn Fields.

The porticoed Royal College of Surgeons stands almost in the middle of the south side of the Fields. The surgeons moved here from their old premises near Newgate in 1797, rebuilding and expanding several times since – in 1806-13 to accommodate the great comparative anatomy and pathology collections built up by John Hunter, again in the 1830s, and after extensive damage from bombing in 1941. The adjoining Nuffield College of Surgical Sciences provides accommodation for visiting surgeons from all over the world. The college's quiet exterior conceals busy

teaching facilities and administrative offices for the major examining body for surgery in England, a fine library, and the Hunterian Museum, which is open to the public. Ask to take the great central staircase with its portraits and busts of famous men as you enter the hall. The museum entrance is on the first floor.

Inside, you will see a glass case containing a huge skeleton. It is over seven and a half feet tall, and was that of a man named O'Brien, known as 'The Irish Giant'. O'Brien had made his living exhibiting himself at fairs and elsewhere (rather as the Elephant Man did later) and knew very well that the anatomists would want his body for their museums. He had such a terror of dissection that, prior to his death in 1783, he had saved £500 to have himself buried at sea in a lead coffin. However, John Hunter paid the undertaker another £500 to deliver O'Brien's body to his rooms.

The museum is brimful of magnificent anatomical specimens and the staff are welcoming. A couple of dissected murderers stand in the gallery, and the dental museum features some remarkable dentures made from 'Waterloo teeth' taken from corpses on the battlefields of the Napoleonic Wars.

It was from a college department in the basement of this building that the artist Anthony Noel Kelly took the body parts that led to his historic prosecution for theft in the summer of 1998. The gilded plaster-casts he made from them have been confiscated.

Behind the college was the notorious Portugal Street burial ground (nothing of which now remains) and King's College Hospital, in whose anatomy school the terrible case of Bishop and Williams was discovered. These men are hardly known today, but in the 1830s they were as notorious as the Edinburgh murderers, Burke and Hare, whose crimes two years previously they copied. Unlike Burke and Hare, the 'London Burkers' had been bodysnatchers. They took to supplying anatomy schools by murder in preference to risking cold nights, attacks from watchdogs or violent treatment at the hands of the enraged public. Whereas Burke and Hare plied their victims with drink before smothering them, these wretches drugged their victims insensible with laudanum and suspended them head-first down a well. They were said to have confessed to 60 murders before their execution in 1831.

Further south stands Somerset House, partly built on an old burial ground and previously the home of the Royal Academy where the *Smugglerius* and crucifixion casts were originally made.

Cross to the north side of Lincoln's Inn Fields (the bandstand is on the site of a place of execution, too) to Sir John Soane's Museum. This wonderful museum, devoted to the structure of buildings, also has numerous stone sculptures on display, and a sarcophagus.

Exit at the north-east corner of the Fields via Newman's Row, then take the little alley called Great Turnstile and turn right into High Holborn. Cross Holborn Viaduct, looking at the resurrection relief on the side of the church of St Andrew Holborn, whose churchyard used to extend right across the current roadway.

Turn north into Giltspur Street. On your left, notice the parish watch-house for the Holy Sepulchre churchyard facing the west flank of St Bartholomew's Hospital. Bodies were liable to be snatched from the church-yard for dissection in the hospital's Medical College opposite. Another famous anatomy school stood east of here in Aldersgate Street, by what is now the Barbican.

Return south along Giltspur Street, and cross Newgate Street into Old Bailey. The present Old Bailey covers the entire site of the old Newgate Prison and the old College of Surgeons, which was a fine building with a double staircase leading to a grand entrance at first-floor level. At street level between the stairs was a door through which executed bodies were delivered for dissection in the college's anatomical theatre. For centuries the Royal College of Physicians also had facilities for ceremonial dissections in its premises nearby on Amen Corner (where William Harvey demonstrated the circulation of the blood in 1616) and Warwick Lane.

The Viaduct Tavern on Newgate Street is said to have a cell from the old prison in its basement. It looks to me no more than a wine cellar created when the Viaduct was built in the 1860s, but I may be wrong.

Between 1783, when the gallows moved from Tyburn, and 1868, when public executions were brought to an end, hangings took place here in the street outside Newgate on the more 'efficient' gallows of the 'New Drop'. The modern reincarnation of the old Magpie and Stump pub, which faces the Old Bailey, features a number of prints of historic hangings, showing the crowds that congregated here on hanging days. The 'London Burkers', Bishop and Williams, were hanged here to the cheers of an enormous crowd in December 1831.

Cross Ludgate Hill to Pageantmaster Court, then along Ludgate Broadway to visit Apothecaries' Hall in Blackfriars Lane. The windows of the great hall – in which many doctors have been examined and awarded their qualifications to practise – can be seen from the lovely inner courtyard of this old livery hall, which dates from just after the Great Fire.

Cross to New Bridge Street by taking the steps up and down in Apothecary Street opposite and find Bride Lane, a crooked alley on the left towards Ludgate Circus. A stair on the left takes you up to the raised level of St Bride's churchyard. If you can, visit the crypt in which are displayed the remains of a patent iron coffin laid open to show the special closure mechanism that rendered the contents secure from bodysnatchers.

Up Ludgate Hill to St Paul's and along Cannon Street. The square mile of the City is peppered with at least 90 old burial grounds, most of which were in regular use until the 1850s. All were raided by bodysnatchers at one time or another. To get a sense of how cheek-by-jowl these churchyards were, cross King William Street, go up Eastcheap and turn south into St Mary-at-Hill. Notice the skulls in the gateway over the rear access to the church on the right. The churchyard to which this alley led has been largely built over. The old Billingsgate Market and the

Anatomical London

Old Bailey

Cooper was entombed in 1841. Sir Astley, a pupil of Hunter, and Keats's tutor, was reputed to have dissected something or someone every day of his working life and probably purchased hundreds (if not thousands) of corpses from bodysnatchers. He was a key witness to the Select Committee that in 1828 investigated the problems of anatomy.

It was Cooper who first proposed to the committee that a much greater supply of corpses than that provided by criminals could be obtained by requisitioning the bodies of people too poor to pay for their own funerals. This idea was enacted in the Anatomy Act of 1832, which swiftly undercut the bodysnatchers and put them out of business and served to stigmatise burial as a pauper even into the 20th century. Cooper's great stone sarcophagus contains at least two, if not three, inner coffins, and is very securely embedded in the crypt floor.

Through the arcade at the rear of the entrance courtyard is a green area that was originally the hospital 'crib' (burial ground), and is now surrounded by the Medical School. One building houses the Gordon Museum, home to thousands of preserved body parts. It is one of the finest medical museums in London, purpose built, much used for teaching and beautifully cared for. It is closed to the general public. The Medical School's dissecting rooms, also closed, use the bodies of public-spirited members of the public who nowadays generously bequeath their bodies to science.

Return to cross St Thomas Street, turning left back towards Borough High Street. A curious Georgian doorway on the right, more or less opposite Keats House, used to provide the students access to the old St Thomas's Hospital. Further up on the right is the former hospital chapel whose loft contains the Old Operating Theatre Museum, well worth visiting, if only to witness the steeply raked stands for the audience at surgical operations.

rather ugly tower of the modern Guy's Hospital can both be seen across the river. Take St Dunstan's Lane left and visit the ruined church of St Dunstan's in the East and its churchyard (no indication of any burials here, though there were certainly thousands). Take Idol Lane back to Eastcheap and King William Street to cross the river at London Bridge on the Monument side. It was on the old London Bridge, just west of here, that the severed heads of traitors were stuck on poles.

When you reach the Southwark side of the river, pass along Borough High Street under the great bridge carrying trains west out of London Bridge Station. After three shops see the plaque marking the site of the old St Thomas's Hospital, which moved to Lambeth in 1863. Its site is now occupied by the station. Turn left into St Thomas Street and walk down its right-hand side, passing a building called Keats House on the site of a house in which the poet lodged while a medical student here in 1816. Further down on the same side of the road are the gates and entrance courtyard of Guy's Hospital. Entering the courtyard, the Hospital Chapel is on your right, in the crypt of which the great anatomist Sir Astley

You will probably need a drink after contemplating these matters. Try the George Inn – a fine old galleried inn in its own yard further along the Guy's side of Borough High Street, much frequented by medical students in the old days. In summer, plays are sometimes performed in the yard. I remember one particularly fine production of *Hamlet* there when I was a child – I never thought to ponder then where Yorick's skull had come from.

Alternatively, try the cosy old Anchor, Bankside tavern. Cross Borough High Street towards the river and take the stairs down on your left to pass beside and behind Southwark Cathedral and then left into Clink Street. Just under the railway arch you will see two gibbets outside the Clink Prison. Both are completely spurious, but give a good idea of the horrible fate that many considered preferable to being dissected. The Anchor is at the junction with Park Street, which, because it skirted a huge and much-used burial ground (now closed and partly built over), used to be called Deadman's Place.

Eating & drinking

Anchor Bankside
34 Park Street, SE1 9EF (7407 1577). **Open** 11am-11pm Mon-Sat; noon-10.30pm Sun. Real ales, river views and fair food.

George Inn
77 Borough High Street, SE1 1NH (7407 2056). **Open** 11am-11pm Mon-Sat; noon-10.30pm Sun. Real ales and pub food in a 17th-century coaching inn.

Magpie & Stump
18 Old Bailey, EC4M 7EP (7248 5085). **Open** noon-11pm Mon-Fri. Food served.

Viaduct Tavern
126 Newgate Street, EC1A 7AA (7600 1863). **Open** noon-11pm Mon-Fri. Standard food and drink served.

Churches

St Andrew Holborn
Holborn Viaduct, EC4A 3AB (7353 3544/www.st andrewholborn.org.uk). **Open** 8.30am-4.30pm Mon-Fri.

St Anne's, Soho
55 Dean Street, W1D 6AH (7437 5006). **Open** *Gardens* 8am-dusk daily.

St Bride's
Fleet Street, EC4Y 8AU (7427 0133/www.stbrides. com). **Open** 8am-5pm Mon-Fri; call for details Sat, Sun.

St Dunstan's-in-the-East
St Dunstan's Hill, EC3R 5DD. Administered by church of All Hallows by the Tower (7481 2928). **Open** 7.30am-7pm or dusk if earlier daily.

St Mary-at-Hill
Lovatt Lane, EC3R 8EE (7626 4184). **Open** 11am-4pm Mon-Fri.

St Paul's, Covent Garden
Bedford Street, WC2E 9ED (7836 5221/www.actors church.org). **Open** 9am-4.30pm Mon-Fri; 9am-noon Sun. *Services* 1.10pm Wed; 11am Sun. *Evening choralsong* 4pm 2nd Sun of mth.

St Sepulchre without Newgate
Holborn Viaduct, EC1A 9DE (7248 3826/www.st-sepulchre.org.uk). **Open** noon-2pm Tue, Thur; 11am-3pm Wed.

Southwark Cathedral
London Bridge, SE1 9DA (7367 6700/www. southwark.anglican.org/cathedral). **Open** 8am-6pm daily. *Refectory* 10am-5pm daily.

Museums & galleries

Apothecaries' Hall
Blackfriars Lane, EC4V 6EJ (7236 1189). For admission contact the Beadle/Hall Manager on the above number.

Clink Prison Museum
1 Clink Street, SE1 9DG (7403 6515/www.clink.co.uk). **Open** *June-Sept* 10am-9pm daily. *Oct-May* 10am-6pm daily. **Admission** £5; £3.50 concessions.

Friends of Benjamin Franklin
Benjamin Franklin House, 36 Craven Street, WC2N 5NF (7930 9121/www.thersa.org/franklin). Opening scheduled for 17 Jan 2006, 300 years after Franklin's birth. More information on the website nearer the time.

Hunterian Museum at the Royal College of Surgeons
35-43 Lincoln's Inn Fields, WC2A 3PE (7869 6560/ www.rcseng.ac.uk/services/museums). **Open** 10am-5pm Tue-Sat. **Admission** free.

Old Operating Theatre, Museum & Herb Garret
9A St Thomas Street, SE1 9RY (7955 4791/www.the garret.org.uk). **Open** 10.30am-5pm daily. **Admission** £4.75; £3.75 concessions; £12 family; free under-5s.

Royal Academy of Arts
Burlington House, Piccadilly, W1J 0BD (7300 8000/www.royalacademy.org.uk). **Open** *Temporary exhibitions* 10am-6pm Mon-Thur, Sat, Sun; 10am-

10pm Fri. *John Madejski Fine Rooms* 1-4.30pm Tue-Fri; 10am6pm sat, Sun. **Admission** Fine Rooms free, exhibitions vary.

St Bartholomew's Hospital Museum

West Smithfield, EC1A 7BE (7601 8152/guided tours 7837 0546). **Open** 10am-4pm Tue-Fri. **Tours** 2pm Fri. **Admission** free. *Tours* £4; £3 concessions.

Sir John Soane's Museum

13 Lincoln's Inn Fields, WC2A 3BP (7405 2107/ www.soane.org). **Open** 10am-5pm Tue-Sat; 6-9pm first Tue of every month. **Tours** 2.30pm Sat. **Admission** free. **Tours** £3; free concessions.

Somerset House

Strand, WC2R 1LA (7845 4600/www.somerset-house.org.uk). **Open** 10am-6pm daily (last entry 5.15pm); extended hours for courtyard & terrace. *Tours* phone for details. **Admission** *Courtyard & terrace* free; £5/£4 concessions for exhibitions.

Somerset House museums

Courtauld Institute Gallery
7848 2526/www.courtauld.ac.uk/gallery
Gilbert Collection
7420 9400/www.gilbert-collection.org.uk
Hermitage Rooms
7845 4630/www.hermitagerooms.co.uk

Open *All collections* 10am-6pm daily (last entry 5.15pm). **Tours** phone for details. **Admission** £5 1 collection; £4 concessions. £8 2 collections; £7 concessions. £12 3 collections; £11 concessions. Free students, under-18s; Courtauld gallery free to all 10am-2pm Mon.

Others

Guy's Hospital

St Thomas Street, SE1 9RT (7188 7188/www.guys andstthomas.nhs.uk). **Open** *Hospital Chapel* 8am-8pm daily. The Gordon Museum is closed to the public.

Lanesborough Hotel

Hyde Park Corner, SW1X 7TA (7259 5599/ www.lanesborough.com).

Lyric Theatre

Shaftesbury Avenue, W1D 7ES (7494 5045).

Old Bailey (Central Criminal Court)

corner of Newgate Street & Old Bailey, EC4M 7EH (7248 3277/www.oldbaileyonline.org). **Open** 10am-1pm, 2-4.30pm Mon-Fri. **Admission** free (no under-14s admitted, 14-16s accompanied by adults only). No cameras, mobile phones, large bags or radios are allowed into the court, and there are no facilities to store them. Stairs may pose a problem for some visitors.

The Herb Garret at the **Old Operating Theatre**.

A monopoly on wealth

Jon Ronson

If Mayfair is good enough for the Sultan of Brunei's brother and Jesus of Nazareth, it should be good enough for you, too.

Start: Portman Square, W1
Finish: Shepherd's Market, W1
Distance: 3 miles/4.5km
Time: 1.5 hours
Getting there: Central line to Marble Arch, exit Oxford Street north side (subway 1), then 5-minute walk
Getting back: 5-minute walk to Green Park tube (Jubilee, Piccadilly or Victoria lines)
Note: Speakers' Corner only operates Sunday mornings, 10am onwards.

My grandparents lived in Mayfair. This was big news for me when I first discovered Monopoly. Admittedly I recognised, even as a child, that an inconsistency existed between the impossibly well-to-do Mayfair of the Monopoly board and the Mayfair of my grandparents' flat, which was somewhat poky and heat-controlled, on the ground floor of a huge mansion block at 15 Portman Square, which is where I begin my walk today.

Portman Square lies between Baker Street and Marble Arch. It is, I like to think, the gateway to Mayfair, although Mayfair is an ill-defined district, sprawling between Park Lane and Piccadilly, somewhere beyond the south side of Oxford Street and the west side of Bond Street. Mayfair is where the double agents, the classy murderers and the international playboys hung out in the 1960s, at nightclubs called the Paramour and such. Those were the days.

Here are some other random facts about Mayfair: the Queen buys her underwear on Conduit Street. Prince Jefri, the brother of the Sultan of Brunei, had his 50-prostitutes-a-night sex parties in a penthouse on Park Lane. And you are forbidden, by law, to beat the dust out of carpets in Berkeley Square. Basically then, aside from the carpet-beating, Mayfair is the home of royalty, sex, international intrigue and murder.

My plan is to walk via Upper Berkeley Street to Marble Arch, down Park Lane, and then cut left into the heart of Mayfair – land of the spies and the embassies and the penthouse pads. But first I shall rest for a moment in Portman Square. Portman Square is home to Selfridges' Food Hall, which contains the Barrier Reef of fish counters. My mother once saw the actor Robert Powell, who starred in *Jesus of Nazareth*, queue for fish here. For many subsequent years, whenever we saw a painting of Jesus at a gallery, for instance, my mother would say: 'I saw Jesus queuing for fish once in Selfridges. Ha ha!'

'Yeah yeah,' I eventually replied, as I entered my teens.

'I was wondering how many people he was hoping to feed with the fish!' my mother would continue merrily. 'Maybe 5,000! Ha ha! Maybe he was going to the bread counter to buy some loaves also!'

'Yeah yeah,' I would mutter.

My grandparents' mansion block is just as large as it was when I was a child. It hasn't shrunk in the intervening years. Mayfair is where the mansion blocks are. Mansion blocks can, of course, be found elsewhere, in Russell Square and Maida Vale, for instance, but they are most at

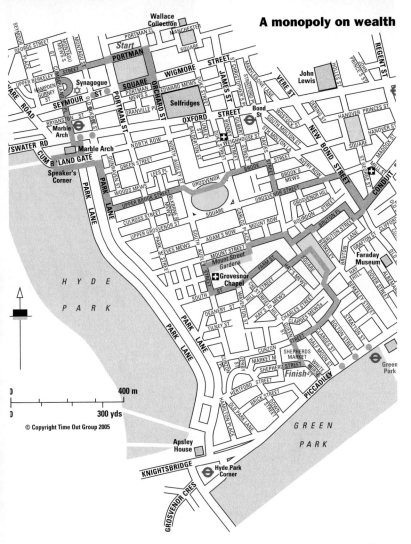

A monopoly on truth

home in Mayfair. They remind me of Staterooms on cruises. Staterooms are, essentially, very small bedrooms with tiny portholes, but they are called Staterooms, and the Queen sleeps in a Stateroom. Mansion blocks are, basically, huge blocks of flats, but they have the word mansion in the title, which gives them, I feel, kudos beyond their intrinsic worth. I am no fan of mansion blocks. The heat is controlled centrally, which diminishes one's sense of personal

freedom, and the porters are invariably surly. They give you looks.

From No.15 I continue into Upper Berkeley Street and I write in my notepad, 'No observations here.' It's the truth. I defy you to find something amusing to observe about Upper Berkeley Street. It's just a street. Then I turn left again into Great Cumberland Place. This is the home of the Marble Arch Synagogue, on the left, which is where my parents were married. Outside the synagogue

Park Lane

Mount Street Gardens

there's a sculpture dedicated to a man called Raoul Wallenberg who, I gather, was an unsung Schindler. He saved Jews from the gas chambers. But nobody made a movie about him. It is unlikely that anyone ever will now, because the film critics will all say, 'They're just jumping on the Schindler bandwagon.'

Right ahead of me is Marble Arch itself. I don't know much about Marble Arch. Like most Londoners, I think of it vaguely as the big marble thing in the middle of the traffic island near the Odeon. I have a vague notion that only the Queen is allowed to walk under it, and if commoners accidentally get too close to its underbelly they will be taken away and beheaded. But then I notice a bunch of tourists wandering back and forth, in and out, so I guess I'm either thinking of a different arch, or they're lax about upholding this particular law. I decide to walk under it myself and see what happens.

Getting to Marble Arch itself – even though it is no more than 20 yards away – proves to be a difficult and horrible task involving urine-sprinkled underpasses and mounds of garbage. I wander around this awful subterrania for 25 minutes,

trying to ascertain which of the 14 exits will take me up to the arch. (See notes at the end.)

In the middle of the underpass is a man selling posters depicting kittens rammed into brandy glasses. Who buys these? It is sadism dressed up as adorableness. If kittens could talk, they would say, 'Please get me out of this brandy glass.' There are also posters of babies, Bob Marley, Liam Gallagher of Oasis, gentle kudu running away from lions on a dusty savannah, and Malcolm X. In total, these posters constitute, I think, an accurate cross-section of the exciting melting pot that is London society, aside from the gentle kudu.

Finally, I make it to Marble Arch, which stands, in a marble manner, among overflowing dustbins, jam-packed with McDonald's wrappers. Why is it all of London's great sculptural monuments become traffic islands? Nelson's Column (pre-pedestrianisation). Wellington Arch. Marble Arch. I look around to see if there's a plaque telling me anything about the arch's undoubtedly intriguing history. But there is nothing. I walk underneath it. Nothing happens.

I move onwards, to Speakers' Corner, that hotbed of constitutional weirdness.

Speakers' Corner is where the lunatics, the Jews for Jesus and so on exercise their democratic right to be heard, the basic flaw being that the audience turns up solely to chuckle benignly at them. This rather defeats the point. If I were a lunatic, I wouldn't pigeon-hole myself in this manner. I'd try to slip unnoticed into the mainstream.

Today, a woman with blonde hair is standing on a soapbox yelling, 'My father is so wonderful, he never fails to give me everything I need'. An old man 20 yards to her left, is hollering, 'Taste and see, young man. Taste is free. You don't have to fall at the feet of the Pope.' I wander from soapbox to soapbox and buy myself an ice-lolly. Speakers' Corner is a wonderful place, of course. It is where the dope smokers gather every year to smoke dope en masse and make a stand, until they get dizzy and sit down again. It's where the religious fundamentalists give their press conferences. Tempers get raised and fights break out, even on lovely sunny days like today.

I could spend all day here, but I must move on, back into the awful underpass, and navigate my way to Exit 6, which will take me to the east side of Park Lane. I have high hopes for the heart of Mayfair. This is one of London's oldest districts, the home to the Spring Fair, which was closed down in 1764 when the neighbours complained about the noise. So not much changes.

It is not a district I know well. Like most people, I have queued for five hours at the visa department of the American Embassy, and I remember it to be an enormously impressive building, combining the brutalist architecture of the post-war years, sprinkled with five-star Eurotrash-hotel gold underneath a huge bald eagle. I decide to make it my next stop. So 20 yards down noisy Park Lane, I turn left on to Upper Brook Street, which leads into Grosvenor Square, home of the embassy.

From far down the street, I see the vast Dwight Eisenhower sculpture, hands on hips, staring outwards. Underneath him is a policeman, hands also on hips, staring in the other direction towards the embassy. A few years ago, there was an architectural scandal when the Americans decided they needed to erect a bunch of unsightly concrete blocks to stop Saddam Hussein bombing the building. Londoners were in uproar, especially after it transpired that we were to pay for the bloody things, but the concrete blocks got erected anyway. After all the fuss, I imagine that the concrete blocks will be huge and ugly, but they turn out to be very small and discreet.

Eisenhower in **Grosvenor Square** and the **US Embassy**.

How can these blocks stop anyone from bombing anything, I wonder? So I ask the policeman.

'Well,' he says, 'they're there to stop suicide bombings. No car or truck can get between the blocks.'

'What about suicide bomber motorcyclists?' I ask.

'In the history of terrorism,' he replies, 'I don't know of any suicide bomber motorcyclists.'

'You know,' I say, 'I've never thought of that. You're right. There are no suicide bomber motorcyclists. Why is that?'

'Well,' replies the policeman, 'suicide bombers like to travel in comfort.'

I walk through Grosvenor Square Gardens and on to Davies Street. This is where the expensive minimalist shops are – furniture shops displaying one chair in the window – and so on. Window shopping is, I think, discouraged here.

A window in Elizabeth Arden offers an intensive full-day spa gift certificate for £180. The poster says, 'She'll love it. We guarantee it. If she doesn't love it, you get your money back.' I think that this guarantee, although well-meaning, may be open to abuse. If I were you, I'd sign up for the full treatment, enjoy it hugely but keep the mmms and ahhhs to yourself. And then simply announce at the end, 'I didn't love it.' What can they do? Love is an arbitrary concept that cannot be tangibly measured.

It is around this point that I begin to get lost and confused (see map). I know that one is supposed to be keeping to a specific, easily duplicable route, but I become overexcited in my window shopping and wander around all over the place for a while, up and down crooked streets and tiny mews rows. I know that I make it, at one point, on to Conduit Street and gaze at the Queen's underwear in Rigby and Peller, but these old and winding central Mayfair streets become a jumble to me now.

This is as it should be. Most visitors get irritated, eventually, by the illogicality of our roads. But the randomness reflects the truth of how this strange city came to be. The map of London is a map of chance decisions and resolutions. Some guy on a horse decides to go left along this field instead of right, and – 500 years later – Conduit Street veers off to the left. Here, in the heart of Mayfair, little roads are called Sheep Walk and Shepherd Place. There's no doubt that Sheep Walk is called Sheep Walk because this is the way they took their sheep to market back then. If the sheep walkers (or shepherds, to give them their accurate title) had decided, haphazardly, to turn left instead of right, this little piece of London would have been for ever slightly different.

So I lose myself until I turn the corner on to Mount Street and stop in my tracks. Three very large slabs of bloody meat stare out at me from a window. Just the three slabs of meat, no adornments. The sign reads 'Allens & Co. Butchers'.

I poke my head around the door. There is always something comforting about seeing a butcher at work. I myself eat beef. My vegetarian friends, I have no doubt, gaze upon us meat-eaters with solemnity, the question on their minds being whether our brains will turn to sponge before our hearts explode into a hundred bloodied mini-fillets. But my reasoned response is this – walk into a wholefood shop, look behind the counter, and you can bet that the young man serving the beans, or whatever, will be pallid and scrawny and lacklustre. Whereas all butchers, with no exception, are rosy-cheeked and full of vigour, laughing heartily at all times with their arms outstretched. This is proof positive, in my book, that meat-eating can only be a good thing in the long run.

And sure enough, the men cutting the meat at Allens & Co fit my utopian description accurately. This is a butcher's from another time, another century. Old wooden panelling, tiles and meat-hooks. Slightly unnervingly, a large, stuffed

Le Gavroche

trophy cow's head glares down from the wall at its descendants lying scattered in bits on the antique slab. But now's not the time for sentimentality. This grand old butcher's, in the heart of ancient Mayfair, stands there like a time-slip, reminding the walker that there was real life here before the mansion blocks descended upon the streets and cut off the sun.

These streets, Mount Street, Shepherd's Market, Bruton Place and so on, are a wonderful little district, besieged by the nearby mansion blocks of Curzon Street and Berkeley Square. I wander into Mount Street Gardens, a lovely shaded public garden, which stands on the site of an old burial ground and is full of Japanese trees. I stop for a while and sit there. It is one of the nicest public gardens I have ever found in London.

Out on to South Audley Street, home of the Grosvenor Chapel, where John Wilkes, the radical MP, is buried. Next to the church and down a little lane stands one of the most beautiful London houses I've ever seen. It is 23 South

Audley Street, cream and detached and strangely tranquil, as if a little bit of the Cotswolds has been picked up and dumped in busy central London.

Have a look, but I don't think you should knock on the door. I get the feeling somebody lives there and they'd be pissed off if they knew they'd been thrust unsuspectingly into the midst of a book about London walks. Still, whoever owns this wonderful house must have had tremendous good fortune in their lives, and they consequently deserve a few months of backpackers standing outside, pointing and gurgling merrily. It will redress the karmic balance a little.

And then on to Berkeley Square, where I listen to see if I can hear any nightingales sing. I can't. There are too many cars. Anyway, I have a sneaking suspicion that nightingales never really did sing in Berkeley Square. The truth is, I don't trust the factual veracity of music-hall songs. I don't think that Flanagan and Allen ever hung around underneath arches either.

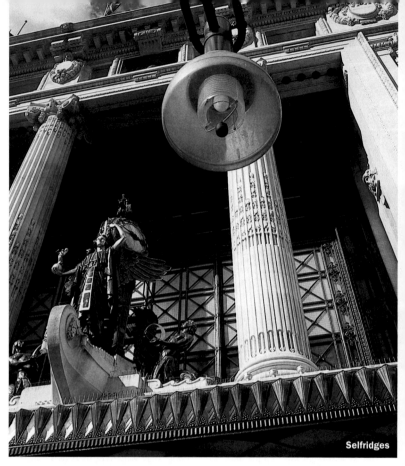
Selfridges

And then on to my final destination, dinner at Shepherd Market, off Curzon Street. This is where, I'm told, the high-class hookers ply their trade. But I can see no high-class hookers, only a strange mix of Arsenal fans and gentlemen in tweed. I sit myself down in the Sofra meze restaurant, order myself a houmous, watch the world go by, and then get a cab home, through the long tall streets where the great big mansion blocks are.

The mansion blocks all around are big and rich and anonymous, with flat façades and hall porters and a general aura that unwelcomes. For those non-Londoners who are predisposed to disliking the city for its closed-door misanthropy, Mayfair could confirm these prejudices. Indeed, when I was in my early 20s, I found

myself one day in a Transit van with a bunch of friends from Manchester, driving through Mayfair on our way to Shepherd's Bush. Just as we crossed Curzon Street, our driver pulled up the van. He wound down the window.

'Excuse me,' he said to a passer-by.

The passer-by stopped.

'Yes?' he said.

'Is this London?' said our driver. There was a short silence.

'Yes,' said the passer-by.

'Well,' said our driver, pointing over his shoulder at the back of the van. 'Where do you want this wood?'

Mayfair was the perfect location to play this joke. It was not impossible to think that the wealthy, insular Mayfairians may believe that this dumb-hick small-town northern Transit-van driver was stupid enough to think that everyone in London would know where the wood had to go. But not only that. Pull up in Highbury, and the passer-by might direct you to the local timber-yard. Pull up in Hampstead and maybe, just maybe, a neighbour may know of another neighbour who needed wood. But Mayfair! Margaret Thatcher once famously said that there was no such thing as society. And here, if you fail to discover the wonderful core of Old Mayfair, it looks as if her dream came true.

Directions for reaching Marble Arch: enter Marble Arch tube on north side of Oxford Street; follow subway 3; emerge by Arch; follow signs for exits 8-14; emerge at Speakers' Corner.

Directions for reaching Park Lane: exit Speakers' Corner by subway exit 5; emerge on to Park Lane east side via exit 6.

Eating & drinking

Angela Hartnett at the Connaught
16 Carlos Place, W1K 2AL (7592 1222/www.gordon ramsay.com). **Breakfast served** 7-10.30am Mon-Fri; 7-11am Sat, Sun. **Lunch served** noon-2.45pm Mon-Fri; noon-3.15pm Sat, Sun. **Dinner served** 5.45-11pm Mon-Sat; 7-10.30pm Sun. A culinary cathedral, devoted to the spirit of haute cuisine. The set dinner costs £55 for three courses.

Le Gavroche
43 Upper Brook Street, W1K 7QR (7408 0881/ www.le-gavroche.co.uk). **Lunch served** noon-2pm Mon-Fri. **Dinner served** 7-11pm Mon-Sat. One of London's grandest, and priciest, restaurants for haute cuisine. Set lunch (£44) includes three courses, mineral water, half a bottle of wine and coffee.

The Guinea Grill
30 Bruton Place, W1J 6NL (7499 1210/www. youngs.co.uk). **Pub Open** 11am-11pm Mon-Fri; 6.30-11pm Sat. **Food served** noon-2.30pm Mon-Fri. **Restaurant Lunch served** 12.30-2.30pm Mon-Fri. **Dinner served** 6.30-11pm Mon-Sat. Friendly, busy and small, with award-winning pies that help to draw the crowds.

Punch Bowl
41 Farm Street, W1J 5RP (7493 6841). **Open** 11am-11pm Mon-Fri; 11am-6pm Sat. **Food served** noon-4pm, 6-9pm Mon-Fri; noon-5pm Sat. Earthy, slightly scruffy, loveable local serving good beer and food.

Sofra
18 Shepherd Market, W1Y 7HU (7493 3320/ www.sofra.co.uk). **Open** noon-midnight daily. Modern Turkish informal bistro.

Ye Grapes
16 Shepherd Market, W1J 7QQ (no phone). **Open** 11am-11pm Mon-Sat; noon-10.30pm Sun. Pricey but handsome corner pub serving decent food.

Film

Odeon Marble Arch
10 Edgware Road, W2 2EN (0871 224 4007/ www.odeon.co.uk).

Information

American Embassy
24 Grosvenor Square, W1A 1AE (7499 9000/ www.usembassy.org.uk). **Open** by appointment only.

Mount Street Gardens
Mount Street, W1. **Open** *Summer* 8am-dusk daily. *Winter* 8am-4.30pm daily.

Speakers' Corner
Hyde Park (7298 2000/www.royalparks.gov.uk). Sunday mornings from 10am.

Shopping

Allen & Co
117 Mount Street, W1K 3LA (7499 5831). **Open** 5am-4pm Mon-Fri; 5am-noon Sat.

Elizabeth Arden Red Door
29 Davies Street, W1K 4LW (7629 4488/ www.reddoorspas.com). **Open** 10am-7pm Mon; 9am-7pm Tue, Sat; 9am-8pm Wed-Fri; 11am-5pm Sun.

Rigby & Peller
22A Conduit Street, W1S 2XT (7491 2200/ www.rigbyandpeller.com). **Open** 9.30am-6pm Mon-Wed, Fri, Sat; 9.30am-7pm Thur.

Selfridges
400 Oxford Street, W1A 1AB (7629 1234/ www.selfridges.co.uk). **Open** 10am-8pm Mon-Wed, Fri, Sat; 10am-9pm Thur; 11.30am-6pm Sun.

Worship

Church of Immaculate Conception
114 Mount Street, W1K 3AH (7493 7811/ www.farmstreet.org.uk). **Open** *Office* 9am-6.30pm daily. **Services** 8.30am, 12.05pm, 1.05pm, 6pm Mon-Fri; 8.30am, 11am, 6pm Sat; 8am, 9.30am, 11am, 12.30pm, 4.15pm, 6.15pm Sun.

Grosvenor Chapel
24 South Audley Street, W1K 2PA (7499 1684/ www.grosvenorchapel.org.uk). **Open** *Office* 9.30am-1pm Mon-Fri. **Services** 11am Sun.

Marble Arch Synagogue
32 Great Cumberland Place, W1H 7TN (7723 7246). Not open to the public.

Museum piece
William Forrester

From Nelson's Column to the Nereid Monument: Trafalgar Square is the launching pad for a tour round London's national galleries and theatres.

Start: Trafalgar Square
Finish: British Museum, Montague Place exit
Distance: 2 miles/3km
Time: 1.5 hours
Getting there: Bakerloo or Northern line, or rail, to Charing Cross followed by short walk
Getting back: short walk to Russell Square (Piccadilly line) or Tottenham Court Road (Central or Northern lines)
Note: check opening times of the galleries.

Begin under Nelson's column looking north to the dome of the National Gallery. Looking from left to right, the first building is Canada House (Sir Robert Smirke, 1824-27). In the foreground is a fountain designed by Lutyens (1939) and, above it, the glass roofs of the new wing of the National Gallery (1991).

Ahead is the gallery's main wing (William Wilkins, 1838), often compared to a cruet set, with salt and pepper pots flanking a mustard pot dome. To the right is the globe-topped Coliseum Theatre and a statue of George IV on horseback by Chantrey. You'll see the spire and portico of St Martin-in-the-Fields (James Gibbs, 1722-24) and, to the right, South Africa House (Sir Herbert Baker, 1933).

Now admire Landseer's lions (1867). They caused the unstable artist no end of grief, not least because the elderly lion he used as a model died and became extremely smelly to work with. They now give joyous piggy back rides to children of all ages.

On the south side, the stainless steel signboard will explain the panorama. Don't miss the statue of Charles I on horseback (Le Sueur, 1633) looking down Whitehall towards the Banqueting House outside which he was executed in 1649, with a single blow of the axe. The clock tower of the Houses of Parliament is just beyond, inside which hangs Big Ben, the famously massive bell.

On the pedestal of the column, the bronze scene shows the moments after Lord Nelson was shot at the Battle of Trafalgar on 21 October 1805. He was carried below decks and learned before he died that his smaller fleet had won a decisive victory over the French and Spanish that put paid to any chances of invasion. The message below the scene, 'England Expects Every Man Will Do His Duty', was sent by Nelson to his sailors as they went into battle. Now turn left around the column and walk up the ramp by the mini plane trees on the west (Canada House) side of the Square. Go along the balustrade on the north side of the Square. Stop at another panoramic signboard. The statue of Nelson (sculpted by Baily, 1840-43) is said to look towards Portsmouth, from where this great little man left England for the last time. Had Hitler taken London in World War II, he planned to re-site the column in Berlin.

Now head for St Martin-in-the-Fields, the setting for many a celebrity's memorial service and candlelit concerts. There's an excellent guide leaflet available in the porch. (Ramped wheelchair access is on the north side, via the mini-market.)

From St Martin's, cross the road by the traffic lights again, but this time walk

Museum piece

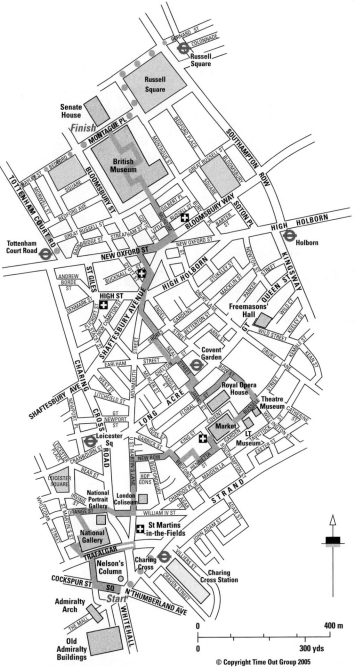

Covent Garden in and around the **Market**.

along the front of the National Gallery.
You'll pass a shrunken statue of George
Washington and (once past the gallery's
main entrance) a statue to Jacobus
Secundus (Grinling Gibbons). This is
James II camping it up as a Roman
Emperor. They seem unusual choices –
a man who kicked the British out and a
king kicked out by the English in 1688.

Beyond James, compare the old and
new wings of the National Gallery. The
architects of the new (Venturi, Scott, &
Brown Associates of Philadelphia) pick up
Wilkins's classical columns and play with
them. The buildings are different, but the
new one matches the old in scale, style
and stone. Enter this new Sainsbury wing,
named after the supermarket family that
paid for it, to take a tour of the gallery's
best views. Paintings' locations do change
– if you cannot find anything, ask one of
the members of staff. But start by picking
up a gallery plan from the information

desk on the ground floor, taking the lift to
level M and turning right out of the lift.

Ahead, in the distance, is *The
Incredulity of St Thomas* by Cima de
Conegliano (1502-4). It is framed between
Robert Venturi's pneumatic classico-
modern pillars. They're made of Italian
petra serena, a stone much used in
Renaissance architecture. In room 60,
turn left and head to *St Sebastian* by the
Pollaiuolo brothers in the southern end
of room 57. He looks moderately bored as
he fills up with arrows like a pincushion.

Return to the lift and on into the centre
of room 9 in the main building. Looking
right, the doorway into room 8 frames the
massive *Raising of Lazarus* by Sebastiano
del Piombo of 1517-19. The doorway is
flanked by two of the four *Allegory of Love*
paintings rendered by Paolo Veronese
in the 1570s, all of them in this room.
Continue to room 10 and admire the
brilliant blues of Titian's *Bacchus and
Ariadne* on your left. In room 11, the view

to the right shows Holbein's majestic *Ambassadors* in room 4.

On to the central hall. A left turn takes you into the centre of room 30. Framed in the doorway is Van Dyck's monumental *Equestrian Portrait of Charles I.* Painted in 1637-38, it dominates this space just as it originally dominated the view down a long gallery at Hampton Court Palace. From here turn left and head all the way to room 15 and the sunny warmth and perfect proportions of Claude's *Seaport with the Embarkation of the Queen of Sheba* of 1648. In the same room is Turner's *Dido Building Carthage* (1815). Turner's sun, neither benign nor gentle, is an apocalyptic fireball.

From here head north into room 18 for the chilly pink splendour of his eminence *Cardinal Richelieu* (1640s). Before leaving the gallery turn left into room 21 and catch the sharp, focused, golden glow of Aelbert Cuyp's landscapes and seascapes of the 1650s on the end wall. Both Cuyp and Claude have long been tremendously popular in England and you can see why. They're the perfect antidote to a grey November day.

From here exit into Orange Street from behind *Cardinal Richlieu.* (If this exit is closed, double back to the Sainsbury wing, exit at the front and walk up under the link between the two National Gallery wings to reach Orange Street.) Turn right and head up the ramp into the National Portrait Gallery. Once inside turn left into the modern gallery (1990 by John Miller and Partners). At the end of the gallery, turn right and right again into the dramatic atrium of the main hall (opened May 2000 – architects: Dixon and Jones). The massive escalator demands ascent. Once up, take the lift up to the Portrait Restaurant for the stunning vista and then back down in the lift to the second floor for the new Tudor galleries (rooms 1-3). Don't miss Holbein's archetypal cartoon of Henry VIII. Beyond room 3, take the lift to the Victorian section (room 21 on the first floor). Here a cast

of a splendidly yucky statue shows Prince Albert saying fond and final farewells to a doting, clinging Queen Victoria (William Theed, 1863-67). This looks down a superb perspective of marble busts of the Victorian great and good which leads on to the World War I section (room 30).

Beyond lies the unexpected delight of a room (No.31) designed by Piers Gough – one of Britain's more successful modern architects. Portraits hang on glass screens under an undulating white ceiling. It's a remarkable achievement – the maximum number of portraits hang within the minimum space without a sense of claustrophobia.

Leave the gallery by the same ramp, turn right along Orange Street and head for the statue of Sir Henry Irving. Arguably the greatest actor of his era, he was the first to be knighted, in 1895. 20 years later, in the ultimate curtain call, his ashes were buried at Westminster Abbey. He looks across to the Garrick Theatre (named after the greatest actor of the 18th century). It opened in 1889 and was funded by WS Gilbert (of Gilbert and Sullivan fame).

Head downhill from Sir Henry and take the second zebra crossing on the left. Stop on the large triangular traffic island and enjoy the memorial to nurse Edith Cavell, shot in 1915 for helping allied soldiers escape from Belgium in World War I. The sculptor is George Frampton, best known for his statue of Peter Pan. Behind to the right is the Coliseum with its dome atop. It was built in 1904 as the largest theatre in the West End, seating 2,358, and is now home to the English National Opera.

Cross towards the Chandos pub and carry on up St Martin's Lane. On your left is the Duke of York's Theatre, where *Peter Pan* had its first night on 27 December 1904. Further up on the left is the Albery Theatre, named after the great theatrical manager Sir Bronson Albery. Sir John Gielgud made his name here.

Now turn right into New Row opposite the Albery. On the corner of Bedfordbury, Arthur Middleton sells antique scientific instruments and rents them out as film props. Turn right down Bedford Street and within 30 metres left through some iron gates, topped with a coat of arms. This belongs to the Russell family (the Dukes of Bedford or Marquesses of Tavistock), who developed the area in the 1630s.

Ahead is St Paul's, Covent Garden (there's a steep wheelchair ramp to the left of the steps). It is a replica of the original of 1633 (by Inigo Jones), which burned down in 1795. WS Gilbert and JMW Turner were baptised here, but it is best known as the actors' church. It is full of thespian memorials, including ones to Vivien Leigh and Boris Karloff (real name William Henry Pratt).

Exit south from the churchyard and turn left into Henrietta Street, named after Henrietta Maria, wife of Charles I. (If the churchyard gates are closed, continue down Bedford Street and take the first left.) Stop at the corner of the Piazza where the paving starts. This area originally grew fruit and vegetables for Westminster Abbey from the 12th century and was then called Convent Garden. A market grew up and the central buildings were put up in 1830. A hint of the past can be seen ahead above the door marked Bar Creperie. The painted sign for 'James Butler Herbalist and Seedman, Lavender Water' still shows through, albeit faintly. The market moved out to Vauxhall in 1974 and the shops moved in.

Head to the columns under the balcony of the Punch and Judy and look back towards the portico of St Paul's. Nobody has ever used that imposing doorway as it is blocked by the altar behind. This was where the professor met the flower seller in *Pygmalion*. Nowadays the area hosts street theatre and buskers. To the right is the gaudy pink façade of Archer House (1717), named after its architect, Thomas Archer (a pupil of Vanbrugh).

Walk through the Market Buildings. At the far end (by yet more columns), look down right towards the former flower market, now the London Transport Museum, a great place for kids.

Up to the left is the new development for the Royal Opera House, occupying a 2.5-acre site and costing a mere £214 million. It remains a profoundly undemocratic building. It's only open to the general public for a few hours a day, and then there's pathetically little to see. Continue straight ahead down Russell Street, on your right passing the Theatre Museum, now with free admission. Cross the zebra crossing and stop near the red telephone boxes.

Ahead is the Theatre Royal, Drury Lane, which showed *Miss Saigon* for years before switching to *My Fair Lady, Anything Goes* and then *The Producers*. A theatre on this site dates back to 1663, though the current building is from 1812. David Garrick and Nell Gwynne, Charles II's mistress, worked here. The classical red niche on the corner holds a bust of Augustus Harris, the theatre's greatest manager in the 19th century. Later he worked at the Royal Opera House, introducing the singer Dame Nellie Melba, after whom Melba toast and Peach Melba are named. The theatre has several ghosts, including the Man in Grey, once seen by a whole cast on stage for a photo call. He walks the upper circle in 17th-century costume and disappears into the wall. Ahead, too, is the Fortune Theatre (1924). Susan Hill's ghost story *The Woman in Black* has been running for 15 years here; ironically, the Fortune isn't haunted.

From here, take a left and cross the road to the Marquess of Anglesey pub. Continue uphill into Bow Street, passing the glass barrel vault of the restored Floral Hall (now an exclusive restaurant), and then the classified façade of the main auditorium of the Opera House of 1858. The original architect for both was Edward Barry, whose father designed the Houses of Parliament.

Stop by the statue of the *Young Dancer* by Plazzotta and just behind is Bow Street Magistrates Court. Its greatest magistrates were Henry Fielding (author of *Tom Jones*) and his brother John. They cleaned up crime and corruption fearlessly in the 18th century. Their Bow Street Runners (set up in 1753) were the first professional police force.

Cross into Floral Street to run down the north side of the Opera House. At the crossroads, turn right up James Street and pass Covent Garden tube station on your left. Turn right and then immediately left to go downhill into Neal Street. Cross Shelton Street and then take a left to head up Earlham Street. Turn right almost immediately up an arcade called Thomas Neal's Shops. (If closed, just continue up Neal Street.) At the end, across Short's Gardens, you will see the water clock (1982) on a Holland & Barrett store. It used to clatter, bang and soak every passer-by, hence the roof above the shop. Sadly, in these boring times, it is no longer working.

Turn right into Short's Gardens and then left to rejoin Neal Street at the fabulous Kite Shop on the corner. At the top turn right into Shaftesbury Avenue. After the pavement turns right round the corner take two pelican crossings to continue uphill on to a triangular traffic island. On your right is the Shaftesbury Theatre of 1911. Its best-known production was the flower-power rock musical *Hair*, complete with daring nude scenes. It ran for just under 2,000 performances from 1968-73, when the ceiling fell in.

Cross uphill so that the Bloomsbury Central Baptist Church (1845-48) is over the road on your left. On the corner with New Oxford Street is James Smith and Sons, 'the oldest and biggest umbrella shop in Europe'. They've been here since 1857 and even make ceremonial maces and umbrellas for African chiefs. Turn right into New Oxford Street and take the second left up delightful Museum Street, brimming with cafés, galleries and bookshops. Ahead stand the columns and railings of the British Museum.

The Museum was founded in 1753 but the current neo-classical building was built between the 1820s and 1840s. The architect, Sir Robert Smirke, also designed Canada House in Trafalgar Square. This building is shaped like a hollow square with a garden in the central courtyard. The garden didn't last long. In 1857 the round Reading Room for the library opened in the centre of the courtyard. Its dome is 43 metres (141 feet) wide, the same as St Peter's in Rome. Book stacks filled the space around it, so goodbye garden. In 1998 the British Library moved out to its new base near St Pancras railway

London Transport Museum

station and the museum commissioned the architects Lord Foster & Partners to rework the redundant book stacks. The end result is the Great Court, a two-acre covered courtyard within the museum, with the magnificent Reading Room in the centre – now open to everybody for the first time.

So, how to tackle this great treasure box? As its brief is World Civilisation, do not attempt to take it all on at once, for that would be the equivalent of trying to eat the whole of a restaurant's menu in one sitting. But some of the rooms that it would be a crime to miss are: to the west of the Great Court the Egyptian Sculpture Gallery (No.4), which holds the Rosetta Stone; the Nereid Room (No.17), which houses what looks like a Greek temple, although it's actually the tomb of a ruler from Xanthos in south-west Turkey (c390-380 BC); the Duveen Gallery (No.18), designed to hold the Elgin Marbles from the Parthenon in Athens (432 BC); and to the east of the Great Court the King's Library (No.1), built to hold the library of George III (of madness fame). As the books are now the centrepiece of the British Library at St Pancras, this has been converted into the Enlightenment Gallery and holds nearly 5,000 pieces. Finally, to the north of the Great Court are the Mexican and African galleries (rooms 27 and 25 respectively).

To leave the Museum, take the north stairs (or north lift) down to the Montague Place exit. In distinct contrast to the old lions panting in Trafalgar Square, this is flanked by two of the most laid-back lions you'll encounter. I hope they leave you feeling the same way.

Eating & drinking

Belgo Centraal
50 Earlham Street, WC2H 9LJ (7813 2233/ www.belgo-restaurants.com). **Open** noon-11.30pm Mon-Thur; noon-11.30pm Fri, Sat; noon-10.30pm Sun. Big, bustling Belgian outfit dispensing pots of mussels and bottles of beer. It's a vast hall that can get noisy, but it's usually fun.

Chandos
29 St Martin's Lane, WC2N 4ER (7836 1401). **Open** 11am-11pm Mon-Sat; noon-10.30pm Sun. Food served.

Marquess of Anglesey
39 Bow Street, WC2E 7AU (7240 3216). **Open** 11am-11pm Mon-Sat; noon-9pm Sun. Tourists and after-work drinkers congregate downstairs; there's a decent pub-restaurant upstairs.

Punch & Judy
40 Covent Garden Market, WC2E 8RF (7379 0923). **Open** 11am-11pm Mon-Sat; 11am-10.30pm Sun. One of the busiest boozers in London. Pub grub available. The upstairs bar has a balcony overlooking Covent Garden piazza towards St Paul's church.

Churches

St George's, Bloomsbury
Bloomsbury Way, WC1E 6DP (7405 3044/ www.stgeorgesbloomsbury.org.uk). **Closed** for refurbishment until spring 2006, when it should be open 10am-5.30pm daily.

St Martin-in-the-Fields
Trafalgar Square, WC2N 4JJ (7766 1100/ www.stmartin-in-the-fields.org). **Open** *Church* 8am-6.30pm daily. *Brass Rubbing Centre* 10am-6pm Mon-Sat; noon-6pm Sun. **Admission** free lunchtime. *Brass Rubbing Centre* £2.90-£15. *Evening concerts* prices vary.

St Paul's, Covent Garden
Bedford Street, WC2E 9ED (7836 5221/www.actorschurch.org). **Open** 9am-4.30pm Mon-Fri; 9am-noon Sun.

Theatre Museum

Royal Opera House

Galleries & museums

National Gallery
Trafalgar Square, WC2N 5DN (7747 2885/www. nationalgallery.org.uk). **Open** *Galleries* 10am-6pm Mon, Tue, Thur-Sun; 10am-9pm Wed. **Admission** free. *Special exhibitions prices vary.*

National Portrait Gallery
2 St Martin's Place, WC2H 0HE (7306 0055/www. npg.org.uk). **Open** 10am-6pm Mon-Wed, Sat, Sun; 10am-9pm Thur, Fri. **Admission** free.

British Museum
Great Russell Street, WC1B 3DG (7636 1555/ www.thebritishmuseum.ac.uk). **Open** 10am-5.30pm Mon-Wed, Sat, Sun; 10am-8.30pm Thur, Fri. *Great Court* 9am-6pm Mon-Wed, Sun; 9am-11pm Thur-Sat. *Highlights tours* (90mins) 10.30am, 1pm, 3pm daily. **Admission** free; donations appreciated. *Temporary exhibitions* prices vary. *Highlights tours* £8; £5 concessions.

Theatre Museum
Tavistock Street (entrance Russell Street), WC2E 7PR (7943 4700/www.theatremuseum.org). **Open** 10am-6pm Tue-Sun. **Admission** free.

London's Transport Museum
Covent Garden Piazza, WC2E 7BB (7379 6344/ www.ltmuseum.co.uk). **Closed** summer 2005-Nov 2006 for major refurbishment.

Other

Bow Street Magistrates Court
28 Bow Street, WC2E 7AS (7853 9241/www. glmca.org.uk). **Open** 9.15am-4.30pm Mon-Fri.

Shopping

James Smith & Sons
53 New Oxford Street, WC1A 1BL (7836 4731/ www.james-smith.co.uk). **Open** 9.30am-5.25pm Mon-Fri; 10am-5.25pm Sat.

The Kite Store
48 Neal Street, WC2H 9PA (7836 1666/www.kite store.uk.com). **Open** 10am-6pm Mon-Wed, Fri; 10am-7pm Thur; 10.30am-6pm Sat.

Theatres

Albery Theatre
85 St Martin's Lane, WC2N 4AH (0870 060 6621).

Duke of York's
104 St Martin's Lane, WC2N 4BG (0870 060 6623).

Fortune Theatre
Russell Street, WC2B 5HH (7369 1737).

Garrick Theatre
Charing Cross Road, WC2H 0HH (7494 5085).

London Coliseum
St Martin's Lane, WC2N 4ES (7632 8300).

Lyric Theatre
Shaftesbury Avenue, W1V 8ES (7494 5045).

Royal Opera House
Covent Garden, WC2E 9DD (7304 4000/ www.royaloperahouse.org).

Theatre Royal, Drury Lane
Catherine Street, WC2B 5JF (7494 5045).

In the shadow of the tower

Robin Hunt

Camden, Regent's Park and Fitzrovia – from Britpop to the bohos of Noho.

Start: Camden Town tube
Finish: Fitzroy Tavern, Charlotte Street, W1
Distance: 4 miles/6km
Time: 3 hours
Getting there: Northern line to Camden Town
Getting back: short walk to Goodge Street (Northern line)
Note: Camden Market is at its liveliest (and most crowded) on Saturday and Sunday.

This walk was invented during a boozy business meeting at the Telecom Tower one May, 520 feet (160 metres) above ground. Business with men in suits from British Telecom was the agenda for the day – hence my privileged access – though I fancied nothing more than getting drunk in the clouds on that languid sunny afternoon. Which, as I recall, was what we did. Looking down from that unmatched viewpoint, it was hard not to think of the city as a series of elements in a SimCity game designed by John Nash, and I made an alcohol-fuelled promise to trace the contours of that aerial perspective on foot.

The walk starts two miles further north, at Camden Town tube station, always a place of singular encounters. In his marvellous book *In Camden Town* (1981) the writer David Thomson noted, 'I have never seen so many destitute people sitting for warmth in Camden

Town tube station as this year – not the usual drunks and winos.' In that year, the first in which I encountered Camden, I found the same thing; Camden had not quite become the HQ for Britpop and those watchful, well-dressed London media folk that it is today. Nor was it quite the mandatory Sunday trip for all tourists – more something of a political battlefield, evoking memories of the Camden Town riots of 1846 when a group of Irish navvies, brought over to build the railways that now run in glorious, privatised ways, famously took on the Camden police. In 1981 the destitute and the politically engaged rubbed shoulders with the likes of Matt Bianco and Madness, and, with the great villain Thatcher to incite us just as Nixon once had in the US, Camden evoked memories of the 1960s and rebellion. The exit from the tube station was the locale for a posse of student Socialist Workers bending their largely smart accents to cry 'Saashallist verka, Saashallist verka', in forlorn attempts to sell their newspaper.

On Sundays today the station is awash with a different kind of activity. The clubbers stepping outside for light and breakfast; the crowds who mill by the exit to meet friends and stay on to watch an extraordinary outdoor evangelical church group dancing and singing as if possessed; the couples and tourists off to search for old(ish) furniture in the market on the canal at Camden Lock, and finding not so pristine copies of old punk anthems at £35 a pop; and the signs for the CCTV, a quiet symbol that perhaps occasional trouble still exists in these parts.

We cross Camden High Street, leaving the crowds to ebb down towards the markets by the Lock, to reach the gently sloping Parkway, a street that starts with a women's toilet wedged in the centre of cars waiting at the traffic lights. Nondescript, in fact slightly grubby, the loo meant much to another old socialist and one-time inhabitant of Fitzroy Square (whose house we will eventually visit). It is here that George Bernard Shaw fought for and won the right to build one of the first ladies' toilets in London. Such things were thought an abomination, he told a meeting in 1927. Now it is an abomination for the usual reasons, my companion advises me.

Parkway was once a location of the Irish riots, now it fights 'brunch wars'. About 60 per cent of the street is taken

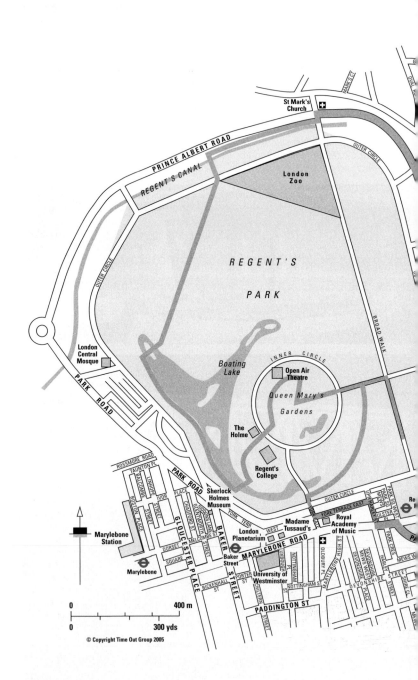

St Mark's Church

PRINCE ALBERT ROAD

REGENT'S CANAL

OUTER CIRCLE

London Zoo

REGENT'S

PARK

OUTER CIRCLE

BROAD WALK

London Central Mosque

PARK ROAD

Boating Lake

INNER CIRCLE

Open Air Theatre

Queen Mary's Gardens

The Holme

Regent's College

ROSSMORE ROAD

TAUNTON PL

BALCOMBE STREET

IVOR PLACE

GLENWORTH ST

PARK ROAD

CRAWFORD

BOSTON PLACE

GLOUCESTER PLACE

MELCOMBE ST

DORSET SQUARE

Sherlock Holmes Museum

YORK TERR

YORK TERRACE EAST

OUTER CIRCLE

WEST

PARK SQ E

PARK SQ W

ULSTER PL

Re

Madame Tussaud's

Royal Academy of Music

London Planetarium

MARYLEBONE ROAD

NOTTINGHAM PL

LUXBOROUGH

OLDBURY PL

DEVONSHIRE ST

PARK CRES

MEWS W

Marylebone Station

BAKER STREET

Baker Street

Marylebone

University of Westminster

BICKENHALL ST

PORTER ST

NOTTINGHAM ST

CHILTERN STREET

LUXBOROUGH ST

DEVONSHIRE PLACE

DEVONSHIRE STREET

HALES

MEWS W

PADDINGTON ST

0 ———— 400 m

0 ———— 300 yds

© Copyright Time Out Group 2005

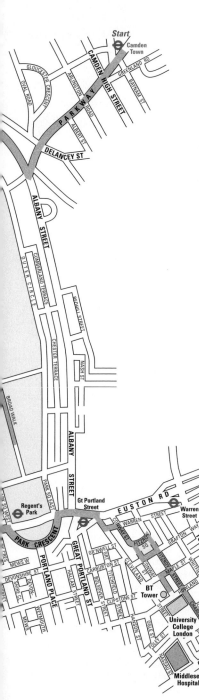

up with pubs, brasseries and restaurants fighting for weekend passing trade. From the Jazz Café, the mellow antidote to the seriousness of Soho's Ronnie Scott's, to the Rat and Parrot, the New Goodfare, the Spread Eagle pub and the Hogshead – to name just a few – visitors are bombarded with chalked 'Sunday lunch all day' signs, or adverts for big-screen sports, care of Sky TV.

We pass a once-fine cinema that I remember for Polish arthouse on Sunday afternoons. These days the cinema is an Odeon. It still has a lovely exterior, but inside it has multiplexed, and post-film diners or drinkers will as likely be tearful from *Titanic* as cut up by Kieslowski. We stop for breakfast a few yards beyond at an old Italian greasy spoon, the New Goodfare Restaurant, filled with a different kind of Camdenite from those gathered around the tube exit, neither trendy nor wasted.

Fed but still thirsty we amble up Parkway towards Regent's Park. We stop again, eschewing the canopies and sophistications of the Hogshead, one of those cod Francophile constructions, to take a pint at the Spread Eagle pub. I remember this place from the 1980s, Socialist Worker friends plotting the downfall of capitalism or justifying the existence of Paul Weller's Style Council over a few pints of Young's best. The atmosphere hasn't changed: it is still resolutely unfazed by Camden's expensive modern ways (the Parkway estate agents don't appear to have houses in the area for less than £300,000) and its older clientele seem glued to their seats as they watch the world

Regent's Park

and its tourists pass by through a splendid four-windowed corner.

We leave Parkway and catch a glimpse of Park Village East and West – good old John Nash, as usual. We turn right into Prince Albert Road, full of white Victorian villas, which only become 'B' league when the true splendours of Regent's Park's crescents come into view.

With the incongruous Chinese restaurant paddle-steamer, the Feng Shang, to the left and the church of St Mark's to the right, we slip down left on to the Regent's Canal footpath. Camden and its traffic noise are gone instantly, to be replaced by the calm and limited horizons of the canal. We enjoy its peace, its almost silent barges and still waters while we can, for after a few hundred yards the hum of the London Zoo aviary (designed in the 1960s by Lord Snowdon, then the husband of Princess Margaret), leads us to look up towards a superannuated birdcage-cum-art-installation filled with exotic birds from India and Africa.

The choice of architect continued a long royal trend: the entire Regent's Park scheme with its palatial terraces was sponsored by George IV when Prince Regent, and designed by his favourite, John Nash, from 1811 onwards. It was designed to be a mini-city within a park with 56 villas for the well-to-do, but

thankfully for us hoi polloi, no more than eight villas were built; otherwise there would be nowhere to walk, lounge, flirt and stare at the sky.

We stop here to think about walking through the aviary, but instead we look across to the giraffe enclosures on the other side of the canal to the left. We then turn right to climb up to the Primrose Hill bridge, cross the canal and take in the zoo.

Officially we are at the Zoological Gardens, founded in 1824 with Decimus Burton its architect. In Peter Høeg's curious novel *The Lady and the Ape*, the zoo is the starting point for a most unusual sexual congress obvious from its title, and other writers from Angus Wilson to Brigid Brophy have used the place as the location for a little light philosophy on animal nature – after all, the entire park was once part of the hunting forest of that most animal of monarchs, Henry VIII.

Most days the zoo and its outbuildings to the left have little resonance – the times have changed, zoos aren't so fashionable – but the smell has the effect of taking you back to those childhood visits and the excitements of animal life. The critic David Piper once wrote that the smell 'may fell the most hardened traveller with an all but unbearable nostalgia for the East' – which may be somewhat overstating the case. Indeed, Parkway

with its many restaurants is more atmospheric in its way. There are some pleasures, it is said, at the Grade I-listed penguin pool – whose occupants were recently moved to new accommodation – where 'the principles of modern architecture, behaviourist research, structural virtuosity and humour' once combined, according to an architectural guide to London. But as neither this eclecticism, nor the smell of animals, nor the history (the cobra that took out the reptile keeper in 1843; the first insect house ever built, in 1881; the circular gorilla house) interested us, we cross the Outer Circle, the narrow oval around the park, and enter the park itself.

Taking the right-hand path, the best place to start in the park is the golf driving range to the right, so perfectly pointless, and by necessity netted-in so as to make the practising players in their tasteless checks appear not dissimilar to the ibis and whatnot in the aviary a few hundred yards away. And perhaps more fun for the amateur anthropologist.

Indeed, on inspection, the entire Regent's Park project is faintly absurd, neither rural like Hampstead Heath or Richmond Park, nor entirely urban like St James's. It is, however, the finest London location for non-athletic rollerbladers and offers a richness of architectural stadia such as Nash's buildings, the mosque, the

gardens of the Inner Circle, and the American ambassador's London residence for spectacle.

On Sunday mornings the best fun is to be found in the schoolboy soccer games, with the odd beanpole up front taking more stick from frenzied parents than most £50,000-a-week Frenchmen playing in the Premiership have to endure. Walking straight on with the brass dome and short minaret of the London Central Mosque to our right, we stop to check the natural jacuzzi in the river that feeds the main lake, which seemingly has been created for the swans and geese to frolic in. We stop to take in the view across the park down to a small bandstand by the main boating lake. The image conjures up visions of clandestine meetings in 1960s spy movies, but more sombrely this was the place in 1982 where seven Royal Greenjackets bandsmen were killed in an IRA bomb attack. Then we turn right and take in the strangely dull features of the London Central Mosque, with its brass dome like some cooking implement from the 1974 Habitat catalogue. In fact, this design, by Sir Frederick Gibberd and his partners, won an open competition in 1978, then was made more 'Arab' before being built. It still seems half-hearted and curiously unspiritual.

We turn left, walking along the side of the main boating lake, observing to our

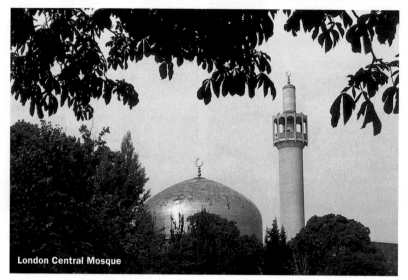

London Central Mosque

left Regent's College. That the park, with its educational riches for those Improving Victorians Who Walked – the exotica of its flora and fauna, its classical friezes and architecture – should now house a business school seems somehow apt. To our right we see the first of the west side terraces, Hanover, with its blue and white reliefs. This is followed by a typically English piece of whimsy, Sussex Place, another long, creamy white terrace with its weird pepperpot turrets.

We cross the first bridge over the lake, and turn left past Regent's College moving towards the Inner Circle and the formalities of Queen Mary Gardens. We pause at the gates of the Holme on the Inner Circle, having admired its front from the park. Gated in and private, it is a Hollywood Hills moment of locked-away privacy and I want to know who lives there. My lottery ticket failed me again last night, but one day, I feel, all this will be mine.

Inside the Inner Circle again we pass the entrance to the Open Air Theatre, whose auditorium looks like a minor league soccer stadium. Inside, the speciality is the Shakespeare-on-a-stick

kind of productions that are either so perfectly right for a balmy evening or lead to early exits back to the pub. We wander down, and right, through the pretty gardens of Queen Mary.

Emerging on to the Inner Circle again, Cumberland Terrace now stands proud ahead of us, via Chester Road and the Broad Walk. It is all columns, pediments and statues on the skyline, evoking Victor Hugo and Paris. This was the location for the last pages of John Fowles's novel *The Magus*. The anti-hero, Nicholas, is here reunited with one of his (several) duplicitous girlfriends. The statues look down on the ill-fated lovers, and – because this is Fowles – become a kind of chorus. 'The afternoon sun made them gleam with light, that Olympian elixir of serene, remote, benign light one sometimes sees in summer clouds.' These gods reveal the futility of life to Nicholas – this was the 1960s, after all.

We turn around and walk along Chester Road, head left to amble down Broad Walk with its aisles of trees, then cut back and leave via York Gate with a view of St Marylebone Parish Church ahead of us across the speeding dual-carriageway that is the Marylebone Road. William Palgrave, who collected all those dull poems for the *Golden Treasury* in Victorian times lived on York Gate, and around the corner young girl violinists sun themselves on the steps outside the Royal Academy of Music. But we turn left before it, into the relative seclusion of York Terrace East, and emerge on Upper Harley Street. Ahead is Park Crescent, intended as a circus, ending up a crescent, but nevertheless dominant and serene amid all the west-bound traffic. This is our favourite Nash – big is beautiful sometimes, you know. Shame, though, about the cars.

Having followed the arc of the crescent, we pass Great Portland Street tube before we move into the top of Cleveland Street. Then, for a more discreet architecture, we take a left into Warren Street, then a right into Conway Street and walk down into Fitzroy Square past the Croatian Embassy. There are many squares in London, but Fitzroy Square is one of the loveliest: it's pedestrianised, and in summer its small grassy park opens for lunchtime flirtations between foreign language students and office workers from Tottenham Court Road. Harts or – on weekdays, even better – Rive Gauche on Warren Street will provide the perfect picnic for such meetings. The square buzzes with a faint Bohemian air: nothing to compare with the full monty that Fitzrovia once enjoyed in the first half of the century, of course, but it is still a welcome place for lunch alfresco.

The south and east sides of the square were built in the 1790s under the eye of the Adam brothers. Robert Adam lived for a time in what is now an office for the architects Ove Arup, at Nos.36/38. Virginia Woolf lived at No.29; the same house that George Bernard Shaw had kept for a decade ten years before; somewhat earlier Lord John Russell, the Prime Minister, was a few doors down at No.21. In fact, the square and its environs have a cultural history to rival anything emanating from the ungenerous villas and squares of

Bloomsbury, a few hundred yards east of Tottenham Court Road. Ford Maddox Brown, Rossetti, Whistler, Sickert, Landseer and Richard Wilson – the painter, not the actor – lived around here, and further down Charlotte Street the Groucho Club of its day, the Fitzroy Tavern, played host to everyone from Augustus John and Dylan Thomas to Tommy Cooper. These days culture is pared down to the offices of Image Bank, a picture agency; French's Theatre bookshop on the corner of Fitzroy Street and Warren Street; the offices of those 'épateurs of the bourgeois', the *Modern Review*, at No.6 Fitzroy Street; and the off-chance of spotting a film star at No.3 Fitzroy Square, which is often hired out to film companies.

Walking past the London Foot Hospital on the south-east corner of the square, we head down Fitzroy Street, across Grafton Way, passing an Indian YMCA on the corner that does amazing cheap lunches. We take a detour down Maple Street to see the somewhat uninspired entrance to BT's eyesore or icon. I've always had a soft spot for the Tower. On puffy-clouded summer days it looks about as real against the skyline as one of those future cities in *Thunderbirds*. It was a defining swinging 1960s symbol for Londoners when it was known as the Post Office Tower. Then it had the same kind of high status as Concorde, Twiggy or Scott Tracey; my father would point it out with pride when we got out of the tube at Tottenham Court Road. Once, the Tower's revolving rooftop restaurant was one of the highest places you could eat in Europe. The revolution of the restaurant took 23 and a half minutes, somewhat shorter than the student revolutions going on below at the time, but, it is said, no less fun. On good days diners could see the evening lights 40 miles away. On bad ones they suffered six-foot lurches caused by high winds. But hell, whatever the weather, it was cool in a velvet loon pants kind of way.

Access to the public has long ended. Since an IRA bomb exploded on the

Park Crescent

31st floor in 1971 the restaurant and cocktail bars have been closed to most people, though the public areas were used as the control room for one of Richard Branson's balloon-fuelled attempts to cross the Atlantic in the 1980s. Presumably the communications possibilities of the Tower were not stretched unduly on that occasion.

Nowadays the Tower has lost some of its symbolic potency to other London behemoths such as Canary Wharf and the Swiss Re Tower ('Gherkin') and returned to a more primary function: it is a place of communication from which are beamed television programmes, telephone conversations and tetrabytes of computer information, of data. I once watched a foetal scan in a Bristol hospital over a particularly sophisticated BT phone line and computer from the 30th floor. It was a girl, eight weeks before birth, getting a quick once-over from a specialist who'd popped in from University Hospital around the corner

in Gower Street. BT calls it remote medicine, and it is a wonderful thing.

We pass further down into Charlotte Street and see that hate-place for the SWP of the 1980s: the offices of Saatchi & Saatchi, who were then deemed the Kings of Advertising. Further down on the right is the new glitzy version of Bertorelli's restaurant, where the old Fleet Street huddled over eight courses, and the location for some of *Sliding Doors*. Around the corner in Rathbone Place is Jerusalem, not the promised land, but a wonderful basement bar and restaurant, ideal for lost Wednesday afternoons consuming a little more than lettuce and Perrier.

We end up at the Fitzroy Tavern on the corner of Charlotte Street and Windmill Street. Once, from the 1930s to the '50s when it was run by one Pop Kleinfeld, this was The Meeting Place for Bohemians. The scientist JBS Haldane, famous for genetics, and for popping around the corner to Broadcasting House in Langham Place to broadcast on the Home service, once wrote a poem that began:

On entering Mr Kleinfeld's portal
One may well find oneself immortal
For I have only got to whistle
To have my portrait done by Bissill
And if he does not do me justice
I'll take a sitting with Augustus…

The place has a long and noted history that is wonderfully captured in Sally Fiber's book *The Fitzroy*. The photographs downstairs tell the story of times when Augustus John sketched 1930s politicians, or later celebrated VE Day with a street party. The Tavern is much diminished these days. It is still full most nights, but the chic have moved south into Soho, and I for one don't miss them. One day I'll look down at them from the Telecom Tower again with the men in suits, and, who knows, perhaps find another part of London to explore.

Eating & drinking

Bertorelli
*19-23 Charlotte Street, W1T 1RL (7636 4174/
www.santeonline.co.uk). Bar* **Open** noon-11pm
Mon-Sat. *Café* **Meals served** noon-11pm Mon-Sat.
Restaurant **Lunch served** noon-3pm Mon-Fri.
Dinner served 6-11pm Mon-Sat. Contemporary
Italian fare in easy-going surroundings.

Feng Shang Princess Floating Chinese Restaurant
*Cumberland Basin, Prince Albert Road, NW1 7SS
(7485 8137/www.chineseboat.co.uk).* **Lunch served**
noon-2.30pm, **dinner served** 6-11pm Mon-Fri.
Meals served noon-11pm Sat, Sun.

Fitzroy Tavern
16 Charlotte Street, W1T 2LY (7580 3714).
Open 11am-11pm Mon-Sat; noon-10.30pm Sun.
Food served noon-2.30pm, 6.30-9.30pm Mon-Thur,
Sat, Sun; noon-2.30pm Fri. No longer the bohemian
hangout of the 1920s, but more an after-work boozer.

Indian YMCA
*41 Fitzroy Square, W1T 6AQ (7387 0411/
www.indianymca.org).* **Lunch served** noon-2pm
Mon-Fri; 12.30-1.30pm Sat, Sun. **Dinner served**
7-8.30pm daily.

Jazz Café
*5-7 Parkway, NW1 7PG (7916 6060/www.jazz
cafe.co.uk).* **Open** 7pm-1am Mon-Thur; 7pm-2am Fri,
Sat; noon-4pm, 7pm-midnight Sun. **Meals served**
7.30-9.30pm daily. **Music** 9-11.30pm Mon-Thur, Sun;
9-10.30pm Fri, Sat. **Club nights** 11pm-2am Fri, Sat.
Admission £12.50-£25. Food is served overlooking
the stage, but diners must pay the entrance fee.

Jerusalem
*33-34 Rathbone Place, W1T 1JN (7255 1120/
www.thebreakfastgroup.co.uk).* **Open** noon-11pm
Mon; noon-midnight Tue, Wed; noon-1am Thur, Fri;
7pm-1am Sat. **Food served** noon-3pm, 6-10.30pm
Mon-Fri; 7-10.30pm Sat. Hoegaarden and Leffe at the
bar, ambitious but reliable dishes from the kitchen.

Rat & Parrot
25 Parkway, NW1 7PG (7482 2309). **Open** 11am-
11pm Mon-Sat; noon-10.30pm Sun. **Food served**
noon-9pm daily.

Spread Eagle
141 Albert Street, NW1 7NB (7267 1410). **Open**
11am-11pm Mon-Sat; noon-10.30pm Sun. **Food
served** noon-3pm, 6-8pm Mon; noon-3pm, 6-9pm
Tue-Sat; noon-9pm Sun. Food is better than average.

Worship

London Central Mosque
*146 Park Road, NW8 7RG (7724 3363/
www.iccuk.org).* **Open** 9.30am-6pm daily.
Admission free.

St Mark's Church
*St Mark's Square, NW1 7TN (7586 1694/
www.stmarksregentspark.org.uk).* **Open** call
for details. **Services** 8am, 10.30pm Sun.

St Marylebone Parish Church
*17 Marylebone Road, NW1 5RS (7935 7315/
www.stmarylebone.org).* **Open** 9am-5pm Mon-Fri.
Services 8.30am, 11am Sun; 1.10pm Wed.

Museums & parks

London Zoo
*Regent's Park, NW1 4RY (7722 3333/www.london
zoo.co.uk).* **Open** Mar-late Oct 10am-5.30pm daily.
Late Oct-Feb 10am-4pm daily. **Admission** £14, £12
concessions; £10.75 3-15s; free under-3s; £45 family.

Regent's Park
*Prince Albert Road, NW1 (7486 7905/www.royal
parks.org.uk).* **Open** 7am-dusk daily.

Theatre

French's Theatre Bookshop
*52 Fitzroy Street, W1T 5JR (7387 9373/www.
samuelfrench-london.co.uk).* **Open** 9.30am-5.30pm
Mon-Fri; 11am-5pm Sat.

Regent's Park Open Air Theatre
*Regent's Park, NW1 (0870 060 1811/www.open
airtheatre.org).* **Season** May-Sept; phone for details.

BT Tower

The full circuit

Margaret Forster

Forget the city and take a hike round Hampstead Heath.

> **Start & finish:** corner of Croftdown Road & Highgate Road, NW5
> **Distance:** 4 miles/6.5km
> **Time:** 2 hours
> **Getting there:** Gospel Oak rail, followed by five-minute walk; 214, C2, C11, C12 bus to Highgate Road (nearest tube: Kentish Town, then 214, C2 bus)
> **Getting back:** reverse of above
> **Note:** it is very easy to get lost on the Heath. You are, however, never far from civilisation.

A long, daily walk has always been of immense importance to me. I find it weird that so many other people seem to see a walk as merely a form of exercise, or a way of getting fresh air, or their least favourite method of getting from one place to another. My walks are like a clever drug, one capable of constant stimulation and yet inducing total relaxation. I can't do without them. So, moving to London in 1960, never having been to the great city and knowing it not at all, I was scared. Where would I walk? Plenty of streets there would be, plenty of parks, but I like country walks best and where would I get those without travelling for miles? Then I found Hampstead Heath. Panic over. On a week-day winter's afternoon, which is when I walk on it, the illusion of proper country can be amazingly convincing.

Not at first, though. I live only two minutes from the Heath, on what used to be called the wrong side, but it's a bad two minutes. There's the horror of crossing Highgate Road and pushing through the hordes of youths and girls posing outside William Ellis and Parliament Hill Schools. I should change the time of my walk to avoid these lunchtime gangs, but that's when I want to walk so I never do. It's not that I'm hostile to these young things, just that they bar the way without seeming to realise it. They're all too busy smoking and strutting about to notice one walker struggling to get through and it puts me in a bad temper. So does all the dog shit on the path they're blocking, and I walk very fast, head down, frowning, until I get to the park-keepers' headquarters. It signals the real beginning of the Heath, but I know I don't look too happy yet, not until I've passed the children's enclosure and reached the first of the Highgate Ponds.

That's where my walk starts to become a pleasure. I slow down a bit. There are always ducks on this pond and children throwing bread for them and it's calming to watch. To the left is the slope of Parliament Hill and along the ridge of it kites fly, kites of unusual shapes these days. There's a 1930s feel to the atmosphere; it's like one of those posters for London transport, everything in sight clean-cut and tranquil.

I saunter on, looking to see if anyone is swimming in the next pond, the men's bathing pond. I didn't know it was only for men when first I came upon it 45 years ago. I didn't know it wasn't wise to enter the water from the side opposite the diving board either, because of the mud and reeds. I found it on a boiling hot day and was so delighted I was preparing to plunge in (my bathing costume was on under my dress, which I'd peeled off in a moment) when a man stopped me. 'You can't go in there,' he said. 'There's nudes.' I couldn't see any nudes, and didn't see why it would matter if there were any, so I waded in for a swim and he had the satisfaction of watching me almost get strangled in the thick weeds under the surface at the edge of the pond. It would have made more sense to warn me about those. But no one can enter from that side now – there's a wooden fence the entire length.

The next pond is used by fishermen in the summer season but in the winter it's taken over by toy boat enthusiasts. This is a surprisingly attractive pond in spite of its concrete rim. The other ponds are fringed with greenery but not this one. It's open, the path round it quite flat, and the expanse of water is bigger altogether. The light seems to hit the surface in a more dramatic way than it does the others. I turn right at the end of it, pausing to peer through the railings and bushes on the left into the nature reserve pond. This is in effect a bird sanctuary with something like 80 species of birds using it. There are regular sightings of kestrels, willow warblers, goosanders and all kinds of other birds whose names sound like poetry. I always think of a woman called Kate Springett here. She was the GLC's Bird Observer and used to plod around the Heath in all weathers, a little white-haired lady wearing sensible shoes and usually with a rucksack on her back and binoculars round her neck. She lived in a council flat in the next street to me and had no training in ornithology – she was a milliner by profession and taught herself. She is dead now, and

Hampstead Heath

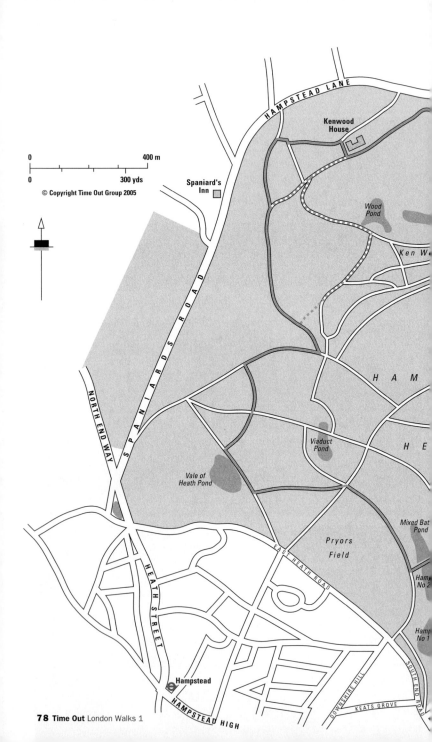

HAMPSTEAD LANE

Kenwood
House

Spaniard's
Inn

Wood
Pond

Ken W

0   400 m

0   300 yds

© Copyright Time Out Group 2005

NORTH END WAY

SPANIARDS ROAD

H A M

Viaduct
Pond

H E

Vale of
Heath Pond

Mixed Bat
Pond

Pryors

Field

EAST HEATH ROAD

Ham
No 2

HEATH STREET

Ham
No 1

Hampstead

SOUTH END ROAD

HAMPSTEAD HIGH

DOWNSHIRE HILL

KEATS GROVE

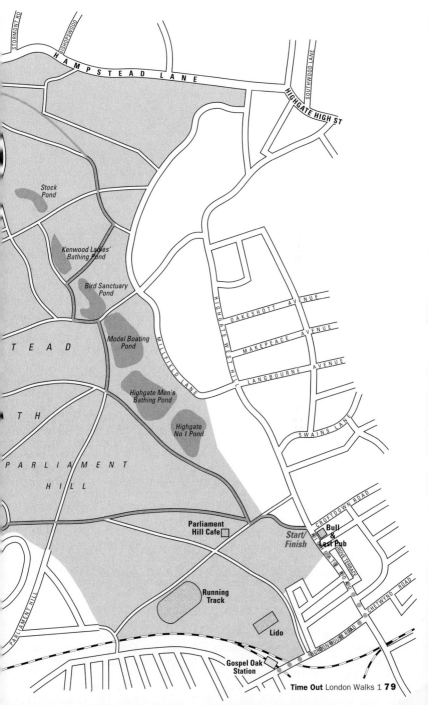

there's a copse somewhere on the Heath named after her. I think about Kate, and her passion for birds, as I climb the slight hill leading up from the bird sanctuary.

There's a path which turns left here, to go down to the ladies' swimming pool, the last in this line of the five Highgate ponds. (One is hidden behind a fence, it's a nature reserve and can only be seen through railings.) Everything changes at this point. The tarmac is left behind, hurrah. The track alongside the ladies' pond is un-made up and though there are houses on the right-hand side, they are mostly concealed. It's a shady path, with trees overhanging it, and there's rarely anyone walking down it except at the height of summer, when I'm never walking on the Heath these days.

The ladies' pond features in quite a few contemporary novels (Esther Freud's *Gaglow*, for example) but is never described on winter days when it's at its most enticing, a grey glint of water through blackened branches, quiet and sometimes even sinister. The bank above is full of ghosts, full of memories of chattering women sunning themselves, languishing half-naked, supposedly (there are often eyes in the bushes) unseen by men. Going there in the early 1960s, it seemed so daring to sunbathe topless, but once an older woman came up to my friend and me and shook her head sadly and said, in a strangely accented English, 'Ah, my young girls, if life were so simple, so simple. Put your clothes on decent, I beg you.' And for some reason we did – well, we put our bikini tops on and rather cheekily said, 'Satisfied?' She trailed away and we took them off and laughed and then felt oddly uncomfortable. But I often hear her voice as I pass, and think about the possible meaning of what she said.

There's a choice after the ladies' pond. Straight on the track leads to Kenwood House and quickly becomes tarmac again, but turning right, which I always do, leads on to a lovely, quite wild corner of the Heath. There isn't much wood left,

but there are some thick clumps of bushes and the grass is thick and tough. It's an area reputed to be a homosexual picking-up place. I've never seen anyone doing any picking up but if it's true then gays show good taste. This is one of the areas where, very briefly, that illusion of real countryside can be enjoyed. The bushes, from certain angles, hide the tarmac paths and all buildings are hidden. I take this patch slowly before slipping over the little muddy plank leading to the next stretch rising up to Kenwood. Good views here, nearing the highest point. The Heath falls away to the distant city and I like the juxtaposition.

Kenwood is not my favourite part of the walk, lovely though the house is, and even though there's another impressive view down to the artificial lake and the white painted false bridge – very Jane Austen. There's a magnificent magnolia tree to the left of the broad path in front of the house, set all on its own, but in winter, of course, it looks plain and humble. I duck through the archway at the corner of the house and walk through the garden, skirting the long flowerbed of shrubs on the other side of the lawn. It's pretty-pretty here, though not as cosy as it used to be when Dr Johnson's hut lay at the end. Dr Johnson never sat here in his life, of course. This hut was built for him in the country garden of some friend of his so that he could write in peace. It was a sweet, circular little wooden structure, open at one side but without a door and rather dark inside.

I always imagined Dr Johnson wasn't so much seeking peace to write in it as hiding from the country, which, as we all know, he didn't think much of. But his house in London, in Gough Square, was so noisy due to all the domestic rows going on – 'discord and discontent reign in my humble habitation as in palaces of monarchs…' – that though he was never tired of the great city he liked escaping to his hut. It was transferred intact to the Kenwood garden and my children loved it though it didn't inspire any of them to write.

The **mixed bathing pond.**

About ten years ago some vandals burned it down and now there is just a rather sad platform, with a couple of benches on it, where it once stood.

People sit a lot on the benches there. They sit and have serious conversations, and as I pass I strain to catch them. A line overheard can keep me musing for ages afterwards – 'I said, what is that for, Bernie, and he said for shrouds, what else?' I see Bernie, small and harassed, staggering under a bundle of heavy material, perhaps loading it into a van, and his friend puzzled, and then shocked when he's told this is material for shrouds. But is Bernie an undertaker? No, I don't think so. A tailor maybe. And it goes out of my head, the speculation, as I finish the Kenwood path and open out again on to the track leading to the car park.

This track is nearly always in the shade but everything to the left of it is in the sun. If I don't do the full circuit, I carry on straight past the house, not going through the arch to the garden, and follow the path round to the left, past the Henry Moore sculpture. At the bottom I turn right over a slatted bridge and follow a narrow path round the far side. This is another area that feels fleetingly countrified. It's one of the best places to sit, hidden in a corner with trees and bushes forming a perfect screen. I look at it longingly from the main

track, but taking that route amounts to a short cut and I want the longer walk. Turning through the gate on my left, I take the right fork, a long foot-trodden path which opens up into a wider track. Another good part, without any track, up and down through the trees towards Hampstead Lane. If there's any sun, this is the place to appreciate shadows and patterns, and if there's any wind to hear rustles and flutters. It's a quiet, quiet part of the Heath even if it ends in a hill over which the noise of a busy road spoils everything.

I drop down, once over it, to the Vale of Health pond. I usually stop a moment and stare, at the back of the house, 9 Heath Villas, where I used to live in a flat when first I came to London. The houses are all painted now, except for number nine. They look quite Italianate, with their pale greens and creams and pinks, and on misty days eerie, not part of London at all. The pub has gone, but the fairground is still there, a sad collection of a few caravans most of the year. The pub was splendid. A bald-headed Scotsman used to shout, on Sunday lunchtimes when the bar was closing, 'Away home, all of ye, away home, your roasts are burning in their ovens!' New flats were built once the pub was knocked down, well weathered by now but still looking new. I like thinking

Kenwood House

of Daphne du Maurier being pushed to this pond in her pram from Cannon Place, her nurse a country girl and like me looking for an illusion.

I don't go to the end of the Vale path, on to East Heath Road. I cut left, past another children's enclosure. There's often a lot of children playing there, from a local private school, all clad in their uniforms, all thrilled to be brought from their expensive establishment to the free Heath. It amuses me to think of it. I cross onto the top end of what we call the avenue of trees – I expect it has a proper other name – and walk down 30 metres and take the downwards sloping path to the right. There, towering over the hill sloping down

to the Hampstead ponds is the Royal Free Hospital. I imagine patients on the top floors staring down at the Heath and wishing they were well and walking on it, pining for it. It's nearly always muddy here, and the noise of traffic permits no illusions, but at least it's open and wide, there's a feeling of freedom and space. The Hampstead ponds at the bottom are not particularly interesting and they are busy. This is where most people get to, coming on to the Heath from the south side. They tend to linger between the two ponds. It's where drunken revellers drown on New Year's Eve, too. They think the ice thick and walk, or stagger, on to it, and crash through. Horror stories abound.

Parliament Hill beckons, though really the full circuit requires turning right at the foot of it and walking down to the playground, but I let myself off that. It would only extend the walk by another ten minutes and it isn't worth it – it's dreary down by the playground and athletics track. I like to pass a bench, just at the start of the hill, that has on it the words of some Iranian poet: 'I was born tomorrow, Today I live, Yesterday killed me'. Very profound, I'm sure. On top of the hill is exhilarating: to the left the broad sweep of the Heath, with beautiful trees, in autumn especially, ahead the Highgate ponds, and to the right the vast expanse of London, all the famous landmarks – the Dome, the Post Office Tower, St Paul's, Centre Point – clearly visible. I stand and stare and then walk very slowly down, not wanting to lose height, and return to where I started.

It's taken me an hour and a quarter this walk, and it never fails to make me feel better even on damp, dark days. It isn't just the physical benefit, the way rapid walking clearly does make the blood circulate more quickly and induces a feeling of well-being; it's the mental rewards that matter most. I get distracted from whatever is preoccupying me, return with a new perspective. On Saturdays I never walk on the Heath – then, I walk across London, across the centre. I trawl the other green areas, Regent's, St James's and Hyde Parks, and though I like this variation I don't benefit from it the way I do from the Heath. I need the absence of buildings, traffic noises and pavements and crowds of people; I need the awareness of greenery, of nature, I suppose, uninterrupted by man. There are only a very few spots on the Heath where I can get this, but I know them and seek them out.

The best is not on the full circuit. The most countrified part is to the left of the end of Highgate ponds, veering off the path leading to Kenwood gate and going up the side of the Kenwood estate. I have a seat of my own there, under a silver birch tree, and walking to it, sitting on it I never fail to be thrilled that such countryside can exist so near to the centre of London. It's possible to sit there, see nothing but trees, and to hear nothing but birds. The greenery seeps through the air, all is fresh and beautiful. I return from the walk to it half in a daydream; it's a shock to reach the dreaded Highgate Road. But when I do, that patch of the Heath is still in my head, an area of calm. The walk has a purpose. It's to reach that state of equilibrium, the calm and the stimulation nicely balanced, though I often wonder, if I didn't live so close to the Heath, would this have disappeared by the time I'd fought my way home? Would a tube journey swallow it up? Wipe out all memory of the walk and what it had given? So I'll have to stay near the Heath, always.

Eating & drinking

Bull & Last
168 Highgate Road, NW5 1QS (7267 3641). **Open** 11am-11pm Mon-Sat; 11am-10.30pm Sun. Gastropub.

Parliament Hill Café
Parliament Hill, NW5 1QR (7485 6606). **Open** *Jul, Aug* 9.30am-9pm daily. *Sept, Oct, Apr-June* 9.30am-6pm daily. *Nov-Mar* 9am-4.30pm daily.

Spaniards Inn
Spaniards Lane, NW3 7JJ (8731 6571). **Open** 11am-11pm Mon-Sat; noon-10.30pm Sun. Food served.

Information

Hampstead Heath
NW3 (Parliament Hill 7485 4491/Golders Hill 8455 5183/www.cityoflondon.gov.uk/openspaces). **Open** 24hrs daily. **Admission** free. *Bathing ponds: men only, women only & mixed.* Summer: 7am-9pm or sunset daily. Winter: dawn to dusk daily; mixed pond closed.

Heath & Hampstead Society
PO Box 38214, London NW3 1XD/www.heathand hampsteadsociety.org.uk.

Kenwood House
Hampstead Lane, NW3 7JR (8348 1286/www. english-heritage.org.uk). **Open** *Apr-Oct* 11am-5pm daily. *Nov-Mar* 11am-4pm daily. The café – the Brew House – is well regarded (open *Mar-Oct* 9am-6pm daily. *Nov-Feb* 9am-4pm daily).

One summer's morning

Peter Paphides

Find your inner child in the cemeteries and parks of Ham and High.

Start: Highgate Village, N6
Finish: The Flask, Highgate
West Hill, N6
Distance: 4.5 miles/7km
Time: 3 hours (including one-hour
guided tour of West Cemetery)
Getting there: Northern line to
Highgate, then 10-minute walk
along Southwood Lane (*see map*);
143, 271 bus
Getting back: reverse of above
Note: West Cemetery is only
accessible by guided tour – see
listings for details. Check opening
times of East Cemetery and
Waterlow Park.

Nature has a way of telling you if you should bother with the day ahead. The trick lies in knowing how to heed her. Sleep with the blinds down and before you know it, you might have missed three hours of premium spring. Keep them up, though, and sunshine will slip beneath your eyelids, turning dreams into the first realisations that Something's Going On. Overcast weather, however, never impinges on slumber. Why bother showing interest in the weekend when it clearly doesn't give a damn about you?

On a radiant morning like this, however, Highgate repays all initial efforts. It's 8.30am when my wife Cate and I begin from the shady peak adjoining North Road and Hampstead Lane, by which time only joggers and dog owners seem to have surfaced. The unimpeded view of London 50 yards behind us seems somehow fitting. After all, few London walks allow you to genuinely feel like

you've left the city behind. But amble alongside the northern border of the Heath and another world takes hold. Left opposite the end of the cricket pavilion and playing fields, into a path surrounded by trees, is a gentle descent that turns into the old Caen Wood Towers farm. Here, a 15-minute drive away from Piccadilly Circus, lies an idyll more commonly found in the paintings hanging at nearby Kenwood House. And it's here for everyone.

Hampstead Heath has a way of surprising you just as you thought you were finally getting to know it. Today it's the trees. Even the gnarled, ancient tree (an arboreal Samuel Beckett) as you descend the left side of the meadow is feminised by the young leaves fluttering in the breeze. That it's actually alive is a mystery in itself. Its roots are formed around a fist of thin air – so that today the area where normally a trunk might be is filled instead by a child hiding from its Posh Parents. Next to rabbits and squirrels, Posh Parents are the most commonly found mammal indigenous to Hampstead Heath. And of these, the most common subspecies is the Well-Scrubbed Young Couple (WSYC). Their markings – matching pairs of starched, light-blue Armani jeans accompanied by Calvin Klein T-shirt (hers), Nike T-shirt (his), stylish shades and cute, tousled Benetton child – make them easy to recognise.

At roughly this point you may notice many WSYCs walking back up towards the wooded area we came in on. They're going towards Kenwood House. While we follow them, you might care to know a little about this wonderful place. Although named after the old Caen Wood, the building and the surrounding area are part of what's now called the Iveagh

Bequest, an estate completed in 1769 to the specifications of the first Earl of Mansfield. Over five years, Kenwood House was remodelled by Robert Adam and furnished with paintings by Rembrandt, Vermeer, Hals, Gainsborough and Turner – all of which still hang.

Today, though, it's to more interactive works of art that our attention must turn. Advance through the rear entrance of Kenwood House and follow your nose. The Brew House is where WSYCs go for breakfast, but it's far too good to be left to them. The walled garden boasts parasols and huge wooden tables, just perfect for leisurely Sunday paper perusal. Combined with the exotic blooms that peer over the walls, the effect is to whisk you away from North London altogether and into the Italianate dreamworld of Portmeirion.

None of which would matter half as much if the Brew House wasn't responsible for quite the most celestial breakfasts in London, the like of which I haven't had since childhood.

It's now about 10.30am, as we turn right out of Kenwood House, carrying on along the path in front of the Orangery. Take the first wooden gate on your right as Henry Moore's reclining woman bares her behind to you on your left. Take the gravel path to your left as it arcs round and another excellent tree encounter awaits us. This time it's an oak with a huge thick branch that veers out sideways, only to dip down almost to ground level, and back up again

– thereby doubling up as some kind of suspended bench that rocks gently beneath our weight.

We're now leaving behind the English country garden ambience of the Iveagh Bequest for something a little wilder. However, any temptation to get increasingly bacchanalian as the terrain gets rougher is kept in check by the notice at the gate listing all the ancient by-laws that continue to preside over the Heath. These seem to swing from the commonsensical down to the utterly surreal. I'll leave you to guess which category the following fall into: Nuisances, No.29: 'No person shall in any open space, sort rags, bones, refuse or matter of like nature, or mend any chair'; No.39: 'Without prior consent, no person is permitted to sing any sacred or secular song except on the sites or site mentioned'. Perhaps 80 years ago, you couldn't move in Hampstead Heath for people mending chairs and sorting rags while humming secular and sacred hits of the day to themselves.

However, these days the Heath has fallen foul of a more insidious problem. Frisbees. Today the Heath is riddled with hordes of Italian-looking frisbee gangs. Which means that any attempt to stray off the path will result in probable decapitation. Instead, seeking perhaps to relocate my inner child in a more dignified way, I decide I'm going to climb a tree. You might even see the tree in question yourself, and decide it looks

The Brew House

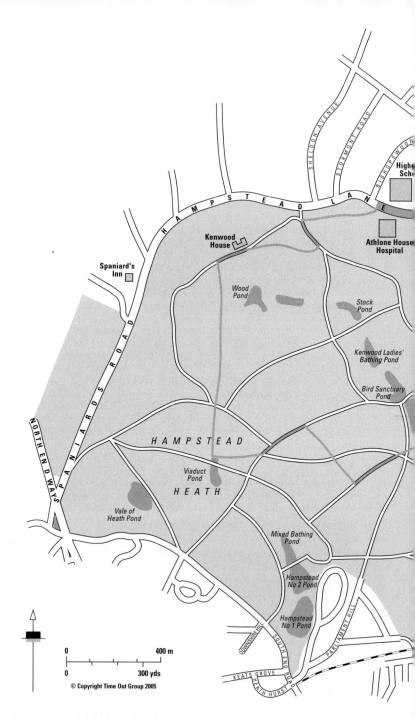

Spaniard's Inn

Kenwood House

Wood Pond

Stock Pond

Kenwood Ladies' Bathing Pond

Bird Sanctuary Pond

Athlone House Hospital

High Sch

HAMPSTEAD LANE

SHELDON AVENUE

STORMONT ROAD

BISHOPSWOOD

PANIARDS ROAD

NORTH END WAYS

HAMPSTEAD

HEATH

Viaduct Pond

Vale of Heath Pond

Mixed Bathing Pond

Hampstead No 2 Pond

Hampstead No 1 Pond

PARLIAMENT HILL

DOWNSHIRE HILL

SOUTH END ROAD

KEATS GROVE

HEATH HURST

0   400 m

0   300 yds

© Copyright Time Out Group 2005

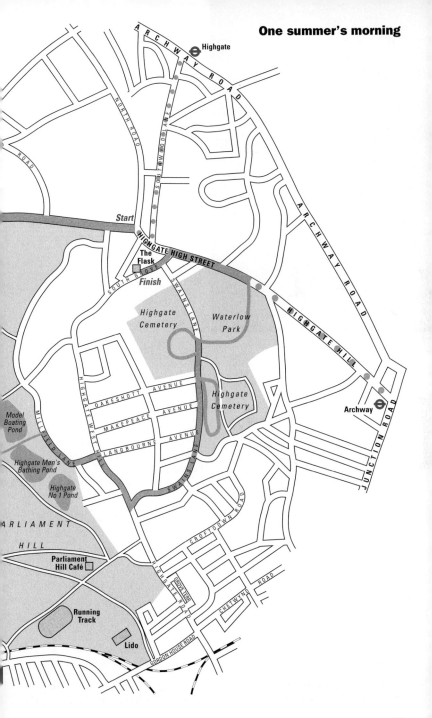

One summer's morning

Highgate

ARCHWAY ROAD

NORTH ROAD

SOUTHWOOD LANE

Start

HIGHGATE HIGH STREET

The Flask

SOUTH GROVE

Finish

SWAINS LANE

Highgate Cemetery

Waterlow Park

HIGHGATE HILL

ARCHWAY ROAD

HIGHGATE WEST HILL

OAKESHOTT AVENUE

MAKEPEACE AVENUE

LANGBOURNE AVENUE

Highgate Cemetery

Archway

JUNCTION ROAD

Model Boating Pond

MILLFIELD LANE

Highgate Men's Bathing Pond

Highgate No 1 Pond

SWAINS LANE

CROFTDOWN ROAD

HIGHGATE ROAD

RETCLIFFE ROAD

PARLIAMENT

HILL

Parliament Hill Café

GROVE TER

CHETWYND ROAD

Running Track

Lido

GORDON HOUSE ROAD

Hampstead Heath

From here, we amble in a north-easterly direction to Parliament Hill, the spiritual home of London's kite-flying fraternity. From the top of the hill you can famously see all of London laid before you and the commuter belt stretching on beyond it. It's also from these lofty peaks that various tributaries fed into the old River Fleet as it began its journey into the city. These days, there's hardly anything left of the Fleet, although the high-walled foundations that prop up much of the buildings in Ludgate Circus act as a reminder of the majestic waterways that flowed from the Fleet Street area into the Thames.

There really is a different Hampstead Heath for every mood: be it the bucolic pastorality of the Iveagh Trust, the sense of new-world triumphalism at the peak of Parliament Hill, or the blasted moorland just beside it. Go back down towards the line of ponds that flanks the eastern end of the Heath and an almost Narnian sense of hyperreality takes hold. Not surprising this, considering CS Lewis came up with the idea for *The Lion, the Witch and the Wardrobe* during a walk in the snow across the Heath. The story goes that amid all this wilderness, Lewis sighted an old-fashioned lamp between the ponds and Parliament Hill which seemed to belong to another world.

The vegetation is lush – lots of ultra vivid greens – and the hedges that afford privacy around the bathing ponds conspire to give this area of the Heath a permanently autumnal feel. We feed the ducks and continue out of the Heath, taking a right down Millfield Lane. This allows us to have a good snoop at all the individually designed houses owned by people with very good accountants – as well as a converted Georgian terrace like the one owned by the family in *Mary Poppins*. Only, this one's horrible.

We turn right at the bottom of Millfield Lane down Highgate West Hill and up to Swains Lane, our approach accompanied by fragrant may tree blossom. Highgate in May is Laurie Lee novels, Lilac Time

climbable. It's situated just to the left-hand side of the path as you approach the bridge over the Viaduct pond. A huge knot in the trunk provides a foothold on to the high branches. The next bit involves walking all the way along a thick branch to the very end, where an additional branch affords greater balance. The only problem is that the drop is about 12 feet, so having made the precarious outward journey, I realise the only way to safety is by turning around and making the scary return journey.

So what do you think happens next? This, I swear, is what happens next.

I begin my balancing act on the branch back to the trunk. Halfway along, I realise that Captain Jean-Luc Picard of the Starship Enterprise – or, if you must, Patrick Stewart – is staring at me quizzically. And because his face is so familiar, it takes a couple of seconds to realise I've never actually met him. By which time, I've said 'Hello' and gotten so flustered at my faux pas that I've slipped and fallen six feet into a bush.

We notice a few seconds later that Patrick is rather taken by a worryingly exposed nest of baby coots over which their mother busily presides.

records and Mini Milks dripping on to fingers – but it takes that moreish aroma to evoke them all. On these tree-lined streets, it's impossible to escape it.

You'll see the Eastern Cemetery of Highgate flanking the right side of Swains Lane before you get to either entrance. That's the one that, famously, plays host to Karl Marx. However, set aside enough time to get lost amid all the overgrown graves and the labyrinthine pathways that snake on to the borders of Waterlow Park – and a minor adventure awaits you. George Eliot, Sir Ralph Richardson, William Friese-Green (the pioneer of cinematography) and Leslie Hutchinson are some of the better-known names that you might find on your travels – as well as Farzad Bazoft, the *Observer* journalist killed by Iraqi authorities for alleged spying. One particular curiosity that

Highgate Cemetery

confronts us on this afternoon is a derelict, damaged grave almost entirely covered by weeds. Look a little closer and you'll see the name WG Grace inscribed on it. The WG Grace? We failed to find anyone who could tell us.

On such a brilliant afternoon, Highgate Cemetery doesn't seem especially scary. The views that appear as we turn every corner are frequently breathtaking: the graves in the foreground, the bluebells and buttercups that sprout randomly between them and the infinite variations of green and yellow that frame the middle distance. Accompanied by a constant soundtrack of song from finches and sparrows, it's an idyll totally at odds with the frenetic feelings more commonly associated with this city.

And yet, I know Highgate Cemetery better than this. I've wandered around here as dark, foreboding skies edge out the blue, and winter nightfall approaches; as the atmosphere thickens and the birdsong starts to appear ever more shrill. I've looked around the place, wondering if I'm actually the only person here. If I weren't, I'd be none the wiser. Highgate Cemetery has a way of swallowing up the living as well as the dead. It may look peaceful here, but remove your sentimentality and what's left is a fierce battle against nature. Of course, if there's one thing that a cemetery serves to remind us of, it's the very fact that nature always has its way, no matter how long you keep her at bay. For the moment, though, it's a close-run thing. The cemetery is just about as wild as it could be without chaos ensuing. The fearsomely aggressive horsetail grows all around here, but look more closely and you'll come across clover, vetch, cow parsley and endless nettles in which the plentiful red admirals, painted ladies and orange tips lay their eggs.

For a time, the older West Cemetery was indeed allowed to run wild, but the Friends of Highgate Cemetery formed in 1975 and set about restoring the place.

The task is never-ending, of course – rediscovering old headstones that had long given way to the pernicious sycamore or the equally ruthless ivy, although that tends to be more readily tolerated given the vital role it plays in providing food and nesting places for the wildlife that thrives unseen in this environment. Much of the money necessary for its maintenance is raised from the proceeds of guided tours around the area.

The best thing about the West Cemetery, though, is the bottomless fund of stories thrown up by the graves. And with a good guide to bring them alive, our allotted hour whizzes by. Those who campaign that boxing has a brutalising effect on society might care to spend a moment by the grave of 19th-century bare-knuckle fighter Thomas Sayers. Despite the illegality of the sport, thousands joined the procession from Tottenham Court Road to see Sayers buried. His death in 1849 came five years after his attempt to steal the world middleweight title from the reigning US champion. The fight lasted 40 rounds and yielded no outright winner, but it did signal Sayers's subsequent retirement from the sport.

Elsewhere on the cemetery tour, you are likely to be shown the Charles Dickens family grave. Unbeknown to himself at the time, Dickens wasn't to end up in Highgate at all – you'll find him at Westminster Abbey – but his wife and daughter reside here. Indeed, Dickens had his young daughter moved here after he had regrets about putting her in the catacombs, where the sunlight couldn't reach her.

Easily the most remarkable sight that awaits any visitor to the West Cemetery is the Lebanon Circle – a raised walled island on which an awesome 250-year-old cedar sits. Around the outside of the Circle itself are the entrances to 20 family catacombs bearing projecting door cases. The effect is magnificent. The final grave we see before the end of our hugely

enjoyable tour is that of Sir George Williams who founded the YMCA. Given the nocturnal ends to which Highgate Cemetery has often been used, some may deem this appropriate.

Following the claustrophobic, chaotic grandeur of Highgate Cemetery, Waterlow Park looks like the set of *Teletubbies* by comparison. Perfectly tended rows of tulips, separated by their respective colours; a neat, colourful children's playground; and two well-tended lakes – all conspire to create the effect of a huge garden. No surprise this, given that the grounds were originally the private estate of Sir Sydney Waterlow, Lord Mayor from 1872-73. On the creation of the London County Council six years later, Waterlow gave his grounds to the people of London – calling it a 'garden for the gardenless'.

As we stroll towards Highgate Hill on the south side of the park beside the railings that separate it from the East Cemetery, we remember that Sydney's admirable compassion toward the 'gardenless' may, at times, have been a touch idealistic. Behold two families engaged in a slanging match while their two dogs attempt to tear each other apart: 'You should learn how to fucking control that animal, mate!'

Henry Moore at **Kenwood House**.

A fetching scene at **Waterlow Park**

'You should fucking watch your mouth!'

'Yeah? And what are you gonna do about it?'

Alas, the squaring-up fails to degenerate into a fitting memorial to Thomas Sayers, but it does at least throw up a diamond one-liner from a nearby father returning from a visit to the East Cemetery: 'You remember what I was telling you about the proletariat, Henry?'

'Yes, daddy?'

'Well, you've just seen why they never got around to seizing the means of production.'

And when hunger strikes in Highgate, head up the hill as you exit Waterlow Park, then turn left into South Grove and get thee to the Flask. The handsome brick façade of this centuries-old boozer hides a labyrinthine interior with tables in all sort of alcoves. It serves chunky sandwiches, various posher dishes and an array of beers. Five hours spent exploring the finest countryside that, erm... London has to offer need to be rewarded by some serious comfort food.

Eating & drinking

The Brew House

Kenwood House, Hampstead Lane, NW3 7JR (8341 5384). **Open** *Mar-Oct* 9am-6pm daily. *Nov-Feb* 9am-4pm daily. Cakes, pastries and hot lunches. Breakfast a speciality. The terrace has pots of flowers.

Café Mozart

17 Swains Lane, N6 6QX (8348 1384). **Open** 8am-10pm Mon-Fri; 9am-10pm Sat, Sun. Fabulous cakes and fine hot dishes at this old-fashioned Viennese café.

Flask

77 Highgate West Hill, N6 6BU (8348 7346). **Open** noon-11pm Mon-Sat; noon-10.30pm Sun. Popular, with excellent beers and fine food.

Parliament Hill Café

Highgate Road, NW5 1QR (7485 6606). **Open** *July, Aug* 9.30am-9pm daily. *Sept, Oct, Apr-June* 9.30am-6pm daily. *Nov-Mar* 9am-4.30pm daily.

Spaniards Inn

Spaniards Road, NW3 7JJ (8731 6571). **Open** 11am-11pm Mon-Sat; noon-10.30pm Sun. Historic, but avoids too much 'ye oldiness'. Food served.

Information

Hampstead Heath

NW3 (Parliament Hill 7485 4491/Golders Hill 8455 5183/www.cityoflondon.gov.uk/openspaces). **Open** 24hrs daily. **Admission** free. A diary of events taking place on the Heath is available at information points. *Bathing ponds: men only, women only & mixed. (Summer: 7am-9pm or sunset if earlier daily. Winter: dawn to dusk daily; mixed pond closed.)*

Heath & Hampstead Society

PO Box 38214, London, NW3 1XD/www.heath andhampsteadsociety.org.uk. Organises themed walks on the Heath on the first Sunday of the month.

Highgate Cemetery

Swains Lane, N6 6PJ (8340 1834/www.highgate-cemetery.org). **Open** *Apr-Oct* 10am-5pm daily. *Nov-Mar* 10am-4pm daily. **Admission** *East Cemetery £2; West Cemetery tours £3.* Booking essential for West.

Kenwood House

Hampstead Lane, NW3 7JR (8348 1286/www. englishheritage.org.uk). **Open** *Apr-Oct* 11am-5pm daily. *Nov-Mar* 11am-4pm daily. *Tours* by appointment only. **Admission** free, donations appreciated. *Tours £3; £2 concessions; £1 under-16s.*

Waterlow Park

Highgate Hill, N6 (Lauderdale House 8348 8716). **Open** 7.30am-dusk daily.

Of kites & Keats

Kate Kellaway

Moments from the fume and roar of Kentish Town Road, an ode to memory lane.

> **Start:** Kentish Town tube
> **Finish:** Hampstead tube
> **Distance:** 3 miles/5km
> **Time:** 2 hours
> **Getting there:** Northern line to Kentish Town
> **Getting back:** Northern line from Hampstead

London is an unnarcissistic city; it does not advertise its beauties. It is marvellously insouciant. It doesn't care if you look the other way. It is not looking at you. Walking through London demands selective sight, editing what you don't want to look at, letting your eye linger only on what you like.

I'm about to take a familiar walk. I grew up with Kentish Town, Parliament Hill and Hampstead – they are my companion places. And yet, I know already that on this particular chill April day, in filthy spring weather, the walk I am about to take will be unlike any I have taken before. In London, you never take the same walk twice.

I'm blown off at the top of the steep escalator at Kentish Town tube station in a draft of stale Northern line air and brace myself for Kentish Town Road, its fume and roar. I partly avert my eyes from the pavilion to the right, which serves as a fancy frame for winos. Two noisy and expansive singers are bawling their street opera into the cold air.

It is easy to give them and the main road the slip. I turn into Leverton Street. There is immediate relief in its relative quiet and surprise at the sight of houses that, painted in ice-cream colours, look almost edible. Lilac, ceanothus and cherries whipped into double blossom conspire to suggest that in this street, spring is a confection. Even the pub on the corner appears to be burgeoning. It is called the Pineapple and is pleasingly spiky.

I turn left again, down Railey Mews, a singular, cobbled street with a view of Victorian backs of houses on one side of it. I love taking London unawares in this way. The mews houses look like old stables.

At the end of Raveley Street, I stop to consider a derelict shop. It is an exotic oddity and easy to miss – it was once 'The Cook Shop'. I cross Fortess Road and into Lady Somerset Road. This is a matronly street, full of late Victorian houses (circa 1880) and dirty pavements. At the end of it, I turn off into College Lane.

I used to walk down this shy lane as a schoolgirl and play the game that I indulge in compulsively on London walks, imagining myself living in the houses I passed and selecting a favourite. Today most of the cottages in College Lane look dainty and spruce, with windowboxes jammed with primroses. The house I used to elect for my imaginary adult life had a spiral staircase. I can no longer find it. But between Nos.13 and 14, I see something I have never noticed before: a faded cream shield, dated 1914-18. It is a disarming, DIY war memorial. I can make out a few names: Biggs, Turner… The others have been rubbed out by time.

College Lane charms because of its secretive quality, although I always used to be a little frightened of it as a child. It was here that schoolgirls from Parliament Hill, the local comprehensive, in purple and grey uniform, used to shout insults at us Camden girls (a grammar school at the time). We wore bottle-green blazers,

College Lane, hidden away and full of secrets and memories.

striped blue and green ties and we knew each other from afar by our uniform, like enemy beetles. Even now, I can't quite shake off a reflex unease. I watch two boys playing and fancy there is something dangerous about their idleness. One of the boys throws a plastic bottle and it ricochets down the lane.

Just off College Lane, on the left, is Little Green Street. I divert to take it in. The street has a Dickensian aura, the houses look like Old Curiosity shops, their bow windows like the sides of bulbous sweet jars. And now I ready myself for seeing again the house where I grew up. Grove Terrace is like a shakily drawn but beautiful bracket alongside Highgate Road. There are four or five Regency houses at one end of the terrace; the remaining houses are Georgian. When I stop outside No.2, I feel furtive, a living ghost. I can remember as a child watching passers-by stop to take our house in and to admire the magnolia. It is an odd sensation to be on the outside of a house that was once your life, now occupied by strangers.

And it looks alien to me: a little too opulent with its gleaming black front door and ruched curtains. The familiar fanlight gives me a feeling of vertigo, as do the dented York stone and the wonderful magnolia tree planted by my uncle. My past has been ruched, almost but not quite painted out by well-applied gloss paint. A fellow resident, an old lady of 100, could recall the days before Highgate Road existed when she looked out from Grove Terrace across fields. How lovely

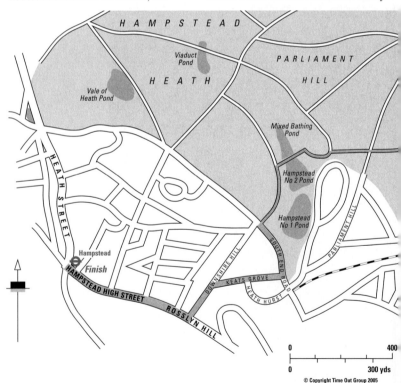

that must have been! I pause outside No.15 where my great-aunt lived. I look from the outside into the first-floor sitting-room where I read *Alice in Wonderland* aloud to her at such speed that she kept asking me to slow down. The first-floor balconies look like stiff, black lace skirts.

At the end of the terrace, round the corner in Woodsome Road, among a group of little shops, there used to be one that was always changing owners – it seemed a doomed location. Its latest incarnation was as a second-hand clothes shop called Change of a Dress, but that has now closed.

I cross Highgate Road to get on to the Heath and proceed down the path that, as children, we nicknamed 'dog poo path'. In spite of the little cans where dog

droppings may now be posted, the path still earns its name. I keep my eyes down, glancing up only occasionally to take in the blowsy pink rhododendrons. There is a NO CYCLING notice and squirrels running between wood palings. There is a fenced grassy area for children to play in with a wooden elephant, camel and pig. Cow parsley is the first reminder that, on the Heath, you are not in an ordinary park. It is almost countryside. I walk through tussocky grass, studded with dandelions and on past an inferior Victorian bandstand.

I used to walk my dog every day on the Heath and I used to think that the wood on the hill just before you reach Parliament Hill itself would make an ideal setting for the witches in *Macbeth*. It has a

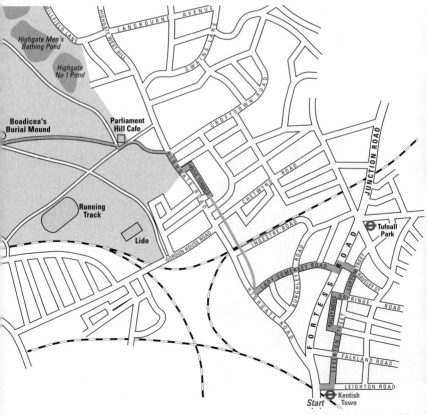

Little Green Street

scrubby, conspiratorial feel. I love the last little climb to the top of the hill. It is like ascending an upturned pudding basin. Although on closer inspection, the outline is slightly asymmetrical – a child could sketch it.

Parliament Hill is known as Kite Hill to its friends and, on windy summer days, the sky is a tangled doodle of kites. Today I see one solitary scarlet kite gamely flying against a grey sky. At the top as I look back down the hill, the view divides into two. I have always thought of the one to the left as the sacred view and the other on the right as secular. To the right, there is a marvellously motley spectacle of London, with the Post Office Tower, St Paul's, the Dome and St Pancras Station all clearly visible. It is a view that is less green and more urban than its neighbour. At sunset, it becomes a study in grey and pink. At all times of day, it is up to the eye to make a unity of the whole.

To the left, there are three spires, St Anne's, St Michael's and St Joseph's – a harmonious trinity of churches. Below them are ponds and weeping willows. I always sit on the same bench to contemplate this view. It is like occupying the front seat of the stalls at a natural theatre, or the front pew of a church, perhaps.

Not far off is Boadicea's burial mound. It is thought that her final battle against the Romans was fought on Parliament Hill and that she was defeated there and slain in the battle. Folklore had it – and still has it – that she was buried here (though some archaeologists think that the exact site is more likely to be under King's Cross Station). The tumulus was dug up in the 18th century and at the end of the 19th century by antiquarians who found Bronze Age relics, suggesting that the tomb was older even than Boadicea. Whatever the case, I trudge off to pay my respects to her. Hail comes down hard on a little circle of trees, including Scots pines, which stand about like mourners. I shelter among taller nearby trees that resemble a company of fine, upstanding

The wide open spaces of **Parliament Hill**.

citizens. The hail makes the hill take on a hazy, silvery look beneath which the grass is intensely green and there is even a faint, fat rainbow in evidence.

I thread through ponds that lead to South End Green. This is the second double view in this walk. On one side is the pond where men swim and dive. On the other, swans and ducks are out in force. I peer into the face of a swan who stares back with a stupid, faintly displeased look, the black bulge over his brow like a small storm cloud.

I leave for East Heath Road and its wide hem of green grass and make my way to Keats Grove. Half way up the street, on the left, is Keats House. It has a pleasing symmetry with two long windows framed by arches. In Keats's day, the street used to be called John Street. Keats House has the look of a haven with its gentle face and sunken lawn. Writers' houses can seem vacated shells, the props – pens and writing desk – no more than sorry souvenirs. But Keats House has held on to its spirit.

It is wonderful to see the old propped mulberry tree and to reflect that it was in this garden that Keats heard the nightingale that inspired his poem. It was here, too, that he wrote an indomitable, less well-known prose companion piece to 'Ode to a Nightingale':

'O there is nothing like fine weather, and health, and Books, and a fine country, and a contented Mind, and Diligent habit of reading and thinking, and an amulet against the ennui – and, please, heaven, a little claret-wine cool out of a cellar a mile deep – with a few or a good many ratafia cakes – a rocky basin to bathe in, a strawberry bed to say your prayers to Flora…' (19 April 1819).

The graceful, arched, ancient lavender bushes are crippled but strong. The Brawne family, including Keats's great love, Fanny, lived on the right of the house and it was in the bedroom on the left that Keats coughed up the blood that he recognised to be arterial. He was reported to have said to his friend Brown in 1820, 'I know the colour of that blood, – it is arterial blood – I cannot be deceived in that colour; that drop is my death warrant. I must die.'

It is impossible not to feel melancholy at the thought of the poet's tragically short life. I walk away from his house towards Hampstead High Street and pass St John's, a pretty church with a handsome clock face. And then to Downshire Hill, the prettiest street in Hampstead. Playing the house game here is not easy. I hesitate between Gothic windows and wisteria-laden balconies – the houses are deliciously varied – while reflecting, also, that

The **Vale of Health**, part of Hampstead Heath.

perhaps they are almost too much of a good thing, too exquisite for common use.

With this encouraging thought in mind, I make my way up Hampstead High Street. It is severely steep but the last lap of the walk. For those with shoes worn out from walking, there is no shortage of expensive footwear to buy in this street. But I am thinking instead of mint tea. One summer afternoon in Hampstead High Street, I sat outside a place called Al Casbah with my family, and a fancy silver tea pot gleamed in the sun. On this fraudulent spring afternoon, I find the place again. It is equally welcome – though dark, warm and deserted. I sit at a table with a hookah (for decorative purposes only). The mint tea arrives and I pour it into a gold glass – a delicious swig of somewhere else – with which to salute north London.

Eating & drinking

Al Casbah
42 Hampstead High Street, NW3 1QE (7435 7632). **Open** 10am-midnight daily. North African restaurant.

Base
71 Hampstead High Street, NW3 1QP (7431 2224/www.basefoods.com). **Lunch served** noon-4pm Mon-Fri; noon-5pm Sat, Sun. **Dinner served** 6-10.45pm Tue-Sat. Café bistro by day; full restaurant by night.

Bull & Last
168 Highgate Road, NW5 1QS (7267 3641). **Open** 11am-11pm Mon-Sat; noon-10.30pm Sun. Mediterranean-style food in one of North London's original gastropubs.

Louis Pâtisserie
32 Heath Street, NW3 6DE (7435 9908). **Open** 9am-6pm daily. This popular Hungarian pâtisserie is a Hampstead institution.

Parliament Hill Café
Highgate Road, NW5 1QR (7485 6606). **Open** *July, Aug* 9.30am-9pm daily. *Sept, Oct, Apr-June* 9.30am-6pm daily. *Nov-Mar* 9am-4.30pm daily.

Pineapple
51 Leverton Street, NW5 2NX (7284 4631). **Open** noon-11pm Mon-Sat; noon-10.30pm Sun. Good food, plus a range of beers and local characters.

Churches

Rosslyn Hill Chapel
3 Pilgrims Place, NW3 1NG (7433 3267).

Saint Benet & All Saints
Lupton Street, NW5 2JB (7485 4231).

Saint John's Church
Downshire Hill, NW3 1NU (7794 8946).

Information

Hampstead Heath
NW3 (Parliament Hill 7485 4491/Golders Hill 8455 5183/www.cityoflondon.gov.uk/openspaces). **Open** 24hrs daily. A diary of events taking place on the Heath is available at information points. **Admission** free. *Bathing ponds: men only, women only & mixed. (Summer: 7am-9pm or sunset if earlier daily. Winter: dawn to dusk daily; mixed pond closed.)*

Museums

Keats House
Keats Grove, NW3 2RR (7435 2062/www.city oflondon.gov.uk/keats). **Open** noon-5pm Tue-Sun. **Admission** £3.50; £1.75 concessions; free under-16s.

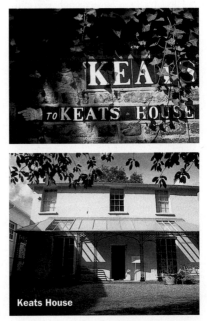

Keats House

Building blocks

Dan Cruickshank

The Square Mile contains a potted history of British architecture.

Start: Tower Hill tube
Finish: Site of Temple Bar
Distance: 7 miles/11km
Time: 5.5 hours
Getting there: District or Circle lines to Tower Hill
Getting back: 10-minute walk to Temple (District or Circle lines)
Note: the City is very quiet at the weekends, and many of the churches and buildings are not open.

Despite destruction by fire in 1666, devastation by bombing in 1940 and ruthless post-war redevelopment, the City of London retains an amazingly rich and varied collection of architecture of the highest quality.

Start at Tower Hill tube. Walk to the Tower of London.

The Tower of London is almost invisible to Londoners but, as is clear to most awe-struck visitors, it is one of the most phenomenal medieval edifices in Europe. It is a great fortress incorporating structures dating from the late 11th century to the 19th century (or even earlier if the slight remains of Roman bastions and wall are included); it has also served as a mint, royal lodgings, armoury and gaol. The Tower is especially remarkable because its individual buildings form a coherent whole – essentially a great keep set in a bailey, now called Tower Green – and are surrounded by two concentric defensive walls strengthened by towers of various sizes and dates. Much has been lost, but much has also been altered. Most of the

eastern portion of the riverside wall is late 19th-century work and stretches of the north wall are post-war reconstruction following bomb damage. But the overwhelming sense of the Tower is that it is of the Middle Ages. The White Tower, started c1077 and completed in 1097, is one of the greatest pieces of Norman, or Romanesque, architecture anywhere. It has a vaguely classical form – elemental and rude, but nevertheless a remote and vigorous memory of the classical traditions of Rome. The walls are given rhythm by the application of tall thin strips of masonry like classical pilasters.

Inside, in the spectacular Chapel of St John, the thick Norman columns with rudimentary capitals are perhaps derived from classical precedent, and the round arches and barrel vaults are as found in Roman buildings. The interior of the White Tower is, apart from the chapel, now something of a disappointment. It was a hall-keep, which means that it contained not just a great hall but several major rooms per floor, with stout timbers supporting floors and ceilings and an internal masonry wall dividing the rooms from each other. Unusually for this early date was the heating of the main rooms by fires placed, not on central hearths, but within wall-mounted fire hoods. However, the Normans had not quite invented the modern fireplace because the smoke was not carried away by tall chimney stacks but curled lazily out of the building through holes in the thick walls behind the fireback. These apartments have been much altered over the centuries and little attempt has been made to restore them. The Tower has been a tourist trap almost as long as it has been a prison, which is why the Beefeaters, who have had centuries to perfect their act, are very good guides indeed.

Walk to Trinity Square. On your right is:

Merchantile Marine Memorial. Sir Edwin Lutyens designed a series of stunning memorials to the dead of World War I, and most are in France or Belgium. This is perhaps his best in London, although far less well known than his Cenotaph in Whitehall. The Merchant Marine memorial, designed in 1926, takes the form of a Doric sanctuary with tunnel vaults.

Follow up Trinity Square to Savage Gardens, then left into Pepys Street. Right on Seething Lane, and on the corner with Hart Street is:

St Olave's, **Hart Street** is a surprising medieval remnant tucked among modern commercial architecture. The entrance to the little graveyard lies

Tower of London

through a massive gate topped with a row of barbarous spikes and huge leering stone skulls. This sombre image prompted Charles Dickens to christen the church St Ghastly Grim in his tale *The Uncommercial Traveller*. The church dates from the 15th century, although a crypt survives from the 13th and the tower was rebuilt in brick in 1731. The church was gutted by fire during the war but much of the joinery was saved and some of it is of the highest quality – especially the pulpit, which is reputedly the work of Wren's favourite carver, Grinling Gibbons. The church survived the Great Fire in 1666 largely due to the presence of mind of Samuel Pepys who referred to St Olave in his Diary as 'our own church'. Pepys – who worked in the Navy Office in Seething Lane – had wooden buildings surrounding St Olave's removed before the fire could get a grip. In 1669 he had his wife Elizabeth buried in the church (her beautiful white marble monument by John Bushnell survives); Pepys himself is buried in the nave beside his wife. Other burials in the church include Mother Goose, who was interned in September 1586, and Mary Ramsey, who is said to have brought the plague to London in 1665. There is also a delightful churchyard complete with a watch house to ward off bodysnatchers.

West along Hart Street to Mark Lane. On the left is:

59-61 Mark Lane is an important and pioneering 19th-century commercial building. It was built in 1864 to the designs of George Aitchison for a company of property speculators, James & John, and marks one of the earliest examples of a now familiar building type – a speculative office block. The stone elevation reflects the influence of the architectural theorist John Ruskin, who during the 1850s had promoted Venetian Gothic as the style for mid 19th-century Britain (*see* 7 Lothbury, *p108*). More interesting is the novel interior structure, which is a frame of cast-iron columns and wrought-iron beams. There

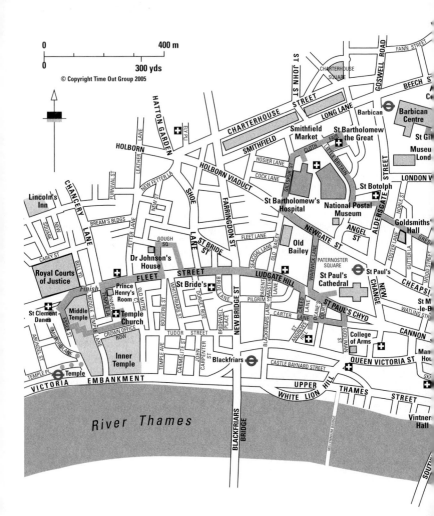

are no internal structural walls but brick arched floors. This type of construction was virtually fireproof and offered flexibility in planning.

North up Mark Lane, cross Fenchurch Street, north along Billiter Street to Leadenhall Street. Turn right to St Katharine Cree Church:

St Katharine Cree Church is one of the wonders of the City; not beautiful perhaps but full of architectural interest. It was built in 1628-31 – a time when few churches were built in England – and

captures the moment when the native tradition of Gothic design was being enriched by the addition of foreign classical details and forms. St Katharine is a remarkable hybrid, perhaps designed by a master mason named John Jackson. The church has the usual basilica plan (that is, a tall nave divided by screens of columns from lower, flanking, aisles), but all is rendered in a delicious mix of idiosyncratic late Gothic and Renaissance-style Classicism. The columns are Corinthian and carry coffered arches,

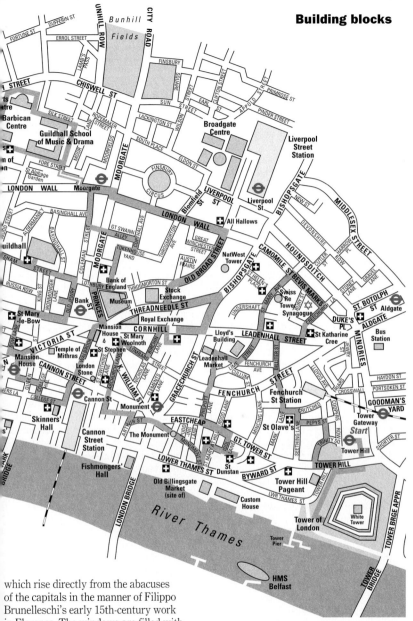

which rise directly from the abacuses of the capitals in the manner of Filippo Brunelleschi's early 15th-century work in Florence. The windows are filled with Gothic tracery, while the ceiling has a flat vault defined by Gothic-style ribs, but all made of plaster not stone. The church also contains some good joinery and monuments, especially the early 18th-century pulpit and the late 18th-century Communion Table attributed to Robert Adam. The organ, of 1686 by the renowned Father Smith, was used by Purcell, Handel and Wesley.

North up Creechurch Lane to Bevis Marks/Duke's Place. North-west (left) along Bevis Marks to turning into court on left in which stands:

Spanish and Portuguese Synagogue, Bevis Marks. There is no other building like this in Britain, and very few elsewhere in Europe. It was purpose-built in 1701 as a synagogue for the Jewish community of rich merchants that had settled around Duke's Place and Aldgate after 1656, when Cromwell formally allowed Jews to resettle in England. The complete state of its preservation and the high quality of its fittings are superb. The synagogue was designed and built by Joseph Avis, a Quaker, who refused to accept a fee for building a house of God. Queen Anne also welcomed the building of the synagogue and, in a symbolic gesture, donated one of the main beams. The synagogue is much like a contemporary nonconformist chapel in its exterior treatment and interior arrangements, and although it lacks the spacial ingenuity of the best of Wren's church interiors, its rich fittings have much in common with the City churches. Most striking are the huge and low-slung brass chandeliers – these, however, are 17th-century Dutch and were the gift of a synagogue in Amsterdam.

Left along Bevis Marks to St Mary Axe. South (left) down St Mary Axe to:

The Swiss Re Tower – officially 30 St Mary Axe, unofficially the Gherkin – was completed in 2004. This 180-metre (591-foot) Sir Norman Foster-designed construction thrusts epically skywards and adds a touch of much-admired cool to the city skyline. Purporting to be London's first environmentally friendly skyscraper, it was designed to reduce energy consumption while also creating a light-filled working environment with views for all. Its circular, tapering build – part pine cone, part cigar – ensures plenty of sunshine reaches the landscaped plaza at its foot.

Continue south down St Mary Axe and across Leadenhall Street to:

Lloyd's was rebuilt between 1978 and 1986 to the designs of the Richard Rogers Partnership in close association with engineer Peter Rice of Ove Arup & Partners. It is one of the most significant European buildings of the post-war period and both encapsulates and develops many of the key ideas underpinning architectural modernism. For example, it is a building of components (prefabricated elsewhere and assembled on site), and it reverses tradition by exposing the services on the exterior of the building – the heating ducts, the lifts – rather than concealing them behind an elegant façade. The apparent logic for this exposure is that a building's services wear out first and need to be accessible for easy renewal.

But Lloyd's is anything but a monument to ruthless functionalism. In reality it is a building full of paradoxes. It is easy to assume that the exposed steel and concrete structure is merely a response to the dictates of engineering, but take a closer look. In fact, it has, in most cases, been exquisitely and expensively crafted to look industrial and functional. The wall-crawling lifts find it difficult to function in the London damp and the ducts are vulnerable to premature corrosion. In short, the look of Lloyd's is as much to do with taste as with function. Rather than being a monument to modernist utility, it is a late product of the Baroque – full of theatre, ambiguity and illusion. And this, of course, is why it remains a pleasure to see in the City landscape and a stunning experience to enter with its atrium, full of activity and illuminated lifts, soaring up to the mighty crowning barrel vault.

South down Lime Street and right along Leadenhall Place to take in Leadenhall Market. Turn left under the central dome and along Lime Street Passage to Lime Street. South across Fenchurch Street and down Philpott Lane. East (left) along Eastcheap to:

33-35 Eastcheap is one of those mid 19th-century buildings which led later

Mary-le-Bow) destroyed in the Great Fire. As with the medieval cathedrals in Edinburgh and Newcastle, Wren's tower is topped by four giant flying buttresses that rise from tall pinnacles and support a slender spire to create an open crown with a powerful silhouette. This tower and spire, along with the walls of the church (which had been rebuilt in 1810), are all that survived war damage. Inside the shell is one of the City's more successful attempts to create a picturesque garden within a gutted church, but this is kept locked.

Along St Dunstan's Lane, slightly north and turn into:

The Church of St Mary-at-Hill, of 1670-76, is the best of Wren's Greek Cross interiors. The columns are Corinthian and carry a delicately detailed dome. St Mary was much rebuilt and altered in the late 18th and early 19th centuries, but until a devasting fire in 1988 it had the appearance of a virtually untouched Wren interior, thanks largely to the sensitivity of restorer James Savage and his carver William Gibbs Rogers. Despite these alterations, St Mary's did retain much early joinery including box pews (the last to survive in a Wren City church), reredos, pulpit and communion rail. Fortunately, most of the joinery survived the fire. The structure has now been admirably reconstructed, with the reredos and pulpit restored, and the interior refurbished.

Pass out of church into Lovat Lane (was Love Lane). South down Lovat Lane to Lower Thames Street and right up Monument Street to:

The Monument, commemorating the Great Fire of 1666, remains one of the most perfect and exciting structures in the City. What could be more pleasing to the sight and to the imagination than a giant and perfectly proportioned Roman Doric column supporting a gilded flaming urn and standing on a tall and handsomely enriched pedestal? Despite ancient precedents (for example Trajan's Column in Rome), the erection of a 202-foot column was still a major engineering challenge in

The Monument

architectural critics to suspect that there had been a cult of ugliness among Victorian 'rogue' architects such as Robert Louis Roumieu, who was responsible for this extraordinary confection, which Pevsner calls 'one of the maddest displays in London of gabled Gothic brick'. Ian Nairn, writing in the 1960s, called it 'truly demoniac… the scream you wake on at the end of a nightmare'. It was built in 1868 as a wine and vinegar warehouse and offices for Messrs Hill, Evans & Co and stands on the site of the famous Boar's Head Tavern, where Shakespeare made Falstaff a regular.

East along Eastcheap and then south down Idol Lane to:

St Dunstan in the East was one of Wren's more interesting Gothic designs with its tower and spire being a conscious attempt on Wren's part to recreate (in 1697) a much-loved medieval spire (that of St the 1670s, especially when it was to be hollow to allow for the insertion of a spiral staircase leading to a viewing platform. Wren and Robert Hooke collaborated and the structure was finally completed in 1677. Climbing the elegant and minimal spiral staircase is still one of the most satisfying architectural experiences to be found in the City. The open well, which adds greatly to the staircase's daring and delight, was not only for visual effect but to allow members of the Royal Society to conduct experiments involving the use of a gigantic pendulum.

The plinth is embellished with a splendid Baroque relief by Caius Gabriel Cibber showing a Roman-garbed Charles II strolling around a building site and 'affording protection to the desolated city and freedom to its builders and inhabitants'. There is also a lengthy Latin inscription, which bewails the calamity of the Great Fire and firmly blamed it all on the Roman Catholics, warning that 'Popish frenzy, which brought such horrors, is not yet quenched'. But a gentler age felt less threatened and these offensive lines were finally expunged in 1830 in the wake of Catholic emancipation.

West across King William Street into Arthur Street then right into Martin Lane. West along alley immediately south of Old Wine Shades, across Laurence Pountney Lane and through alley to Laurence Pountney Hill for:

1 & 2 Laurence Pountney Hill. These are among the finest very early 18th-century houses surviving in London. They were built as a mirror-plan pair and are distinct to the City. They stand on a steep island site (they have no gardens or yards) and are each L-shaped in plan. In the centre of the entrance façade are a pair of magnificent semi-circular, round-topped and barrel-backed shell hoods, enriched foliage friezes around the doors, cherubs and the date 1703. Typical of grand City houses of this date, the doors are approached up a long flight of stairs, which means that the 'ground' floor is raised high above a deep, well-lit basement that is virtually at ground level. The elevation, of rich brickwork, is topped by a deep and handsome timber cornice.

North up Laurence Poutney Hill, across Cannon Street to Abchurch Lane. North along Abchurch Lane to Lombard Street, right and left up Birchin Lane. Right on

St Giles Cripplegate, surrounded by the Barbican Arts Centre.

Cornhill, then right almost at once into Ball Court for:

Simpson's Tavern is a remarkable survival. It is one of the last and best preserved of a great and once numerous City institution – the chop house and the coffee house. These were the places where business was done and deals struck in the 17th- and 18th-century City and, in the case of Mr Lloyd's coffee house, they grew into great business institutions in their own right. The buildings occupied by Simpson's date from the late 17th or very early 18th century, with a good 19th-century shopfront wrapped around the ground floor. The interior has been much altered since 1757 (when Simpson's claims to have been established) but diners still sit back-to-back on regimented rows of benches.

Past Simpson's to Castle Court and left for:

The **George & Vulture** is the City's other surviving chop house. The building looks as if it dates from the 1730s but the interior has been much altered. It retains some Georgian half panelling in the main dining room and the interior has a solid, old-fashioned atmosphere. Busts of Dickens abound because it was here that Mr Pickwick dined with Sam Weller.

Left along Castle Court and north up St Michael's alley to rejoin Cornhill. East (right) along Cornhill, north (left) up Bishopsgate to north corner with Threadneedle Street for:

Gibson Hall, **13 Bishopsgate** is the most noble of the City's mid 19th-century bank buildings. It was designed in 1863 for the National Provincial Bank by John Gibson and aspires to the unassailable classical grandeur of the nearby, and earlier, Bank of England buildings by Sir John Soane. Like Soane's bank, Gibson's building is a mere, and majestic, single storey. It is stone-built, pierced by large arched windows lighting the tall-ceilinged banking hall, dressed by tall Corinthian columns that support a deep entablature. Below the entablature is a series of carved panels (modelled by John Hancock), which illustrate man's activities and aspirations – the arts, commerce, science, manufacture, industry, agriculture and navigation.

West along Threadneedle Street and right up Old Broad Street to:

NatWest Tower (now **Tower 42**) is a crass construction, which, because of its sheer size, has managed to wheedle its way into Londoners' affections. It rises 600 feet (183 metres; for ten years it was the tallest building in Britain) and was constructed between 1970 and 1981 to the designs of Richard Seifert. This incredibly long construction period ensured that, in many ways, the office was commercially out of date before it was completed and the National Westminster Bank has now abandoned it following bomb damage in 1993. The plan is one of the building's curiosities – it takes the form of three overlapping half hexagons and looks much like NatWest's logo in the 1970s.

Continue north along Old Broad Street to London Wall/Wormwood Street. Turn left to:

All Hallows, London Wall is the most exquisite neo-classical building in the City. It is a pioneering work, designed in 1765 by the 24-year-old George Dance, which introduced many of the forms and details – seen by Dance on his Grand Tour – that were to become common currency among later 18th-century European designers. The exterior is brick-built and sombre, with giant blank arches and semi-circular thermal windows inspired by Roman bath architecture. The interior, by comparison, is light, delicate and finely detailed. It has a barrel vault, pierced by the semi-circular windows and supported by Ionic columns attached to the wall. At the east end is an apse with a half-domed top, of the sort found in Roman temples or basilicas. Another rational, if somewhat odd, innovation is the placing of the pulpit within an opening on the north wall from which it is reached by a concealed staircase.

Continue west along London Wall until just after the junction with Moorgate. Take the raised pedestrian walkway on the north side of London Wall (Gate 4). Wander round the walkways of:

The Barbican Centre. Just north of London Wall is the City's massive Barbican development – built between 1959 and 1981 to the designs of Chamberlain, Powell & Bon – which incorporates concrete-built housing towers, and an arts centre with library, theatres, exhibition space and restaurants. Pedestrians are accommodated on a raised walkway and podium with the focus being a lake around which are clustered pleasing, low-rise housing, the City of London Girls' School, more bastions of the City wall and the church of St Giles Cripplegate (dating from 1550 but gutted in World War II, it contains the graves of Martin Frobisher and John Milton). Despite being completed at a time when such megastructure developments were deeply unfashionable, the Barbican has always been popular in the City.

Return to exit at Gate 4, turn south down Coleman Street then left (east) along Great Swan Alley to:

The Institute of Chartered Accountants is one of the outstanding buildings of late Victorian Britain. It was designed in 1888 by John Belcher with his pupil Beresford Pite and was one of the earliest expressions of the return to the traditions of the English Baroque. Its appearance confirmed a new architectural direction. The building is designed in a light-hearted and picturesque neo-Baroque with lots of rich and original exterior detail, including a wonderfully composed corner with a cantilevered and columned oriel window, delightful caryatids above the ground-floor windows and a frieze of sculptured figures, which, at the witty suggestion of the clients, are 'balancing' themselves. The interiors are magnificent (sadly altered in the 1960s) with a mighty arched and domed council chamber and a splendid barrel-vaulted

entrance hall. The inspiration behind the details are intriguing and eclectic, ranging from Wren and Hawksmoor to Soane. The building was extended in the 1930s and again in the '60s when William Whitfield created (on Copthall Avenue) one of the most satisfactory works of that decade in the City.

South down Copthall Avenue, right along Telegraph Street and left down alley in Cazenove building. Down Tokenhouse Yard to corner with Lothbury:

7 Lothbury is the best Victorian Gothic building in the City. It was built in 1866 to the designs of George Somers Clarke senior, for the General Credit Company, a firm founded in 1863 that presumably wanted to make its mark in the City landscape by occupying a modish Gothic pile rather than the standard Italian Renaissance palazzo. This building, which embraces most of the architectural, structural and decorative ideas promoted in Ruskin's *Stones of Venice*, would look well on the Grand Canal. There is structural polychromy (the pink and white colouring of the building is achieved by combining stones of different colours rather than by paint or stucco), much well-carved detail and a sculptured frieze. Each storey is treated differently to reflect the hierarchy of occupation, with the best offices on the lower floors. The handsome main door was moved at a later date to the Lothbury frontage from the long Tokenhouse Yard elevation.

West along Lothbury, then turn south down Princes Street past:

Tivoli Corner and the west elevation of the screen wall of the Bank of England. Sir John Soane's rebuilding of the Bank of England, which began in 1788 and was not completed until 1833, created one of the most significant neo-classical public buildings in Europe. It was an immensely powerful and original composition and a project that allowed Soane to develop his distinct, and in many ways idiosyncratic, brand of neo-classic design. The bank required a series of high, single-storey halls that would be safe from thieves and rioters (the Gordon Riots of 1780 had had a sobering effect on many London institutions) and this need for security, along with the earlier top-lit rooms on the site designed by Sir Robert Taylor, stimulated Soane to design a series of spectacular, top-lit, arched and domed spaces, which created the most original and exciting series of interiors in the City since Wren's churches of 100 years earlier. Unfortunately, of this work, virtually nothing is left beyond parts of the screen wall. The Bank chose to do away with Soane's halls in the 1920s and commissioned the second-rate architect Sir Herbert Baker to pile multi-storeyed classical buildings behind Soane's wall. These Baker buildings have lame elevations but contain a reasonably interesting, if pompous, set of interiors including a few parodies of Soane's halls. Soane's screen wall is a grotesquely inadequate memorial to this lost masterpiece (and of this wall only the west and south sections are Soane's) but is well worth examining. It dates in part from the early stage of Soane's commission (the Lothbury section was begun in 1795) and is still embellished with the ornaments of classicism. The columns are Corinthian, derived from the Temple of Vesta at Tivoli, and the Lothbury/Princes Street corner (built in 1805) originally had a curved and columned corner composition inspired by the round Roman temple at Tivoli. This was altered and rebuilt by Baker utilising Soane elements. Understandably racked with guilt over its act of barbarism, the bank reconstructed a Soane hall in the 1980s. They chose the earliest and most characteristic – the Bank Stock Office of 1791-92 – and the work is well done. This room is part of the Bank's excellent museum.

Continue down Princes Street to Poultry – the 'Heart of Empire'. Proceed clockwise, from left to right past the south elevation of the screen wall of the Bank of England and past the south end of Bartholomew Lane in which is located the entrance to the Bank of England Museum.

The Royal Exchange is one of the great institutions of the City but not one of its great buildings. It attempts to dominate the heart of the City with its great portico – inspired by that of the Pantheon in Rome – which was intended to transform this interchange of busy streets into the 'Forum Londinium'. The building was designed in 1841 by Sir William Tite and was the result of a hotly contested and notoriously mismanaged architectural competition in which, as is often the case, the least demanding, but not the best, design won. Most informative now is a progress around the building that reveals the decline and fall of British classicism.

The Roman portico, with its fine sculpture by Richard Westmacott Junior, is handsome. The side elevations become decadently fussy with a meaningless mix of classical motifs from different epochs, with the Baroque dominating. And, most distressing of all, the rear elevation has rounded corners and, in its middle, two pairs of columns, one pair of which is attached to the building while the other pair, for no rational reason, is detached. Above these sits a rather small and meaningless Baroque tower.

Slightly set back from the junction is:

St Mary Woolnoth is one of the City's most rewarding and intriguing buildings. It was built between 1716 and 1727 to the designs of Nicholas Hawksmoor and occupies a key and unusual position in that great architect's astonishing repertoire of church designs. Hawksmoor's east London churches (notably Christ Church, Spitalfields and St Anne's, Limehouse) are characterised by a sublime scale, a sculptural massing of forms and a powerful abstraction of the conventional classical language of decoration. At St Mary's all is slightly different, although no less powerful. The scale is reduced and the direct debt to historic classical precedent is more obvious. For example, the north elevation – one of the great architectural thrills of the City – is embellished with three great rusticated arches containing concave entablatures and columns set on curved and diagonally placed pedestals. Below the arches are massive key stones set among more rustication – it is certainly the best wall in Britain. This remarkable composition is the nearest you can find in London to the works of Bernini or Borromini. The south wall, pierced with windows set within giant arches, is now sadly mostly obscured by a later screen wall. Inside, St Mary's is, if anything, even more original and reveals Hawksmoor's obsession with simple and primary volumes used in a rational manner.

The interior is effectively a large cube from which rises a smaller cube supported on four groups of three Corinthian columns – a form probably inspired by Serlio and Palladio's reconstructions of the Roman author Vitruvius's description of what was termed an 'Egyptian Hall'. The walls of the smaller, higher, cube are pierced by huge Roman bath-style semi-circular windows to capture light from the congested City streets. The area of the larger cube, behind the groups of columns, works as aisles to the north and south and chancel to the east. Hawksmoor's joinery is equally original, especially the astonishing black Baldacchino modelled on that in St Peter's in Rome. But the interior was much altered in 1878 when William Butterfield reordered it with a particularly heavy hand. John Newton was the incumbent of St Mary's from 1780-1807 – he was an ex-slaver who converted to Evangelical Christianity during a storm, inspired William Wilberforce and wrote the hymn 'Amazing Grace', which was, presumably, first performed in this church.

The Mansion House is a cross between a palace, a town hall and a law court – complete with lock-up. Its prime role, however, is as the official residence of the Lord Mayor, and to fulfil this function it is provided with a superb succession of state rooms. The design for the Mansion House was secured through an architectural competition in 1737 when the City chose a submission by the City's own Clerk of Works and member of the Merchant Taylors' Company, George Dance. The site is awkward and Dance did not really succeed in realising a Palladian mansion in the heart of the City. There is a fine Roman portico and the building sits on a rusticated base, but the portico does not relate easily to the side elevations. Despite his best efforts, Dance betrays his taste for flamboyant detail by veering towards an idiosyncratic Baroque in some of his external ornament. The interior (not completed until 1753) is superb and a worthy monument to merchant taste in the early 18th-century City. The straight axis from the portico leads to a vestibule, hall, saloon and then through another vestibule to the Egyptian Hall, which should not be missed. (*See* St Mary Woolnoth, *p109*.)

Midland Bank HQ (now **HSBC**) is the most distinguished building of its type and date in the City. It was built from 1924-27 to the designs of Sir Edwin Lutyens and shows that the language of classicism was alive and well between the wars and could realise the potential offered by new building technology – the bank has a steel frame with Portland stone used only as a cladding. The elevation is worth close scrutiny to see how Lutyens managed to achieve such a tall composition while keeping his classical details proportionate. There is much layering of the stone surface; there are mezzanines, tall arches that contain more than one storey, and when the elevation has run its classical course and finally reaches the cornice, Lutyens starts again with another, separately composed, classical pavilion on the roof. And then there is Lutyens's famous wit – the fat boy with a goose

Bank of England

logic and proportion. It is an oblong slightly longer than wide within which Wren created a square volume defined by four groups of three columns, with the inner eight columns supporting a dome. This forest of columns is linked by a beautifully embellished entablature from which spring the eight semi-circular arches that support the dome. Light floods in from oval windows set high in the walls, from windows set above the entablature and from a tall lantern set in the centre of the dome. The dome itself is a perfect creation – a half sphere embellished with large-scale plaster ornament. The surviving joinery is fine, particularly the reredos and the real focus of the interior, the massive pulpit with its sounding board. However, in recent years a massive and formless stone altar, wrought by Sir Henry Moore, has been placed beneath the dome. Moore's sculpture may or may not be a work of aesthetic merit but what is certain is that it gravely disturbs Wren's interior. The focus should be on the pulpit and on the altar and reredos against the east wall, not on the space below the dome, which should be serenely empty.

Continue south down Walbrook, cross Cannon Street and south down Dowgate Hill past, on south-west corner with Cloak Lane:

Tallow Chandlers' Hall (4 Dowgate Hill), built 1670-72, is one of the great surprises of the City. The front to Dowgate Hill is unpromising – a nondescript late 19th-century building – but there is an arch and when you enter that you enter the City of the late 17th century. The first impression is of impossibly large ideas realised on an impossibly small scale. The arch leads to a short passage at the end of which lies a tiny courtyard, which is formed by loosely uniform brick elevations (lightly tricked up with inappropriate details in 1871 by E Norton Clifton) unified by a massive timber cornice and a Doric arcade on all four sides. Get inside if you can, for there

carved by Sir William Reid Dick – and clever interior planning. Most memorable is the circular marble basin that stands where the interior axis between the Poultry and Princes Street elevation meet and, instead of containing water, offers an entertaining view into the safe deposit vault below.

Continue south down Walbrook to:

St Stephen, Walbrook, built between 1672 and 1679, is generally regarded as Wren's finest City church. Certainly it was highly regarded at the time, and Wren, who controlled the design and execution of all the interior details, was rewarded by the parishioners with a gift of 20 guineas in a silk purse for his 'great care and extraordinary pains taken in contriving the design of the church'. So what is so remarkable? Certainly not the exterior, which, in Wren's time, was largely obscured by houses and narrow alleys. That is why there are no windows at low level and why much of the walling is rough and unadorned. The only exceptions are the handsome entrance portal and the spire, completed in 1717. The interior is a mathematical exercise in are some remarkable interiors and details, notably the staircase (you can just glimpse it from outside), the panelling and Corinthian-columned reredos in the hall, the panelled parlour and the Court Room with its original seating. Also be sure to see the fine (if somewhat restored) 1670s hooded doorcase on Cloak Lane.

Continue south down Dowgate Hill to junction with College Street. Turn right (west) along College Street to College Hill. Turn right (north) up College Hill to, on the right:

21-22 College Hill contain a stupendous pair of large, late 17th-century stone-built doorcases, each supporting segmental pediments packed with flamboyant mannerist carvings of masks, swags, scrolls and the like. Between the arches is squeezed a small late Georgian-style shop front (now a private members' bar) and above each arch is a round window. The whole composition is incredibly pleasing. Pass through the southern arch and another surprise awaits – a fine large house of around 1700 with an excellent mid 18th-century doorcase. Turn and look at the rear elevation of the College Hill buildings and another delight – a late 17th-century domestic elevation complete with some good brickwork, eaves cornice and a projecting staircase bay in which the stout balusters of a fine staircase can just be detected.

Continue north up College Hill and turn west (left) along Cloak Lane to Queen Street. Cross Queen Street and continue west along Great St Thomas Apostle to Garlick Hill. North up to the junction of Cannon Street and Queen Victoria Street. Cross junction and head north up Bow Lane. Continue north up Bow Lane to Watling Street. Turn left (west) into Watling Street to see:

24-26 Watling Street is a rare surviving example of a galleried warehouse and showroom, designed in 1871 by Herbert Ford for a manufacturer of trimmings and braids. This building is a reminder that banks and offices did not

entirely dominate the Victorian City and that there were still areas of warehousing, manufacturing and housing. This building has an internal structure of cast iron and timber and a very meticulously detailed classical façade with pilasters framing large windows and ferocious lion masks framing the doors. The building now houses a bar.

Return to junction with Bow Lane and turn left (north) up Bow Lane. Go left (west) down Groveland Court to:

Williamson's Hotel stands on the site of Sir John Fastolfe's house – the knight whom Shakespeare unfairly caricatured as Falstaff. The existing building dates in part from the late 17th century, although greatly rebuilt after the war, and has been known by its present name since 1753 when Robert Williamson made it a hotel.

Return to Bow Lane, turn left (north) up to Cheapside. Turn right along Cheapside and turn left (north) up Old Jewry and left into:

Frederick's Place is the remains of a small but elegant and uniform residential development undertaken by the Adam brothers in 1776. The best preserved houses, which reveal the design of the Adam scheme, are 1, 4 (although somewhat altered in the early 19th century), 6 and 8, which has a good original doorcase and a Venetian window lighting a first-floor room.

Return to Old Jewry and continue north to Gresham Street. Turn left (west) at Gresham Street and continue west along Gresham Street. Turn right (north) at St Lawrence to see:

The Guildhall. The most extraordinary thing about the Guildhall is that it is there at all. By a miracle it survived the Great Fire, which raged around it, and somehow or other it came through the Blitz. But it did not survive unscathed – in fact, war damage was extremely severe – nor has the medieval building, erected c1411-40 by John Croxton, been treated lightly by successive generations of restorers.

But the Guildhall remains an extremely moving testament to the architectural ambitions of the early 15th-century City merchants. The grand porch survives with its two bays of stone vaulting (called tierceron vaulting). The masonry shell of the great hall – which is over 150 feet long – is also original and some windows survive. The roof has been remade to the designs of Sir Giles Scott. Below the hall is the building's most impressive medieval space, the undercroft. This is a splendid room with nave and aisles and, again, stone tierceron vaults. The entrance front to the Guildhall is, perhaps, the most surprising aspect of the building. It was added in 1788 by the usually sober and exquisitely neo-classical City Corporation surveyor George Dance the Younger. But what on earth are we to make of the style he has chosen? It is symmetrical and thus classical in feel and even has a few Grecian details. But the majority of the forms and details, particularly the finials and the pointed windows, have a distinctly Gothic look – but a Gothic that bears little relation to authentic Gothic. The façade has been called 'Hindoo' – for which there was a fashion in the late 18th century – but which it certainly is not. It may be an attempt at north Indian Moghul architecture and as such is a tribute to the source of much of the City's wealth in the late 18th century. If so, then the Guildhall façade is the first example of the influence of Indian taste on British architecture.

Return to Gresham Street and continue west along Gresham Street to St Martins le Grand/Aldersgate. Turn right (north) and on the left is:

St Botolph, Aldersgate Street is a gaunt little brick box of a church, built between 1788 and 1791, with a pretty stuccoed and pilastered east façade added in about 1830. But this vernacular exterior conceals a delightful neo-classical interior with good galleries, barrel-vaulted ceiling and delicate plasterwork. The designer was Nathaniel Wright. Adjacent is

Postman's Park – a pleasant retreat created in 1880 from the burial grounds of three nearby churches. In 1887 the painter GF Watts had the idea of turning the place into a mini Valhalla with memorials to heroic men and women. These memorials – ceramic plaques of admirable typographic design – now line one wall and the heroes whose praises are sung are pleasingly humble. There is the daughter of a bricklayer's labourer who saved three children from a fire 'at the cost of her own life', and the particularly poignant memorial to Soloman Galaman who died aged 11 in 1901 in Commercial Street, Spitalfields, while saving his brother from hurtling traffic and whose last words were: 'Mother, I saved him, but could not save myself.'

Go through Postman's Park and right on King Edward Street. Continue north and turn west along Little Britain to West Smithfield to see on the right:

St Bartholomew's-the-Great church was founded in 1123 by Rahere, Henry I's former court jester, who became a pilgrim and had a vision in which St Bartholomew saved him from a winged monster. This is the only surviving fragment of the resulting, once extensive Augustinian priory. In fact, only the crossing and part of the transepts and chancel of the priory church survive, but it is, nevertheless, the most evocative early medieval fragment in London. The interior is wonderfully gloomy, dominated by massive Norman columns and with a curved chancel (much restored) with a splendid Lady Chapel at the east end. To the south are the stunted remains of the priory cloister. The church was much restored and gently extended from the 1860s-90s by Aston Webb.

Exit the church and follow Cloth Fair west. Before Giltspur Street, enter left into:

St Bartholomew's Hospital was also founded by Rahere in 1123. The oldest structures now on the site of Rahere's hospital are the 15th-century tower and vestry of the hospital chapel

– St Bartholomew-the-Less (now with a pretty octagonal nave designed in 1823 by Thomas Hardwick) – and the impressive gateway, dated 1702 but rebuilt and extended in 1834. The most architecturally significant buildings are the three ranges that form the inner court. These were built from 1730-59 to the designs of James Gibbs and, stone-clad and correctly classical, have great gravity and grandeur. Inside the north-western block is one of the most spectacular Georgian interiors in London. There is a Great Hall, panelled and with a coffered ceiling and a grand staircase with wall paintings of 1735 by William Hogarth. They show appropriate emblematic scenes – for example, the Good Samaritan – and figures suffering from the sort of wounds and ailments treated in the hospital, supposedly based on studies of contemporary patients. Gibbs's quadrangle, with the gatehouse and chapel, give the hospital the feel of a rather grand Oxbridge college, which was the monastic-inspired building type thought suitable in the 18th century for hospital design.

Follow down Giltspur Street, east (left) down Newgate, and then south down Warwick Lane. At the bottom turn east along Ludgate Hill to:

St Paul's Cathedral is one of a half dozen great classical churches of the world and compares well with St Peter's in Rome, which for Wren was both an inspiration and – as a great Roman Catholic cathedral – also a challenge. St Paul's was built between 1675 and 1714, which means that work of reconstruction did not start until nearly ten years after the medieval cathedral was severely damaged during the Great Fire. Wren was made Surveyor-General of the cathedral in 1669 and produced no fewer than five schemes for reconstruction. After his first three designs had been ruled out, Wren produced a plan in 1675 that received the Royal Warrant for construction. This design – known as the Warrant

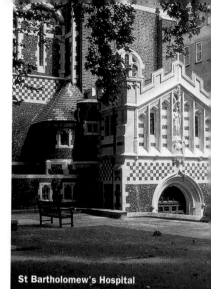

St Bartholomew's Hospital

Design – and the process by which Wren built it shows him at his most pragmatic and politically astute. He erected a huge screened scaffolding around the site when work started in June 1675 and the construction of St Paul's became one of the great secrets of Stuart London. Behind this hoarding rose a fifth design, which combines elements from the earlier efforts but is clearly not the Warrant Design. To achieve this sleight of hand Wren seems to have utilised a clause in the warrant which gave him 'the liberty… to make some variations rather ornamental than essential, as from time to time he would see proper'.

To understand the cathedral as built, you should first walk around its exterior. Wren always fantasised that his cathedral would stand in a great piazza like St Peter's in Rome. But when work started, Wren knew this was not to be – merchants had already rebuilt on their old sites and the cathedral was closed in by red-brick houses that re-established the medieval street pattern. So Wren's great design had to be made to work in a cramped and architecturally humble context. He used two tiers of smaller columns so that the lower Order corresponded in height to surrounding houses while the upper Order sailed above the roof tops with the top half of the cathedral, when seen from afar, looking like a self-contained classical temple rising above the roof tops – the City's Parthenon on its Acropolis.

The other, obvious point about the exterior is its huge scale. Wren was determined to create the grandest Protestant church in Europe. The dome got ever higher and, to stay in proportion, the body of the cathedral had also to grow in height. Indeed, most of the upper elevations above the aisles are merely screen walls that both raise the height of the perimeter walls of the cathedral and hide the visually disturbing flying buttresses. Most famous is the dome, which is, essentially, a great and wonderful illusion. Outside it is a perfect hemisphere – an ideal shape for a dome but a form incapable of supporting the huge weight of the stone structure (called 'the cross') that rises above. In fact, the dome does not carry this stone structure at all, but it is supported by an immensely strong but ugly brick cone concealed within the beautiful outer dome. This cone, strengthened by the use of great iron chains set in stone bands, also supports the timber structure of the outer dome. A third dome, placed below the cone, conceals it from within the cathedral. It is possible to clamber between these domes and cones – an exhilarating adventure among 17th-century engineering that should not be missed.

The interior of the cathedral is a vivid reminder that Wren had to achieve his great Protestant temple by working with the architectural language of the Roman Catholic counter-reformation. As with his City churches, Wren used light streaming through large windows of plain glass to create a suitably rational Protestant atmosphere and focused the interior on the great pulpit – where the word of God was expounded – as much as on the altar. Nevertheless, the vast scale and the richness of the interior, and the Renaissance and Baroque references in

its details (the arcade of the nave and the richness of the chancel are reminiscent of St Peter's) retain a powerful, Catholic atmosphere. The quality of the interior fittings are of the highest standard: Wren not only created a great classical building, but he created a school of craftsmen who were to apply the lessons learned at St Paul's to the design and construction of buildings throughout the country.

Walk along south part of St Paul's Churchyard and turn south down Godliman Street and right into Carter Lane, then north into Deane's Court to see:

St Paul's Deanery is the best 17th-century mansion in the city and suggests the type of house that the more prosperous post-fire merchant would have occupied. It is virtually a freestanding house, low and wide, but set over a tall basement. As was typical of the time, the front door – here embellished with a magnificent hooded and consoled doorcase – is reached via a flight of steps. To give a touch of extra grandeur, the windows are framed with rubbed brick jambs. Most charming of all, the house sits behind a cobbled forecourt separated from the street by a tall wall and gate. The house was designed in 1670 by Wren's office, or even by Wren himself.

Return to Carter Lane and turn right (west) and then left (south) to see:

Wardrobe Place, a delightful wide court dominated by tall plane trees and, on its west side, two groups of houses that date from the late 17th or very early 18th century. This is the best preserved of a once common City arrangement and reveals how pleasant these residential courts must have been.

Return to Carter Lane and turn left (west) and then north up Creed Lane to Ludgate Hill. Turn left (west) at Ludgate Hill towards Ludgate Circus and Fleet Street. Head west along Fleet Street. and turn north into Wine Office Court to see:

Cheshire Cheese Inn is a fine building, probably of the late 17th century, with an early 19th-century shopfront. It is famous as one of Dr Johnson's favourite retreats and inside it contains a fine pair of bars – particularly that to the east, which retains early half panelling, settles and a fire-surround with a breast supported on large stone consoles. The staircase is also early.

Continue north along Wine Office Court, then left (west) into Gough Square to see:

Dr Johnson's House is one of the area's few surviving late 17th-century domestic buildings. The pretty doorcase dates from around 1775. The house is now a museum in honour of Samuel Johnson, who lived here from 1748-59 and compiled his dictionary on the top floor. Unfortunately, this garret was gutted by fire during World War II but otherwise the interior retains much panelling, a good staircase and panelled walls on the first floor that hinge back to create one large room for entertaining.

Turn south through Johnson's Court to Fleet Street. Walk west along Fleet Street and then turn left (south) into the Temple via Inner Temple Lane.

The Temple is an entertainment in itself. It is named after the Knights Templar, who in about 1160 were gifted the land. After their downfall in 1308 it passed to the Knight Hospitallers and finally into the hands of lawyers to become one of the Inns of Court. The Templars' church survives with a round nave of 1160-85, modelled on the Holy Sepulchre in Jerusalem (including a spectacular Norman west door) and a wide chancel of 1220-40. The church was gutted during World War II (when the famous stone effigies of knights were damaged) but the reconstruction of 1948-58, by Walter Godfrey, is exemplary. The Temple (divided into the Inner Temple and Middle Temple) comprises a series of large spaces of various sizes and forms connected by courts and alleys. Much was reconstructed after the Great Fire. The most important early secular building is the Middle Temple Hall of 1562-70, with

a double hammer beam timber roof and a spectacular Elizabethan timber screen. It was here that Shakespeare's *Twelfth Night* was produced for the first time in February 1601 in the presence of the aged and ailing Queen Elizabeth. Also early is the Inner Temple Gateway, bridging Inner Temple Lane leading from Fleet Street; it dates from 1610 (although much restored in 1906) and is built in the medieval timber-frame tradition although with classical details. Inside is the panelled Prince Henry's Room with an ornate plaster ceiling of c1610. Another gate, that over Middle Temple Lane to the west, is a fine pedimented and brick-built affair designed in 1684 by the bencher and gifted amateur architect Roger North.

From Devereux Court pass to the west out of the Temple and north up Essex Street to the junction of the Strand and Fleet Street, the site of Temple Bar and the western edge of the City of London.

Eating & drinking

Old Cheshire Cheese
145 Fleet Street, EC4A 2BU (7353 6170).
Open *Bar* 11am-11pm Mon-Sat; noon-2.30pm Sun. *Ground floor restaurant* noon-9pm Mon-Fri; noon-2.30pm, 6-9pm Sat; noon-2.30pm Sun. *2nd floor restaurant* noon-2.30pm Mon, Tue; noon-2.30pm, 6-9.30pm Wed-Fri. Charmingly creaky old establishment, and one of Fleet Street's most famous pubs.

Simpson's Tavern
off Ball Court, Cornhill, EC3V 9DR (7626 9985).
Open 11.30am-3pm Mon-Fri. **Food served** noon-3pm Mon-Fri.

George & Vulture
3 Castle Court, off Cornhill, EC3V 8DR (7626 9710). **Open** noon-2.45pm Mon-Fri. British cuisine.

Williamson's Tavern
1 Groveland Court, EC4M 9EH (7248 5750).
Open 11am-11pm Mon-Fri. **Food served** noon-9pm Mon-Fri.

Buildings & museums

Bank of England Museum
Entrance on Bartholomew Lane, EC2R 8AH (7601 5545). **Open** 10am-5pm Mon-Fri. Tours by arrangement. **Admission** free.

Barbican Centre

Silk Street, EC2Y 8DS (7638 4141/www.barbican. org.uk). **Open** *gallery* 11am-8pm Mon, Fri-Sun; 11am-6pm Tue, Thur. **Admission** varies according to event.

Dr Johnson's House

17 Gough Square, off Fleet Street, EC4A 3DE (7353 3745/www.drjohnsonshouse.org). **Open** *May-Sept* 11am-5.30pm Mon-Sat; *Oct-Apr* 11am-5pm Mon-Sat. **Admission** £4.50; £1.50-£3.50 concessions.

Guildhall

off Gresham Street, EC2P 2EJ (7606 3030/www. cityoflondon.gov.uk/guildhall). **Open** *Guildhall* 9am-5pm Mon-Sat. **Admission** free.

Mansion House

Walbrook, EC4N 8BH (7626 2500). **Open** for group visits by written application, at least two months in advance (min 15, max 40 people).

Middle & Inner Temple

Middle Temple *Middle Temple Lane, EC4Y 9AT (7427 4800).* **Open** phone for details on the variable opening hours. **Admission** free.
Inner Temple *Inner Temple Treasury Office, EC4Y 7HL (7797 8250).* **Open** group tours of the hall costing £10 can be booked by phone (min 10 people).

Monument

Monument Street, EC3R 8AH (7626 2717). **Open** 9.30am-5pm daily. **Admission** £2; £2 concessions.

Prince Henry's Room

17 Fleet Street, EC4Y 1AA (7936 4004). **Open** 11am-2pm Mon-Sat. **Admission** free.

St Bartholomew's Hospital Museum

West Smithfield, EC1A 7BE (7601 8152/guided tours on Fridays 7837 0546). **Open** 10am-4pm Tue-Fri. **Admission** free.

Tallow Chandlers Hall

4 Dowgate Hill, EC4R 2SH (7248 4726/www.tallow chandlers.org). **Open** office 8am-5pm Mon-Fri. Available for private hire.

Tower of London

Tower Hill, EC3N 4AB (7709 0765/www.hrp. org.uk). **Open** *Mar-Oct* 10am-6pm Mon, Sun; 9am-6pm Tue-Sat. *Nov-Feb* 10am-5pm Mon, Sun; 9am-5pm Tue-Sat. *Tours* every 30 mins daily. **Admission** £14.50; £9.50-£11 concessions; free under 5s; £42 family.

Information

City Information Centre

St Paul's Churchyard, EC4M 8BX (south side of the Cathedral) (7332 1456). **Open** *Easter-Sept* 9.30am-5pm daily. *Oct-Easter* 9.30am-5pm Mon-Fri; 9.30am-12.30pm Sat. A source of information on sights, events, walks and talks within the Square Mile.

Worship

All Hallows

83 London Wall, EC2M 5ND (7588 2638). **Open** 11am-3pm Fri.

St Bartholomew-the-Great

West Smithfield, EC1A 7JQ (7606 5171/www.great barts.com). **Open** *Mid Nov-mid Feb* 8.30am-4pm Tue-Fri; 10.30am-1.30pm Sat; 8.30am-1pm, 2.30-8pm Sun. *Mid Feb-mid Nov* 8.30am-5pm Tue-Fri; 10.30am-1.30pm Sat; 8am-1pm, 2.30-8pm Sun.

St Botolph without Aldersgate

Aldersgate Street, EC3N 1AB (7606 0684/7283 1670/www.stbotolphs.org.uk). **Open** 10am-3pm Mon-Fri, Sun.

St Dunstan's in the East

St Dunstan's Hill, EC3R 5DD. Administered by church of All Hallows by the Tower (7481 2928). **Open** 7.30am-7pm or dusk if earlier daily.

St Katharine Cree

86 Leadenhall Street, EC3A 3DH (7283 5733). **Open** 10.30am-4pm Mon-Fri.

St Mary at Hill

Lovatt Lane, EC3R 8EE (7626 4184). **Open** 11am-4pm Mon-Fri.

St Mary Woolnoth

Lombard Street, EC3V 9AN (7626 9701). **Open** 9.30am-4.30pm Mon-Fri

St Olave

Hart Street, EC3R 7NB (7488 4318). **Open** 9am-5pm Mon-Fri.

St Paul's Cathedral

Ludgate Hill, EC4M 8AD (7236 4128/www.st pauls.co.uk). **Open** 8.30am-4pm Mon-Sat. *Galleries, crypt & ambulatory* 8.30am-4pm Mon-Sat. Hours may change, special events may cause closure; check before visiting. Tours 11am, 11.30am, 1.30pm, 2pm Mon-Sat. **Admission** *Cathedral, crypt & gallery* £8; £3.50-£7 concessions. *Audio guide* £3.50; £3 concessions.

St Stephen Walbrook

Walbrook, EC4N 8BN (7283 4444). **Open** 10am-4pm Mon-Thur; 10am-3pm Fri.

Spanish & Portuguese Synagogue

Bevis Marks, EC3A 5DQ (7626 1274). **Open** *Winter* 11am-1pm Mon-Wed, Sun. *Summer* 11am-1pm Mon-Wed, Fri, Sun. **Admission** £2; £1 children.

Temple Church

Inner Temple, King's Bench Walk, EC4Y 7BB (7353 3470/www.templechurch.com). **Open** Times vary; call to check before visiting.

Transition & reinterpretation

James Miller

Take a walk through the city-as-palimpsest, where change is endemic.

> **Start:** Old Street tube/rail, exit 5
> **Finish:** Waterloo tube/rail
> **Distance:** 4 miles/6.5km
> **Time:** 2.5 hours
> **Getting there:** Northern line to Old Street
> **Getting back:** Bakerloo, Jubilee and Northern lines from Waterloo
> **Note:** the area north of the river is quieter at the weekends.

This walk revisits those places around the City, the tower blocks and demolition sites, that express a sense of the city as a living, changing presence.

They reflect a dynamism that always seems lacking from the atrophied atmosphere of the traditional sights. Sure, the Houses of Parliament, Buckingham Palace, St Paul's and the Tower are all wonderful buildings, capable, when viewed from a certain angle or bathed in one of London's surreal smog-scented sunsets, of impressing even the most jaded urbanite. However, this walk sets out to see the city in a different way: not as an achieved or static form, to be carefully preserved (like Venice or Rome), but as a city that is continuously evolving. This very process of evolution, as a city constantly destroying, rebuilding, renovating and reinterpreting itself, is

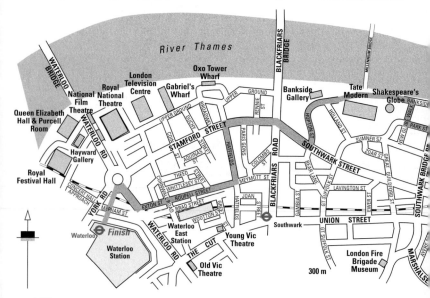

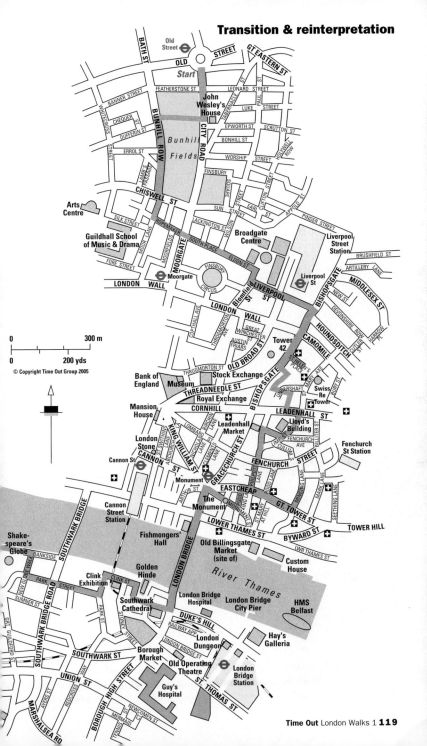

Transition & reinterpretation

The vast hulk of the **Swiss Re Tower**.

part of London's essential character, a process to delight in. London is neither beautiful nor architecturally harmonious, but dramatic and frantic, thriving on its unresolvable tension between immense antiquity and extreme modernity.

Start by taking the Northern line to Old Street, just north of the City. Take exit 5 to emerge on to the southbound City Road. The traffic is bad today, but then the place has always been busy. On either side of the underground station was once a Roman road that allowed the legions to bypass London. This is border territory, skirting the racial and economic confusion of Hackney, the vibrant gentrification of Islington and the City's wealthy citadels. But it is in these transitional districts that so much of London's essential character exists, the unseen centres, where the city of the past lies neglected and buried, and the city of the future struggles to be born.

This can be graphically demonstrated by Bunhill Fields, 100 yards down City Road. The fields were 'walled in' in 1665, while the name derives from 'bone's hill' and is the resting place of three of the capital's greatest visionaries: John Bunyan, Daniel Defoe and William Blake. A large office block (once home to the *Independent* newspaper) overlooking the cemetery has been converted into luxury flats, green glass and terracotta cladding replacing the drab concrete. It was something the empty office towers on Bunhill Row, on the other side of the cemetery, were crying out for. One of London's most encouraging trends has been this process of redevelopment. Instead of carving up what remains of the countryside with alienating suburban cul-de-sacs, councils and property speculators have finally had the good sense to start turning some of the capital's empty office buildings into new flats and lofts that promise to bring a sense of life and community back to what, at night, are some of the quietest streets.

Continue down Bunhill Row, pausing to glance through some railings at the HAC ground on the left. The ground, which is completely out of bounds, has been in existence since 1642 and, in the 18th century, was home to some of the first cricket matches ever played. The Honourable Artillery Company itself was granted a charter by Henry VIII in 1537 and is the oldest military body in the city.

From Bunhill Row walk across Chiswell Street into Moor Lane, then turn left along Ropemaker Street, gazing up at the 410-foot blue-green glass façade of City Point Tower. Formerly Britannic House, the old headquarters of BP, the original 1960s building has been completely re-structured and re-built, a new building materialising out of the old.

Keep walking along into South Place, where the throng of grey suits declares as clearly as the surveillance cameras and police checkpoints that you are entering the City proper. The police checkpoints were started after IRA bombs added to the City's history of sudden destruction and subsequent restoration and reconstruction. They ensure that every vehicle entering the City is monitored and catalogued.

The Broadgate Centre, on the left at the end of Eldon Street, built around and over Liverpool Street station, is a genuinely strange piece of architecture. It seems to take a perverse delight in its ability to alienate the people who move through it. I can't help thinking the architects must have been satirising their client's pretensions. The tinted and dark steel buildings, partly camouflaged by ivy and shrubs, resemble a high-tech ruin. This impression is enhanced by the ice-rink arena at the centre. The ivy-smothered concrete evokes the faded marble of a Roman ruin, but it is pure façade. There is nothing behind it. The centre attempts to deconstruct traditional architectural values of unity, harmony and stability. An ironic comment, perhaps, on the nature of modern business, where notions of value have ceased to have any real connection with production or demand. Or a realisation that the modern city is a place of pure momentum and any attempt

to preserve a sense of permanence or continuity is illusory. If you can actually handle this place, take a look at a few of the statues decorating its open spaces: a faceless man wrestles down a Pegasus, their bodies conflating into a single twist of limbs; monolithic slabs of metal, like an industrial Stonehenge, dominate the entrance to Liverpool Street; and, most surreal of all, a cluster of anonymous figures wrapped in long overcoats, facing the same direction. How do the people who work here feel, seeing themselves as faceless, dehumanised abstractions? In keeping with the mood there is little evidence of the artists or architects responsible.

So, following the signs, walk through Liverpool Street Station and turn right down Bishopsgate. Bishopgate marks the route of the main northern Roman road out of London. Stop to look at St Botolph, Bishopsgate on the right. This small church is not one of the City's most beautiful or famous, but nonetheless embodies the very process of transition, destruction and reinterpretation traced throughout this walk. The original Norman church that occupied this site was replaced by a medieval church, which was demolished in 1724 for the present church, completed in 1728. After surviving World War II it suffered extensive structural damage following the IRA Baltic Exchange and Bishopsgate bombs, as did the Hong Kong and Shanghai Bank tower opposite.

Cross over Wormwood Street, glancing down London Wall, where remains of the old Roman fort can be glimpsed beneath the office towers. Continue down Bishopsgate, passing St Ethelburga's at No.78, which was reduced to rubble by the IRA blast and is now a Centre for Reconciliation and Peace, before pausing to step inside St Helen's Place on the left. The site is occupied by the Leathersellers' Livery Hall, a City guild that has existed for 800 years and now makes money by letting property on the land it owns. Originally growing from the 'Great

Twelve', there are now a hundred livery companies, from the more traditional guilds such as the Mercers or Fishmongers, to Chartered Accountants, Actuaries and even Information Technologists.

Leaving St Helen's Place, take the next left into Great St Helen's. Towering above the 12th-century St Helen's is the giant Swiss Re Tower – or 'Gherkin', as it is fondly known – designed by Sir Norman Foster and the first environmentally friendly skyscraper in London. Between St Helen's, Bishopsgate church and the tiny church of St Andrew Undershaft (at the corner of St Mary Axe and Leadenhall Street), which dates from 1520, is the 387-foot Chicago-style Aviva Tower and the massive high-tech bulk of Richard Rogers's Lloyd's Building, built between 1978 and 1986 (it looks better at night, bathed in blue and white light). The area was seriously damaged by the Baltic Exchange IRA bomb. Foster's proposed Millennium Tower, on the site of the ruined Exchange, would have stood taller than the Empire State Building and severely altered the scale and skyline of the City. However, when walking through this quarter of the City, with its radical contrasts in size and epoch, the very incongruity of such a building seems ideal. Sadly, the proposal failed for a variety of reasons – one criticism was that the tower would compete with St Paul's, as if an ideological line can be drawn with Sir Christopher Wren. Walking around London demonstrates how it thrives on sudden contrast and evolution – few other cities could accommodate such continuity and change at the same time, in the same place.

Turn left past the Lloyd's Building into Leadenhall Market, a Victorian mall designed by Sir Horace Jones in 1881. There has been a food market here, originally the site of the Roman forum, since the Middle Ages. Traditional pubs and cafés in the market make a welcome change from the fast-food sandwich shops, wine bars and pseudo-olde-England pubs that service most of the City's 500,000 workers.

Leave the market by crossing Fenchurch Street and walking down Philpot Street. Turn left along Eastcheap and walk along Great Tower Street, taking a brief detour up Mincing Lane to look at Minster Court, a massive art deco/Gothic office complex nicknamed Dracula's castle.

Walk back along Eastcheap, and turn left down Pudding Lane to the Monument, designed by Wren and built between 1671 and 1677 to commemorate the Great Fire of London. The tower is 202 feet high, the exact distance between it and the source of the fire. A plaque at the base of the Monument once aportioned blame for the fire to the Catholics, an unfounded allegation (deleted in the 19th century following the Catholic emancipation) that reflected the anti-papist sentiment of the time. There are 311 steps up a narrow spiral staircase, but the view from the top (not for the faint-hearted) is one of the best in London. The Great Fire is symbolic of the City's ability to convert destruction into creative change. From the top one can see how this process continues. The City maintains its chaotic medieval street plan (Wren's proposal to replace it with a rational grid was rejected), but it is no ancient Oxford, York or Durham. Up here it's the modern skyline that catches one's eye. Despite the brutality or gaudy hubris of these buildings, their great glass and steel bodies reflect London's raw energy, and we should see in them an attempt to exaggerate, parody or perfect the essential character of the city around them.

From the Monument cross over King William Street, then walk over London Bridge towards the mishmash of Southwark and Bankside. The present London Bridge might not be very eye-catching but this is the oldest Thames crossing, its history dating back to the first century AD. The previous bridge can now be found at Lake Havasu, Arizona, having been bought in 1971 by a wealthy American. At the end of

London Bridge turn right down the steps to Southwark Cathedral.

The church only became a cathedral in 1905, but there has been a church on this site for a thousand years and some parts of the building still date from the 12th century. Those buried here include the poet John Gower, while stained-glass windows depict scenes from Shakespeare (who worshipped here) and Chaucer (whose Canterbury pilgrims set out from Southwark). The founder of Harvard University was baptised here in 1607 and is commemorated in the Harvard chapel. Despite the persistent rumbling from the adjacent railway line it is a peaceful and soothing place to sit for a few minutes and recover from rushing up the Monument. The Diocese of Southwark has always been sympathetic to homosexual issues. The chapel of St Andrew, located to the rear, is dedicated to those who suffer with HIV/Aids and their families.

Leave the cathedral and turn right (heading west from the cathedral), going down Cathedral Street into Pickford's Wharf, with its replica of the *Golden Hinde*. Then continue down Pickford's Wharf into Clink Street, named after the prison attached to Winchester House, the remains of which are visible on the left, sunken beneath the looming warehouses and dark railway bridges that give this district its distinct atmosphere. The notoriety of the place led to 'the clink' becoming slang for prisons in general. Winchester House was the palatial home of the Bishop of Winchester from the 12th century until 1626. The south bank was under the jurisdiction of the bishop and was London's red-light and theatre district. 'Winchester Geese' or prostitutes worked from brothels licensed and regulated by the bishop, while Shakespeare's plays were first performed in theatres in the area.

Pass the Clink museum and under a railway bridge, turn left up Park Street (the Anchor pub at the end of the street dates from 1676 and is a good place for a refreshing pint with magnificent riverside views), first right, across Southwark Bridge Road, and right down New Globe Walk. The reconstruction of the Globe

The view north across the river from the **Oxo Tower**.

The reconstructed and incongruous **Globe Theatre.**

Theatre is a curious attempt to recreate an 'authentic' Elizabethan theatre, although its authenticity may not extend to throwing abuse and fruit at actors and having pre-pubescent boys playing the female roles. Walk left along the river in front of the tremendous brick behemoth of what was once Bankside Power Station. Designed by Sir Giles Gilbert Scott and completed in 1955, this cathedral of power (directly opposite St Paul's) now houses the Tate Gallery's modern art collection, and provides a new focus of activity on the South Bank. With the construction of the Millennium Bridge crossing over to St Paul's, this neglected area is in the process of becoming one of London's most fashionable. Follow through to Hopton Street and up to Southwark Street and turn right.

Negotiating the relentless rush of traffic zooming over Blackfriars Bridge, cross to Stamford Street. High-rise offices and apartments crowd the riverfront, including the Oxo Tower, a co-operative development incorporating social housing with a trendy top-floor restaurant. Turn left up Hatfields, past depressing tenements, then right into Roupell Street

and the atmosphere changes again. The dark workers' terraces evoke the London of Charles Dickens and Wilkie Collins.

The walk ends with a disorientating twist at the ugly concrete roundabout outside Waterloo Station. The 'cardboard city', where the homeless used to shelter in the underpass, has been replaced by an Imax cinema. The conversion of parts of the massive Shell Centre, opposite, and neighbouring County Hall into more luxury flats, along with the Jubilee line extension, give a glimpse of how the South Bank is finally realising its tremendous potential and seems set to rise like a concrete phoenix from the ashes of decades of neglect and bad development. The London Eye, the newest and already one of London's most popular attractions, is a vivid example of this. The world's largest Ferris wheel takes half an hour to complete a circuit, carrying visitors to a height of 450 feet, and the experience is awesome.

From Waterloo, a tube or train can be caught to anywhere, even Paris, whose south (or I should say left?) bank couldn't be more different.

Eating & drinking

Anchor Bankside

34 Park Street, SE1 9EF (7407 1577). **Open** 11am-11pm Mon-Sat; noon-10.30pm Sun. **Food served** noon-10pm Mon-Sat; noon-9pm Sun. Real ales, river views and fair food.

Chez Gérard

64 Bishopsgate, EC2N 4AJ (7588 1200/www.sante online.co.uk). **Breakfast served** 8-11am, **lunch served** 11.45am-3pm, **dinner served** 5.45-10pm Mon-Fri. One of the many pleasant French restaurants in the chain.

Leadenhall Wine Bar

27 Leadenhall Market, EC3V 1LR (7623 1818). **Open** 11.30am-11pm Mon-Fri. **Food served** 11.30am-10pm Mon-Fri. Good and varied wine selection in tapas bar.

Old Thameside Inn

Pickfords Wharf, 1 Clink Street, SE1 9DG (7403 4243). **Open** 11am-11pm Mon-Sat; noon-10.30pm Sun. **Food served** noon-10pm daily. Riverside views, real ales and a restaurant.

Churches & churchyards

Bunhill Fields Burial Grounds

38 City Road, EC1Y 1AU (7374 4127/www. corpoflondon.gov.uk). **Open** Apr-Sept 7.30am-7pm Mon-Fri; 9.30am-4pm Sat, Sun. *Oct-Mar* 7.30am-4pm Mon-Fri; 9.30am-4pm Sat, Sun.

St Andrew Undershaft

St Mary Axe, EC3A 8BN (7283 2231/www.st-helens.org.uk). **Open** by arrangement only.

St Botolph, Bishopsgate

Bishopsgate, EC2M 3TL (7588 3388). **Open** 8am-5.30pm Mon-Fri. *Services* 1.10pm Wed; 12.10pm Thur.

St Helen's, Bishopsgate

Great St Helen's, EC3A 6AT (7283 2231/www.st-helens.org.uk). **Open** 9am-12.30pm Mon-Fri; call for afternoon opening times. *Services* 10.15am, 7pm Sun.

Southwark Cathedral

Montague Close, SE1 9DA (7367 6700/tours 7367 6734/www.dswark.org/cathedral). **Open** 8am-6pm daily (closing times vary on religious holidays). *Audio guide* £2.50. Donations welcome.

Cinema

Imax Cinema

1 Charlie Chaplin Walk, SE1 8XR (0870 787 2525/ www.bfi.org.uk/imax). **Open** *Phone bookings* 10.30am-7.30pm daily. **Admission** *Standard presentations* £7.90; £6.50 concessions; £4.95 under-15s. *Digitally remastered presentations* £12; £11 concessions; £6 under-15s.

Museums

Clink Prison Museum

1 Clink Street, SE1 9DG (7403 6515/www.clink. co.uk). **Open** *June-Sept* 10am-9pm daily. *Oct-May* 10am-6pm daily. **Admission** £5; £3.50 5-15s.

Monument

Monument Street, EC3R 8AH (7626 2717). **Open** 9.30am-5pm daily. **Admission** £2; £1 5-16s.

Shakespeare's Globe

21 New Globe Walk, SE1 9DT (7902 1500/www. shakespeares-globe.org). **Open** *Tours & Exhibitions* May-Sept 9am-noon daily; Oct-Apr 10am-5pm daily. **Admission** £8.50; £7 concessions; £6 5-15s.

Tate Modern

Bankside, SE1 9TG (7887 8000/www.tate.org.uk). **Open** 10am-6pm Mon-Thur, Sun; 10am-10pm Fri, Sat. *Tours* 11am, noon, 2pm, 3pm daily. **Admission** free.

Shopping

Leadenhall Market

Whittington Avenue, off Gracechurch Street, EC3. **Open** 7am-4pm Mon-Fri.

Globe Theatre

In the mix

Pratibha Parmar

Loft apartments and an artists' community – Hoxton as centre of cool, or is it all talk?

Start: Old Street tube, exit 2
Finish: Highbury & Islington tube
Distance: 4 miles/6km
Time: 2 hours
Getting there: Northern line or rail to Old Street
Getting back: Victoria line or rail from Highbury & Islington
Note: countless eating and drinking opportunities.

London has earned a reputation as the hippest European city, primarily because of its rich multicultural diversity created by generations of settlers from Africa, India, Pakistan, Bangladesh and the Caribbean. In a recent survey of Londoners' views, the city's racial and cultural mix was the major factor attracting people to the capital. The fact that a popular 1998 World Cup song was named 'Vindaloo' after the most popular 'ethnic' food is an indication of the changing identity of Englishness and all things British.

This diversity is to be found all across London, but one area that has a particularly interesting 'melting pot' is east London. Setting out from the borough of Tower Hamlets, our walk takes us through histories and time frames and a contemporary popular culture that is unique to this part of London.

Arrive at Old Street station and walk quickly through the rather desolate, dingy passages. As you emerge from exit 2 and walk east along the busy road, look behind you. The strange edifice hanging over the roundabout might be considered by some as an interesting piece of design, but to me it is a bland indicator of the urban, commercial nature of the area south of Old Street. However, tucked away on the other side of the roundabout is a little gem – Fresh & Wild, an organic food hall, natural remedy centre and wholesome takeaway all housed in the East West Centre.

Only backtrack if you are in desperate need of any of the above, otherwise continue past the fire station and some 1960s housing estates on your left. These are fast being replaced by new loft apartments for the city slickers from the financial district only a stone's throw away. It is ironic that within spitting distance of the capital's smartest office blocks lies some of London's poorest housing.

Our first detour is into Charlotte Road, on your right at the second traffic lights you come to. This charming street with old cobbled alleyways coming off it illustrates how old, Dickensian London is being renovated by property developers looking to create a new 'West End'. Towards the bottom of the street is the Cantaloupe Bar, a good place to drop in for Sunday brunch if you are in need of a little kick-start for the walk ahead. There is no shortage of places to stop for a fortifying drink either. At the corner of Charlotte Road and Rivington Street is the Bricklayers Arms where they serve a wonderful pint of Beamish Stout, or further up, the Barley Mow if you fancy a Caffrey's Irish Ale. Cut across to Curtain Road if it's an espresso you are looking for – the Bean Espresso Bar was an early sign of the trendification of the area.

Cotton's Gardens

White Cube² on Hoxton Square.

Walk left up Curtain Road and back on to Old Street. Opposite is the 333 Club, once the infamous London Apprentice, London's oldest gay bar, mostly frequented by men in leather chaps and whips. Beyond is Hoxton Street.

For now, walk east down Old Street, past Shoreditch Town Hall on the right and under the bridge. Look back on to the bridge and check out the colourful graffiti – there was a rat saying 'it's not a race' and some soldiers in riot gear, as we went to press.

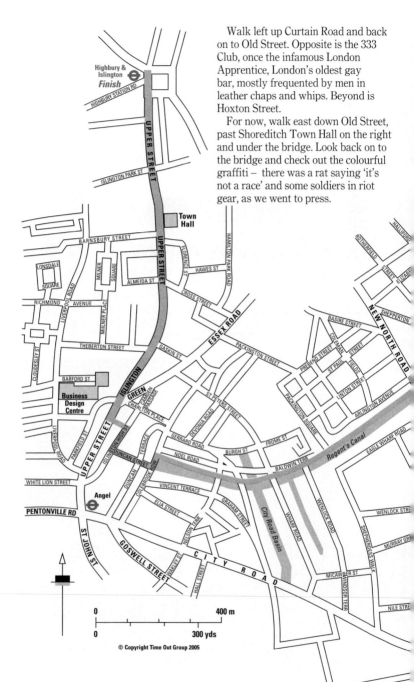

Make your way over the junction to St Leonard's, Shoreditch almost opposite the bridge. It has everything you would wish to see in a typical English church – stained-glass windows, pretty gardens and a magnificent giant brass-tubed organ built in 1756 by Richard Bridge. It still works and gets played. The day we went, a local resident and volunteer caretaker pointed out the original clock designed by Chippendale in the late 1780s that is now valued at almost a million pounds. If it's local history you want, this is an excellent first stop. A

makeshift exhibition of original drawings and parish documents teaches us that Shoreditch appears to have originated as a settlement at the junction of two important Roman roads – Kingsland Road and Old Street. The earliest mention of Shoreditch occurs in the middle of the 12th century, although the origin of the name is unknown.

If churches are not your fancy, then turn on to Kingsland Road, going under another railway bridge and past little cobbled streets – Crooked Billet Yard and Cotton's Gardens – where old warehouses are rapidly being modernised into cool bars and trendy clothes shops. Stop only when you come to Viet Hoa at 70-72 Kingsland Road, one of the best and most authentic Vietnamese restaurants in this part of London. This unpretentious café/restaurant/community centre looks like

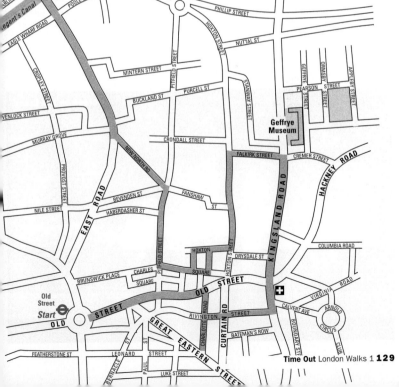

a school canteen, but produces top-quality food for just £10 a head.

Walk across from Viet Hoa and take a left into Falkirk Street, past housing estates and the Hackney Community College, then left again into Hoxton Street. Here, during the week, a lively market sells everything from food and clothes to potted plants. It's a typical London market where you can spend time browsing and eavesdropping on the many conversations between stallholders sharing cups of tea and a cigarette.

Walk through the market and cut through Mundy Street on your right to Hoxton Square. In recent years this little square became oh-so-hip it hurt, where cult films could be seen and the newest sounds could be heard. It is a pleasant square with a park in the middle, refurbished in 1995. Take time to sit and watch the variety of people who hang out here – one or two loud drunkards, trendy girls sitting reading on the benches or maybe even a film crew or a photo shoot for some style magazine. Neil Jordan, the Irish filmmaker, shot a scene here for *The Crying Game*.

Regrettably, the main draw for the square's nightlife has moved. The Blue Note was the birthplace of the 'new Asian underground' music where the immensely talented Talvin Singh (who worked with Madonna) started out with his Anokha club nights. Every Monday this was the club to hang out in. Björk, Jarvis Cocker and Simon Le Bon were all known to frequent the Blue Note, listening to the drum 'n' bass sounds mixed in with sitar and tabla riffs. Anokha moved on to be replaced by Swaraj (meaning 'self-rule'). DJ Pathan and club promoter Ash continued to pack in the crowds, which at one point included David Bowie, who whisked DJ Pathan off on a tour of Europe.

The mid 1990s saw Asian music, fashion and club culture make a significant impact with their vibrancy and fresh style. Certainly, India and all things Indian have finally become cool, achieving mass appeal. Media attention on the 'new Asian cool' has been no bad thing for a new generation of Asian youth, although both Anokha and Swaraj rightly insist that they are about being multicultural rather than Asian. Their styles borrow from many

Screen on the Green

Islington Green

Cantaloupe

cultures and are global rather than a
clichéd fusion of Asian and British. Once
you have sampled some of the music from
the 'Asian underground', Kula Shaker's
rather weak attempts to sound 'ethnic'
get shown up as the crass pastiches they
are. The Blue Note was at the hub of this
scene. The first time I went there I was
impressed by the mix of people – from
white girls with sarongs and bhindis,
Asian girls in trendy Adidas tracks with
sari blouses, and handsome blokes of
deep black hues to brown-skinned Asian
boys throwing moves to the music that
leave you mesmerised.

I wonder what James Parkinson,
a physician and geologist who lived
here from 1755-1824 and who is
commemorated by a blue plaque outside
the building, would have thought of this
transformation? He might have been less
perturbed by the new premises – eight
flats and a bar. The Blue Note moved to
bigger premises in Islington for a while
but didn't survive.

Another scene that Shoreditch is
particularly known for is the local artists'
studios and galleries – the opening of
White Cube^2 gallery in Hoxton Square
(Tracey Emin, Damien Hirst and Anthony
Gormley are among those in the gallery's
stable) indicates how the area's star is risen.

Behind the square, Coronet Street
houses the offices of Britain's largest
Gujarati newspaper, *Gujarat Samachar,*
as well as a base for creative circus
performers at the Circus Space (No.15).
Turn right at the end of Coronet Street
and walk up Pitfield Street until you
come to the New North Road. You may
hear some rather beautiful sounds
coming from an old library building,
now the rehearsal space of the English
National Opera. Walk up New North
Road past the diminutive Shoreditch
Park and over the bridge, then take a
right on to Baring Street and up to
the junction with Shepperton Road.

Here you will come to the Rosemary
Branch – a pub with an upstairs theatre.

The present Victorian building was renowned for its music hall where it's rumoured that Charlie Chaplin played. More recently, both series of the BBC comedy *Happiness*, starring Paul Whitehouse, were shot here. It was completely refurbished in 1992 with the aim of preserving the tradition of presenting an eclectic range of art and entertainment along with excellent food and drink. As well as theatre, there is a constantly changing exhibition of sculpture, paintings, photographs and uncategorisable works by local artists.

Having fortified yourself with a real ale or a Belgian beer, walk across to the entrance to the Grand Union Canal (also known as the Regent's Canal along this

King's Head on Upper Street.

stretch). Coming down the stairs you will see cyclists, fishermen and all manner of people walking along the waterway. Take a right along the canal towards the Angel and enjoy the quiet and the lines of warehouses in various states of renovation or decay.

As the canal path ends in a cavernous tunnel, you come out on to Colebrooke Road in Islington. Cross over and walk straight up Duncan Street to Upper Street, stopping off at the antiques arcade in Camden Passage. This is ideal for those who love to browse through old furniture and jewellery – a real aficionado's paradise. But beware – the prices are only for those serious about their antiques.

Then on to Upper Street. In the next mile or so you can eat, drink and spend in a frightening array of venues; and satisfy your culture craving in the cinema, or in the theatres and bookshops that punctuate the route. Alternatively, Islington Green itself is another one of those quiet, sweet little greens where on a hot summer's day you may find a little oasis of shade and a bench to rest your weary feet.

But back to consumerism. Waterstone's, at the far end of Islington Green, often has interesting writers giving readings. Once I happened to walk in and the photographer Del La Grace Volcano was launching her controversial queer photography book with a riveting slide show of her work. One is not likely to walk into something quite this eventful anywhere else in London.

For film buffs the Screen on the Green is the place to check out the latest Hanif Kureishi film, or walk on to the King's Head, the first pub-theatre in London. It has seen John Hurt and Victoria Wood tread its boards on the way to West End openings, and the bar has the peculiarity of charging in the old currency of pounds,

Viet Hoa

shillings and pence. Further up, the newly refurbished Almeida Theatre has played host to the likes of Cate Blanchett, Juliette Binoche, Kevin Spacey and Ralph Fiennes.

This also used to be Tony Blair's neighbourhood before his move to Downing Street. He is rumoured to have struck a few significant secret deals in the Granita restaurant, which was at No.127 but has been replaced by a Turkish eaterie. The variety is endless, not least in the proliferation of cafés spilling out on to the pavement – one of the finer imports from the Continent.

Having walked the length of Upper Street, you will arrive at Highbury & Islington tube. You have crossed many cultural, geographical and scenic borders and got to know different parts of London along the way – where the variety of colours, smells and sights transport you into different worlds.

Eating & drinking

Barley Mow
127 Curtain Road, EC2A 3BX (7729 3910). **Open** noon-11pm Mon-Thur; noon-midnight Fri; 4pm-midnight Sat; 3-10.30pm Sun. Small and cosy, with a good range of beers on tap.

The Bean
126 Curtain Road, EC2A 3BG (7739 7829). **Open** 7am-7pm Mon-Thur; 7am-6pm Fri; 8am-5.30pm Sat; 8.30am-5.30pm Sun. Coffee and light snacks.

Bricklayers Arms
63 Charlotte Road, EC2A 3PE (7739 5245/ www.333mother.com). **Open** 11am-11pm Mon-Fri; noon-11pm Sat; noon-10.30pm Sun. **Food served** noon-3pm, 6-11pm Mon-Fri; 2.30-11pm Sat; 1.30-9pm Sun. Hugely popular with the Hoxton crowd; downstairs is shabby, upstairs serves the food.

Cantaloupe
35 Charlotte Road, EC2A 3PB (7613 4411/ www.cantaloupegroup.co.uk). **Open/food served** 11am-midnight daily. Very busy, with fine Mediterranean food in the restaurant and tapas at the bar.

King's Head
115 Upper Street, N1 1QN (7226 0364/www. kingsheadtheatre.org). **Open** 11am-1am Mon-Thur; 11am-2am Fri, Sat; noon-1am Sun. **Food served** (pre-booked theatre dinner only) 7-8pm Tue-Sat. A mix of theatre bar, late-night pub and music venue.

Pasha
301 Upper Street, N1 2TU (7226 1454). **Lunch served** noon-3pm Mon-Fri. **Dinner served** 6-11.30pm Mon-Thur; 6pm-midnight Fri. **Meals served** noon-midnight Sat; noon-11pm Sun.

Rosemary Branch
2 Shepperton Road, N1 3DT (7704 2730/ www.rosemarybranch.co.uk). **Open** noon-11.30pm Mon-Thur; noon-midnight Fri, Sat; noon-10.30pm Sun. **Food served** noon-2.30pm, 6-9.30pm Mon-Sat; noon-6pm Sun. Good selection of beers.

Viet Hoa
70-72 Kingsland Road, E2 8DP (7729 8293). **Open** noon-3.30pm, 5.30-11.30pm Mon-Fri; noon-11.30pm Sat, Sun. Fine and well-priced Vietnamese food in this big Shoreditch café.

Church

St Leonard's, Shoreditch
119 Shoreditch High St, E1 6JN (7739 2063). **Open** 10am-7pm Sun. Phone for access on other days.

Cinema, gallery & theatres

Almeida Theatre
Almeida Street, N1 1TA (7359 4404/www.almeida. co.uk). **Open** *Box office* 10am-7pm Mon-Sat.

Screen on the Green
Islington Green, N1 0NP (7226 3520/ www.screencinemas.co.uk).

White Cube
48 Hoxton Square, N1 6PB (7930 5373/ www.whitecube.com). **Open** 10am-6pm Tue-Sat.

Nightlife

333 Club
333 Old Street, EC1V 9LE (7739 5949/ www.333mother.com). **Open** 8pm-midnight Wed; 10pm-4am occasional Thur; 10pm-5am Fri, Sat; 10pm-4am Sun.

Shopping

Camden Passage
Camden Passage, off Upper Street, N1 8EE (7359 0190). **Open** *Antiques* 7am-4pm Wed, Sat. *Books* 9am-5pm Sun. *Mixed* 11am-5pm Sun.

Fresh & Wild
196 Old Street, EC1V 9FR (7250 1708/www.fresh andwild.com). **Open** 9.30am-7.30pm Mon-Fri; 10am-6pm Sat.

Waterstone's
10-12 Islington Green, N1 2XH (7704 2280/ www.waterstones.co.uk). **Open** 9.30am-8pm Mon, Wed-Sat; 10am-8pm Tue; noon-6pm Sun.

Walk like a Huguenot

Ben Richards

Retrace the ever-changing face of the East End.

> **Start:** Bricklayers Arms,
> 63 Charlotte Road, EC2
> **Finish:** Prospect of Whitby,
> 57 Wapping Wall, E1
> **Distance:** 4.5 miles/7km
> **Time:** 2.5 hours
> **Getting there:** Northern line or
> rail to Old Street, exit Old Street
> East, south side (subway 3),
> then five-minute walk
> **Getting back:** five-minute walk
> to Wapping (East London line)
> **Note:** the markets are only open
> on Sunday at the weekend, when
> many of the shops are closed.

Among the many amusing aspects of the letters pages of local East End papers is the hotly debated topic of the exact parameters of the area. This issue, which always has the purists and the pedants scrambling for their pens, has raised its head over such weighty issues as whether *EastEnders* is a fraudulent title for the popular soap opera or whether the borough of Tower Hamlets has the right to rename itself the East End. I do not hold strong views on where the East End starts and finishes, although I would be prepared to stick my neck out and exclude Ladbroke Grove. But this walk will take you through some of the best bits of the East End – from Shoreditch to Limehouse.

The walk starts in the Bricklayers Arms, not part of the 'official' East End, where Rivington Street meets Charlotte Road, just off Old Street. (Sunday is the best day to do this walk because then the various markets around Shoreditch and Spitalfields will be open.) Shoreditch is the

epicentre of a widely proclaimed cultural feel-good factor with property prices rocketing as the newspapers trumpet the area as the capital of Cool Britannia, the new Soho, a loft with a view for those who, according to one fashion magazine, 'love the grittiness of city life'. One of the unfortunate consequences of this gritty-chic is that those who have lived in the area for... well, I guess you know the rest.

We begin by heading from the pub down Rivington Street, across Curtain Road and on to Shoreditch High Street. Walk down until you get to the junction with signs for Whitechapel and bear off to the left down Commercial Street, which runs all the way down to Aldgate East. This has always been an area where women have sold sex to men and where some men have responded by intimidating and sometimes murdering them. I was determined not to mention Jack the Ripper, but it was around here that he murdered prostitutes – one in nearby Hanbury Street – decorating cheap lodging rooms with their intestines. On top of the usual hazards of street trade, women are now being 'hassled' by groups of moral, not-in-our-neighbourhood vigilantes.

On the right-hand side of Commercial Street – in between Lamb Street and Brushfield Street – is Spitalfields Market. A market area for centuries, it was granted its first charter under Charles II, although the current building dates from 1928. It is a good place on a Sunday to nurse a hangover with a beer and food from one of the stalls offering eclectic mixes such as 'a taste of Mexico, Hawaii and the Pacific'. You will find everything from clothes and records to shops selling transparent plastic armchairs, sunflower purses and various other daft-punk items – shops full of shite, as my brother-in-law accurately labels them.

When you have finished browsing, cross back over Commercial Street to have a look at the first Hawksmoor church on the walk – the unmissable Christ Church. The Hawksmoor churches were built during the reign of Queen Anne – work began around 1714. The result of the Fifty Churches Act, introduced to cope with London's rapidly expanding population, they stand out for their similar dimensions and huge western towers.

A plaque at the entrance to Christ Church testifies to the generosity of one Jane Brown who left a large sum of money to promote Christianity among the Jews. The desire to convert and reform others has always been strong in the East End; it is a missionary magnet.

Next, turn into Fournier Street, which runs down the church's right side. We are now in Spitalfields (which started life as the Priory of St Mary of the Spittle). I should mention a text that will serve as an invaluable accompaniment to this walk: *The Streets of East London* by WJ Fishman with photos by Nicholas Breach. (Although slightly dated now, the book gives a huge amount of detail about local history.) Fournier Street is one of my favourites in London, the dwelling place for many of the first wave of refugees to arrive in the East End – the Huguenots fleeing from France in the 17th century. The Huguenots were silk-weavers, bird-fanciers, name-changers (the Leblancs became Whites, the Lenoirs Blacks); they had a reputation for having small heads as well as a predisposition to riot when their interests were threatened.

At the corner of Fournier Street and Brick Lane is a building erected in 1742, which has been a Huguenot Chapel, Methodist Chapel, Jewish Synagogue and is now the Jamme Masjid Mosque. This building is a perfect palimpsest produced by the ebb and flow of immigration for which the East End is so famous. Check what appears to be an elegant sundial on its wall, although we were quite unable to work out the time from it. Then turn right

Spitalfields Market

from Fournier Street into Brick Lane – now, not without some controversy, renamed Banglatown – where the huge selection of Asian restaurants testifies to the presence of more recent arrivals. The only problem at this point is resisting the temptation to stop the walk here and dive in for something to eat.

Carry on walking down Brick Lane, noting the community-friendly-looking police station, before turning left into Old

Montague Street. At the corner of Old Montague Street and Greatorex Street in a state of abandonment is what used to be the office of the Federation of Synagogues – testimony to the diaspora of the Jewish community that had given so much vibrancy to the East End at the beginning of the 20th century. Turn into Greatorex Street and you will arrive at Whitechapel Road, which you should turn left into. Across the road you will see the

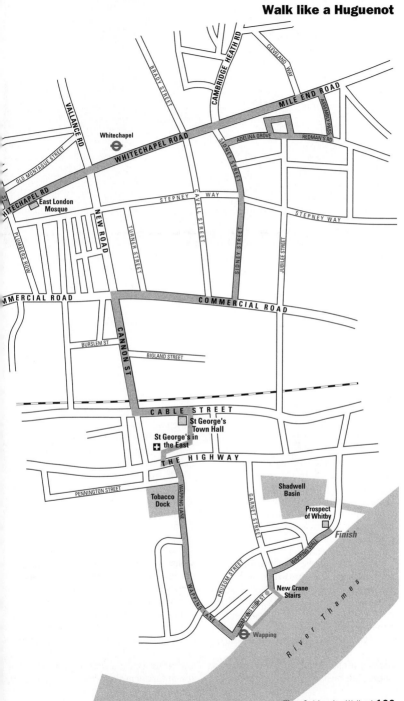

Trinity Almshouses

Whitechapel Bell Foundry to your right and the East London Mosque to your left.

Whitechapel Road has wide pavements, it is the road out of London to Essex, and if you look down as far as you can see, there is a huge tree that appears almost to be exploding in the middle of the road. Keep walking east on the left-hand side of the road. You will see on the right the London Hospital – home to the Elephant Man – with its huge helicopter pad. Walk past Whitechapel tube station on the left, noting the small market and the plethora of sari shops, immigration practitioners and halal food stores that indicate the area's racial diversity. Continue past the entrance to Sainsbury's and the huge ex-brewery now converted into flats until you arrive at the junction with Cambridge Heath Road. On your left is the Blind Beggar pub where, as everybody knows, George Cornell was shot in March 1966 by Ronnie Kray and which is now a smart pub with a conservatory beer garden.

Carry on along the tree-lined street – the junction marks the division between Whitechapel Road and Mile End Road. A little further on the left, set back from the road, are the Trinity Almshouses built by Wren in 1695. Don't miss the stone ships that stand at the entrance. A touch further and note the statue of William Booth, founder of the Salvation Army, and a less impressive bust of Edward VII erected by

local Freemasons. The bust reminds me of my favourite history book, *The Strange Death of Liberal England* by Edward Dangerfield, which opens with a comet and the king's death. There is also an excellent Chinese restaurant here, the Sinh Le, which does buffet lunches on Sunday.

Cross over the main road and look for the plaque that commemorates Captain Cook's old residence, then look carefully for Assembly Passage, a narrow alleyway opposite the Blockbuster video shop and the DIY emporium. Turn right into Assembly Passage, which leads down on to Adelina Grove. Turn right again into Adelina Grove and walk towards Sidney Street past O'Leary Square, which does boast something of interest – Rinkoff's Bakery, purveyor of cakes and bagels since 1911.

Adelina Grove leads into Sidney Street, where you turn left. Sidney Street is home to a great legend – the Siege of Sidney Street. Apart from its philanthropists and criminals, the East End was fertile ground for a radical tradition, in part inspired by the immigration of Russian and Polish anarchists and Communists at the beginning of the last century. This was territory that attracted Eleanor Marx, Sylvia Pankhurst and Lenin. It produced trade unionists Ben Tillet (dockers' strike) and Annie Beasant (match-girls' strike). A recent Freedom Press book documents the

Converted warehouses near **Wapping Wall**.

childhood of Fermin Rocker, son of Rudolf Rocker, a German anarchist involved in the garment workers' strike of 1912.

Back in Sidney Street in 1911, three fugitive Jewish radicals were holed up in a house owned by doughty Jewish landlady Mrs Gershon. Bill Fishman, in his account of the siege, notes that the rebels removed her skirt and boots on the assumption that, as a respectable Jewess, she would not try to escape in her undergarments. Self-preservation overcame religious modesty, however, and Mrs Gershon did a bunk at the first opportunity. The police attacked, then the army, ostentatiously directed by Home Secretary Winston Churchill, who would later distinguish himself for his wartime rhetoric and his enthusiasm for putting down any kind of working-class rebellion or protest. Finally, the house caught fire, but when the charred bodies were retrieved, one was missing. Peter Piatkov, aka Peter the Painter, had slipped the net, escaped Mr Churchill and passed into legend.

You have to imagine this as you walk down Sidney Street because all you will see are council estates plus some recent refurbishments. The last block on the street is called Siege House, but this was not, in fact, where the siege took place. At the bottom of Sidney Street turn right into Commercial Road and cross on to the other side (don't be confused, as

Commercial Road is totally different from Commercial Street). There is little to recommend in Commercial Road, but you don't have to put up with it for long. At the next main lights, turn left into Cannon Street Road, a mix of saris, sweets, grocers and travel agents. At the bottom of this road, a railway bridge crosses it. Turn left under the bridge into Cable Street and we are now approaching the two best bits of the walk.

On the wall of St George's Town Hall, on the right, is the mural commemorating the battle in October 1936 that ensued when Mosley's blackshirts attempted to march into the East End from Royal Mint Street. Phil Piratin, Communist MP for Stepney (1945-50), gives an excellent account of the battle in his book *Our Flag Stays Red*. Barricades and a human mass consisting of Irish dockers, orthodox Jews and other local anti-fascists blocked the entrance to Cable Street. Despite repeated charges by the police, many arrests and much blood spilled, access to the East End could not be gained. Finally, the police commissioner wearied of the struggle and told Mosley he could not march as planned, sending him to the Embankment where the fascists dispersed.

The files held by the British state on the events of this day are confidential. Why? Given that many Labour Party members fought alongside Communists, anarchists and workers with no other objective than to stop Mosley, it would be nice if New Labour remedied this anomaly. Also on the side of St George's Town Hall is a worn plaque to those from Tower Hamlets who went to fight for the International Brigades in Spain. One of the organisers of the defence of Cable Street was Harry Gross, later killed in Spain. The plaque ends with the slogan 'NO PASARAN!'

But we shall pass and turn immediately right alongside the Hall and into the churchyard of St George in the East, another magnificent Hawksmoor church, completed in 1726 and consecrated for worship in 1729. It was partly destroyed by the bombs of Mosley's mates in the Luftwaffe in May 1941. Walk around the churchyard, then take a look inside the church. On the walls of the church when I was last there, local kids had put up their own personal ten commandments. Alma (satisfyingly, it means 'soul' in Spanish) considered it necessary not to push people, not to swear at God and not to cut her friends. All very sensible advice and I'm sure God would appreciate not being sworn at. The best commandment, however, came from Shuhana: if someone makes a face at you, ignore them.

Leaving the church, turn left towards the masts of the ship that can be seen over Tobacco Dock and walk out on to the Highway. We are coming into Wapping, where Charles I once hunted down a stag and pirates were hanged in chains to 'abide the washing of three tides'. Now, the heavy hand of 1980s development is stamped all over it – luxury riverside housing complexes and harsh-angled glass buildings break up the skyline. Turn right down Wapping Lane to the Ornamental Canal outside Tobacco Dock. This is a good place to pause if you have kids, as there are two sailing ships and a café. If you go up on to Discovery Walk, you will also see an incredible skyline with almost every type of building imaginable – enough to reduce Prince Charles, self-appointed guardian

of the nation's architectural standards, to a gibbering wreck.

Continue down Wapping Lane towards the river, past the White Swan and Cuckoo. Continue until you come to a sign for the Riverside Walkway, accessed through a housing complex. The doors look as if they don't open, but they do, and they open out on to a great sweep of the Thames. It is like the moment when children are going to the seaside and feel that tremendous anticipation of water, of sudden openness. Forget swinging or moaning London, this is the city's magnificent timeless asset. A city without a river is not a proper city and this is the mighty river that fed Dickens's vast imagination, that gave us Gaffer Hexham and his boat that was 'more allied to the bottom of the river than its surface by reason of the slime and ooze with which it was coated'. Now the rich and powerful take advantage of their riches and their power to have a daily window on to its splendour. Follow the path, until you come to New Crane Stairs, where at low tide you can hop down the algae-slimed steps to the riverbank and look towards Canary Wharf on the Isle of Dogs and the third Hawksmoor church on the horizon, St Anne's in Limehouse.

From New Crane Stairs, come back out on to Wapping Wall. Turn right and you will arrive at the Prospect of Whitby pub where you can get a reasonable Sunday lunch or sample grander fare in the upstairs restaurant. It is also a good place for kids as there is a terrace overlooking the river. For more top-end nosh, cross the road to Wapping Food, housed in an old hydraulic pumping station which also hosts an interesting exhibition.

This really is the end of the walk, but for those who wish to continue there are plenty of options. You can walk up to Shadwell Basin with its tasteless property development and from there follow the signs along the Thames Path back to St Katharine's Dock. Or you can cross Shadwell Basin to King Edward's Park and from there carry on to Limehouse Basin and Marina. Alternatively, Shadwell and Wapping tube stations on the East London Link are nearby. Whatever you do, follow those modern commandments: don't push people, don't swear at God and don't cut your mates. And if somebody makes a face at you, just ignore them.

Eating & drinking

Blind Beggar
337 Whitechapel Road, E1 1BU (7247 6195). **Open** 11am-1am Mon; 11am-11pm Tue-Sat; noon-10.30pm Sun. **Food served** noon-2.30pm Mon-Sat; noon-3pm Sun. Sofas, conservatory, restaurant and large garden – one of the East End's best outdoor drinking areas.

Bricklayers Arms
63 Charlotte Road, EC2A 3PE (7739 5245/www.333 mother.com). **Open** 11am-11pm Mon-Fri; noon-11pm Sat; noon-10.30pm Sun. **Food served** noon-3pm, 6-11pm Mon-Fri; 2.30-11pm Sat; 1.30-9pm Sun. Busy with Hoxton groovers, and trendy pub grub to match.

London Hospital Tavern
176 Whitechapel Road, E1 1BJ (7247 8978). **Open/ food served** noon-midnight Mon-Wed, Sun; noon-1am Thur-Sat.

Prospect of Whitby
57 Wapping Wall, E1W 3SH (7481 1095). **Open** 11.30am-11pm Mon-Sat; noon-10.30pm Sun. **Food**

served 11.30am-9.30pm Mon-Sat; noon-8.30pm Sun. An historic pub that retains much of its original interior, and also fine river views and a restaurant.

Rinkoff's Bakery
222-226 Jubilee Street, E1 3BS (7790 1050). **Open** 8am-4pm Mon-Fri; 8am-2pm Sun.

Sinh Le
41 Mile End Road, E1 4TP (7790 1154). **Open** noon-11.30pm Mon-Thur; noon-12.30am Fri; 4pm-12.30am Sat; 1-11pm Sun. Chinese restaurant.

Wapping Food
Wapping Hydraulic Power Station, Wapping Wall, E1W 3ST (7680 2080). Bar **Open** noon-11pm Mon-Sat; noon-6pm Sun. *Restaurant* **Brunch served** 10am-12.30pm Sat, Sun. **Lunch served** noon-3pm daily. **Dinner served** 6.30-11pm Mon-Fri; 7-11pm Sat. Modern European restaurant and gallery space.

White Swan & Cuckoo
95-97 Wapping Lane, E1W 2RW (7488 4959). **Open** 11am-11pm Mon-Sat; noon-10.30pm Sun. **Food served** 11am-3pm Mon-Fri.

Information

Docklands Light Railway
(7363 9700/www.dlr.co.uk). Trains run 5.30am-12.30am Mon-Sat; 7am-11.30pm Sun.

Riverside Walkway
Open 8am-dusk daily.

Shopping

Brick Lane Market
Brick Lane, Sclater Street, Bacon Street, E1; Cheshire Street, Chilton Street, E2. **Open** 8am-2pm Sun.

Spitalfields Market
65 Brushfield Street, E1 6AA (7247 8556/www.visit spitalfields.com). **Open** 10.30am-4.30pm Mon-Fri; 10am-5pm Sun.

Worship

Christ Church Spitalfields
Commercial Street, E1 6LY (7247 7202/www.christ churchspitalfields.org.uk). **Open** 11am-4pm Tue; 1-4pm Sun; also occasional Mon, Fri.

East London Mosque
82-92 Whitechapel Road, E1 1JQ (7247 1357/www. eastlondonmosque.org.uk). **Open** by appointment only.

Jamme Masjid Mosque
59 Brick Lane, E1 6QN (7247 6052). **Open** daily, phone for details.

St George in the East
16 Cannon Street Road, E1 0BH (7481 1345). **Open** 9am-5pm daily. Occasional early closures.

Christ Church Spitalfields

Crafts & conversions
Janet Street-Porter

Clerkenwell for the bookish, peckish and parched.

Start and finish: Farringdon
tube/rail
Finish: Farringdon tube/rail
Distance: 2 miles/3km
Time: 1.5 hours
Getting there and back: Circle,
Hammersmith & City and
Metropolitan lines, or rail, to
and from Farringdon
Note: countless eating and
drinking opportunities.
Significantly quieter at weekends.

I came to live in Clerkenwell in 1986,
although my career as a journalist started
round the corner in Farringdon Street, on
the long-departed *Petticoat Magazine* back
at the end of the 1960s. I worked in Fleet
Street till 1973 and used to stroll round
the area occasionally after a particularly
large lunch. Then the Farringdon book
market still consisted of several stalls
just up from Clerkenwell Road, and all
the buildings were full of engravers,
watch and clock repairers, photo
lithographers and scientific instrument
makers. Little or nothing happened at
ground-floor level. The streets were home
to thousands of craftsmen not interested
in the retail trade.

Now everything has changed, and my
walk around Clerkenwell reveals just how
much of the old place has gone for ever,
but been replaced with an equal number
of small businesses and craftspeople. It's
very much alive and in the middle of a
giant building boom.

Clerkenwell's roots stem from the priory
built by the Knights of St John in the 12th
century, just to the south of what is now

Clerkenwell Green. The River Fleet ran
under what is now Farringdon Road.
Craftsmen first came to the area in
the 17th century when it was home to
jewellers, furniture makers, clock and
watchmakers. These days Clerkenwell
provides work spaces for photographers,
and in the cheaper workshops provided
by the Clerkenwell Green Association
(a charity providing affordable studios
and business advice for small crafts
businesses) some of the old trades live
on. Because the area is so close to the
City, every street is having former office
or warehouse buildings converted into
trendy lofts or flats for upwardly mobile
people who want to live in what is
becoming London's answer to New
York's SoHo. There's a lot of dust, noise
and mess. Too many wine bars and
not enough grocery stores; too many
restaurants and not enough galleries;
but all that will change. When I moved
in the area was dying, now it's buzzing
with life, so I'm prepared to sit through
the noisy birth pangs.

For my walk you need an empty
stomach (there are lots of food places
and bars) and a rucksack (to carry the
great book bargains you'll pick up en
route). With meals, coffees and drinks,
it could be an all-day affair, the perfect
urban stroll, the opposite of one of my
rural roams in the wilderness.

Our walk starts at Farringdon station,
one of London's busiest, with the tidal
wave of workers that spew out of it at
9am. It opened in 1863, with a banquet,
and now there are plans for it to be
massively refurbished. Opposite the
station is a great second-hand bookstore
where journalists from the *Guardian* and

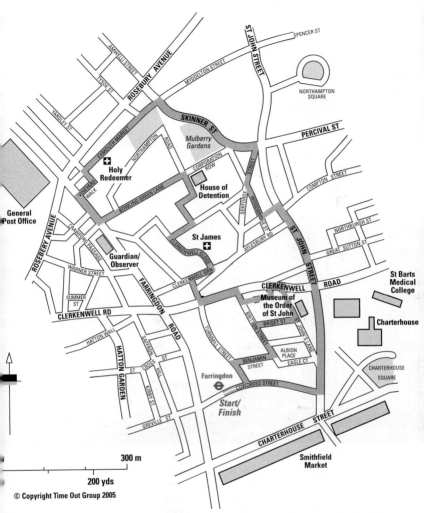

© Copyright Time Out Group 2005

Observer take in their review copies. This was once a red-light district, now it's full of sandwich bars and supermarkets serving commuters rather than locals. Go left along Cowcross Street and then left up Turnmill Street, which runs over the River Fleet. Turn right up a little passage that opens out into Benjamin Street. On your left are gardens, once an overflow burial ground for St John's Church. On the corner of Benjamin Street and Britton Street is an eccentric modern

house with a bright blue roof, designed for me by Piers Gough in 1987 (I have since moved elsewhere in Clerkenwell). Turn left up Britton Street leaving an ugly modern development behind you, and pass some fine 18th-century houses on both sides of the road. Turn right along Briset Street and left into St John's Lane.

Here the medieval archway contains a plaque explaining that this was the Gateway to the Priory of the Knights of St John and was built in 1504. It's now

Headquarters of the **Order of St John**.

the headquarters and museum of the Order of St John, with guided tours and an imposing vaulted chapter hall, but existed as a priory until the Dissolution of the Monasteries under Henry VIII. After that the gate was a coffee house and a public house, the Old Jerusalem Tavern. A wine bar in one of the 18th-century houses on Britton Street has adopted the name. To the north of the Gate is the Church of St John, with a fine Norman crypt, the remains of the original priory buildings. St John's Square is ruined by parked cars and traffic wardens. It's worth admiring the work displayed in the windows of Pennybank Chambers on the east side

of the square, the headquarters of the Clerkenwell Green Association. (You can shop here too if you make appointments in advance – call the Association for a list of the craftspeople.) Now retrace your steps slightly and take a narrow passageway (St John's Path) west out of the square and back through to Britton Street. This gives you an idea of what the 18th-century street pattern must have been like.

Carry on north (right) up to Clerkenwell Road. 59 Britton Street is particularly fine, though further down there's a hideous new building with a mock 1930s top level on the corner on your left. Clerkenwell's springs attracted breweries to the area and a large Gordon's Gin factory stood nearby. Now it's been demolished and its 1920s murals have been placed on a block of flats in Britton Street.

Cross over Clerkenwell Road and enter Clerkenwell Green, a focal point locally, and an open space used for public meetings going back centuries. The large Georgian (built 1782), stone, double-fronted mansion on the west end looks as if it could do with refurbishment at street level. Once Middlesex's county courthouse, now it's the home of the London Masonic Centre and you can see men creeping in and out in dark suits and white shirts in the early evening. To your left (if you stand on the steps of the Centre) is an imposing putty-coloured building, dating from 1737 when it was a charity school. Now it's the Marx Memorial Library and contains a collection of socialist literature. A few yards up Farringdon Lane you can make a detour to see the Clerk's Well (if you want to go in, apply to Islington's Local History Centre), near the corner with the Green.

You cross Clerkenwell Green by the firmly locked public lavatories (very few are open in the borough of Islington, and there is a local campaign to prevent them being sold) and walk up Clerkenwell Close. 3 Things Coffee Room on your right sells amusing papier-mâché items, dog lamps and coffee and on your left is the Three Kings pub, with its exotic sign made by local craftspeople. On the right is St James Church, rebuilt by Hawksmoor in 1792. In the church is a memorial to the Protestant martyrs burned at the stake by Mary Tudor, as well as a fine organ. In the church wall there's a memorial plaque to the poor wife and four children killed by one John Steinberg in 1834.

As you carry on up Clerkenwell Close, note the seating in the park on your right which was made by students from different design colleges. Then on the same side you pass the site of two prisons built in the 17th century. You used to be able to visit some of the cells and see the records of the inmates, who were subsequently sent to Australia. Sadly, the museum has now closed.

At this point I always take a little detour left along Bowling Green Lane. There are two famous architects in the street: Zaha Hadid's office is Studio 9 at No.10 in a converted school and CZWG – Piers Gough's office – is at No.17 in a converted warehouse. Clerkenwell's industrial buildings are home to dozens of design companies, from architects to graphic designers to furniture makers.

Now you have to face the brief horror of Farringdon Road, surely one of the most charm-free traffic thoroughfares in central London. Just down on your left are the offices of the *Guardian* and *Observer* newspapers. Behind them is an interesting warehouse conversion on Summer Street, with Viaduct Furniture selling avant-garde design on the ground floor.

Turn right up Farringdon Road and you have a choice of eating places, both equally fine. The Eagle pub serves great food (sadly it's very crowded between noon and 2pm) on your left, and on your right is the Quality Chop House. If you go in here, don't moan about the hard wooden benches: the food is delicious and the portions huge. Opposite is G Gazzano, my favourite of the two remaining family-owned Italian grocery stores in the area. The shop assistants have north London accents but all speak fluent Italian to their regulars. They have a fine range of cheeses and fresh pasta and a deli bar. I would turn right just before the Quality Chop House up Vineyard Walk and left up Pine Street. Here you pass a 1930s building, Exmouth House, which was home to trendy magazines *The Face* and *Arena*. Next door is the Finsbury Health Centre, an architectural gem designed in 1937 by Berthold Lubetkin.

This brings you into Exmouth Market, which has slowly turned from a run-down shopping street into a trendy pedestrian zone with bars, cafés and restaurants such as Moro (which I like but find too noisy in the evening) – all those loft conversions mean a rapidly growing number of middle-class residents. In the 18th century this area was popular for all kinds of entertainment at the local taverns, from bear- and bull-baiting to fist fights. On your right is Our Most Holy Redeemer Church, a fine red-brick Victorian building, which is the centre for the Clerkenwell Music Festival every November. Café Kick on your left features table-football, and Clark & Sons Pie and Mash at No.46 with its fine tiled front is where the diehard locals eat, although personally I can't see the attraction – I could never eat pie and mash as a child growing up in Fulham and I'm not going to start now.

Leave Exmouth Market and turn right down Skinner Street, where in 1390 the Skinners' Livery Company performed a play lasting three days for Richard II. There's an attractive park on your right, where the Mulberry Pleasure Gardens opened in 1742. On the corner of St John Street is the Ingersoll building, which has been turned from a watchmaker's into apartments. Opposite is the Peasant, once a pub, now a bar and restaurant, and a bit lacking in atmosphere, although the food can be quite good. Now turn right down Sekforde Street, easily one of the prettiest streets in Clerkenwell with its terraces of fine double-fronted Georgian cottages, many of which have the original doorways and entrance columns. The street itself is named after Thomas Sekforde, a lawyer in the 16th century. What was the Finsbury Savings Bank (1840) at No.18½ is a splendid Victorian edifice, now converted into a grand private residence and known as The Bank. Take a left-hand fork down Woodbridge Street, past the charming Sekforde Arms and left down Hayward's Place. You can still get a real sense of Clerkenwell as a village here, unlike the chaos that will greet you as you emerge on to St John Street.

Turn right and start heading south towards Smithfield. Down on the left at Nos.140-142 is the Real Greek Souvlaki & Bar with its industrial-chic decor and periscope ventilators. Next door at No.144 is a tattooist, Cicada (a trendy, noisy bar, but with fine Thai-inspired food) and there's a good florist, McQueen's. I often go to Da Andrea in Great Sutton Street, one of the few remaining old-fashioned Italian cafés, for my lunch.

Now cross Clerkenwell Road and you are in the part of St John Street where the Clerkenwell revival started. To your left, further along Clerkenwell Road, is the huge Metro colour processing centre and a bit further along the Wyvern Bindery, which will rebind books for you and make portfolios for photographers. On the corner of Clerkenwell Road opposite Metro is Tim Tim, a tiny takeaway place that sells fantastic spicy noodles. Heading down St John Street, there are interesting little courtyards

Moro and Exmouth Market.

and passageways off St John Street (Passing Alley and Hat and Mitre Court are opposite each other after a few yards, whereas Smoke House Yard is further down on the left where the street opens out). At No.66 is a trendy new apartment building, home to avant-garde art dealer Jibby Beane.

Next you pass Vic Naylor's bar, the nearest thing in the area to something from *Cheers*. It's quiet at the start of the week and a riot by Fridays – City boys and girls having fun after work. I really like its brick interior and the barmen are great. Back on the road, look right on the corner of St John Lane and peer down Peter's Lane to see the fantastic warehouse with ornate weathervane which has been converted into the Rookery boutique hotel. The award-winning St John restaurant (on your left) is a stark, white, converted factory with a bar selling good snacks and cocktails and a dining area serving hearty meaty and fishy fare: new English cuisine. I always think the monosyllabic menu is a scream. A dozen kinds of freshly baked bread are sold in the bar area.

Now you have the chance to explore the fine Victorian Smithfield meat market. Designed by Horace Jones in 1878, the corner towers were originally pubs. St John Street was the wide drovers' route for cattle coming into the market. Take Cowcross Street and you'll soon be back at Farringdon station, hopefully feeling well fed and slightly intoxicated, with a rucksack containing souvenirs of the new Clerkenwell – a St John loaf and a second-hand book, a little piece of modern silver or perhaps a hand-woven scarf from one of the people at the Clerkenwell Green Association.

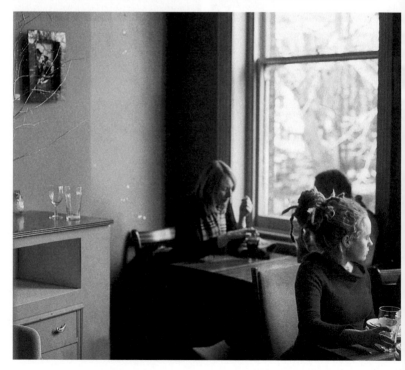

Eating & drinking

Café Kick

43 Exmouth Market, EC1R 4QL (7837 8077/
www.cafekick.co.uk). **Open** noon-11pm Mon-Sat;
5-10.30pm Sun (spring/summer only). **Food served**
noon-3pm, 6-10.30pm Mon-Fri; noon-10.30pm Sat.
Happy hour 4-7pm Mon-Sat. Shambolic gem of
a bar where table-football is king.

Clark & Sons

46 Exmouth Market, EC1R 9AL (7837 1974).
Open 10.30am-4pm Mon-Thur; 10.30am-5.30pm
Fri; 10.30am-5pm Sat. Pie and mash.

Cicada

132-136 St John Street, EC1V 4JT (7608 1550/
www.cicada.nu). *Bar* **Open** noon-11pm Mon-Sat.
Food served noon-10.30pm Mon-Sat. *Restaurant*
Lunch served noon-3pm Mon-Fri. **Dinner**
served 6-10.45pm Mon-Sat. Pan-Asian food is
served in the open-plan bar or the heavily stylised
restaurant area with open kitchen.

Da Andrea

30C Great Sutton Street, EC1V 0DU (7253 0130).
Open 6am-4.30pm Mon-Fri. Italian café.

Eagle

159 Farringdon Road, EC1R 3AL (7837 1353).
Open noon-11pm Mon-Sat; noon-5pm Sun. **Lunch**
served 12.30-3pm Mon-Fri; 12.30-3.30pm Sat, Sun.
Dinner served 6.30-10.30pm Mon-Sat. Famous for
sparking the fashion for gastropubs; there's a good
selection of wines.

Jerusalem Tavern

55 Britton Street, EC1M 5UQ (7490 4281/
www.stpetersbrewery.co.uk). **Open** 11am-11pm
Mon-Fri. **Food served** noon-3pm Mon-Fri.
London's sole outpost for Suffolk's St Peter's
Brewery in this one-time coffeehouse.

Moro

34-36 Exmouth Market, EC1R 4QE (7833 8336/
www.moro.co.uk). *Bar* **Open** 12.30-11.45pm Mon-Fri;
6.30-11.45pm Sat (last entry 10.30pm). *Restaurant*
Lunch served 12.30-2.30pm Mon-Fri. **Dinner**
served 7-10.30pm Mon-Sat. Excellent traditional
Spanish food, albeit with influences from North
Africa. Book well in advance – it's deservedly busy.

Peasant

240 St John Street, EC1V 4PH (7336 7726/
www.thepeasant.co.uk). *Bar* **Open/food served**
noon-11pm daily. *Restaurant* **Lunch served** noon-

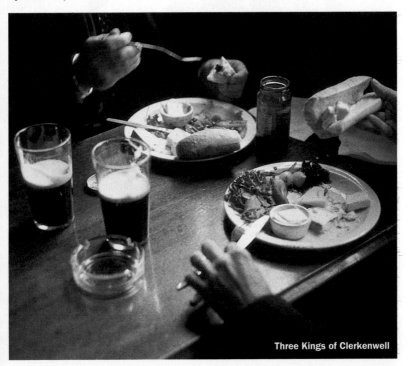

Three Kings of Clerkenwell

3pm, **dinner served** 6-11pm Tue-Sun. A gastrobar where modern European food is very much the draw – drinking tends to be the secondary activity.

Quality Chop House

90-94 Farringdon Road, EC1R 3EA (7837 5093). **Lunch served** noon-3pm Mon-Fri; noon-4pm Sun. **Dinner served** 6-11.30pm Mon-Sat. **Meals served** noon-10pm Sun. An updated, upgraded version of the working man's canteen, although the proliferation of City suits at lunchtime hints at the more ambitious remit of the kitchen. It's excellent value for money and the pared-down surroundings are charming.

The Real Greek Souvlaki & Bar

140-142 St John Street, EC1V 4UA (7253 7234/ www.therealgreek.co.uk). **Open** noon-11pm Mon-Sat. Bar/restaurant concept with seating either at tables for two or at long counters.

Leafy, villagey **Clerkenwell Green**.

St John

26 St John Street, EC1M 4AY (7251 0848/4998/
www.stjohnrestaurant.com). Bar **Open/food**
served 11am-11pm Mon-Fri; 6-11pm Sat.
Restaurant **Lunch served** noon-3pm Mon-Fri.
Dinner served 6-11pm Mon-Sat. Offal-oriented
menu in an old smoke-house – home to fans of
British meat and bone, although there's always
a vegetarian dish and at least one fish option.
A pioneering gem.

Sekforde Arms

34 Sekforde Street, EC1R 0HA (7253 3251).
Open 11am-11pm Mon-Fri; 11am-6pm Sat; noon-
4pm Sun. **Food served** noon-9.30pm Mon-Fri;
noon-3pm Sat, Sun. A charming local that bucks
the style bar trend, and is at the top end of the
pub grub scale.

Three Kings of Clerkenwell

7 Clerkenwell Close, EC1R 0DY (7253 0483). **Open**
noon-11pm Mon-Fri; 7.30-11pm Sat. **Food served**
noon-3pm Mon-Fri. A strong contender for the best
boozer in Clerkenwell. Real ales and food (lunchtimes
only) available. The music is excellent, too.

Tim Tim

21 Clerkenwell Road, EC1M 5RD (7251 1433).
Open 10am-10pm Mon-Fri. Spicy noodles.

Vic Naylor

38-42 St John Street, EC1M 4AY (7608 2181/
www.vicnaylor.com). Bar **Open** 5pm-1am Tue-Sat.
Restaurant **Lunch served** noon-5pm Mon-Fri.
Dinner served 5-11pm Mon-Sat. High-quality
bistro food, a good wine list and selection of beers
from around the world. Very busy from Thursday
to Saturday.

Books & publishing

Guardian

119 Farringdon Road, EC1R 3ER (7278 2332/
www.guardian.co.uk).

Marx Memorial Library

37A Clerkenwell Green, EC1R 0DU (7253 1485).
Open 1-6pm Mon; 1-8pm Tue-Thur; 10am-1pm Sat.
Tours by prior appointment.

Observer

119 Farringdon Road, EC1R 3ER (7278 2332/
www.observer.co.uk).

Wyvern Bindery

56-58 Clerkenwell Road, EC1M 5PX (7490 7899/
www.wyvernbindery.com). **Open** 9am-5pm Mon-Fri.

Churches & museums

Our Most Holy Redeemer Church

24 Exmouth Market, EC1R 4QE (7837 1861/
www.holyredeemer.co.uk). **Open** 8.30am-6.30pm
daily. **Services** 11am, 6pm Sun.

The Order of St John Museum

26 St John's Lane, EC1M 4DA (7324 4005/
www.sja.org.uk/museum). **Open** 10am-5pm Mon-Fri;
10am-4pm Sat. **Admission** free; donations
appreciated.

St James Church

Clerkenwell Close, EC1R 0EA (7251 1190/www.jc-
church.org). **Open** *Office* 8.30am-6pm Mon-Fri.
Phone for opening times. **Services** 11am Sun.

Services

Clerkenwell Green Association

Pennybank Chambers, 33-35 St John's Square,
EC1M 4DS (7251 0276/www.cga.org.uk). **Open**
9am-5pm Mon-Fri. Phone for information on events.

Clerkenwell Historic Trail

Details are available from **3 Things** (*see below*).

Clerkenwell Visitor Centre

53 Clerkenwell Close, EC1R 0EA (7251 6311/
www.clerkenwell.org). **Open** 11am-6pm Mon-Sat.

Islington Local History Centre

7527 7988/www.islington.gov.uk. **Open** 9.30am-8pm
Mon, Thur; 9.30am-5pm Tue, alternate Sat; 9.30am-
1pm Fri. Appointment-only service.

London Masonic Centre

Old Sessions House, Clerkenwell Green, EC1R 0NA
(7250 1212/www.sessionshouse.com/masonic).
Open 9am-1pm Mon-Fri.

Shopping

G Gazzano

167-169 Farringdon Road, EC1R 3AL (7837 1586).
Open 8am-5pm Mon, Sat; 8am-6pm Tue-Fri; 10am-
2pm Sun.

McQueens

126 St John Street, EC1V 4JS (7251 5505/
www.mcqueens.co.uk). **Open** 8.30am-6pm Mon-Fri;
9am-3pm Sat.

Metro Imaging

76 Clerkenwell Road, EC1M 5TN (7865 0000/
www.metroimaging.co.uk). **Open** 24 hrs daily.
Exhibitions in the reception area.

3 Things

53 Clerkenwell Close, EC1R 0EA (7251 6311).
Open 9am-6pm Mon-Fri.

Smithfield Market

Farringdon Street, EC1 (7248 3151/
www.cityoflondon.gov.uk). **Open** 4-10am Mon-Fri.

Viaduct Furniture

1-10 Summer Street, EC1R 5BD (7278 8456/
www.viaduct.co.uk). **Open** 9.30am-6pm Mon-Fri;
10.30am-4pm Sat.

A river runs through it
John Vidal

Follow the Thames as it wends its way past millennial follies, sterile developments, beaches, parkland and pubs.

Start: Thames Barrier
Finish: Hampton Court Palace
Distance: 29 miles/46km
Time: two days/seven hours by bicycle. Some parts are 'no cycling'
Getting there: rail to Charlton, then taxi/long walk
Getting back: rail from Hampton Court
Note: the route can be followed by bicycle or on foot. It's probably best done in stages, unless you're fit or foolhardy. The following rail and/or tube stations are close to the route: Greenwich, Rotherhithe, London Bridge, Waterloo, Vauxhall,

Battersea Park, Wandsworth Town, Barnes Bridge, Richmond and Kingston. Note that the pace of building development is so great that the map is likely to become out of date, particularly between the Dome and Rotherhithe. However, the Thames Path should always be labelled, so even when you sometimes have to leave the river to avoid developments you can always rejoin it at a later point. For a truly quiet riverside walk along a towpath, head west from Putney Bridge, though note there is little chance of 'escape' between bridges.

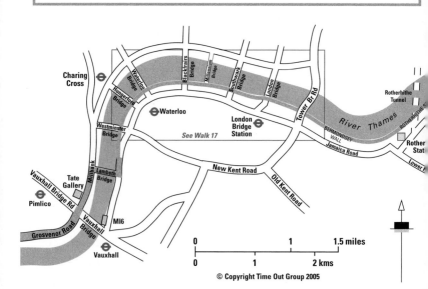

© Copyright Time Out Group 2005

A river runs through it

From the Thames Barrier in the east, 30 miles to Hampton Court in the west, there more or less runs a pathway that should be recognised as one of the world's great walks. People rarely go the full distance, let alone up to the source of the Thames or down to the sea, but to complete this stretch of Britain's longest waterway can be as satisfying as any trek through mountain or forest.

Prepare in advance as you would for any long tramp. You need two days at least and more if you like to stop or hive off along the way. Aim to spend a night en route, perhaps in the centre of London. Take guides, binoculars, an *A-Z*, water, rucksack, even gifts. Travel with friends. Treat it as a hike through foreign lands, and do not underestimate its length, its changing topography or the appeal and detail of its distractions.

The places you will pass through have their own climate and lore. The path is mostly clearly marked but when you are on the river shore remember that it is a different world, sometimes wild and potentially dangerous. At many points you will be disorientated because your direction will keep changing. You will meet people from different tribes with their own cultures and languages. Some will be hostile and defensive, others welcoming. You will need good shoes and much stamina.

My advice is to start dead early at the Thames Barrier, the true modern outer wall of the natural city that is the river and its banks to the west. Head for Charlton on the train or bus and then take a cab ride through run-down back streets to reach the £500 million engineering spectacle that gleams gold on its eastern side in the early morning

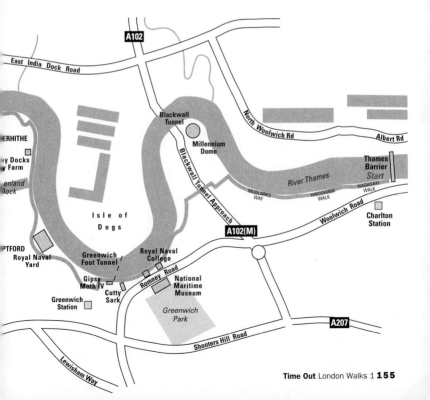

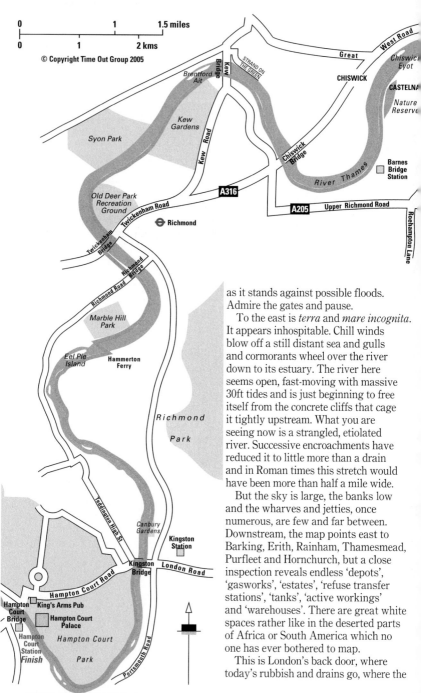

0   1   1.5 miles

0   1   2 kms

© Copyright Time Out Group 2005

Kew Bridge

STRAND ON THE GREEN

Great   West Road

Brentford Ait

Chiswick Eyot

CHISWICK

CASTELNA

Kew Gardens

Syon Park

Kew Road

Chiswick Bridge

Nature Reserve

River Thames

Barnes Bridge Station

Old Deer Park Recreation Ground

A316

Twickenham Road

A205   Upper Richmond Road

◉ Richmond

Roehampton Lane

Twickenham Bridge

Richmond Bridge

Richmond Road

Marble Hill Park

Eel Pie Island

Hammerton Ferry

Richmond Park

Teddington High St.

Canbury Gardens

Kingston Station

Kingston Bridge

London Road

Hampton Court Road

King's Arms Pub

Hampton Court Bridge

Hampton Court Palace

Hampton Court Station
Finish

Hampton Court Park

Portsmouth Road

as it stands against possible floods. Admire the gates and pause.

To the east is *terra* and *mare incognita*. It appears inhospitable. Chill winds blow off a still distant sea and gulls and cormorants wheel over the river down to its estuary. The river here seems open, fast-moving with massive 30ft tides and is just beginning to free itself from the concrete cliffs that cage it tightly upstream. What you are seeing now is a strangled, etiolated river. Successive encroachments have reduced it to little more than a drain and in Roman times this stretch would have been more than half a mile wide.

But the sky is large, the banks low and the wharves and jetties, once numerous, are few and far between. Downstream, the map points east to Barking, Erith, Rainham, Thamesmead, Purfleet and Hornchurch, but a close inspection reveals endless 'depots', 'gasworks', 'estates', 'refuse transfer stations', 'tanks', 'active workings' and 'warehouses'. There are great white spaces rather like in the deserted parts of Africa or South America which no one has ever bothered to map.

This is London's back door, where today's rubbish and drains go, where the

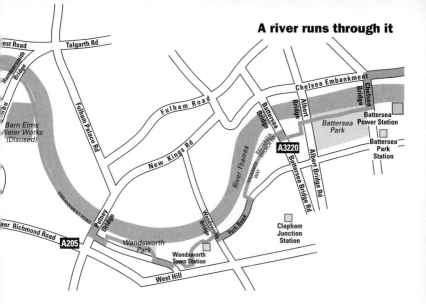

tradesmen come, the sewage heads and where archaeologists are finding ancient forests in the mud. Here are car compounds, waterworks, power stations and the belching, farting hinterlands. Beyond, *terra nullius*, is a place of wild unexplored marshes, mud and bleak windswept reaches, dearly loved by those who live nearby but otherwise ignored.

Turn your back, reluctantly, on the estuary. To the west, where we are heading, are the first signs of cosmopolitan life. Towers, peaks, domes, spires, cranes, skyscrapers. The air feels warmer. The river is changing here from estuary to channel, the water is salty and the city we think we know is starting to close in. You can sense it in the river's quickening currents, the higher walls that have progressively moved in and bound it, the first new housing developments on the northern banks and the first sound of traffic.

The barrier is a fit place to start because it is no man's land, a hail and farewell spot for the millions who have left and entered the city by boat in the past 500 years. This reach of the river would have marked the end of the old world for those heading for Australia, the Americas and Africa. Here, the goodbyes over, the city

behind them and a chill wind coming off the unprotected banks of the river, who would not have gone below decks to prepare for the long voyage ahead? And for the waves of Huguenots, Jews, Flemish, Indians and others fleeing persecution or looking for betterment through the ages, here, just before the

Thames Barrier

Millennium Dome

first sharp bend in the river, would have been the heart-beating start of the new.

The footway to London from this frontier post is paved in concrete: head through the underpass enlivened by a 100-yard-long frieze depicting the length of the Thames, pass down Hiroshima and Nagasaki walks and through alleyways of corrugated iron and wasteland primed to be housing estates.

When, at low tides, you can see the foreshore through railings and fences, it is unremarkable, except that it is there twice a day, shingly, modest and unannounced. The foreshore is one of the great archaeological sites in Europe with traces continually being found of London's origins, but it is also vital to the river, providing irreplaceable feeding and resting places for fish, birds and innumerable invertebrates. It is, however, almost impossible to reach at most points, ever since the Victorians built their high embankments for flood defences and to claim ever more land for development.

The Thames Barrier Yacht club bustles with enthusiasts. How soon before this is

marina-and-blazerland, priced out of reach for everyone except executives? Enjoy it before the developers come. It is old and resonant. There are old ropes everywhere. Old boats. Old men. Old haunts of Arthur Daleys. Take your time here. It's human. Much of the Thames is not.

The lure of New Britain draws you on to the Millennium Dome. Never mind the politics or the cost of the great white jellyfish of a building now looming, this is a giant London landmark and never better seen than from this stretch of the Thames. You get the scale a mile away and from there it grows on you. The ecological exchange involved in its construction seems unjust; even as hundreds and thousands of tons of contaminated soil were being quietly exported through east London to waste sites around England, so other trucks imported mountains of hardcore from quarries in the countryside.

But the millennium site is an ecological work in progress and far more than a political statement. The peninsula is one of the best points for birdwatching along the river. And as part of the new Greenwich Peninsula development, £11 million has been invested in ecological terracing, which will encourage plants and nesting. On top of that, 50 acres of the new site will be parkland and 12,000 trees are being planted.

Away from the development there is a sense of danger on the walk. The path, clearly marked, skirts the Dome and cuts through the Blackwall peninsula, crossing the Tunnel Approach Road via a concrete bridge. It is an inhuman, machine-dominated place of trucks, speed, noise, signs, sirens and every modern pollution. After the lull of the river, the reality of street London is good preparation for the next short step, which involves following the path through a chemical works.

Phwoar. The buildings hiss and rumble, stink, squeak, steam and stench. Just in time you are back on a quiet river that has narrowed and become more intimate, offering a remarkable view of Greenwich ahead. The scale, light and direction have changed. Now you can see why Greenwich grew in its sheltering crook of the river.

But before the classical buildings and the masts comes a mile of raw London to traverse. Antiseptic 1980s riverside housing lines the north bank, replacing the many Victorian wharves, docks and jetties. Here on the south is the graveyard of old ro-ro ferries, rubbish and pleasure barges, rusty cruisers, broken cranes and hoppers. It pleases enormously. The scale is human, the people who live this way say they are the best and you can believe them. Behind high, corrugated walls are old yards with old cars, falling roofs, lifebelts, butane cylinders. Ropes and polystyrene line the way and old men with grey beards walk shaggy dogs.

How long before a great tide of money comes and washes this second-hand, recycled world away? Catch this last fling of the smallscale before it's made mean, tidy and emotionally inaccessible.

From the Barrier to the *Cutty Sark* in the centre of Greenwich takes about an hour. It takes half that time to loiter in any one of the many riverside pubs, the same to dodge the sightseers and briefly check out the Royal Naval College and the *Cutty Sark*. From here the scenery,

the pace, and the walk are going to change dramatically. So pause.

What is this great flow that at this point has already wound 120 miles from the Cotswold Hills? We see the Thames usually only from its bridges in central London, or perhaps from a favourite stretch. It is for most of us little more than a view, something untouchable, without life or function beyond the aesthetic pleasure it brings or the hassle involved in crossing it. Only a handful of Londoners live on it, fewer still work on it. Yet the Thames is the sink of southern England, the longest, most important British river and the reason why every village and industry that has ever grown up in what is now London started life. When boat people and others call for it to be dammed to make a giant lake above Tower Bridge, or try to build roads along the foreshore well away from the cramped town centres along the river's reach, they seek to kill all our history and geography.

If, once, the tide of history was in the direction of developers and industrialists who would infill, encroach and cage the river without a second thought, today there is a new awareness of the value of the Thames as an ecological unity and the protectionists are beginning to win the arguments. The shift is as significant as the progress that has been made cleaning up what was once one of Europe's most polluted waterways.

Only 48 years ago the river was biologically dead to the point that only eels could survive in it. The introduction of the water closet in the 1830s started the real damage and by 1957 there was no marine life whatever in the tidal Thames between Kew and Gravesend. The great muddy flow became the cleanest it had been for 200 years, although it took a few retrograde steps in the summer of 2004 when flash floods caused 600,000 tons of raw sewage to enter the water as the sewers backed up. On a good day, however, there are 115 species of fish, and some 350 species of invertebrates.

HMS Belfast

It is a great ecological success story and there is much educating to be done.

But the industrial river clings on. Lines of lighters and barges still take London's rubbish downriver to the Essex marshes. Paper comes up to Deptford from Finland, and steel heads for the Isle of Dogs. But there is little else in the way of trade these days apart from the pleasure boats. Only 40 years ago there would have been great ships lining each bank. Today, two of the last and best-known boatyards on this Greenwich stretch have fallen to the developers, the cement and corn lighters have given up and the river is being inexorably homogenised.

Remember this, for we shall soon enter some of the foulest, most unfriendly places in Britain. Not the next mile or three, where the well-signposted path wiggles around run-down housing estates, sweeps you into Greenwich town via waste and breakers' yards, crosses parks and jumps back to the river every so often, but as we reach the new world of private estates.

First some history. Drake's Steps, between Royal Naval Yard and Greenwich Dock at Deptford Strand, commemorate not only where Sir Walter Raleigh reputedly threw his cloak to save his queen from mud, but also where the English slave trade started. From here the infamous Admiral Hawkins (his coat of arms had three black men shackled together by the neck) and his fragrant young nephew Sir Francis Drake headed for West Africa to take slaves to the Dominican Republic, bringing back ginger and spices. A nasty triangle.

A few hundred yards further on, there's a statue of Peter the Great, erected in 2001 to commemorate his sojourn – famous for its wild parties – in Deptford in 1698. Beyond this, the Surrey Docks surprise. Dutch barges, gaff riggers, old fishing smacks and a floating pub are cosy. A community of houseboats, refugees from the marina mentality upstream, huddle together for security, and nearby, at Dog and Duck Stairs, a plaque commemorates the Mudlarks. These riverside scavengers hauled out coal, timber and anything else from the shoreline that they could sell.

Hold your breath. We are entering new London's slums for the young, rich and lonely. New housing developments, each more expensive and grotesque than the last, line the river. The most common signs are 'No bike riding', 'No dogs', 'No ball games' and 'No driving'. New Caledonian Wharf, Traders Wharf, Crane Wharf, Metropolitan Wharf and a dozen others with their mock Victorian lamps, dinky squares and net curtains were once the site of the workhouses of London. Even the developers recognise that they got it wrong here. Today they are a grim homage to the power that corporate salesmen have over people and they reflect some pretty sad values and aspirations.

Grandiose neo-classical steps and porticos pompously announce people-free, play-free communities. Who lives here? Where are they? Are they all infertile? Why are the people who can afford to see the Thames from their pretty windows so silent? Do they like it here? What do they see? Are they dead from their footings up? Let's ask them. Press the intercoms at random and wait expectantly. No one is in or at least no one will answer. Shame. It seems such a lonely, ghostly world, built in a few years for the few, to be regretted at leisure by many.

But what's this? Right in the middle of the Dead Zone is an incongruous, wonky city farm – Surrey Docks Farm – which positively squeals with children and patient animals. No straight lines here, no grilles or security fences. The three acres in the wilderness of developments burst with life and self-expression. Broken windmills and solar panels reflect old enthusiasms. There are yurts and winding footpaths with herb gardens and sculptures. Geese, pigs, goats, ducks and kids roam equally. Want to learn bee-keeping or how to make a willow cabin? Where else in central London? Seagulls sit and contemplate the river on old mooring piers.

The riverside path is occasionally barred by the developments, but the way is obvious and always leads back to the water. Shortly, you are in Rotherhithe, from where the Pilgrim Fathers left for America. If it's not too early, you could enjoy a first tipple at the Blacksmith's Arms. Narrow Dickensian streets and alleys are being tarted up in an orgy of plasterboard, reclaimed brick and lofts. A few latter-day mudlarks can be found by the water's edge, lost in a private world of plastic cups and shopping trolleys. The streets hold pointed graffiti: 'Build your helicopter pad in your own back garden.' Tower Bridge looms into view, behind it St Paul's and the Post Office Tower.

And then goodbye Barratland and on past Butler's and New Concordia Wharves into the Pool of London and the city proper. A fine Paolozzi sculpture is welcome respite from the luxury apartments. Just 15 years ago the buildings on this stretch were tumbling and the decay was noticeably London-ish. Today it is Anywhereville and the style is Euro-uniform. The brasseries could be Hamburg, the spice shops Paris, the pizzas and piazzas, coffee bars and restaurants Amsterdam or Copenhagen. They are equally efficient and uniformly expensive.

Tower Bridge framed the City for the Victorians as the Thames barrier does today. Now it seems small and in scale with the narrowing river, which is becoming dominated by office blocks and the frenzy of new international money. Only 45 years ago there was a beach here to which thousands of Londoners went to picnic.

The river is noisy now, if a faint echo of pre-war days when freighters would queue up here to unload in the docks. The sirens and hooters of pleasure craft, party boats and police launches compete for attention. On your left, the squiffily sloping City Hall is the rented home of the London Assembly. This environmentally friendly structure, designed by Lord Foster, uses just one quarter of the energy of a conventional office building. Beyond this you may wonder whether *HMS Belfast* is a real warship or a theme park model. The tone of three massive 1980s developments is set by a replica of the 16th-century *Golden Hinde*, in permanent gloomy drydock. This is no film-set model, however; it claims to have

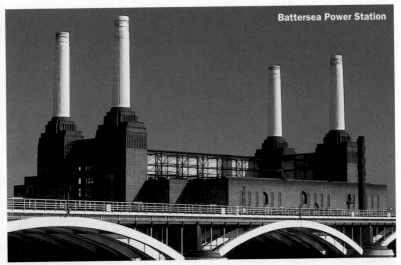

Battersea Power Station

sailed 140,000 miles. It is confusing. Is this ruin of Winchester Palace new or did they build it with just one gable end? Only old, grey Southwark Cathedral seems unchanging and inviolable.

From here through to and beyond Westminster, there is little or no foreshore, the developments are going in different directions and the city is metamorphosing as it tries to turn away from its industrial past. The Globe Theatre is worth a visit if only for its construction in oak and traditional materials; the massive old Bankside Power Station is now Tate Modern, sister gallery to Tate Britain; opposite St Paul's is the visionary Millennium footbridge.This part of London is the most architecturally fluid, with new plans always being mooted. But the Environment Agency, the government's statutory advisers on nature and controllers of pollution, vehemently resists developments which would adversely affect the river's natural functions.

The individual buildings in the city centre are more or less known but the curious walker can stop at many notice boards that name names and can choose which bank of the river to follow, which bridge to cross and which from a host of bars and pubs to stop at. The eastern banks of the city are not architecturally static,

which gives this approach to central London an air of excitement and transience. Coin Street, the most successful community development in Britain, the victory of locals over corporate Britain in the 1970s, still looks vulnerable beside the giant developments that surround it, but it faces both ways in the new politics of London: one way to designer restaurants and fashion; the other to the faintly hippyish market and lively summer weekend music festivals.

Beyond the National Theatre, the National Film Theatre and Hayward Gallery (all good staging posts for a meal or tea), the river turns sharply south past the London Eye, the giant Ferris wheel that sticks out into the river at Jubilee Gardens just by the old County Hall at Westminster. Follow the Albert Embankment opposite the Palace of Westminster and then go west over Lambeth Bridge. At low tides you can just see stumps in the mud on the east side. They are the remains of the first Saxon bridge. Set in the river walls underneath a modernist cold store are old bronze lion heads. When the river rises to their open mouths, the signal is given for the Thames barrier to rise. Every building here accurately reflects its times. In a short stretch you can move from the medieval, through to Victorian and so on to the post-modernity of the MI6 building.

Eel Pie Island

The best route for the moment is probably along Millbank and then into Grosvenor Road as far as Chelsea Bridge. It is noisy and there are grand views of Battersea Power Station, another monument awaiting development and a path along its frontage. Its old cranes and wharves are some of the last on the river and there are moves to preserve them. Duck south across Chelsea Bridge and into Battersea Park with its Peace Pagoda. At low tide here you can just see ancient stumps of former forests.

The only option is now to stay on the south bank, go down Battersea Church Road, along Vicarage Walk and then along Vicarage Crescent, Lombard Road and York Road. On the north bank are some of the most expensive houseboats on the Thames, and the cold and impersonal Chelsea Harbour development. At low tide, below the houseboats, you can just see the remains of a Saxon fish trap.

Just before Wandsworth Bridge is high corrugated fencing. In 1996 this land was occupied by eco-activists in protest against yet more supermarkets and massively expensive flats along the Thames. The community was finally cleared in 1997.

Stay on the south bank for Wandsworth Park and see the inlet of the Wandle, a chalk stream river that starts on the South Downs, once fed the Thames and was inexorably turned first into a ditch and then into a drain. New ecological thinking and co-operation between the council and the Environment Agency has led to a revamp of much of the Wandle and the mouth is slowly returning to its state of 200 years ago.

You still have a daunting 15 or more miles to go from Putney Bridge to Hampton Court, but the path is clear the whole way, there are fewer human distractions, increasing bird life and you can build up a good pace, even if the walk to Kew seems never-ending.

The stretch from Putney towards Hammersmith is Barn Elms, probably established as an ancient river crossing and now a great expanse of football fields. This is the first part of the river without high concrete or stone walls and the natural gradations down to the water have a calming effect. Further on, and stretching to the west, natural reed beds have started to form in the past ten years and shingle beaches appear. This is the site of the London Wetland Centre, which offers a wetland wildlife environment within easy reach of central London.

The tidal Thames, which runs up to Teddington, is a 100-kilometre wildlife corridor. Where downstream, beyond the barrier, there are mudflats, lagoons and salt marshes, here there are oases in an urban desert. The foreshore is easier to reach from here on and it is well worth getting your feet wet if you've not brought wellies. The gravel and shingle are refuges for crabs, small fish, shrimps, snails and worms galore. The wetland plants include hemlock, wild angelica, meadowsweet and ragworts. Mute swans, herons, cormorants and kingfishers are all to be found, with the many small islands providing extra shelter.

From here on look for the many holes in the clay banks. They are from Chinese mitten crabs – so named because they have velvety, glove-like claws – that have colonised the Thames in the past 20 years. Many millions have moved up the river in great submarine armies with the tides, and for unknown reasons, probably due to their population having built up to a critical level, they began to burrow into the banks in 1997-98. Now they threaten the riverbank stability in places and there is no hope whatsoever of containing them. One of the few crabs in the world that can take to the land without dehydrating, they are expected to move up to the Cotswolds. Nevertheless, they are a culinary delicacy and Londoners can expect them on the menu before long. In Germany, where they are heading for the Alps, thousands of tons of mittens a year are pulled out of the Rhine and turned into fertiliser.

And look, beside the boats at Chiswick Pier, for a low brick building. It is the home of the Thames Explorer Trust, where Ali Taylor and others regularly and in all weathers take children and adults down to the foreshore to teach them about the ecology and archaeology of the river. It is a model community centre and one that could be an inspiration to other London boroughs.

At Strand on the Green, over Kew Bridge, all the houses still get flooded, but the locals have decided they don't want high embankment walls. The flood defence line is a black line on the local pub and the front doors face the river. Even the post office stresses the fact that the river was a high street and people came and went across and down it by boat until very recently.

Brentford Ait is a graveyard for boats and there is evidence of at least 14 that have sunk here. The north bank, where the Grand Union Canal joins the river, is under intense development pressure but there is little likelihood now that the basins will be filled in or that the river will be further narrowed.

We are entering boat and playing field land. Aim to stop in Kew Gardens before the beautiful Syon Reach of the river, the only stretch that is more or less natural on both sides and much as Londoners would have seen it 500 years ago. The great house in its own park is out of sight on the other bank. The peace is remarkable, the river calm, the birds numerous and other walkers – for the first time in miles – return greetings.

The river is becoming more natural, so anywhere along the towpath is fine to contemplate the other populations of the river, each of which have their seasons and migrations. In March and April, the Thames is a corridor for the young eels; in May, it is the flounders' turn to swim upstream; June finds bass coming into the river from their spawning grounds in the English Channel. And in November the

fry of thin grey mullet enter the river. The river could now support commercial fisheries for several species.

But head ever westwards, for there are several more miles to complete. After the Old Deer Park and Richmond Lock, cross Twickenham Bridge and follow what is now the north bank through Marble Hill Park and then take Hammerton's humble ferry. Head past Eel Pie island and all the way on to Kingston. As you approach this plush town you will pass swans and ducks and a particularly ugly block of new flats in Canbury Gardens. This was the site of a colourful protest in early 1988 supported by 20,000 people. Fifty mature poplars once masked the old power station and gave the public park an intimate feel. But the developer got his way, local democracy proved inadequate and despite tunnels, tree houses and river protests, the poplars were summarily felled. Those flats with a river view appreciated by £30,000 each in the time it took to cut them down.

Cross Kingston Bridge speedily. This is the home stretch and the feet are weary. The city has come and gone, the river has dwindled and halved in size and its banks have become progressively less steep and forbidding. There hasn't been much natural topography along the way, but

Kew Gardens

that is changing as people learn to value the river as London's greatest natural asset.

In human terms, the river has made us all Londoners. It is the reason for London past and London future. It has stitched four or five distinct Londons together, gone from drainage canal and channel to harbour, port, estuary and pool. It has led the walker through suburbia to visionary world capital and back to front gardens, all in 30 miles. It has been Victorian and futuristic, medieval and post-modern, sublimely ugly and famously romantic, alternately imposing, pompous, stern and subtle.

But it is all one river, vulnerable to pollution, overdevelopment and theft at every point, and what happens anywhere along its stretch affects its whole ecology. Until it is experienced at some length and seen as an asset for everyone, mistakes will continue to be made in its development.

We started with a modernistic barrier in no man's land and it is right that this walk should end with a palace that has long been open to the people and home to the most famous maze in the world. You will be forgiven if you skip the last mile of towpath, cut west across Hampton Court Park and head for the great Tudor pile built for Cardinal Wolsey and its gardens inspired by Versailles. My advice is to congratulate yourself for having come so far, head for the old King's Arms pub and put your feet up. You well deserve it.

Pubs

Anchor Bankside

34 Park Street, SE1 9EF (7407 1577). **Open** 11am-11pm Mon-Sat; noon-10.30pm Sun. **Food served** noon-10pm Mon-Sat; noon-9pm Sun. Real ales, river views and fair food.

Blacksmith's Arms

257 Rotherhithe Street, SE16 5EJ (7237 1349). **Open** noon-11pm Mon-Sat; noon-10.30pm Sun. **Food served** noon-3pm, 6.30-10pm daily. A decent, no-nonsense boozer serving pub grub and good beer.

Boaters Inn

Canbury Gardens, Lower Ham Road, Kingston-upon-Thames, KT2 5AU (8541 4672). **Open** 11am-11pm Mon-Sat; noon-10.30pm Sun. **Food served** noon-9.30pm Mon-Sat; noon-9pm Sun. Standard pub grub and lazy river views.

Duke's Head

8 Lower Richmond Road, SW15 1JN (8788 2552). **Open** 11am-11pm Mon-Sat; noon-10.30pm Sun. **Food served** noon-2.30pm, 6-10pm Mon-Fri; 11am-10pm Sat; noon-9pm Sun. A riverside patio for fine weather and a thoughtful menu.

King's Arms

Lion Gate, Hampton Court Road, East Molesey, Surrey KT8 9DD (8977 1729). **Open** 11am-11pm Mon-Sat; noon-10.30pm Sun. **Food served** noon-3pm, 6-9pm Mon-Fri; noon-5pm, 6-9pm Sat, Sun.

Mayflower

117 Rotherhithe Street, SE16 4NF (7237 4088).
Open noon-11pm Mon-Sat; noon-10.30pm Sun.
Food served noon-3pm, 6.30-9pm Mon-Sat; noon-
4pm Sun. Historic pub with floorboards (reputedly)
from the *Mayflower* ship.

Morpeth Arms

58 Millbank, SW1P 4RW (7834 6442). **Open**
11am-11pm Mon-Sat; noon-10.30pm Sun. **Food
served** noon-9pm Mon-Fri; 12.30-4pm Sat, Sun.
Perfect for Tate Britain; good beers and food served.

Old Thameside Inn

*Pickfords Wharf, 1 Clink Street, SE1 9DG (7403
4243).* **Open** 11am-11pm Mon-Sat; noon-10.30pm
Sun. **Food served** noon-10pm daily. Spectacular
views at this otherwise unremarkable pub.

Spice Island

163 Rotherhithe Street, SE16 5QU (7394 7108).
Open 11am-11pm Mon-Thur; 11am-midnight
Fri, Sat; noon-10.30pm Sun. **Food served** noon-
9.30pm Mon-Sat; noon-8.30pm Sun. Cavernous
old warehouse converted to popular boozer and
upstairs restaurant.

Trafalgar Tavern

*Park Row, SE10 9NW (8858 2437/www.trafalgar
tavern.co.uk).* **Open** noon-11pm Mon-Thur; noon-
midnight Fri, Sat; noon-10.30pm Sun. **Food
served** noon-3pm, 6-9pm Mon-Sat; noon-4pm
Sun. Upmarket food and views of the Dome in
this historic tavern.

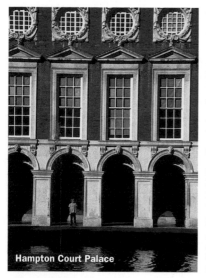

Hampton Court Palace

Cafés & restaurants

Café Rouge

*Hays Galleria, 3 Tooley Street, SE1 2HD (7378
0097).* **Open** 9am-10pm Mon-Fri; 9.30am-10pm Sat,
Sun. Formulaic French(ish) food.

The Depot

*Tideway Yard, 125 Mortlake High Street, SW14
8SN (8878 9462).* **Open** 10am-11pm Mon-Sat;
10am-10.30pm Sun. **Lunch served** noon-3pm
Mon-Sat; noon-4pm Sun. **Dinner served** 6-11pm
Mon-Sat; 6-10.30pm Sun. Slick brasserie in a
riverside warehouse.

Gourmet Pizza Company

*Gabriel's Wharf, 56 Upper Ground, SE1 9PP
(7928 3188).* **Meals served** noon-11.30pm daily.
Overambitious pizzas, with the river nearby.

Oxo Tower Restaurant, Bar & Brasserie

*8th floor, Oxo Tower Wharf, Barge House Street,
SE1 9PH (7803 3888/www.harveynichols.com).*
Bar **Open** 11am-11pm Mon-Sat; noon-10.30pm Sun.
Brasserie **Lunch served** noon-3.15pm Mon-Sat;
noon-3.45pm Sun. **Dinner served** 5.30-11pm
Mon-Sat; 6-10.15pm Sun. *Restaurant* **Lunch
served** noon-2.30pm Mon-Sat; noon-3pm Sun.
Dinner served 6-11pm Mon-Sat; 6.30-10pm Sun.
Interesting and classy modern European cuisine,
and wonderful views.

Le Pont de la Tour

*Butlers Wharf Building, 36D Shad Thames, Butlers
Wharf, SE1 2YE (7403 8403/www.conran.com).*
Lunch served noon-3pm, **dinner served** 6-11pm
daily. Sir Terence Conran's top-notch (in price and
quality) modern European restaurant. Next door you
can try his take on British food – Butlers Wharf Chop
House – or Mediterranean – Cantina del Ponte (the
least expensive).

Tidetables Café

*2 The Arches, beneath Richmond Bridge, Riverside,
Richmond, Surrey TW9 1TH (8948 8285).* **Open**
Winter 9am-6pm daily. *Summer* 9am-8pm Mon-Fri;
9am-9pm Sat, Sun. Vegetarian food.

Galleries, museums & sights

For further South Bank listings, *see p168*
Freewheeling.

British Airways London Eye

*Riverside Building, next to County Hall, Westminster
Bridge Road, SE1 7PB (0870 500 0600/www.ba-
londoneye.com).* **Open** *Oct-Apr* 9.30am-8pm daily.
May, June, Sept 9.30am-9pm daily. *July, Aug* 9.30am-

10pm daily. **Admission** £12.50; £10 concessions (not applicable weekends or Jul, Aug); £6.50 5-15s; free under-5s.

Cutty Sark

King William Walk, SE10 9HT (8858 3445/ www.cuttysark.org.uk). **Open** 10am-5pm daily (last admission 30min before closing). **Admission** £4.50; £3.25 concessions; £3.20 5-16s; free under-5s; £12 family.

Golden Hinde

St Mary Overie Dock, Cathedral Street, SE1 9DE (0870 011 8700/www.goldenhinde.co.uk). **Open** daily, times vary; phone for details. **Admission** £3.50; £3 concessions; £2.50 4-13s; free under-4s; £10 family.

Hampton Court Palace

East Molesey, Surrey KT8 9AU (0870 751 5175/ www.hrp.org.uk). **Open** *Palace* Mar-Oct 10.15am-6pm Mon; 10am-6pm Tue-Sun; Nov-Feb 10.15am-4.30pm Mon; 9.30am-4.30pm Tue-Sun (last admission 1hr before closing). *Park* dawn-dusk daily. **Admission** *Palace, courtyard, cloister & maze* £12; £9 concessions; £7.80 5-15s; free under-5s; £35 family (max 5 people). *Formal gardens only* £4; £3 concessions; £2.50 5-15s.

Hayward Gallery

South Bank Centre, Belvedere Road, SE1 8XX (9870 169 1000/www.hayward.org.uk). **Open** *During exhibitions* 10am-6pm Mon, Thur, Sat, Sun; 10am-8pm Tue, Wed; 10am-9pm Fri. **Admission** £9; £4 concessions; £3 12-16s; free under-12s.

Old Royal Naval College

King William Walk, SE10 9LW(8269 4747/ www.greenwichfoundation.org.uk). **Open** 10am-4.45pm daily. **Admission** free.

Surrey Docks City Farm

Rotherhithe Street, SE16 5EY (7231 1010). **Open** 10am-1pm, 2-5pm Tue-Thur, Sat, Sun. **Admission** free; donations welcome.

Tate Modern

Bankside, SE1 9TG (7887 8000/www.tate.org.uk). **Open** 10am-6pm Mon-Thur, Sun; 10am-10pm Fri, Sat. *Tours* 11am, noon, 2pm, 3pm daily. **Admission** free.

Thames Barrier Information & Learning Centre

1 Unity Way, SE18 5NJ (8305 4188/www. environment-agency.gov.uk). **Open** *Apr-Sept* 10.30am-4.30pm daily. *Oct-Mar* 11am-3.30pm daily. **Admission** £1.50; £1 concessions; 75p 5-16s; free under-5s.

Information

Environment Agency

0870 850 6506/www.environment-agency.gov.uk.

Hammerton's Ferry

(8892 9620). **Open** 10am-6pm, or dusk if earlier Mon-Fri; 10am-6.30pm, or dusk if earlier Sat, Sun. **Tickets** 60p; 30p children; £1.10 person with bike.

Low & high tide information

Thames Barrier Visitors' Centre, 1 Unity Way, SE18 5NJ (8305 4188/www.environment-agency. gov.uk & www.portoflondon.co.uk/hydrographics).

Thames Explorer Trust

The Pierhouse, Corney Reach Way, W4 2UG (8742 0057/www.thames-explorer.org.uk). Or contact Chiswick Pier Trust (8742 2713/ www.chiswickpier.org.uk).

Thames Path

Leaflets, with map, are available from Tourist Information Centres in central London. You can also try **National Trails** (01865 810224/ www.nationaltrails.gov.uk) or **The Heart of England Tourist Board** (01905 763436/ www.visitheartofengland.com).

Parks

Battersea Park

SW11 4NJ (8871 7530/www.wandsworth.gov.uk). **Open** 8am-dusk daily.

Marble Hill Park

Richmond Road, Twickenham, Middx TW1 2NL (Park 8892 1900/Marble Hill House 8892 5115/ www.english-heritage.org.uk). **Open** 7am-dusk daily.

Richmond Park

Richmond, Surrey (8948 3209/Royal Parks police 7706 7272/www.royalparks.org.uk). **Open** *Mar-Sept* 7am-30min before dusk daily. *Oct-Feb* 7.30am-30min before dusk daily.

Royal Botanic Gardens (Kew Gardens)

Kew, Richmond, Surrey TW9 3AB (8332 5000/ www.kew.org). **Open** *Late Mar-Aug* 9.30am-6.30pm Mon-Fri; 9.30am-7.30pm Sat, Sun. *Sept-late Oct* 9.30am-6pm daily. *Late Oct-early Feb* 9.30am-4.15pm daily. *Early Feb-late Mar* 9.30am-5.30pm daily. **Admission** £10 adults; £7 concessions; free under-17s.

Wandsworth Park

SW18 (8871 6000/www.wandsworth.gov.uk). **Open** dawn-dusk daily.

Freewheeling
William Forrester

There's a relatively smooth ride for wheelchair users on the South Bank. In fact, it's probably the most accessible stretch in London.

Start: County Hall
Finish: London Bridge station
Distance: 2.5 miles/4km
Time: 1.5 hours
Getting there: Northern, Bakerloo, Jubilee or Waterloo & City line or rail to Waterloo, then short journey to the London Eye
Getting back: Jubilee or Northern lines or rail from London Bridge

Note: unless otherwise stated, all venues are generally accessible to wheelchair users and have an accessible café and toilets. An unavoidable problem is cobbles, making for a particularly rough ride near Southwark Cathedral and the Oxo Tower. Ironically, these cobbles often replace flat paving to give an area 'heritage appeal'.

Start under the London Eye, the fully accessible 135-metre-high (443-foot) Ferris wheel near where Chickeley Street joins Belvedere Road. Turn left for the London Aquarium in County Hall and

continue through the tunnel under Westminster Bridge for the view of the Houses of Parliament. Turn back to continue the walk. At Hungerford Bridge, two new walkways give great views and

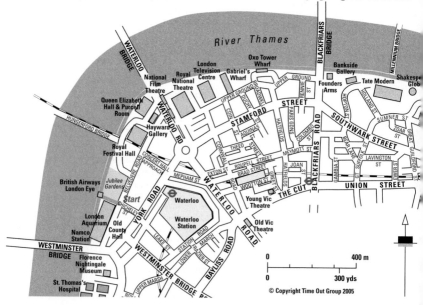

are accessible by lift. Past the bridge and opposite the Festival Pier you can deviate from the riverside. A ramp takes you down to cafés and shops (being built as we went to press) beneath the Royal Festival Hall, which will be closed for redevelopment work until early 2007. Return to the lift at Hungerford Bridge and go up to level 2 and out on to the high walkway. Turn right then left along the terrace and you will pass the Queen Elizabeth Hall and Purcell Room foyers, and the newly refurbished Hayward Gallery. After Waterloo Bridge, the Royal National Theatre's lifts get you down to the riverside level again (except on Sundays, when the theatre is closed). The upper floors of the Royal Festival Hall (only accessible from 2007) and the Royal National Theatre are great for views.

If you stick to the riverside, continue on under Waterloo Bridge, where there's a second-hand book market and the riverside entrance to the National Film Theatre. (Just beyond, turn right and head straight for 150 metres if you want to visit the IMAX cinema). On past the Royal National Theatre and the Gourmet

Pizza Company to the red-brick Oxo Tower. There are lifts at the back of the building and a viewing area at level 8. It is a great place for class war barfing as Harvey Nichols restaurant is next door. There is also a café on the ground floor for much cheaper food. Behind the Oxo Tower the Mallside exhibition space is worth a peep and they have a wheelchair lift.

Once beyond Blackfriars road and rail bridges, the walk goes round the back of the Founders Arms pub. A ramp up to the left takes you to the pub's riverside terrace. A ramp down to the right takes you to the Bankside Art Gallery (no wheelchair toilet or café, but there's a Starbucks next door).

Beyond the pub is the enormous chimney of the Bankside Power Station, now converted into the dramatic Tate Modern. There are fabulous views from level 7, but they've closed off the viewing gallery to the east of the chimney with the best of the views – a profoundly undemocratic move in a public building. The Tate overlooks the new Millennium footbridge across to St Paul's Cathedral. Just before the Globe Theatre, take the ramp down off the riverside to the roadway (called Bankside; it's partially cobbled). In my experience, you cannot see or hear Globe performances well from a wheelchair either in the Gentlemen's Rooms or the Yard. The Yard is cheaper

and has more atmosphere, but is 'standing' only. A platform is urgently needed here so wheelchair users can see over the heads of the crowd. But there are no problems with the excellent exhibition and guided tour.

Continue on under Southwark Bridge for the Anchor Tavern. Nearby is Vinopolis, an exploration of the world's wines (complete with tastings). On under Cannon Street railway arch into Clink Street. Here the Clink Prison Museum and the *Golden Hinde* replica are completely inaccessible. Console yourself with the Old Thameside Inn by the replica instead.

The roadway beyond takes you to the west end of Southwark Cathedral. To get in, enter through the south-west door. Double back to the lift on the north side of the nave, which takes you to the new café, shop and exhibition area. Once inside, take the south side up into the south transept. Ask staff for the ramp into the choir area and for the cunningly concealed ramp into the retrochoir.

To continue, return to the roadway and turn right (if the cathedral is closed follow round its north side into Montague Close). Some 50 metres (165 feet) beyond London Bridge, turn left (just before St Olaf's House) to rejoin the riverside at Queen's Walk. Beyond London Bridge City Pier, Hay's Galleria opens to the right. The key for the wheelchair toilet is available at Shackleton House behind the Horniman at Hays.

HMS Belfast is far from easy but is possible in parts with considerable assistance. Once aboard, an extremely steep ramp leads up to the Boat Deck where café service is available. One extremely steep up-and-over ramp takes one to zone 7 and the living quarters and another to the wheelchair toilet.

I recommend ending the walk with a view of Tower Bridge – still stunning, especially at night. Beside you is the rotund HQ of the Greater London Authority where there are stunning views from the ninth floor. However, if you want to go half a kilometre further, go under Tower Bridge

Approach into Shad Thames. In 75 metres (250 feet) a passageway (Maggie Blake's Cause) takes you back into the Thames Path. Along here is the Design Museum and the furthest one can get along the riverside – the elegant stainless steel bridge over St Saviour's Dock.

To return, go back to Hay's Galleria, walk through Tooley Street and turn right. Within ten metres is a grocery (Absolutely Starving) for cheap food. Within 50 metres (165 feet) is a well-concealed lift. Take it for the walkway into London Bridge station. Follow the wheelchair signs in the station for the underground and take the Jubilee line, which is accessible to Waterloo and Westminster.

Eating & drinking

Anchor Bankside

34 Park Street, SE1 9EF (7407 1577). **Open** 11am-11pm Mon-Sat; noon-10.30pm Sun. **Food served** noon-10pm Mon-Sat; noon-9pm Sun. Real ales, river views and fair food.

Founders Arms

52 Hopton Street, SE1 9JH (7928 1899). **Open** 9am-11pm Mon-Sat; 9am-10.30pm Sun. Decent pub with better-than-average food and gorgeous views.

Gourmet Pizza Company

Gabriel's Wharf, 56 Upper Ground, SE1 9PP (7928 3188). **Open** 11.30am-11.30pm Mon-Thur; 11.30am-midnight Fri, Sat; 11.30am-11pm Sun. Overambitious pizzas, but there's a sunny terrace with river views.

Old Thameside Inn

Pickfords Wharf, 1 Clink Street, SE1 9DG (7403 4243). **Open** 11am-11pm Mon-Sat; noon-10.30pm Sun. **Food served** noon-10pm daily. Riverside views, real ales and a restaurant.

Oxo Tower Restaurant, Bar & Brasserie

8th floor, Oxo Tower Wharf, Barge House Street, SE1 9PH (7803 3888/www.harveynichols.com). *Bar* **Open** 11am-11pm Mon-Sat; noon-10.30pm Sun. *Brasserie* **Lunch served** noon-3.15pm Mon-Sat; noon-3.45pm Sun. **Dinner served** 5.30-11pm Mon-Sat; 6-10.15pm Sun. *Restaurant* **Lunch served** noon-2.30pm Mon-Sat; noon-3pm Sun. **Dinner served** 6-11pm Mon-Sat; 6.30-10pm Sun. Interesting and classy modern European cuisine, and stunning views.

Galleries & museums

Bankside Gallery

48 Hopton Street, SE1 9JH (7928 7521/www. banksidegallery.com). **Open** 11am-6pm daily. **Admission** free.

Clink Prison Museum

1 Clink Street, SE1 9DG (7403 6515/www. clink.co.uk). **Open** *June-Sept* 10am-9pm daily. *Oct-May* 10am-6pm daily. **Admission** £5; £3.50 concessions, 5-15s; free under-5s; £12 family.

Design Museum

28 Shad Thames, SE1 2YD (7403 6933/www. designmuseum.org). **Open** 10am-5.45pm Mon-Thur, Sat, Sun; 10am-9pm Fri. **Admission** £6; £4 concessions; free under-12s; £16 family.

Golden Hinde

St Mary Overie Dock, Cathedral Street, SE1 9DE (0870 011 8700/www.goldenhinde.co.uk). **Open** daily, times vary; phone for details. **Admission** £3.50; £3 concessions; £2.50 4-13s; free under-4s; £10 family.

HMS Belfast

Morgan's Lane, Tooley Street, SE1 2JH (7940 6328/ www.iwn.org.uk). **Open** *Mar-Oct* 10am-6pm daily. *Nov-Feb* 10am-5pm daily. **Admission** £7; £5 concessions; free under-16s.

Hayward Gallery

South Bank Centre, Belvedere Road, SE1 8XX (0870 169 1000/www.hayward.org.uk). **Open** *During exhibitions* 10am-6pm Mon, Thur, Sat, Sun; 10am-8pm Tue, Wed; 10am-9pm Fri. **Admission** £9; £4 concessions; £3 12-16s; free under-12s.

London Aquarium

County Hall, Riverside Building, Westminster Bridge Road, SE1 7PB (7967 8000/www.londonaquarium. co.uk). **Open** *Term-time* 10am-6pm daily). *School holidays* 10am-7pm daily. **Admission** £8.75; £5.25-£6.50 concessions; £3.50 wheelchair users; free under-3s; £25 family.

Tate Modern

Bankside, SE1 9TG (7887 8000/www.tate.org.uk). **Open** 10am-6pm Mon-Thur, Sun; 10am-10pm Fri, Sat. *Tours* 11am, noon, 2pm, 3pm daily. **Admission** free. *Temporary exhibitions* prices vary.

Film, music & theatre

IMAX Cinema

1 Charlie Chaplin Walk, SE1 8XR (0870 787 2525/ www.bfi.org.uk/imax). **Open** *Box office* 10.30am-7.30pm daily. **Admission** *Standard presentations* £7.90; £6.50 concessions; £4.95 under-15s. *Digitally remastered presentations* £12; £11 concessions; £6 under-15s.

National Film Theatre

South Bank, SE1 8XT (box office 7928 3232/www. bfi.org.uk/nft). **Open** *Box office* 11.30am-8.30pm daily. **Admission** £8.20; £6.20 on the day; £5.25 under-16s.

Royal National Theatre

South Bank, SE1 9PX (box office 7452 3000/ www.nationaltheatre.org.uk). **Open** *Box office* 10am-8pm Mon-Sat. **Tickets** £10-£35.

Shakespeare's Globe

21 New Globe Walk, Bankside, SE1 9DT (7902 1500/www.shakespeares-globe.org). **Open** *Tours & Exhibitions* May-Sept 9am-noon daily. Oct-Apr 10am-5pm daily. **Admission** £8.50; £7 concessions; £6 5-15s; free under-5s.

South Bank Centre

South Bank, Belvedere Road, SE1 8XX (08703 800400/www.rfh.org.uk). **Open** *Box office* 9.30am-8pm daily. Royal Festival Hall closed till Jan 2007; Queen Elizabeth Hall, Purcell Room and Hayward Gallery remain open.

Other

British Airways London Eye

Jubilee Gardens, next to County Hall, SE1 7PB (0870 500 0600/www.ba-londoneye.com). **Open** *Oct-Apr* 9.30am-8pm. *May, June, Sept* 9.30am-9pm. *July, Aug* 9.30am-10pm. **Admission** £12.50; £10 concessions (Mon-Fri); £6.50 5-15s; free under-5s.

Greater London Authority

City Hall, The Queen's Walk, SE1 2AA (7983 4000/ www.london.gov.uk). **Open** *Second floor and below (incl café)* 8am-8pm Mon-Fri. *Ninth floor and Chamber* check website for details.

Southwark Cathedral

Montague Close, SE1 9DA (7367 6700/tours 7367 6734/www.dswark.org/cathedral). **Open** 8am-6pm daily (varies). *Audio guide* £2.50.

Shopping

Absolutely Starving

51 Tooley Street, SE1 2QN (7407 7417). **Open** 7am-10pm Mon-Fri; 9.30am-9pm Sat, Sun.

Vinopolis

1 Bank End, SE1 9BU (0870 241 4040/www. vinopolis.co.uk). **Open** 10am-9pm Mon, Fri, Sat; 10am-5.30pm Tue-Thur, Sun (last entry 2hrs before closing). **Admission** £12.50; £11.50 concessions; free under-16s.

Black sabbath

Darcus Howe

Ghanaian togas, Nigerian dashikis, Brockwell Park and a Peace Garden –
take your pick from the Brixton bazaar.

Start: Brixton tube/rail
Finish: St Matthew's Parish
Church
Distance: 3 miles/4.5km
Time: 1.5 hours
Getting there: Victoria line
or rail to Brixton
Getting back: short walk to
Brixton (Victoria line or rail)
Note: the walk describes a
Sunday morning in Brixton,
although it could be followed
any day of the week.

Brixton

In the still of a Sabbath's morning the
train trundles into Brixton on its long
run from north-east London. Time enough
to consider the Pope's encyclical pleading
with his flock to reclaim Sundays from
the rising tide of entrepreneurship. The
escalator lifts a handful of passengers
from the bowels of the underground
where the Effra River once irrigated
London's rural surrounds.

The call of the Azan drifts across
from the local mosque, the pentecostalist
couple with reluctant offspring in tow
hurry along to celebrate yet another
remembrance of the huge myth of the
resurrection. Face left and the chimes
of the local Big Ben draw the eye to the
Town Hall, the seat of local government,
which once boasted a black phalanx
of radical councillors who earned the
sobriquet 'the loony left'. This imposing
structure with its classical clock tower
was opened in 1908 with additions in 1938.

Stroll along in the direction of the town
hall and the anxious eye is puzzled by

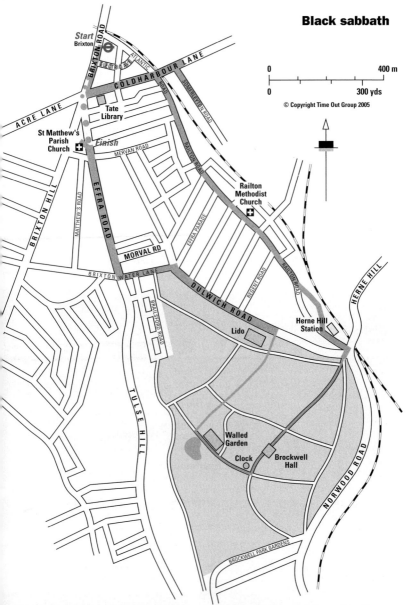

Black sabbath

Start
Brixton

Tate Library

St Matthew's Parish Church

Finish

ACRE LANE

BRIXTON ROAD

COLDHARBOUR LANE

ELECTRIC AVENUE

ATLANTIC ROAD

SOMERLEYTON ROAD

MERVAN ROAD

BRIXTON HILL

MATTHEWS ROAD

EFFRA ROAD

RAILTON ROAD

EFFRA PARADE

Railton Methodist Church

MORVAL RD

BRIXTON WATER LANE

DULWICH ROAD

REGENT ROAD

RAILTON ROAD

HERNE HILL

BRAILSFORD ROAD

TULSE HILL

Lido

Herne Hill Station

Walled Garden

Clock

Brockwell Hall

NORWOOD ROAD

BROCKWELL PARK GARDENS

0 — 400 m
0 — 300 yds

© Copyright Time Out Group 2005

deserted cobbled streets where the barrow boys chant their sales pitch on market day. Ignore the lure of emptiness and proceed to the traffic lights and straight over. Sitting easily on the corner is the Ritzy, the oldest cinema in south London and the second oldest in the capital. It

was purpose-built and welcomed its first buffs in 1911 as the Electric Pavilion. The initials EP are displayed on the corner wall. The billboards advertise the latest both in popular and haute cinema.

Just next to the Ritzy is another historical monument, the former Tate

Library (now Brixton Library). The Tate name recalls deep associations with the local black population, settled now after a mass migration from the Caribbean 50 years ago. The Caribbean is sugar and slavery and the Tate family were slave owners. Sir Henry Tate, the inventor of the sugar cube, also bequeathed the Tate Gallery to the nation. In 1892, only 50 years after the abolition of slavery in the Caribbean, he offered this library to the locals. You may rest awhile, peruse the Sunday newspaper in the comfort of the Tate Library Gardens, sheltered by an old plane tree and in the presence of a bust of Sir Henry. You are at the junction of Coldharbour Lane going east, Brixton Hill and the long haul to

Streatham due south, and west along Acre Lane to Clapham Common.

I recommend a short stroll along Coldharbour Lane, the heartbeat of Caribbean Brixton. Now there is no longer a trickle of churchgoers but a procession of finely attired Caribbean women dressed to the nines in Ascot couture with a host of children who have barely drifted from last night's sleep. Coldharbour Lane now assumes the image of a Caribbean Sunday where the Sabbath is obeyed *sans réservation*. The smells are from Saturday's market and the jollity of Saturday night's party. The shutters are drawn on almost every shopfront creating an air of desertion or perhaps solitude.

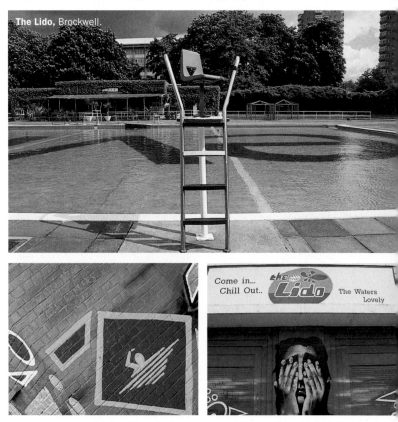

The Lido, Brockwell.

Come in... Chill Out.. *the* **Lido** The Waters Lovely

Walk past the Granville Arcade on your left. Turn around and look back at a bold and intriguing mural entitled *Nuclear Dawn*. Continue along Coldharbour Lane and witness an architectural hazard at the corner of Coldharbour Lane and Somerleyton Road. It has been named Southwyck House, and it is unarguably one of the ugliest buildings in human history. It houses, or rather imprisons, council tenants. It was designed, if we can call it that, in 1970, to shelter the Moorlands Housing Estate from the traffic noise of a proposed ring road. Local councillors then moved in mysterious ways their wonders to perform – the ring road plan was abandoned and Brixton is left with this eyesore.

Skip along Somerleyton Road for a while and absorb a warren of cottages in drab brown bricks. Stop for a moment or two, close your eyes and imagine some 50 years ago a hive of Caribbean music and immigrants infused with the spirit of Bacchus in an elegant line of Victorian terraced houses. Most black Brixtonians can trace their antecedents to someone who lived here in the last 50 years. However council plans and avaricious builders have together transformed this street into one of London's monstrosities.

Retrace your steps to the railway bridge, turn left and within 40 yards you are in Railton Road and the womb of recent history. You are in fact strolling along the pavement which was once notoriously named the 'Front Line', a boundary across which the local police and a community in revolt eyeballed each other through the late 1970s and into the early '80s. Skirmish after skirmish disturbed the peace until in mid April 1981 some clever senior police officer set in train 'Operation Swamp'. A band of plain clothes police officers swamped the area, searching every black male in sight. The author, who then lived on the street parallel to Railton Road, was searched on more than six occasions that week. The bubble burst and Brixton was transformed into a violent insurrection. The shopping centre was destroyed by firebombs. The burnin' and a lootin' immortalised years before in the lyrics of Bob Marley came alive in Brixton for 72 hours and then spread to almost every community throughout the United Kingdom. Almost as historical coincidence, Bob Marley Way is directly opposite the spot where the riots started.

Thereafter Brixton assumed its place in history as the leadership of the black community in the UK.

You ease forward out of history's troubled waters along Railton Road. Walk on the right-hand side and just before Harmony Bar, the local watering hole where a former mayor presided as the landlord, are the St George's residences built in 1878 and currently under restoration. Continue along Railton Road and old Brixton is celebrated in the names of the streets which cross Railton into Mayall on the left and Dulwich on the right. First Chaucer, then Spenser; Shakespeare and Milton follow.

Brixton has a fine past in literature and drama and housed players who brought a theatrical stamp to the neighbourhood. John Major's forebears played at the local circus. Between Chaucer and Shakespeare sits the Methodist church with its resident youth club, and Sheppards, which poet Linton Kwesi Johnson evoked in metaphor and simile in his poem *Five Nights of Bleedin'*. Here on Railton Road in the quiet of the Sabbath's morning, Chaucer's ghost breaks silence as he recites the *Complaint of Troilus*:

From thennesforth he rideth up and down,

And everything come him to remembrance,

As he rode forby places of the town
In which he whilom had all his pleasance.

and Spencer can barely hold his tongue:

For, all that moveth, doth in Change delight:

*But thence-forth all shall rest eternally
With Him that is the God of Sabbaoth
hight;
O that great Sabbaoth God, graunt me
that Sabbaoth's sight.*

The clouds break into a shower and
Shakespeare exclaims:

*Why didst thou promise such a
beauteous day
And make me travel forth without
my cloak,
To let base clouds o'ertake me in
my way,
Hiding thy bravery in their rotten
smoke?*

And just as one seeks shelter in the
doorway of 165 Railton Road, contemplate
the fact that CLR James (1901-89) once
lived here – although the plaque in his
honour is on Shakespeare Road. He was
perhaps the Plato of his generation:
a West Indian philosopher, novelist,
playwright and revolutionary associate of
Leon Trotsky who spent his last ten years
on earth in a tiny flat atop this building.

Past Poets' Corner and Railton Road
leads you to Herne Hill where the road
bends sharply to the right. On the left
you are confronted with a litter-strewn
footpath overhanging with thick
vegetation, which leads straight to Herne
Hill railway station. The station was
built in 1862 for the London, Chatham
and Dover Railway Company. It is
Venetian Gothic and has only recently
been restored.

The railway station sits close to
the junction. You cross over and are
welcomed to Brockwell Park, 124 acres
of undulating parkland in the middle
of south London. Perched at the top is
Brockwell Hall, built between 1811-13
for John Blades, a glass manufacturer
in the city. When one of his descendants
wished to sell the estate in 1891 the
London County Council acquired it. So
here we are early on a Sunday morning,

free of the patter of joggers' feet and of the
canine species dropping their waste and
fouling this green and pleasant space.

A soft wind blows across the parkland
as you follow the path up the slope to the
Georgian House now being restored after
a fire. On the approach to the house you
turn to savour the view of Brixton and
Herne Hill, and at the top admire Canary
Wharf straight ahead, and the Houses of
Parliament and Battersea Power Station
to the left. Cedars abound – a young blue
Atlas on the left, a Deodan in the centre
and a Lebanon on your right. At the back,
past two English oaks, is the old stable
block topped by a weather vane. The
path approaches a turret clock presented
in 1897 by Sir Ernest Tritton, MP for
Norwood, not unlike the clock at the
Victoria end of Vauxhall.

Continue left of the clock towards a
white shelter, behind which is a small
chamber with pointed windows. This
was once the private chapel where the
Bladeses worshipped. Just left of the
shelter is an iron gate leading into the
old, walled, beautifully tended garden.

Tour the garden, carefully taking
note of the range of rosebuds and the

Brockwell Park

sunflowers tossing in the morning breeze. Poppies with thin stalks dance in conversation. Then pause a while on one of the benches where nature-lovers stamped their dedication to loved ones who have passed away into the night.

There was once an aviary close by here that charmed with a variety of clucking fowl, but it is now gone after persistent protest from bird-lovers. In the adjoining pond are Canada geese, tufted duck, moorhen and coot. Two more ponds nearby support a variety of wild life fussing at each other in the morning sunlight. A small stream babbles along, a tributary of the Effra River, which flows beneath Brixton to discharge in the Thames near Vauxhall. Weeping willows hug the stream and a Judas tree is prominent.

The way back to Dulwich Road offers an Olympic-sized open-air swimming pool, the Brockwell Lido, where you may join any number of local dignitaries who share this marvellous facility.

Turn left into Dulwich Road and walk up to Brixton Water Lane. All the houses along here form a small conservation group. They were built in the 1830s to house staff from Brockwell Park. Water Lane is so named because the whole area from Herne Hill and along Dulwich Road formed gravelled beds of small rivers that were often used as cart tracks.

At the top of Water Lane turn right at Effra Road on your way back to central Brixton. Perhaps one of the most dramatic encounters on the walk is St Matthew's Church on your left, now transformed into the Brixton Village and shorn of almost all religious icons. Once the pillar of Anglicanism, it was converted into a multi-purpose centre as a result of its declining congregation. It was consecrated in 1824 as St Matthew's Church and in the following year a new Parish District of St Matthew's was created. CP Porden was the architect who broke with the classical Greek portico and bell tower and steeple. Porden places the tower at the eastern end – Effra Road – and the portico to the west. The building now houses two churches, the original St Matthew's and its established Anglicanism sitting uneasily alongside the happy clappy New Testament Assembly. Here the Sabbath is celebrated in shifts, an ecumenical mystery.

It's the end of the walk and you may rest your tired feet in the peace garden, a former burial ground, that adjoins the church. It is rather spacious and accommodates a curious stone monument erected by Henry Budd in 1825 (his father Richard was buried here). A local writer expressed the enthusiastic view that the memorial was 'without doubt the finest sepulchral monument in the open air in the metropolis, and perhaps not equalled by any one in the kingdom'.

Poor Richard Budd would perhaps turn in his grave at the knowledge that the church which sent him off to St Peter's gate now houses a theatre, offices and restaurant, with the presence of the sacrament as a bare reminder of a glorious past.

Now transport yourself in time to a Friday, market day. You emerge from the underground to be greeted by revivalists both ancient and modern. A seemingly demented African lady inveighs against the demon drink and a white Malcolm X chants the scriptures summoning the sinners to repent. To the left outside the station and a small group of Muslims accost passers-by with the virtues of the Koran. The empty cobbled streets of Electric Avenue are now filled with the chants of barrow boys offering fruit and vegetables imported from tropical isles and the farms of Kent. Further down, a cluster of shops, the Kashmiri yam boys cater for both meat-eaters and veggies. Huge slabs of muscle and flesh in the halal tradition whet the appetites of some and churn the stomachs of others. This is the Brixton Market so much like Thackeray's *Vanity Fair*.

There is a great quantity of pushing and shoving along narrow passages. Stallholders shouting in dialects and languages, at the last count more than 100 in number – finest Coxes, spotty bananas, Arab jellabas, Ghanaian togas and Nigerian dashikis; arts and crafts from every continent, the sounds and smells of different nationalities. Rastas and Ethiopians, women in yashmaks, all with something to sell in a spiel that would hardly be recognisable to the original inhabitants of late 19th-century Brixton.

Brixton offers a walk through time, through the changing scenes of life in trouble and in joy.

Ritzy Cinema

Eating & drinking

Brockwell Café
Brockwell Hall, Brockwell Park, SE24 9BJ (8671 5217). **Open** *Mar-Oct* 9am-6.30pm daily. *Nov-Feb* 9am-dusk daily.

Bug Bar
The Crypt, St Matthew's Church, Brixton Hill, SW2 1JF (7738 3366/www.bugbrixton.co.uk). **Open** 6pm-3am Mon-Thur, Sun; 6pm-6am Fri, Sat.

Dogstar Bar
389 Coldharbour Lane, SW9 8LQ (7733 7515/ www.thedogstar.com). **Open** noon-2am Mon-Thur, Sun; noon-4am Fri, Sat. **Food served** 6pm-midnight Tue-Sat; noon-7pm Sun. **Admission** £3 10-11pm, £5 after 11pm Fri, Sat. A Brixton institution that's loud and boisterous, particularly at weekends.

Satay Bar
447-450 Coldharbour Lane, SW9 8LT (7326 5001/ www.sataybar.com). **Open** noon-11pm Mon-Thur, Sun; noon-2am Fri; noon-3am Sat. **Food served** noon-5pm, 6-11pm daily. The Indonesian food is still a winner here, even if its popularity as a nightspot might be waning.

Churches

Railton Methodist Church
141 Railton Road, Herne Hill, SE24 0LT (7274 4823). **Open** *Services* 11am Sun.

St Matthew's Church
Brixton Hill, SW2 1ND (7733 9605). **Open** *Services* 10am Sun.

Other

Brockwell Park
Brockwell Park Gardens, SE24 (7926 6200/ www.lambeth.gov.uk). **Open** 7.30am-dusk daily.

The Lido
Brockwell Park, Dulwich Road, SE24 0PA (7740 7500/www.fusion-lifestyle.com). Now under new management, but the lido should be open by summer 2005 (and every subsequent summer). See website for details and prices.

Ritzy Cinema
Brixton Oval, Coldharbour Lane, SW2 1JG (7733 2229/www.picturehouses.co.uk). **Open** *Telephone bookings* 9.30am-8.30pm daily.

Tate Library Brixton
Brixton Oval, SW2 1JQ (7926 1056/www.lambeth. gov.uk). **Open** 1-8pm Mon; 10am-8pm Tue, Thur; 10am-6pm Wed, Fri; 9am-5pm Sat; noon-5pm Sun.

Shopping

Brixton Market
Electric Avenue, Pope's Road, Brixton Station Road, Atlantic Road, SW9. **Open** 8am-6pm Mon, Tue, Thur-Sat; 8am-3pm Wed.

Chainy walk

Rick Jones

Follow in the footsteps of Chaucer's pilgrims, Dick Turpin's fellow highwaymen and legions of marching trees.

Start: Erith rail
Finish: Falconwood rail
Distance: 6.5 miles/11km
Time: 3.5 hours
Getting there: Train from London Bridge station

Getting back: Train from Falconwood station
Note: Long stretches without refreshment opportunities. Much of this is a Green Chain walk. Muddy paths, so wear boots.

This walk may begin and end with train journeys from and to London Bridge station. It covers ancient tracts of common land in south-east London that have never been touched by either lord or developer. It plots a course through wild, unruly nature lying between the jaws of the enclosing city. It visits a ruined abbey and a bluebell wood. It is used by lovers, ramblers and dogs exercising their owners. As an

official Green Chain walk, it is staked out by regular green or yellow arrows and mileage posts. It is considered a complete waste of time by anyone under 15.

The walk proceeds westwards from Erith, to which ancient suburb we take a train from London Bridge. The north side of the carriage affords a view of Canary Wharf and the Millennium Dome swelling like a pustule on the marshland north-east

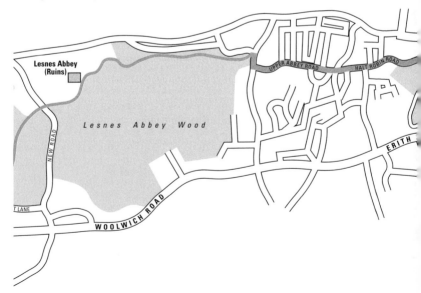

of Greenwich.

Erith had a reputation in the days of sail. Victorians took the waters here and pleasure boats moored at the pier. The river was busy day and night with ocean-going cargo vessels, tea clippers and coal smacks, arriving at and departing from the world's greatest port. In 1874, 700 people drowned in a collision off Erith. Nowadays, everyone comes to London by plane and the Thames is quiet.

Having disembarked, we leave Erith station and walk under the bridge, turn left along Stonewood Road through a new housing estate and cross West Street. We mount the bank on the other side by the public footpath and take in a view of the placid estuary bereft of boats. The north bank is even bleaker, being nothing more than uninhabited Rainham Marshes. We turn left and continue north along the fenced-in riverside footpath towards cranes and industrial plumes of smoke. The skeleton of a pier stretches out into the mud. Seagulls perch on half-submerged supermarket trolleys.

We come to the first of the Green Chain signs and follow this away from the river

towards Corinthian Manorway lower walkway, keeping an eye out for the church spire to which we are heading. We turn left between some flats and a car park and come to the small, wooden-spired church of St John the Baptist with its lychgate entrance, ancient graveyard, 800-year-old yew tree and day-glo Jesus Saves posters on the notice board. The church is locked except for services. Local beneficent Victorian industrialists are commemorated within. Past the church to the left the route leads through Jessett Close over an iron footbridge across the roaring A2016, which takes the traffic to and from London that the river once took.

Turn left along Pembroke Road and take the first right, following bungalow-bordered Valley Road up to the top tree. We arrive at the entrance into Frank's Park, observing the council's No Metal Detecting directive now obliterated by smut. We enter ancient woodland for the first time. Wood pigeons coo. Unseen wildlife rustles the undergrowth. Other tracks diverge but we must keep to the straightest and best-trodden track (marked always by Green Chain arrows)

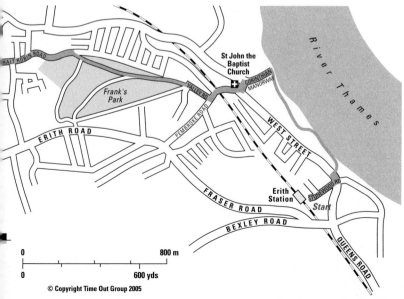

0 — 800 m

0 — 600 yds

© Copyright Time Out Group 2005

until we come to a broad, open space featuring a children's playpark which has been fenced in to protect Erith's young from wild dogs and perverts. In the middle, a milepost indicates a right turn, which we duly follow.

We re-enter the woods along a muddy path. To our left, nature; plunging away to our right, the industrial city. A distant police siren down among the strange-shaped factories mingles with nearby birdsong which imitates it. At the end of the park the footpath grows into a tarmacked track (Halt Robin Road), as footpaths always do – even the A1 was a dirt track once. The tarmacked track soon acquires pavements.

BOSTALL

B o
W

WICKHAM LANE

Woolwich
Cemetery

DRYDEN ROAD

GLENMORE ROAD

East Wickham
Open Space

SHOOTERS HILL

BELLGROVE ROAD

Oxleas
Wood

WELLING WAY

ROCHESTER WAY

Falconwood
Station

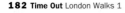
Finish

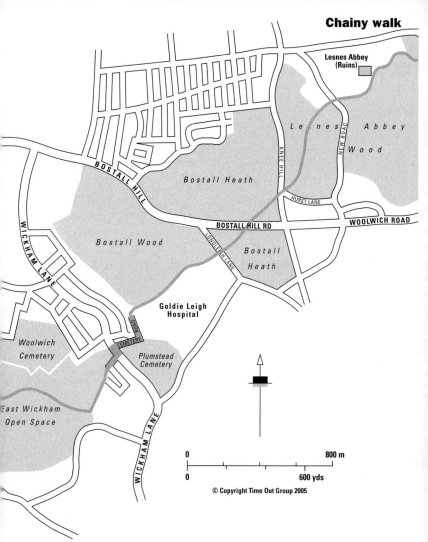

Lesnes Abbey (Ruins)

L e s n e s   A b b e y   W o o d

Bostall Heath

BOSTALL HILL

KNEE HILL

NEW ROAD

HURST LANE

BOSTALL HILL RD

WOOLWICH ROAD

WICKHAM LANE

Bostall Wood

TONGUE IN LANE

Bostall Heath

Goldie Leigh Hospital

CEMETERY ROAD

Woolwich Cemetery

Plumstead Cemetery

East Wickham Open Space

WICKHAM LANE

| 0 | | 800 m |
| 0 | | 600 yds |

© Copyright Time Out Group 2005

At the end of Halt Robin Road, we cross steep, wide Picardy Road (B250) and continue west along Upper Abbey Road. The end of this road is marked by a convenience store and a pub, the Leather Bottle.

The Abbey in question is ruined Lesnes Abbey which lies on the outskirts of Lesnes Abbey Woods and towards which we now head. We enter the woods by skirting the pub car park to the right and heading along a mud track behind the backs of garages towards an acre of allotments, quickly turning left along a path where a metal bar prevents vehicles from further progress. Guided ever by green arrows, we take the path around the northern periphery of the forest that remains within sound, if not sight, of the bordering houses. A van door slams and a nail is hammered in somewhere out of sight.

Lesnes Abbey Woods is crossed by a network of broad and narrow, unmarked footpaths whose course and destination are known only to locals. We pass beech trees with National Front symbols and bull terrier teeth marks carved and scratched into the bark.

The green arrow marker posts lead uphill away from the back gardens into the greater solitude of the trees where municipal authorities display their almost oppressive concern for nature with log-bordered paths and litter bins with roofs. But we leave the Chain walk here and continue hugging the northern edge of the wood. We bear left to come to a place where several paths meet, then turn right and rejoin the Chain walk opposite the stepped path. On our left we find the first fenced-off wild flower bed. A patchwork of them stretches deep into the forest. In spring the beds are thick with short, wild daffodils of the sort the poet Wordsworth would have known, rather than the tall, overgrown, horticultural, market garden variety boosted by nitrates and growth hormones and bought at petrol stations. Lesnes Abbey daffs are more nosegay material, although anyone who dares pick them is liable to the most stringent penalties. A month later, bluebells replace the wild narcissi with even more profusion. The beds are a quilt of blue throughout April. We follow up and over the hill, left at the bottom and then right. At the signpost (Bostall Woods 1, Oxleas Woods 3½) we turn right into Lesnes Abbey.

The flattened Abbey lies on a mown open space overlooking council estates, distant factories and the River Thames glinting between the high-rises. Canary Wharf stabs the horizon. Tower Bridge is a tiny 'H' in the north-west. Planes like gnats make circles in the sky above City Airport.

Lesnes Abbey was built in 1178 by one Richard de Luci, Chief Justiciar of England, as a penance for the prominent part he played in the murder of the turbulent Archbishop of Canterbury, Thomas à Becket. Canterbury-bound pilgrims passed this way. Chaucer might have stopped here for some bawdy board and lodging. In those days, the Abbey was a haven far removed from the city which now laps at its door. Societies fortified within cities aim to keep unruly, irreverent and unpredictable passions in check, so confined metropolitans make for the country to spoon and indulge their fancies. An environment of daffodils is more conducive to romance than cold grey concrete and lovers record their visits on trees and rocks.

The shape of the Abbey buildings is mapped out in stone. Kevin and Emma have chalked their names in the chapter house. Some of the walls rise to 12 feet; most are no more than a doorstep. The ground within is mown grass dotted with daisies. The chapel has patches of floor tiles and stumps of columns. The altar is raised slightly and marked by a small plaque which records that de Luci's daughter, who loved the place, is buried nearby. A hole in the wall in the refectory is said to be the serving hatch. The monks' dorms are horribly narrow. The cloister is a pleasant and contemplative square, as well tended as a bowling green. In the grilled and gated dungeon, a discarded Valentine's rose, not even taken out of its polythene sheath, lies among the Coke tins and crisp packets.

We retrace our steps through the Abbey's well-tended formal gardens and back into the woods whence we came. We follow the Green Chain arrows passing the signpost to Crystal Palace Park, across New Road and then crunch through stony paths past bluebell beds until we come to the first of two artificial ponds. The lower one on our right is weedy and barely visible. The left one is deeper and surrounded by a barrier.

Further on, emerging at Hurst Lane, we follow the signs, turn right and continue for a short way until its junction with Knee Hill, a pavement-less main road to be crossed between thundering country buses. On the other side, Green Chain arrows point two-ways – take the path to your left and go through Cooperative

Lesnes Abbey Wood

Plumstead Cemetery

Woods leading to Bostall Heath. The track passes the secluded Belvedere Private Clinic which has expensive cars in the drive and surveillance cameras on the gateposts.

The woods open onto Bostall Hill Road; we turn right and aim for the small car park on the other side of the cricket green. Here a hot dog stall offers refreshments and chatting opportunities.

Fortified, we cross Longleigh Lane directly in front of the car park and bear left following the signs downhill keeping the Goldie Leigh Hospital to our left and Bostall Woods to our right. At the bottom, a short diversion to the right affords a look at Turpin's Cave, but it is a disappointingly small hole and one doubts the famous highwayman spent much time there. He was in part responsible for the name Shooters Hill, which we are now approaching.

Turning left, the route leads us onto Cemetery Road, alongside Plumstead Cemetery which is terraced and formal and bounded by walls topped with iron railings. The noise of a mechanical grab excavating the graves breaks the silence. Even gravediggers modernise. Emerging at wide Wickham Lane we turn left and then right into Highbanks Close, which leads uphill to the raised plateau of East Wickham Open Space.

This ancient, untouched land is a thoroughfare for locals whose homes lie the other side of a margin of allotments around the perimeter. After 200 yards we cut towards a second graveyard – Woolwich Cemetery – and continue with this on our right. Bearing left and down we head towards a park exit, passing some allotments on our right as we descend.

The Green Chain arrows now attach themselves to lamp-posts through a council estate built during the socialist housing boom of the 1950s when post-war idealists sought to educate the masses by christening the roads after Shelley, Wordsworth, Tennyson, Milton and others. The walk follows Dryden to its junction with Keats where we diverge and continue until the houses up to our left end, and past concrete bollards into what looks as if it were once a wheat field. There was a farm here until the 1980s.

The path follows the edge of the field and halfway along passes through a gate into more open land. It follows beside a barrier of blackberry bushes and a muddy stream which the walker eventually crosses, either on foot in dry weather or via a low wooden platform if there has been rain. Further on, we come out at the main road (A207), the aforementioned Shooters Hill, fizzing with traffic, which we cross when we can and walk westwards (to the right) until we come to the entrance to Oxleas Wood. Here a gallows once stood ready to effect immediate summary justice on highwaymen like Dick Turpin, if not Dick Turpin himself.

Oxleas Wood is all that is left of a huge and ancient forest dating back to the last Ice Age 12 millennia ago. As the ice receded, so trees from mainland Europe made their way north in its wake, marching like armies, seedling after seedling. Trees are only life forms which have not learnt how to uproot themselves and walk about. Why bother when you can get bees, dogs and even the wind to do your seed dispersal for you? Man only

moves around to mate and to go to work, and he only does the latter in order to finance the former.

The forest canopy is high, the undergrowth thick, the birdsong thrilling and the paths fairly clearly marked by the Green Chain markers. Middle-aged women forbid unleashed dogs to run too far. Young girls on ponies leave horseshoe tracks along the bridleway. At a cross-road, where many paths meet like spokes at a wheel-hub stands the tallest, most majestic and informative Green Chain signpost yet, directing hikers on to many destinations in south-east London.

Follow the sign headed 'Eltham Park North' towards Falconwood railway station only 12 minutes away. We continue to the end of the avenue and then follow the Green Chain sign to the left until we arrive at the junction of Welling and Rochester Ways. A left down Rochester Way takes us to Falconwood station.

Eating & drinking

Ye Olde Leather Bottle
Heron Hill, Belvedere, Kent DA17 5HJ (01322 432066). **Open** 11am-11pm Mon-Sat; noon-10.30pm Sun. Food served.

Churches & cemeteries

Lesnes Abbey
Abbey Road, Belvedere, Kent (Bexley Council 8303 7777/www.bexley.gov.uk/service/parks/lesnesabbey.html). **Open** 24hrs daily.

Plumstead Cemetery
Wickham Lane, SE2 0NS (8856 0100). **Open** *Apr-Sept* 9am-7pm daily. *Oct-Mar* 9am-4pm daily. **Admission** free.

St John the Baptist Church
West Street, Erith, Kent DA8 (01322 332555). **Open** 10am-noon Sun.

Woolwich Cemetery
Camdale Road, SE18 2DS (8856 0100). **Open** *Apr-Sept* 9am-7pm daily. *Oct-Mar* 9am-4pm daily. **Admission** free.

Information

South East London Green Chain
Information Line 8921 5028.

Common people

Yvonne Roberts

South London commons of Clapham and Wandsworth – a class act of Us and Them.

Start: Clapham South tube
Finish: Clapham Common tube
Distance: 5 miles/8km
Time: 3.5 hours
Getting there: Northern line
to Clapham South
Getting back: Northern line
from Clapham Common
Note: good for children, except
for the long walk between the
commons. Go on Saturday to
catch Northcote Road at its best.

Parks are posh – manicured, orderly, under control – commons aren't. Or, rather, they shouldn't be. A common is literally land for the free use of the people, doing things that people like to do – football, cycling, fishing, walking, playing chess, tanning, dancing, dossing, reading, demonstrating. No self-respecting common has time or space for floral beds as horticultural haute couture or signs that begin, 'Do not…'. A common, in short, is a park on the wild side, proud of its history of rowdy rough trade. It's a place for all sorts, from the metaphorical man on the Clapham omnibus, a timeless Dick Decent, to representatives of the rabble with no particular place to go.

That was and remains Clapham Common, described a mite snobbishly in the 1950s by the writer EM Forster as 'full of… facilities and infelicities…' and here is the conundrum through which this walk will wander.

Minutes away from Clapham Common, laced to it by row upon row of suburban semis, lies Wandsworth Common. This rectangular clump, divided by a railway track and road, has been conquered and

colonised by the kind of person who, upper-middle class for several generations, or aspiring to be, slips out of the womb and straight into a sleeveless parka, pearls, Alice band and future betrothal to a banker called Jeremy.

In short, Wandsworth Common, unlike Clapham, gives the impression that it is not so much for all sorts as Our Sort. Wandsworth is a well-tended garden for the mainly white and wealthy. Of course, sporadic pockets of resistance remain – the cricket field, the bowling green and tennis courts in summer; the pond during the fishing season; the adventure playground at the northernmost tip near Chivalry Road; and the area occupied, once the sun comes out, by drinkers from the pubs and wine bars on Bellevue Road. But overall, Wandsworth Common gives the appearance of being a one-class act.

What emerges on our walk is that in the past and in the present, for demographic and topographic reasons, Clapham Common has been for the underdog and Wandsworth for the more aspiring pooch. Or, to put it more simply, we're following in the footsteps of Us – and Them.

Before we move forward, we should first step back in time. Clapphem is Old English for village or enclosure on a hill. In the 17th century, the site of Wandsworth Common was rural countryside in which wheat and barley grew, around Bolingbroke Farm, while Clapham was 'a wild and marshy tract'. Local people used it for fuel, water and grazing (even at the beginning of the 20th century, sheep still chomped around the bandstand), and, on windy days, to dry their smalls. In literature Clapham was viewed as pious in the extreme. William

Clapham Common

Holy Trinity, Clapham Common

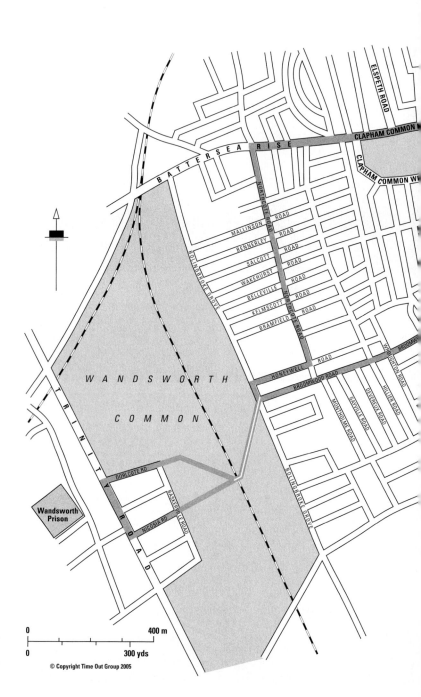

Thackeray wrote of Clapham in *The Newcomers*, 'It was a serious paradise. As you entered… gravity fell on you; and decorum wrapped you in a garment of starch.' In the 1940s, Noel Coward, briefly a Clapham resident, wasn't much kinder to the then suburban middle classes in his play, *This Happy Breed*, set at 17 Sycamore Road, Wimbledon.

During the Civil War, Clapham Commoners, the have-nots, banking on reward if not now then in the future, were for Cromwell; Wandsworth remained Royalist. Puritanism, however, didn't

Northcote Road

from one end of Rookery Road to the other. 'As time went on, the crowd became larger, the riders more numerous and frolicsome,' he recorded. 'These meetings had to be abolished; and in 1873 they were officially put an end to, and further action taken for regulation of the control of the Common.'

Conflict still exists between those who wish to make the most of Clapham Common and those who like to regulate. Every spring, the area used to see an outbreak of opposition to the Gay Pride festival, which occurred on one day in the summer until the cancellation of 1998's event. Those who argued weakly, 'Some of my best friends are gay… but look at the litter/leather/ loucheness,' should bury their heads in shame. What's a common for if it isn't to be used? And come to that, why can't we see a revival of the best days of the Common, which came after the London County Council took responsibility in the 1890s?

At that point, London's population had doubled in 40 years. Lambeth, of which Clapham Common is a part, soaked up labourers via the waterworks, gasworks and factories. Wandsworth, home of the Huguenots, offered employment for the skilled: silk-dyeing, millinery, beer-brewing. Employment meant a little more money in hand while the advent of public transport (Clapham Junction and its myriad trains opened in the 1860s, electrified trams and tube trains came to Clapham Common in the 1900s) encouraged the London County Council to turn the Common into a pleasure dome for the people. On offer was open-air ballet, gymkhanas, boxing, theatre in a tent, festivals, story-telling and concerts on the bandstand – much of it free. In 1946, the Common hosted the people's Victory party. Now, apart from the occasional conclusion to a march or the annual Lambeth Show, the opportunity to be 'frolicsome' en masse is sadly a much more limited affair.

Begin at Clapham South tube station, opened in 1924. Take a look up, remove

remain Clapham Common's style for long. The highwayman Robert Forrestor, 'a notorious sinner', delighted in patrolling the Common dressed in ladies' nighties holding up those who had something to give, while the whores released from Wandsworth Prison resumed business not on the Common on their doorstep, but on Clapham 'among the furze'.

Clapham Common has always enjoyed a creative tension between the wealthy – who live on its fringes and who, in the 18th century, made attempts to annex hunks of the Common as their private domain – and the proles. The upper crust preferred a nicer sort of neighbour; the plebs were determined to use and abuse their communal grounds as they chose. In Victorian times, for instance, a solitary keeper was hired at 23 shillings a week to prevent 'gross outrage to females committed in broad daylight'.

Again, on Rookery Road, in the early 1800s, wooden slums accumulated, and donkeys and horses were tethered for hire. Thomas Parsons, born in 1838, describes how these pony rides were 'wild scurries'

Westbury Court, the now grim tiers of flats that were added in the 1930s, and imagine the clean, clear lines of the new tube station, when it first went into business – it brought the plebs, working six days a week, with no holidays and living in overcrowded housing, to 'their' open space, their bit of backyard. Turn left, and follow the line of Clapham Common along South Side, once Stane Street, an old Roman road. The boarded-up South London Hospital is on the right, its overgrown grounds home to a family of foxes that will soon be evicted by a new supermarket on the site.

Pass Eagle Pond, the first of Clapham Common's four ponds, most of which were created in the 19th century, when gravel was dug for local road making. In the 1980s, when Clapham Common looked in danger of going to seed, the ducks often wore plastic handcuffs made from the discarded rings round beer cans. Now it's clean and relatively rubbish free.

Next is the depressing Windmill pub – an inn since the 17th century – on the site of one of two windmills that used to operate on the Common. It's large and cavernous and packed in summer. Walk on, but stop at the point where South Side meets Rookery Road and turn to take a good look at the Common.

What you see today is cycle tracks, trees, a bandstand and café with decor, strong on 1950s lino and formica, that once had a strong whiff of Bulgarian bus depot cafeteria about it, but has now been modernised. Outside the café, chess and draughts are played. In the distance, to the café's right, the chimneys of Battersea Power Station poke above the rim of grand houses now rapidly being transformed into small private schools with grandiose names.

In front of you, as you stand on Rookery Road, is Long Pond, the longest-serving model boat pond in London. It was once enclosed for his private use by the Lord of the Manor and only opened up to the public in the 1870s (when local people also tried unsuccessfully to take over the Common and run it themselves). The Lord of the Manor, a Colonel Bowyer, instead relinquished the lease of the Common for £8,000 to the Metropolitan Board of Works.

Model Yacht HQ (more accurately a graffiti-covered concrete bunker) is a lock-up next to the pond where some 'boaters' keep their craft, but since it also offers a bench under shelter, it's also a favourite berth for the dedicated all-weather drinker. Next door, close to the basketball courts, is another café – with a sign for 'refreshments' – one that likes children, cooks well and is decorated in casbah-hippy style, so baby-boomers who live off the Common in heavily mortgaged homes can console themselves that the 1960s are alive and well – at least for the time it takes to eat a cheap Sunday brunch.

If you face the Long Pond, your back to South Side, in the distance to the left, disguised by clumps of greenery, is the council dump. A children's playground and skate park is also visible – Disney-bright, advanced gear with a constant traffic jam of children in the holidays. And, of course, dog shit lies everywhere.

On Wandsworth Common, if you are out walking the dog and wish to avoid ostracism, a passport carried visibly is essential: a plastic bag. Clapham, in contrast, is divided into those dog owners who literally couldn't give a shit and the greenies who, as their Labradors and Alsatians evacuate their bowels, will argue at length that excreta is part of life's grand recycling theme. So, on the occasion that you tread on a turd, as you surely will on this walk, try to see it not as the blight of urban life but nature's picnic for the birds. It's hard, I know.

Walk (gingerly) past the netball courts on Rookery Road, cross Long Road and we move into a segment of the Common in which the Clapham Sect congregated to work on the souls of the less fortunate. The Sect was a group of friends, rich, religious do-gooders, led by William Wilberforce, MP first for Hull and then for nearby Southwark, who fought against slavery for two decades. Holy Trinity Church was their place of prayer. Built in 1746, it's simple but moving in its austerity. John Venn was its rector for 20 years – his name is now given to a street close by. His ally, Zachary Macaulay, editor of the *Christian Observer*, who owned a home on the Pavement, two minutes from the church, had observed the effects of slavery in Sierra Leone. (He also has a street named after him, across the road from the church, on North Side.) While at No.8 Rectory Grove, off Clapham Common Old Town, Macaulay set up an 'African Academy', home to 25 black children brought from Jamaica (most of whom died from the cold).

Zachary's son, Tom, born in 1800, wrote *The History of England* in five volumes. His biographer and nephew, Sir George Trevelyan, describes how the young Tom played on Clapham Common, 'a region of inexhaustible romance and mystery'.

Next to the church is Cock Pond, bombed in the war, now a paddling pool in summer used by every colour, class and creed. Walk almost the length of North Side, past Trinity Hospice, once called the Hostel of God, and past the football pitches where once, perhaps, Clapham Rovers trained – the team that won the FA Cup in 1880. Turn left on the Common before it hits the Avenue and walk through an archway of trees. Take a right on the zebra crossing and arrive at Clapham Common West Side. Here, on what is now Canford Road, the Thornton family, bankers, philanthropists and founders of the Clapham Sect, lived in a massive house with 34 bedrooms, and a library designed by William Pitt. Here too, somewhere in a private garden, is a tulip tree that Mariane Thornton (EM Forster's great aunt, who left him £8,000, sufficient to finance his life as a writer) feared that Napoleon would cut down if he invaded.

On West Side, cross back into the main body of Clapham Common and take a right through Battersea Woods. 'Woods' gives the area ideas above its station. This battered clump of trees lost its pulse for some Commoners once the gents' loo nearby was closed several years ago. For others, it remains their favourite copse for cottaging. In summer, in G-strings, men sunbathe and wait. In winter, they just wait, a set of human statues.

Next to the woods are yet more football pitches that, on a Sunday, resemble a glorious outpost of Latin American family life. Spanish-speaking teams play against each other while food is prepared, children play, women gossip, salsa booms and beer is drunk. Here, too, are the so-called Alps – more like giant molehills – which partially hide Mount Pond. In Edwardian times, naked boys were allowed to swim in the pond. Now, it's left to the occasional dog that plunges in and emerges smelling of cesspits and last night's hamburgers.

Close by, before Windmill Drive separates the Common in two, is the site on which fairgrounds, circuses, evangelists, salesmen and film crews park themselves. Also here, but now without a voice, is Clapham's own Speakers' Corner.

Somewhere in this area, on 6 September 1852, an entertainer named Madame Porteri allegedly went up in an air balloon and parachuted down again – on the back of a horse. Clapham Common's joy is that you never know who might drop in.

Although the circle of Clapham Common is not quite complete, it's time to veer off right and descend the gentle slopes into 'Nappy Valley' via Broomwood Road. 'Nappy Valley' is an area between the Commons in which, according to myth or more probably local estate agents, exists the highest concentration of aspiring couples with young children in England (or Western Europe, depending on how determined the estate agent is to make the sale). Part of the attraction is a couple of excellent state primary schools – Honeywell and Belleville – part is the mushrooming of the fee-paying sector, establishments that teach their children to curtsy and whose rules frown on females in trousers.

Broomwood Road, like almost all those between the Commons, is a street in which most of the houses are heavily accessorised – sparkling stained-glass doors, impeccable tiling, façades like frosting on a wedding cake. The streets dip down and up again, curving gently like a boomerang, all leading to Bolingbroke Grove, which marks the eastern perimeter of Wandsworth Common.

Halfway down, cross Wroughton Road and look at the side of 111 Broomwood Road. Here is a small plaque telling you that on this site William Wilberforce lived for ten years until 1807, when, aged 50, he finally succeeded in banning the slave trade. 'Well, Henry,' Wilberforce asked his friend Henry Thornton with whom he lived when he first came to Clapham in his late 20s, 'what shall we abolish next?'

At the top of Broomwood Road, cross on to Wandsworth Common, walk over the railway bridge, and enter a different and, to me, blander, land. To the right are tennis courts, bowling green, a nature centre and co-ordinated flowerbeds. To the left is the pond, swans and cygnets patrolling, the children's playground and, a few minutes' walk away, Bellevue Road, a handful of shops that deal mostly in the pleasures of life – clothes, booze, books, knick-knacks and food. Here, too, is Wandsworth Common railway station, where on an average day commuters leave their Bentleys and Porsches, as well as more mundane motors.

On Wandsworth Common, your back to the railway bridge, pond to the left, walk straight ahead. Still on the Common, you are walking towards an enclave of five parallel streets, known as the 'toast rack', topped by Trinity Road (where, at No.179, David Lloyd George lived when he first came to London) and tailed by Baskerville Road. The gardens of the Baskerville Road houses back on to the Common. Most have pools, conservatories, follies and extensions; a mini-Hampstead in the south.

At the end, you'll come to a small alleyway that leads to Nicosia Road. Follow through it. Local tribal insignias are people-carriers, private school uniforms, curtains ruched like a cancan dancer's skirt and rural chintz glimpsed through front windows with rarely a hint of minimalism. The eclectic mix of housing that marks out Clapham Common – flats, bedsits, housing estates, DSS and posher hotels, large and small family homes – is absent. This is mostly mansion territory.

At the top of Nicosia Road, take a right on Trinity Road. At the corner of Trinity Road and Dorlcote Road, opposite the County Arms, stop and look to right and left. On the right is Wandsworth Prison, home to almost 1400 men, mostly on remand. It is large and looming, a Victorian monstrosity. Opened in 1851, as the Surrey House of Correction, its architecture failed to impress even at the time: 'as uncommanding as a Methodist College,' wrote one critic. It had five wings for men and three for women. Oscar Wilde spent six months there in 1895; Ronnie Biggs did a bunk in 1965.

Nicosia Road

Wandsworth Common

Wandsworth Prison

Shortly after the prison opened, a commentator wrote of the growing number of its inmates, 'This lamentable state of affairs appears to have risen from the indifference shown by parents as to the manner in which their children's lives are spent.' Plus ça change.

If you turn right down Dorlcote Road, returning to the Common, on your left are a squadron of ugly high-rise flats, privately owned, and the graceful spires of a Gothic building opened in 1857 as the Royal Victoria and Patriotic Asylum. Now it houses a drama school, restaurant, wine bar and luxury apartments in which apprentice celebs and pop stars occasionally live. It seems ironic that residents of Wandsworth Common, the majority of whom have the money presumably to choose any site in London, have opted for an area with two such strong reminders of the nastier side of traditional working-class life – the madhouse and the clink.

On the Common, retrace your steps over the railway bridge to Broomwood Road. When you meet Bolingbroke again, take a left, then go right down Honeywell Road. When it meets Northcote Road, turn left.

This part of the walk is best done on a Saturday, when Northcote Road teems. Head towards Battersea Rise and prepare to spend. Wine bars, delis, bakeries, organic butchers, a café called Boiled Egg & Soldiers (offering food that nanny used to make, also available in transport caffs), jewellery, charity shops, toys, books and wonderful antiques. And, of course, the street market. It almost died a few years ago, but seems revived again – fruit, veg, plants, eggs. Boom or bust, broke or flush, young or old, single or otherwise, Northcote Road caters majestically to the needs of residents of both the Commons.

At the northern end of Northcote Road, at Battersea Rise, take a right, straight up the hill, and keep on going. Follow Clapham Common round again on the North Side and keep walking until the Clock Tower, unveiled in 1906, comes into view above Clapham Common tube. Along Clapham High Street there are a dozen or more pubs, cafés and wine bars. So, if you're so inclined, raise a glass to Us and Them; distinctly common kind of people.

Eating & drinking

Boiled Egg & Soldiers
63 Northcote Road, SW11 1NP (7223 4894). **Open** 9am-6pm Mon-Sat; 9am-4pm Sun. Kid-friendly café.

Café on the Common
2 Rookery Road, Clapham Common, SW4 9DA (7498 0770). **Meals served** *Summer* 11am-6pm daily. *Winter* 11am-4pm daily. Simple snacks.

County Arms
345 Trinity Road, SW18 3SH (8874 8532/ www.countyarms.co.uk). **Open** 11am-11pm Mon-Sat; noon-10.30pm Sun. Food served.

Holy Drinker
59 Northcote Road, SW11 1NP (7801 0544/ www.holydrinker.co.uk). **Open** 4.30-11pm Mon-Fri; noon-11pm Sat; 1-10.30pm Sun.

Pepper Tree
19 Clapham Common South Side, SW7 7AB (7622 1758). **Meals served** noon-3pm, 6-10.30pm Mon; noon-3pm, 6-11pm Tue-Fri; noon-11pm Sat; noon-10.30pm Sun. Good Thai food at low prices.

Windmill on the Common
Clapham Common South Side, SW4 9DE (8673 4578). **Open** 11am-11pm Mon-Sat; noon-10.30pm Sun. Solid pub food, and perfect for a summer pint.

Churches

Holy Trinity Church
Clapham Common North Side, SW4 0QZ (7627 0941/www.holytrinityclapham.org). **Open** times vary, phone for details.

Trinity Hospice
30 Clapham Common North Side, SW4 0RN (7787 1044/www.trinityhospice.org.uk).

Information

Clapham Common
Clapham Common Long Road, SW4 (7926 6214/ www.lambeth.gov.uk).

Wandsworth Common
Bolingbroke Grove, SW18 (8871 6347/ www.wandsworth.gov.uk).

Shopping

Northcote Market
Northcote Road, SW11. **Open** 7am-6.15pm daily.

Wombling free

Liz Jensen

Tiptoe through the horse manure to Wimbledon Village, before encountering a walled garden, a windmill, a Buddhist temple – and no stupid, furry animals.

Start & finish: Wimbledon tube/rail
Distance: 5 miles/8km
Time: 3 hours
Getting there & back: District line
Note: though long, this walk is suitable for children. Cannizaro Park is particularly spectacular in spring. The Windmill Museum and Buddhist temple are open only at weekends.

Wimbledon is internationally famous for its tennis tournament, but my favourite local walk gives all that forehand drive malarkey a wide berth.

This is a rhododendron-strewn, feel-good, knickerbockerglory of an outing, especially perfect if you have a dog or a kite, or you need some horse dung to fertilise your garden, or you fancy meditating on the Four Noble Truths of Buddhism before returning home. There are also opportunities for widening your appreciation of food, horticulture, booze, windmill engineering and retail therapy. And not a tennis racket in sight.

As you turn right out of Wimbledon tube station, marvel at the contemporary urban architecture – all assembled in minutes from a flatpack with a simple Allen key – that surrounds you on all sides. If there were to be a competition for Classic of its Genre, there are four strong candidates all parked on the crossroads immediately to the right of the station, within spitting distance of each other. My money's on the Argos building,

notable for its 1950s-style retro sundial. But crossing over to it and continuing straight on up the main road, you'll soon see vestiges of old Wimbledon such as the Wimbledon Library with its black bell-tower, and the old brick Bank Buildings, the colour of sun-dried tomato paste. Look out for a recent embellishment on the library's side wall: a beautifully simple ceramic bas-relief ensemble of books on shelves, a reminder that less is more.

Hold on to this idea as you head up Wimbledon Hill Road towards a new stratosphere of property prices. A brisk ten-minute walk (or a brisk one-minute bus ride on a number 93) will lift you up where you belong, on that Olympian plateau of refinement that is Wimbledon Village, whose snaking High Street – continue along it – features such phenomena as a Japanese property leasing agency and Estilo Kitchen, one of those kitchen boutiques that sells stainless steel rubbish bins, pasta machines, pistachio chutney and groovily shaped bottles of fancy vinegar with red berries in. And because this is practically the countryside, there's often a trail of steaming horse dung in the road, from Wimbledon Village Stables behind the Dog & Fox – and indeed often a trail of horses, too.

If you're peckish after mountaineering your way up the Hill, stop for a stupendous Indian lunch at Rajdoot by the mini-roundabout, then stagger on down the High Street, manoeuvring your way past outdoor cafés, designer boutiques and clumsily parked Range Rovers until you come to the war memorial, where you can re-tie the laces of your hiking boots because this is where the serious walking begins.

First, cross to the other side of the bumpy treeless heath, which is notable for its absence of any features at all except Rushmere, an expanse of water that's either a large pond or a small lake, depending on whether it's half full or half empty. From here you can get a feel of the generous geography of this part of Wimbledon. It's a good place to sunbathe, fly a kite, sail your remote-controlled yacht or let your dog go crazy – but be aware that, like much of this walk, it's only suitable for the more rugged type of pushchair.

From Rushmere, cross Cannizaro Road (which bisects the heath diagonally) and a further triangle of heath, then follow West Side, still heading away from Wimbledon Village, until you come to the gates of Cannizaro Park, sedate cousin to the wilder Common.

Cannizaro Park forms the grounds of the immensely posh Cannizaro House, which dates back to 1705 and was once the home of Count St Antonio, 'an impoverished Sicilian'. (The mind boggles. Where would he have lived if he'd been rich?) Later the house was frequented by glitterati such as Oscar Wilde, Alfred Lord Tennyson and the last Maharajah of the Punjab, but it was destroyed by fire in 1900 and emerged, phoenix-like, first as a World War I convalescent hospital and later a home for the elderly. Its most recent incarnation is an exclusive hotel favoured by the tennis elite.

Ignoring all this nonsense, begin your culture 'n' horticulture tour by entering the park gates next to the hotel entrance, and then bear right at a white wooden pagoda, home to a chirping flurry of budgies and parakeets. Follow the path to the bottom right corner of the park, where there's a stone sculpture of a woman caressing a fawn (in summertime, it's joined by a wilder and usually arresting collection of outdoor sculptures made by final-year students at the Wimbledon School of Art), then head gently downhill to the duckpond. Here you'll find the entrance to a large walled garden, where every summer there's a magical two-week festival of theatre and jazz in the open air. With the sound of saxophones and thespians drowning

Wimbledon Common

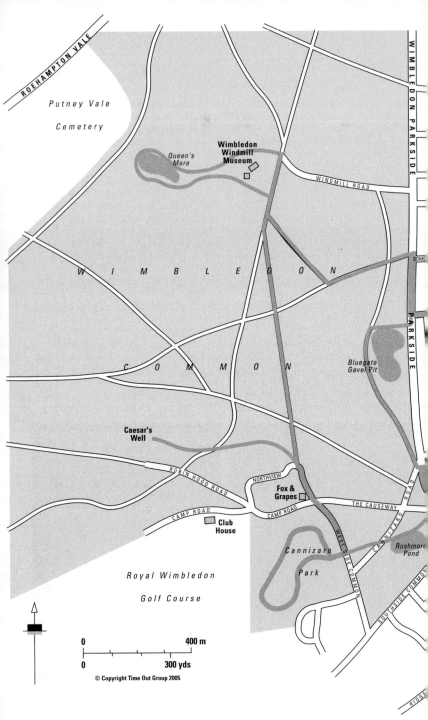

Putney Vale

Cemetery

ROEHAMPTON VALE

Queen's
Mere

Wimbledon
Windmill
Museum

WINDMILL ROAD

WIMBLEDON PARKSIDE

SOME

W I M B L E D O N

PARKSIDE

C O M M O N

Bluegate
Gavel Pit

Caesar's
Well

ROBIN HOOD ROAD

NORTHVIEW

Fox &
Grapes

THE CAUSEWAY

CANNIZARO ROAD

ROAD

CAMP ROAD

CAMP ROAD

Club
House

WEST SIDE COMMON

Cannizaro

Park

Rushmore
Pond

SOUTHSIDE COMMON

Royal Wimbledon

Golf Course

RIDG

0   400 m

0   300 yds

© Copyright Time Out Group 2005

out the buzz of traffic, and the scent of flowers in the air, it's so sympatico it feels like abroad.

Passing through the portals at the far end of the walled garden, you'll find yourself in a marsh area, where two streams feed an array of ferns, azaleas and rhododendrons and some spectacularly huge, primaeval, rhubarby-looking bog plants with spiky webbed leaves. From here, enter a maze of fenced paths. Continue straight on and follow the outer path through even more extravagant rhododendrons, azaleas and camellias leading up to the coniferous section, where there's an impressive range of trees (including one that looks like a frog doing a handstand) and a rather staid folly, made up of stone balustrades and pillars. *'My name is Ozymandias, king of kings, Look on my works, ye mighty, and despair!'* Complete your circuit by heading uphill, past Cannizaro House and out where you came in, then gird your loins for the next phase of your Odyssey.

Turn left out of Cannizaro Park, and follow West Side until you reach Camp Road; stop there for a big and boisterous second lunch at the Fox and Grapes, then tip yourself back out in the direction you came from, past the row of picturesque and chi chi cottages on West Place, and find yourself at the entrance to Wimbledon Common, famous as the home of those

Cannizaro House

notorious TV creatures – part dishcloth, part beaver – the Wombles.

'Underground, overground, Wombling free, The Wombles of Wimbledon Common are we!

'Making good use of the things that we find, Things that the everyday folks leave behind…'

The Wombles – who are still occasionally recycled on children's television, should nostalgia grip you – live in a tunnel system under the Common, and they clear up people's sweet wrappers, fag-ends, used condoms and so on and give them new life. The ringleaders are Orinoco, Tobermory and Uncle Bulgaria – who chose their cute names by sticking a pin in an atlas. The theme tune to the show has a horrible tendency to stick in your head.

Try to banish these wretched gonks from your mind if you wish to enjoy this section of your walk.

Wimbledon Common – site of some celebrated duels – was historically a wasteland, used as a grazing ground for cattle and sheep and as a place to hunt. It also provided wood and water for local inhabitants. In the 19th century

Earl Spencer, head of the National Rifle Association (whose members turned it into a no-go area by using it as a shooting range) claimed that as lord of the manor he was its legal owner. But after much local and parliamentary argy-bargy he finally relinquished the lot to a Board of Conservators in 1871 – in return for a fat fee. Now, over a century later, the Common continues to sport an unusual mixture of nature wild and tamed, giving it a strangely split personality. One moment you'll be thrashing through unkempt woodland, the next you're tiptoeing across a pristine stretch of that pricey outdoor carpeting known as a putting green. You almost need two different outfits – or perhaps a reversible jacket would do. This schizophrenia arises because Wimbledon Common is now home to the London Scottish Golf Club. Not as dangerous as in the heyday of the National Rifle Association, you might think – but I once read a newspaper article about a Tory politician who was in a scrape over some sexual peccadillo. It showed a picture of his wife. Her nose was at a very strange angle. The accompanying article mentioned in passing that she had been hit on the nose by a golf ball while walking on –

I don't even need to say it, do I? You have been warned.

As the map at the entrance to the Common will show you, there are many circuits you can do; if you are feeling energetic – and are not afraid to get slightly lost – bear left, walk across the golf course, past some tall conifers and you may be able to find Caesar's Well (what else do you christen a Roman spring?) and the horse-ring, a sunken training area for dressage, notable for some impressive soil erosion, which has left whole trees clinging grimly to its rim, apparently more by faith than by physics. Otherwise, take a more leisurely stroll along the bicycle track in a straight, no-nonsense line across the Common. One of the most beautiful sights here is that of the silver birch trees, which always seem to shimmer in a very inspirational sort of way, particularly in sharp sunshine. Within ten minutes or so – by which time you may well have spotted a Park Ranger on horseback patrol and thought: holy mackerel, we're in Yosemite! – you'll be approaching the white sails of Wimbledon Windmill hidden behind the trees. Turn right onto the main path and continue as far as the green gate, where you'll see the white sails. Circumnavigate the windmill, and in the far right corner of the car park head down the shady path to Queensmere Lake – from where a brief detour up a small stream will take you to some wonderful trees for climbing.

Queensmere is one of the focal points of Wimbledon Common, and it's used by the locals – Canada geese, ducks, coots and Labradors – as a sort of lido area. Circle the lake, taking note of the memorial inscription on one of the wooden benches: *'Lady Bubbles of Wimbledon. 16.9.1967-25.3.1989, a dear friend who loved this Common. Followed by Lord Bimbo, her son. 4.9.1980-8.8.1990.'* Is this, you

wonder, some tragic tale of premature death among the local aristocracy? Or might Lady Bubbles and Lord Bimbo actually be dead dogs?

As you ponder this question, complete your circuit of the lake and bear straight uphill back towards the windmill, stopping for tea or a third lunch at the Windmill Café next to the car park, where they do a hearty baked potato that you can eat indoors or out.

Wimbledon Windmill, next door to the café, was constructed as a public corn mill in 1817 by a carpenter, Charles March, 'for the advantage and convenience of the neighbourhood', and it's thought to be the only remaining example of a hollow post flour mill in this country. To discover what a hollow post flour mill is, exactly, and how it differs from say a tower mill or a smock mill, a visit to the museum is in order. The Windmill Museum, housed in the millhouse itself, provides a fascinating tour d'horizon of windmill engineering – complete with beautifully crafted working models of different types

Buddhapadipa Temple

of windmill, including Wimbledon Mill itself. There's also an exhibition of antique wooden tools with names like the Button Chuck Brace, the Old Woman's Tooth and the Lamb's Tongue Plane. Climbing the ladder to the second floor, you can see the rafters and the machinery of the sails – all that remains of the original mill mechanism after the building was converted into flats. The census of 1871 shows that 15 adults and five children lived in these dwellings, but in reality there were probably more, because female children were not included in the census. I wonder if Lord Baden-Powell, 'Chief Scout of the World', would have approved. In 1908, when the riff-raff had been turfed out, he borrowed the windmill from his sister and used it to write part of 'Scouting for Boys'.

So banish the Wombling song from your mind, and burst into 'Ging Gang Gooly' mode as you leave the windmill, heading back across the Common along the cycle track that runs parallel to the horse track. Bear left at the first

Wimbledon Village

opportunity, then take a left turn at the bench (commemorating 'Our Loved Ones, Tubby and his daughter Linda who both loved this Common' – more dead dogs?), following the well-fertilised horse track until you hit Parkside, the main road that runs north-south along the Common from Putney. (Somerset Road should be on the opposite side.) Turn right and continue until you see the signpost to the Buddhapadipa Temple. Cross Parkside into Calonne Road, and a five-minute walk through swish suburbia will land you at the entrance to the temple grounds. And suddenly you could almost be in the Orient – because there on the slope above you, up three broad flights of steps, stands a gorgeously decorated temple in crimson, white and gold.

This is Uposotha Hall; it opened in 1982, and is visited by Buddhists from all over the country. Remove your shoes – an essential sign of respect – and enter the temple. On either side of you there are carpeted benches with cushions where the orange-clad, shaven-headed Thai monks sit cross-legged. You may talk to them, addressing them as Bhante or Venerable Sir – but don't offer to shake hands, as they must avoid physical contact. Inhale the incense and take time to behold the shrine before you – a multicoloured extravaganza of candles, artificial flowers, joss sticks and little twinkling mirrors, with a statue of the Enlightened One seated in the middle. Note the murals, too, hand-painted by Thai artists using a phantasmagoric palette featuring much mauve and red. But if you sit on the carpet to admire them, take care not to allow the soles of your feet to face the dha, as this as disrespectful as, say, spitting at the Queen or showing your bum to the Pope.

After the garish exuberance of the Hall, give your eyes a rest by taking a tour of the grounds, bursting with horticulture and urban wildlife – ducks, squirrels, Koi carp, the whole shebang – then visit the monks' residence, housed in the main building at the foot of the Hall. Again, you must remove your shoes before entering. The two main rooms are the dining area and the shrine room – the equivalent of a chapel – where offerings of flowers and fruit are placed before a statue of the Buddha. The monks eat only one meal a day, provided and served by lay people who are practising Dada (giving). Lay people are welcome to eat at the residence, too, once the monks have finished their meal. There's a friendly, welcoming atmosphere, and in the porch you'll see a notice board giving details of special festivals and introductory talks on Buddhism.

This is one of the things I love about Wimbledon. One minute you're on horseback. The next you're battling across some windswept moonscape of a heath, or marvelling at plants that look like special effects for a sci-fi movie. Then you're getting pissed in the Fox & Grapes, or inspecting Baden-Powell's peculiar work-station. Then, before you know it, you're eating a baked potato and flying a kite. And then suddenly – whoosh – you're practically in Thailand.

Your Buddhist meditation over, retrace your steps up Calonne Road, cross Parkside again, and head back towards Wimbledon Village for about 40 metres, before re-entering the Common by taking a small path into the woodland. Pass the shallow pond on your left, cross the horsetrack and then follow the main path (which is parallel to, and beyond, the horsetrack), bearing left by the bench. Within ten minutes you'll be back in the Village, where you can treat yourself to burgers and shakes at Jo Shmo's before leaving the country plateau that is upper Wimbledon for reality and the station.

Then go home and try to get those irritating songs out of your head. Underground, overground, wombling free… Ging gang gooly gooly gooly gooly wotcha, ging gang goo, ging gang goo…

Eating & drinking

Dog & Fox
24 High Street, SW19 5DX (8946 6565). **Open** 11am-11pm Mon-Sat; noon-10.30pm Sun. Food served.

Fox & Grapes
9 Camp Road, SW19 4UN (8946 5599). **Open** 11am-11pm Mon-Sat; noon-10.30pm Sun. 18th-century inn.

Jo Shmo's
33 High Street, SW19 5BY (8879 3845/www.jo shmos.com). **Meals served** noon-11pm Mon-Thur, Sun; noon-11.30pm Fri, Sat. Modern diner.

Rajdoot
72 High Street, SW19 5EE (8946 0238). **Lunch served** noon-2.30pm, **dinner served** 6-11.30pm daily.

Rose & Crown
55 High Street, SW19 5BA (8947 4713). **Open** 11am-11pm Mon-Sat; noon-10.30pm Sun.

Wimbledon Tea Rooms
Windmill Road, SW19 5NQ (8788 2910). **Open** 9am-5.30pm daily. Food served until 2.30pm.

Houses & museums

Buddhapadipa Temple
14 Calonne Road, Wimbledon, SW19 5HJ (8946 1357). **Open** 1-6pm Sat, Sun.

Cannizaro House Hotel
West Side, Wimbledon Common, SW19 4UE (8879 1464/www.cannizarohouse.com).

Cannizaro Park
West Side, Wimbledon Common, SW19 4UD (8545 3657). **Open** 8am-dusk Mon-Fri; 9am-dusk Sat, Sun.

Wimbledon Windmill Museum
Windmill Road, Wimbledon Common, SW19 5NR (8947 2825/www.wimbledonwindmillmuseum. org.uk). **Open** Apr-Oct 2-5pm Sat; 11am-5pm Sun.

Information

Wimbledon Society Museum of Local History
22 The Ridgway, SW19 4QN (8296 9914/www. wimbledonmuseum.org.uk). **Open** 2.30-5pm Sat, Sun.

Wimbledon Village Stables
24A-B High Street, SW19 5DX (8946 8579). **Open** 10am-4pm Mon-Fri; 9am-3pm Sat, Sun.

Shopping

Estilo Kitchen
87 High Street, SW19 8TR (8944 6868). **Open** 10am-6pm Mon-Sat; noon-5pm Sun.

THEN TURN LEFT INTO **WHITE POST LANE**, HIGH OVER BROCKBANK ROAD...

BUT WATCH OUT! THIS IS ALSO KNOWN AS "DOG SHIT ALLEY"...

ALONG HERE YOU GET A **CLEAR** INDICATION OF THE **LOCAL** TOPOGRAPHY... CARRYING ON OVER THE END OF **OVERCLIFF** ROAD INTO THE **STEEP & COBBLED** CONTINUATION OF **WHITEPOST LANE**, THE BACK GARDENS OF **TYRWHITT** ROAD LOOM **HIGH** OVER **SANDROCK RD.** TO THE WEST, WHILE **SHELL** ROAD RISES OVER **UNDERCLIFF RD.** TO THE EAST. THE UNDULATING LANDSCAPE, HIDDEN BENEATH THE TARMAC & THE ROWS OF HOUSES, IS **PARTLY** EXPLAINED BY THE FACT THAT THIS WHOLE AREA WAS A **QUARRY** BEFORE BEING DEVELOPED IN THE LATE 19th CENTURY.~ HENCE THE **STREET** NAMES: "SHELL" ROAD, "FOSSIL" ROAD, "SANDROCK", & SO ON, WITH "**LOAMPIT VALE**" JUST TO THE NORTH. INCIDENTALLY, THE ONLY REASON **HILLY FIELDS** WASN'T DEVELOPED TOO WAS BECAUSE OF **LOCAL AGITATION**! IT BECAME A MUNICIPAL PARK IN 1897 (although they say SHEEP SAFELY GRAZED there before~) — AND IN CASE YOU HADN'T GUESSED, THE BOURGEOISIE LIVED ON THE HILLS, THEIR **SERVANTS IN THE VALLEYS...**

BUT ENOUGH OF SUCH **MARXIST** ANALYSES OF **LOCAL HISTORY!** FROM WHITEPOST LANE KEEP ON STRAIGHT DAHN **SANDROCK** ROAD, THEN TURN LEFT ONTO **LOAMPIT VALE!** OPPOSITE YOU IS THE CELEBRATED **PAINTED HOUSE**: WHETHER LEGACY OF **HIPPY MUDDLE-HEADEDNESS** OR LOCAL **LOOP-**NESS, IT PROVIDES **WRID JOY** TO A MILLION CARBOUND COMMUTERS **DAILY!**

THEN IT'S A **SHORT TROT** BACK TO **ST. JOHN'S** STATION. THE WALK LASTS ABOUT **45 MINUTES** IF YOU SLOUCH. **ST. JOHN'S STATION** IS 12 MINUTES FROM **LONDON BRIDGE STATION** ON THE **HAYES LINE**. IT'S CLOSED AT WEEKENDS, SO GO TO **LEWISHAM STATION** OR GET A **36** BUS FROM **VICTORIA**. THERE'S A MAP OF THE AREA ON P. **93** OF THE **A-Z** (REF: L & M/123). **ENJOY!**

LOAMPIT HILL8G

@Martin Rowson 92

A short walk in south-east London

Start and finish: St Johns rail
Distance: 1.5 miles/2.5km
Time: 45 minutes
Getting there and back: St Johns
rail (from London Bridge); 36 bus
Note: St Johns station is closed
at weekends, but Lewisham
station is open. The views from
Hilly Fields are spectacular.
There are no refreshments
until the end of the walk.

Eating & drinking

The Talbot
2-4 Tyrwhitt Road, SE4 1QG (8692 1640).
Open noon-11pm Mon-Sat; noon-10.30pm Sun.
No food served.

Churches

St John's with Holy Trinity
*corner of Lewisham Way & St John's Vale,
SE8 4EA (8692 2857/www.sjht.org.uk).* **Open**
call for details. **Services** 10.30am, 7.30pm Tue;
10.30am, 6.30pm Sun.

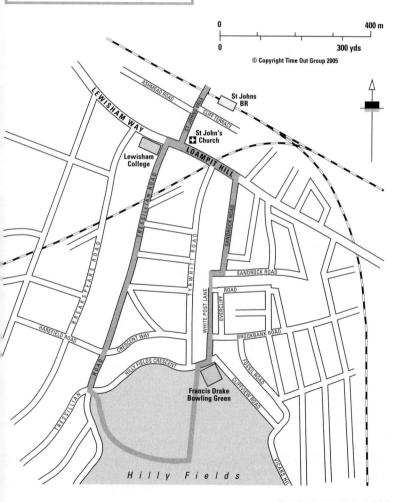

© Copyright Time Out Group 2005

From tree to tree

Thomas Pakenham

Medieval oaks, landscaped plantations, rare specimens and hothoused plants punctuate the route from Richmond Park to Kew Gardens.

Start: Mortlake rail
Finish: Kew Gardens tube/rail
Distance: 11 miles/18km
Time: 5 hours
Getting there: Mortlake rail
Getting back: District line from Kew Gardens
Note: the first opportunity to stop for refreshments once in Richmond Park is at Pembroke Lodge. The walk could be split in half at Richmond. Take boots – this can get muddy.

Leave Mortlake station and turn right down Sheen Lane. Either follow this main road direct to Richmond Park or take the prettier route by two quiet suburban streets – Milton Road and Richmond Park Road – which rejoins Sheen Lane shortly before East Sheen Gate. Arrive at the East Sheen Gate to Richmond Park.

Walk 150 yards left to Adam's Pond. Here you will see the first five of the medieval oak trees (*Quercus robur*) with which Richmond Park abounds. Like the majority they are pollards; until about 1750 the heads were regularly cropped to get small poles; subsequently they grew several large trunks. You will also see waterfowl – mallard, Canada geese, swans and so on – and perhaps some of the 400 fallow deer and 300 red deer that roam the park.

Now turn right and head for Dean's Coppice about 600 yards to the south-west, following the riding track until off to the left you see a metal gate into Two

Storm Wood and the Dean's Coppice. Inside the enclosure are about 15 medieval oaks, some of the oldest and largest in the park. The majority are notable for not having been pollarded: they must have been grown as standard oaks (suitable for planking timber) among a coppice of smaller trees such as hazels, alder and field maple (suitable for infilling timber frames and for fencing). Go down to the south-west corner and you will find the biggest, a medieval boundary tree, preserved to mark the edge of the coppice. Go out through the metal gate just north of it and head along through Barn Wood towards Holly Lodge. On the way you will see several examples of medieval lanes, still marked by lines of ancient oak trees. Indeed, of the 1,300 ancient trees in the park, 1,000 are oaks.

Pass along the north side of Holly Lodge; the back entrance to the farm is lined with trees planted (or self-sown) about the time of the Black Death in the mid 14th century, which greatly reduced the need for corn fields in what is now the park.

Cross the main tarmac road and head up the slope with Sawpit Plantation to your left. This largely consists of sweet chestnuts (*Castanea sativa*) planted in the early 19th century. The timber is even more durable than oak, and the nuts are, of course, delicious when roasted.

Cross two riding tracks of cinders and reach the Queen's Ride, a long grassy vista curling up from the White Lodge which you can see to your left. The building itself, designed by Roger Morris for Lord Pembroke in 1727 with additions by Wyatt and others, is architecturally a mess and best seen from afar. But the Ride is a magical place, particularly in winter when no one's about. This was the private drive through old woodland cut for Queen Caroline (wife of George II) to go from Richmond Lodge to White Lodge, and the latter became her favourite residence where she hatched her political intrigues with the Prime Minister, Sir Robert Walpole.

Continue southwards to the causeway between the Upper and Lower Pen Ponds and cross to the south side. These ponds have the richest collection of waterfowl in the park. If you are lucky you might catch a glimpse of a kingfisher.

Now swing right and head for the Isabella Plantation about 800 yards away. Enter by the east gate. The Isabella Plantation is the only place in the park where there is a collection of rare trees. It was originally planted with oaks in 1831 by the then Deputy Ranger, Viscount Sidmouth (better known as Henry Addington, the famously dim Prime Minister of 1801-4). At first it had only a small pond fed by a spring. But since 1950 it has been developed as a large-scale woodland garden, with three large ponds and a stream 500 yards long fed by pumped water. Specialities include birch (*Betula*), maples (*Acer hersii, Acer* 'Silver Vein'), hornbeam (*Carpinus*), Pieris

'Forest Flame', swamp cypresses and gigantic scarlet rhododendrons (50 species and 120 hybrids). The azaleas would make a rainbow blush.

Leave the garden by the west gate and head for the 'main' road, then cross the tarmac at the crossroads and take the path northwards, parallel to the main road to Richmond Gate. (Don't take the yellow gravel track nearest the main road but a grass one, which is quieter, 100 yards beyond – *see map*.)

The track passes several splendid medieval oaks, including a dead one like a font, and two half-dead dinosaur oaks. Continue down the hornbeam walk towards Pembroke Lodge; notice that the biggest hornbeams are the size of beech trees. (As for beech trees themselves, they are conspicuous by their absence, although there is a fine old one below the hornbeam walk.)

Arrive at Pembroke Lodge by the metal gate on the west side of the garden. This is the grace-and-favour house built for Lady Pembroke, to whom poor mad George III was devoted, in the 1790s. Sir John Soane was the architect, but it is an unpretentious building rather like a large rectory. Its chief claim to fame is that it was the childhood home of Bertrand

Isabella Plantation

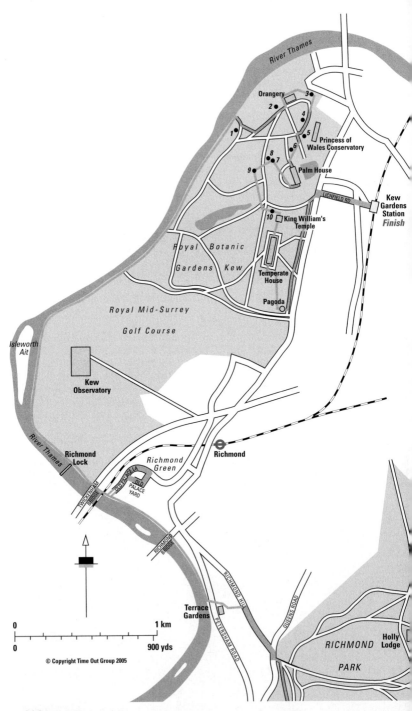

Orangery

Princess of Wales Conservatory

Kew Gardens Station Finish

LICHFIELD RD

Palm House

King William's Temple

Royal Botanic Gardens Kew

Royal Mid-Surrey Golf Course

Temperate House

Pagoda

Isleworth Ait

Kew Observatory

River Thames

Richmond Lock

Richmond Green

Richmond

OLD PALACE LA

OLD PALACE YARD

TWICKENHAM BRIDGE

RICHMOND BRIDGE

Terrace Gardens

RICHMOND HILL

QUEENS ROAD

PETERSHAM ROAD

Holly Lodge

RICHMOND PARK

0   1 km
0   900 yds
© Copyright Time Out Group 2005

From tree to tree

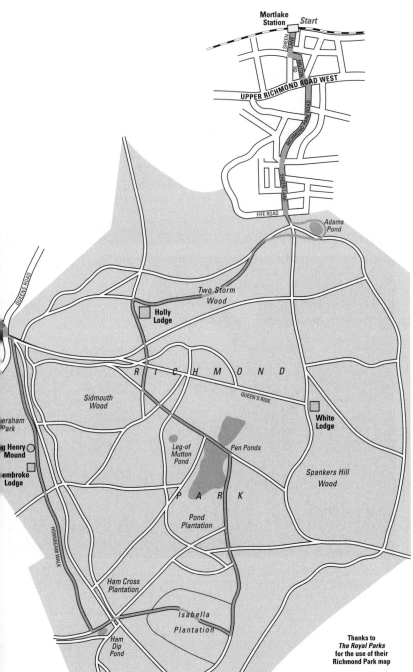

Mortlake Station

Start

SHEEN LANE

RICHMOND PARK ROAD

UPPER RICHMOND ROAD WEST

SHEEN LANE

QUEEN'S ROAD

FIFE ROAD

Adams Pond

Two Storm Wood

Holly Lodge

R I C H M O N D

QUEEN'S RIDE

Sidmouth Wood

White Lodge

...ersham Park

...g Henry Mound

...embroke Lodge

Leg-of-Mutton Pond

Pen Ponds

Spankers Hill Wood

HORNBEAM WALK

P A R K

Pond Plantation

Ham Cross Plantation

Isabella Plantation

Ham Dip Pond

Thanks to
The Royal Parks
for the use of their
Richmond Park map

Richmond Bridge

The **Thames**, from Richmond.

Russell, the philosopher and crusader, when his grandfather, Lord John Russell, then ex-Prime Minister, was lent it by Queen Victoria. There is a fine hollow oak on the front lawn that Bertrand Russell must have climbed as a boy. Children can still shelter from the rain inside the trunk.

Follow the path north through the garden till you reach Henry VIII's Mound. From here you will see the famous 'keyhole' framing the view of St Paul's dome ten miles away. The keyhole is made of holly and the trick is that this shrubbery, and a plantation beyond, exclude all the other buildings in the

City skyline. Look the other way, towards Windsor Castle, and the view is utterly banal by comparison.

Continue east past the poet James Thomson's oak (a medieval tree next to a memorial in his honour). He was buried in Richmond Churchyard below.

Leave Richmond Park by Richmond Gate and proceed down Richmond Hill along a broad gravel walk commanding a famous view of the Thames. Halfway along, opposite the great bend in the river, is the best viewpoint, and there are helpful plans and photographs on display. Go to the end of the walk and through the iron gate leading to Terrace Gardens, then descend to the river walk by way of this small but elegantly planted public garden. Two notable trees are the maidenhair trees (*Ginkgo biloba*) at the top and bottom; they are younger versions of the famous one at Kew. Notice also the Coadestone figure of a river god designed in 1784 by the sculptor John Bacon and restored by the Richmond Society in 1992.

Cross Petersham Road and look out for a fine young Metasequoia, the Chinese 'fossil tree' only discovered in Sichuan in 1941. Then follow the Thames Path along the riverbank towards the five great stone spans of Richmond Bridge 300 yards to the north. On the right of the path you will see one of the tallest trees in the London area, a 38-metre (125-foot) London plane (*Platanus x hispanica*); it is bravely maintaining itself in the garden of Canyon, a North American restaurant overlooking Richmond landing stage.

Walk under Richmond Bridge, past three more towering London planes (unfortunately pollarded when they were young) and along the waterfront with more pubs (the Slug and Lettuce and the White Cross) until you reach Old Palace Lane, just before the railway bridge. Here is a good place to make a diversion to Richmond. Go up the lane past the White Swan and turn right through Old Palace Yard. This is a delightful cache of grace-and-favour houses including the Palace

Gate House, which leads to Richmond Green. Note the magnificent old umbrella pine (*Pinus pinea*) and the huge bay tree in the front garden.

Return to the path beside the Thames by way of Old Palace Lane. Continue along the path and go under the railway bridge and Twickenham Bridge, then pass below the arch of Richmond Lock. For the next mile and a quarter you will be following the Thames Path with the river on your left. It is surprisingly wild and the path is badly potholed as you approach Kew Gardens. Don't miss the fine view of Syon House and its park on the left. Take Brentford Ferry Gate into Kew Gardens – it's at the southern end of the riverside carpark.

Kew Gardens is so rich in trees and plants and structures of all kinds that a personal selection must be entirely arbitrary. I have chosen a route that highlights most of the oldest trees and some of the best buildings.

Pass the ticket kiosk and go straight on a few yards till the fork, where on your right is the large, many-headed Zelkova (*Zelkova carpinifolia*) [1]. Despite their close links to the elm genus, these trees have so far stayed free from the Dutch elm disease that has destroyed most of the great elms in the south of Britain. This one, the largest at Kew, looks like an arboreal firework in the autumn.

Follow the left fork and, leaving the eucalyptus grove on your left, head for the sumptuous white Orangery straight ahead. This is the finest of the buildings designed by Sir William Chambers for the Princess of Wales, when Kew was originally laid out as a royal botanic garden in the early 1760s. Opposite it is the newly restored 'Dutch House' – or Kew Palace – built in 1631. It is a red-brick affair with heavy-handed Dutch gables, hardly what you would expect to find in this arcadia. But the Princess used it as her HQ. Notice the old oriental plane tree (*Platanus orientalis*) [2] on the lawn between the two buildings. The species is squatter and less elegant than the common hybrid, the London plane.

Pass north-east of the Orangery and follow the path leading to the main gate. There's a fine young Indian horse chestnut here (*Aesculus indica* 'Sydney Pearce') [3] that makes a dazzling spectacle in June, the branches buried in a mound of white-and-pink 'candles'.

Turn right before reaching the main gate and head back to an ancient locust-tree (*Robinia pseudoacacia*) [4] that looks like a bundle of half-rotten stakes tied together with metal bands. This is one of the Kew originals – a tree dating from the 1760s. Normally the locust tree is short-lived and this is a prodigy best seen when its ancient head is white from flowers. Of much the same date, but still looking remarkably fit, is the famous maidenhair tree behind. This is one of the first of these Chinese 'fossil trees' to be planted in Europe. Their leaves look like ferns, hence the English name, and in fact they evolved 300 million years ago in the age dominated by ferns, long before the first dinosaurs were flying over Kew.

Beyond this ginkgo and beside the path is a third original: an ancient pagoda tree (*Sophora japonica*) [5], also from China, despite its botanical name. For years it has been a stretcher case, recumbent on a steel frame; in 1997 it was locked into a cage like a zoo animal. But it still flowers every year and perhaps produces fertile seeds.

Now head for the great Palm House designed by the English architect Decimus Burton and the Irish engineer Richard Turner and begun in 1845, six years before the Crystal Palace was erected at the Great Exhibition in Hyde Park. Before entering look at the lace-bark pine (*Pinus bungeana*) [6] just to the north. This is a rare Chinese pine with elegantly mottled bark, best seen across a snowy landscape like the famous example outside the Imperial Palace at Beijing.

Inside, the Palm House is stuffed with tropical oddities and oldies. My favourite is a cycad that was brought back from South Africa in the 1770s by Francis Masson, Kew's first overseas plant explorer, and is claimed to be the oldest pot-plant in the world. But don't miss the giant bamboo by the central staircase. Sometimes it grows three feet a week: care has to be taken to see that it does not escape through the 18-metre-high (59-foot) roof.

North-west of the Palm House is Kew's tallest tree, the 35-metre (115-foot) chestnut-leaved oak (*Quercus castaneifolia*) [7] from the Caspian, the first and finest specimen of the species in Britain. West of this lies an exceptionally picturesque group of black pines, including the variety from the Cevennes, *Pinus nigra cebennica* [8]. Cross the path to the new azalea garden. Beyond this you will see the tallest and oldest of many American tulip trees in the gardens (*Liriodendron tulipfera*) [9]. It is at its best in June, when the 33-metre (108-foot) tree is decked with tulip flowers from top to toe. Now cross the avenue of evergreen oaks (*Quercus ilex*) and stop at the small neo-Greek temple built in honour of William IV.

On a corner of the lawn in front is a hybrid strawberry tree (*Arbutus andrachnoides*) [10], which flowers in the autumn and keeps its berries until the following year; appropriately, this hybrid comes from Greece. On to the Temperate House, a later and less distinguished glasshouse by Decimus Burton. It is claimed to be the world's largest, and is stuffed with rarities arranged geographically. One of the most sinister is the dragon tree (*Dracaena draco*) from the Canaries and Madeira. When the flesh is cut, the wound bleeds sap the colour of blood.

End the tour with a visit to the Pagoda, the most spectacular of Sir William Chambers's mid 18th-century follies. Although some killjoy has pruned off the dragons at the corner of each storey and the gilt finial on the 50-metre (164-foot) summit, the Pagoda remains the first and

The Orangery

Pembroke Lodge

finest Chinese skyscraper in Britain.

Turn left and northwards to the exit at the Victoria Gate, passing Chambers's sham Roman arch (a good 1760 joke) and averting your eyes from the 58-metre (190-foot) flagpole, hacked out of one of the tallest Douglas firs that ever graced the forests of Canada.

Now head across the main road and it's a five-minute walk to Kew Gardens station.

Kew Palace, Palm House (below) and Kew Gardens (opposite).

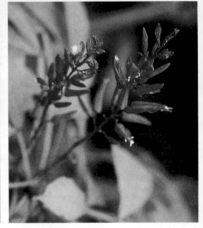

Eating & drinking

Canyon

Riverside, The Tollpath, near Richmond Bridge, Richmond, Surrey TW10 6UJ (8948 2944). **Open** noon-4pm, 6-10.30pm Mon-Fri; 11am-4pm, 6-10.30pm Sat, Sun. An easy-going restaurant offering a relaxed mood and a modern menu with an excellent brunch.

Kew Gardens Cafés & Restaurant

Kew Gardens, Richmond, Surrey TW9 3AB (8332 5000/www.kew.org.uk). **Open** *Kitchen at White Peaks* 10am-1hr before gardens close daily. *Pavilion* 11am-1hr before gardens close daily. *Victoria Gate Coffee Shop* 10am-1hr before gardens close daily.

Pembroke Lodge

Richmond Park, Richmond, Surrey TW10 5HX (8940 8207/www.pembrokelodge.co.uk). **Open** *Winter* 10am-30mins before park closes. *Summer* 10am-5.30pm Mon-Fri; 9.30am-6pm Sat, Sun.

Slug & Lettuce

Riverside House, Water Lane, Richmond, Surrey TW9 1TJ (8948 7733/www.slugandlettuce.co.uk). **Open** *Winter* 11am-11pm Mon-Sat; noon-10.30pm Sun. *Summer* 10am-11pm Mon-Sat; 10am-10.30pm Sun. One of the reliable chain. Food served.

Tidetables Café

2 The Arches, beneath Richmond Bridge, Riverside, Richmond, Surrey TW9 1TH (8948 8285). **Open** *Winter* 9am-6pm daily. *Summer* 9am-8pm Mon-Fri; 9am-9pm Sat, Sun. Vegetarian food.

White Cross

*Water Lane, Richmond, Surrey TW9 1TH (8940
6844).* **Open** 11am-11pm Mon-Sat; noon-10.30pm
Sun. Grand river views and a good wine selection.
Food served.

White Swan

*26 Old Palace Lane, Richmond, Surrey TW9 1PG
(8940 0959).* **Open** 11am-midnight Mon-Sat; noon-
10.30pm Sun. Extensive wine list and elegant
upstairs restaurant.

Parks & gardens

Richmond Park

*Richmond, Surrey TW10 5HS (8948 3209/
www.royalparks.gov.uk).* **Open** *Mar-Sept* 7am-
30mins before dusk daily. *Oct-Feb* 7.30am-30mins

before dusk daily. There are free guided walks
available throughout the year; these last about
90 minutes.

Royal Botanic Gardens (Kew Gardens)

*Kew, Richmond, Surrey TW9 3AB (8332 5000/
www.kew.org).* **Open** *Late Mar-Aug* 9.30am-
6.30pm Mon-Fri; 9.30am-7.30pm Sat, Sun. *Sept,
Oct* 9.30am-6pm daily. *Late Oct-early Feb* 9.30am-
4.15pm daily. *Early Feb-late Mar* 9.30am-5.30pm
daily. **Admission** £10 adults; £7 concessions;
free under-17s.

Terrace Gardens

*Petersham Road, Richmond, Surrey TW10 6UX
(8831 6115/www.richmond.gov.uk).* **Open** 7.30am-
dusk Mon-Fri; 9am-dusk Sat, Sun.

Green thoughts by the gasometer

Margaret Drabble

From Venetian aspirations of funerary splendour to the Apocalypse Hotel.

Start and finish: Sainsbury's car park, Ladbroke Grove, W11
Distance: 3.5 miles/5.5km
Time: 1.5 hours
Getting there: Bakerloo line to Kensal Green then ten-minute walk, or Hammersmith & City line to Ladbroke Grove then 15-minute walk; 23 or 295 bus
Getting back: reverse of above or, if you take the alternative finish down Portobello Road, the Central, District or Circle lines from Notting Hill Gate
Note: May is the month for baby Canada geese.

This walk sets out from Sainsbury's car park on the junction of Harrow Road and Ladbroke Grove. The car park is a popular spot with many attractive facilities, including the superstore itself, a low white model of its kind, which we have now forgiven for causing years of traffic jams when it was under construction. When I took my aunt from out-of-town round it on a sightseeing shopping spree she was overwhelmed by the variety of produce, far greater, she assured me, than that available in Safeway in Grantham, hitherto her idea of Trimalchian excess. It also has a distinguished clientele – on this occasion we met one famous actress and one of my ex-editors, who passed the time of

Grand Union Canal

Wormwood Scrubs

lay pleasantly. One is not always so lucky, but it's as well to be on guard: somebody you know may be watching you as you hesitate by the ravioli and the microwave sauces. It is wise to stock up here with a sandwich if you expect to need a snack en route, as there is not much to eat on the first half of this walk. After admiring the mosaic murals for old folks near the turnstiles leading on to the Grand Union Canal, you set off along the towpath, turning to the left.

Here begins the water walk. Beware of cyclists and joggers, and look out for herons. Last time we walked along here we saw one standing on the first longboat we passed, long and thin and grey and about four feet high, looking prehistoric and proud. A little further on we saw another, solid, fat and hunched and streaked with yellow. Could they have been of the same species? Carrion rooks were assembling noisily like vultures in the trees in the cemetery over the canal, where, if you train your binoculars towards the far shore, you may be able to spot Lucinda Lambton or other aesthetically inclined graveyard-haunters admiring the beauties of Kensal Green Cemetery. But we are on the industrial side, on the side of the living, and come shortly to the extraordinarily handsome grey/green gridwork of the gasometers. If you stand quite still and silent here, you can sometimes hear them creak and grind and clank as a few thousand North Kensingtonians cook their Sunday lunch. Shortly after this you come to a view of the sleeping place of Eurostar trains, resting in their dark blue and yellow glow amidst miles of track and electric angle and metal fencing. How they get here from Waterloo is a mystery and it is better not to ask. There is much on this walk that is inexplicable, giving me the impression that one lives in a world lost in the Piranesi maze of its own mad technology – rail tracks that go nowhere, signs that mean nothing, pylons and towers and spikes and fences

that nobody seems to own or tend. Maybe each brick, each barrier, each strand of barbed wire is loved and counted, but I doubt it. An intricate randomness reigns.

There have been attempts by the authorities to make this a conventionally pleasant canal walk, but they have met with resistance. The notice board (now deceased) that gave information about wildlife was completely obliterated by graffiti. It showed sketches of the original plans for the cemetery: there was to have been a grand watery approach from the canal through great funereal gates, a death voyage of almost Venetian majesty, which, alas, was never constructed. Nevertheless, despite the best efforts of vandals, there is much along the way to interest and delight. Connoisseurs of garbage will note the fine displays of polystyrene boxes, drinks cans, old stockings and abandoned shopping trolleys that accumulate in odd corners, and nature lovers will admire the bravery with which the elder and the ivy, the nettle and the dandelion, the buddleia and the chickweed fight back.

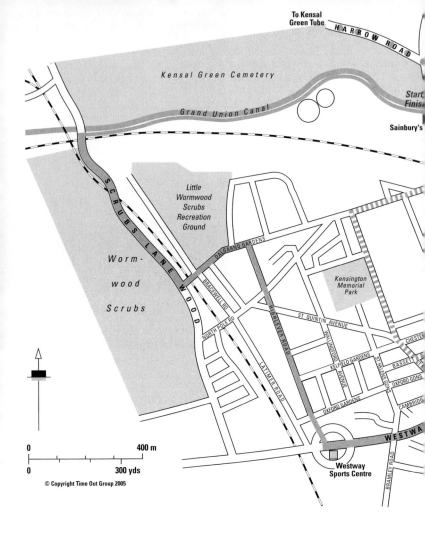

Moorhens, ducks and ferociously large and threatening Canada geese dispute the slick wet runway, and there are fish, for I have seen them, lurking beneath the oily iridescence. Once a bright blue budgerigar appeared suddenly, as in a conjuring trick, at our feet on the towpath. We spoke to it sympathetically, but it flew away, over to the far green side, to perch in loyalty, perhaps, on its dead owner's grave.

After 20 minutes or so of strolling, we come to two bridges, one rail, one road: between them on the far bank, after the

Tyre Mountains, is a little pleasure garden with a bench for the pilgrim, sprouting with pale green euphorbia, my favourite plant species. We ascend now from the towpath to Mitre Bridge, admiring the pink, blue and yellow metalwork, which makes it resemble a giant Meccano set. Its flanks are adorned by a mixture of highly coloured murals depicting herons and anglers, and a sign saying 'Grand Union Canal 1801'. This is the Scrubs Lane exit, and you now find yourself on Scrubs Lane

Start/
Finish

..bury's

Westbourne
Park

Ladbroke
Grove

Pembridge
Villas

Notting Hill
Gate

...self. Pause to admire the view. A few miles to the east you can see the Post Office Tower, reminding you of your location, and also, nearer but in much the same direction, a more local landmark, the bulky elevation of the Pall Mall Deposit, a historic building that the evasive Wyndham Lewis used to give as his postal address to correspondents he did not wish to hear from too frequently.

We now proceed along Scrubs Lane, heading southwards (right). Impossible to describe or comprehend the strange

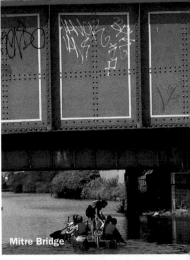
Mitre Bridge

mixture of elevations here – you have to see them for yourself. Over your head, as it were, rumble slowly along their tracks Universal Express Intermodal Logistics, and Bell and Seaco, and Contship Overland, and other strange conveyors of who-knows-what-to-where. Follow under the bridge to the green open space of Wormwood Scrubs itself, where you can follow a pretty little landscaped winding red-brick path that runs parallel to the road through groves of poplar and hazel, past banks of flowering white dead nettle. From this you can see the dog walkers, the footballers, and the distant block of the infamous Scrubs. Is that immensely tall tower a lookout post for watching escaping prisoners? Probably not. We used to go to the Scrubs for its Christmas show and sale when a friend of ours was visiting her prisoner there, and a very fine occasion it was, with some excellent actors: we own a huge bird table made out of authentic Scrubs prison wood by a genuine lifer, but for some reason the birds have never taken to it and rarely perch upon it.

At the end of the path, as you approach the dismally, memorably and inexplicably entitled North Pole Road, you see on your right a pony farm, which smells pleasantly of pony. This is truly *rus in urbe*. There is also a Linford Christie stadium.

Some years ago, if I remember rightly, a schoolboy won a prize for his survey of the surprising biodiversity of the Scrubs – I don't think the word biodiversity had been invented then, but the concept had, and he had been a pioneer in the field. I wish I could remember his name. I wonder where his passions led him. I think it was my smoky suburban Sheffield childhood, followed by seven years of early married life just off the Blackstock Road in N5, that gave me my affection for desperate urban wasteland and its courageous blossoming. Anyone can like Hampstead Heath. You need an eye to like Wormwood Scrubs.

I suppose at this point you could pop into the Pavilion pub on the corner of

North Pole Road, which advertises Hot and Cold Food. Instead, cross Scrubs Lane and go along past the red-brick mansions of Dalgarno Gardens, past Little Wormwood Scrubs, which is not a children's penal colony but a Stay and Play playground. On, past well-defended shops with grilled windows, one of which advertises Thai breakfasts, past the Sutton Housing Trust endowed by William Richard Sutton, carrier of Golden Lane, EC1, who died in 1900, and turn right into Highlever Road. You are now approaching small-scale domesticity and civilisation, manifested in a delightful variety of two-storey dwellings with porches, wooden chalet balconies and other original decorative features, with gardens full of roses, tulips, clematis, ceanothus, daffodils and glimpses of cosy interiors. Some have bookcases and no doubt copies of *Time Out* on the coffee table. Continue along Highlever, which is planted with a pleasing variety of municipal trees, making your way carefully across a triangular junction with confusing crossings, and on past slightly larger, older three-storey houses that, after Scrubs Lane, look imposingly grand. They have intriguing names, some of them – Salutatia, La Vapies. At the end of Highlever, turn right along Oxford Gardens towards Latimer Road.

We are now making for the area under the motorway, which you see looming above you, inviting you to the M40 and Oxford. But we are not going to Oxford, we are going to the Westway Sports Centre. There are many ways into this area, and many ways out. It is best to wander and wonder, among the heavily decorated concrete columns bearing the names of many loved ones, gazing up from time to time at the great dripping underbelly of the monster, enjoying the impressive range of activities – tennis, multicultural soccer, traditionally sedate equitation and, most impressively, mountaineering. Some genius who has read his Ballard has built some extraordinary spiked miniature Matterhorns, which rear up at jagged angles to the very brink of the motorway itself; they are studded with what I at first take to be mosaics, but which on closer inspection turn out to be coloured hooks of green, turquoise, yellow, blue, each colour denominating presumably some carefully designated route upwards. Here, for £6.50 an hour, you can aspire. This whole Climbing Centre area has been expensively refurbished with smart new buildings and now boasts some vertical white billows made of Millennium Dome material (freshly made, not recycled) which add a touch of Sydney Opera House glamour. I'm not sure what they are for. Maybe they are planning some new skyward routes.

I prefer to stay on the ground, wandering past the Westway Wildlife

Portobello Road and **Market**.

Westway Sports Centre

Corner with its pond and frogs and kingcups, its painted portraits of slugs and dormice, to the Westway Wildlife Garden, whose sinuous path echoes the snaking curve of that other roaring mechanical wildway above. Here grow bluebells and green alkanet. Stay under the motorway and try to find Maxilla Walk and the Maxilla Nursery Centre, with pleasingly professional murals of parrots and pink and blue palm trees, and a garden with a Wendy house – a far cry this from Peter Pan and Kensington Gardens, but we are still in Kensington, in an area that flourishes largely thanks to the Westway Development Trust.

The work of this body deserves a diversionary paragraph. It has reclaimed more than 20 acres of derelict land and provided space for a variety of activities – charity offices, lunch clubs, small businesses. But it was born out of conflict. The creation of the motorway caused years of noise, dirt and devastation from 1964, when demolition began, to 1970, when it opened to traffic. Roads were cut in two, communities were uprooted, housing stock was destroyed, dead ends were created. The Greater London Council and the Royal Borough of Kensington and Chelsea, both of which had given planning permission, were reviled by local activists, and a revolutionary spirit of protest and self-help was born. The Trust was launched in 1971, facing unprecedented problems of urban regeneration. The rest is not quite history, because problems continue and solutions are disputed. Some of us even have moments of regret about the ordering of the chaos and the municipalisation of the spirit of free enterprise. Once, near the squatters' Apocalypse Hotel (long-since demolished and neatly redeveloped by a Housing Trust), I had a close encounter with a car driven by a ten-year-old who was careering along brilliantly, though he was so small he could hardly see out of the front window. He seemed like a symbol of something. As I was myself at the time a nervous middle-aged learner-driver with L plates, I had reason to be impressed. This neighbourhood had its own anarchic quality. Some it retains.

Let us return to the space between the stilts. You are probably well lost by now, but there are usually plenty of people around to tell you the way and to send you on it with a blessing. (Don't ask for 10 Rillington Place, where John Christie committed his murders – you are very near it, but it has mysteriously vanished and been reborn under a new name, and people don't want to remember.) Carry on until you emerge on St Mark's Road, and turn right, past a convenient and well-patronised bottle bank under the bridge. Pause here and look at the doors in the side of the bridge and listen to the ominous noises from within. They terrify. What can be in there? Then pick your way through the pigeon shit and proceed to Lancaster Road, where you turn left. On the left-hand side of this stretch, before you hit Ladbroke Grove, have a look at No.158, once the garden of publishing pioneer Carmen Callil, and winner of a prize for being Best Kept Small Front Garden. On the other side of the road the red-brick beacon of the London Lighthouse is a historic monument to late 20th-century London life, and to the efforts of many dedicated people.

You are now nearing the end of the trail, as you emerge on to Ladbroke Grove itself, where you can admire on the far corner the fine traditional Public Library, which continues to provide a fine traditional service. On the opposite corner, a flower shop, with good stock. If you go straight ahead here, you come shortly to Portobello Road, Portobello Market and all its wares, some of which are rotten. You have to watch out – those avocados may not be as edible as they look. If you were to turn right, you come on the next corner to a pub called the Elgin.

Cast your eyes upwards, beyond the pub, and you are gazing towards Holland Park and Ziegler-land, where the houses are grand, indeed extravagant. But that is another story, another walk. Yours is almost over. You can now turn left to Ladbroke Grove tube station and escape from Martin-Amis-land by train. Or you can walk back up to your car at Sainsbury's, making a short detour along Bassett Road to the left to see the two stone basset-hounds that wittily sit yearning on their pedestals outside No.19. If you divert further along Bassett Road to St Mark's Road, and turn right, you will come to a little park where I once was allowed to take my grandson. Oh, the years I have spent in public parks with small children! But I had lost the knack, and this was a humiliating experience: young Stanley, who has a gracious disposition, was very patient with me, but I couldn't get the brake off his pushchair and had to ask for help from a group of young mothers. This made me feel my age.

I sometimes wonder how many miles I have tramped round London, first with a pushchair, then, when I grew up, on my own, or with adult company. It never ceases to astonish, delight and appal. When I first came to London, as a schoolgirl from the north, I was almost sick with excitement. And some of that excitement can still be recaptured.

Eating & drinking

The Elgin
96 Ladbroke Grove, W11 1PY (7229 5663). **Open** 11am-11pm Mon-Sat; noon-10.30pm Sun. **Food served** noon-10pm daily.

Garden Café
London Lighthouse, 111-117 Lancaster Road, W11 1QT (7816 8520). **Open** 9-11am, noon-2pm Mon-Fri.

Number One Café
1 Dalgarno Gardens, W10 5LL (8968 0558). **Open** noon-3pm, 6-10pm Mon-Fri; 6-10pm Sat, Sun.

Pavilion
Wood Lane, W12 0HQ (8743 3913). **Open** 11am-11pm Mon-Sat; noon-10.30pm Sun. **Food served** noon-8pm Mon-Fri; noon-2.30pm Sat; 1-3.30pm Sun.

Information

Kensington Memorial Park
St Mark's Road, W10 (7471 9814). **Open** *Summer* 7.30am-9.30pm daily. *Winter* 7.30am-5pm daily.

Westway Development Trust
1 Thorpe Close, W10 5XL (8962 5720/www. westway.org.uk). **Open** 9.30am-5.30pm Mon-Fri.

Shopping & services

Bramley's Big Adventure
136 Bramley Road, W10 6TJ (8960 1515/ www.bramleysbig.co.uk). **Open** 10am-6.30pm daily. *Last admission* 5pm. Indoor playground.

North Kensington Library
108 Ladbroke Grove, W11 1PZ (7221 2917). **Open** 9.30am-8pm Mon, Tue, Thur; 9.30am-1pm Wed; 9.30am-5pm Fri, Sat.

Portobello Road Market
Portobello Road, W10; Golborne Road, W10 (www.rbkc.gov.uk). **Open** *General market* 8am-6.30pm Mon-Wed, Fri, Sat; 8am-1pm Thur. *Antiques* 5.30am-4.30pm Sat.

Westway Sports Centre
1 Crowthorne Road, W10 6RP (8969 0992/ www.westway.org). **Open** 8am-10pm Mon-Fri; 8am-8pm Sat; 10am-10pm Sun.

Mind, body, spirit, soul

Dan Fielder

A new age for a new millennium.

> **Start:** High Street Kensington tube
> **Finish:** Primrose Hill, or Camden Town tube
> **Distance:** 10.5 miles/17km
> **Time:** 5 hours
> **Getting there:** Circle or District line to High Street Kensington
> **Getting back:** Northern line from Camden Town
> **Note:** this mighty walk passes several tube stations should you want to cut it short at any point.

Turn right out of High Street Kensington tube and continue along Kensington Road until you reach Kensington Gardens. Cross the road, enter the park and head straight for the gates of Kensington Palace, the London residence of Diana, Princess of Wales.

Diana's extraordinary funeral, which began its procession to Westminster Abbey from here, provided a focal point for an unprecedented outburst of national grief, and on the anniversary of her death, people come to the palace to lay flowers or be photographed at the gates. Throughout the year children will enjoy the delightfully chaotic Peter Pan-themed adventure playground built in Diana's memory, or you can follow signs to the memorial fountain near the Serpentine.

Diana was, among many other things, a sort of patron saint of the New Age, a firm supporter and consumer of everything from aromatherapy to astrology. (She even had her apartments here rearranged by a specialist in *feng shui*, the oriental art of ordering living space to promote good fortune.) 'Diana was really a healer,' says Craig Brown, a GP and President of the National Federation of Spiritual Healers. 'Just by walking into a room and touching people and paying them attention, she healed them. Their illness may have continued but they felt better for it.' Diana must surely have contributed to the UK's burgeoning passion for alternative and complementary therapies: we now live

Freud Museum

Mind, body, spirit, soul

QUEENSWAY

LEINSTER TERR

Queensway

BAYSWATER ROAD

Children's Playground

Cafe

Elfin Oak

Peter Pan Statue

KENSINGTON

THE BROAD WALK

Round Pond

Kensington Palace

GARDENS

KENSINGTON CHURCH ST

KENSINGTON PALACE GDNS

PALACE AVE

LAND ST

St. Mary Abbots

SINGTON HIGH ST

KENSINGTON ROAD

Albert Memorial

Start

High St Kensington

YOUNG ST

DERRY

KENSINGTON CT

PALACE GATE

KENSINGTON GORE

Royal College of Art

JAY MEWS

Royal Albert Hall

EXHIBITION ROAD

VICTORIA ROAD

DE VERE GDNS

HYDE PARK GATE

HYDE PARK GATE

ALBERT COURT

QUEEN'S GATE

PRINCE CONSORT ROAD

Royal College of Music

PRINCES GDNS

ST ALBANS GR

QUEEN'S GATE TERRACE

Goethe Institute

VICTORIA ROAD

LAUNCESTON PLACE

GLOUCESTER ROAD

Imperial College of Science and Technology

ELVASTON PLACE

IMPERIAL COLLEGE RD

Science Museum

EXHIBITION ROAD

Victoria & Albert Museum

CORNWALL GARDENS

GRENVILLE PLACE

QUEEN'S GATE GDNS

EMPEROR'S GATE

Baden Powell House

Natural History Museum

CROMWELL ROAD

EXHIBITION PL

Gloucester Road

Institut Français

CROMWELL RD

SQUARE

THURLOE

Gloucester Road

STANHOPE

QUEEN'S GATE

HARRINGTON ROAD

REECE MEWS

CROMWELL RD

S. Kensington

S TERR

PELHAM ST

400 m

300 yds

© Copyright Time Out Group 2005

GLOUCESTER ROAD

COURTFIELD ROAD

STANHOPE GDNS

GLOUCESTER

CLAREVILLE GR

CLAREVILLE STREET

QUEEN'S GATE

BUTE ST

OLD BROMPTON ROAD

ONSLOW SQUARE

ONSLOW ROAD

ONSLOW GDNS

ONSLOW SQUARE

ONSLOW PLACE

FOULIS TERR

FULHAM

SELWOOD TERR

SELWOOD GR

Royal Marsden Hospital

in a country with significantly more healers and therapists than GPs.

The park itself was not opened to the public until Victoria's reign. The Jacobean palace became a royal residence under William and Mary in 1689; today the Kents and the Gloucesters have apartments here. Past the pretty Sunken Garden and Orangery there is another charming curiosity to show any children with you. Just by the Broadwalk children's playground stands the charming Elfin Oak, a huge 500-year-old tree stump inhabited by elves, pixies, fairies and woodland animals. Carved by sculptor Ivor Innes in 1911, it was restored with the help of comic Spike Milligan.

Leave the park where you came in,

cross Kensington Road and turn down Palace Gate opposite. Follow it as it turns into the upmarket parade of shops on Gloucester Road, among them Queens healthfood shop, which has a good range of natural cosmetics, dietary supplements and wholefood snacks.

Turn left into Cromwell Road and continue until you reach the Cromwell Mint casino, with the Natural History Museum opposite. Turn right down Queensberry Place, where, at No.16, stands the increasingly popular College of Psychic Studies, an educational charity founded in 1884 'to promote spiritual values and a greater understanding of the wider areas of human consciousness'.

Given its ecumenical aim of demonstrating that 'human personality

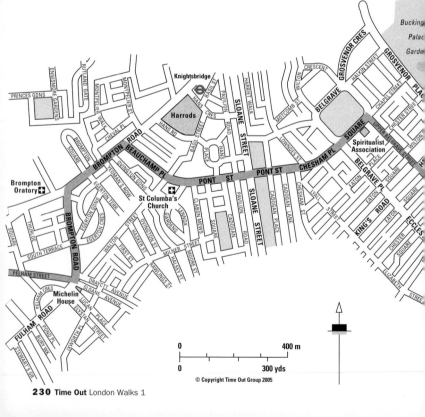

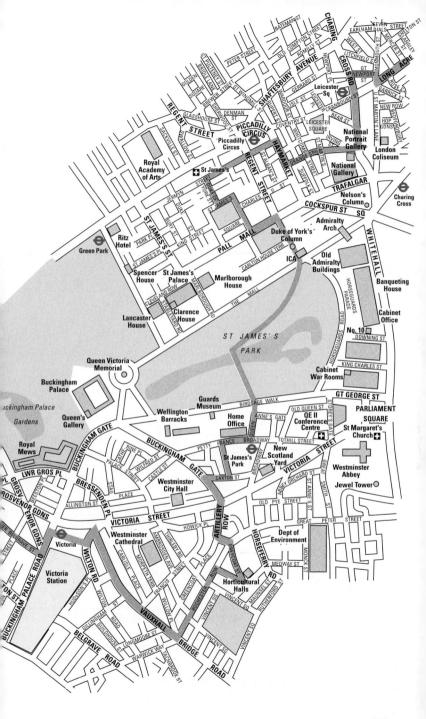

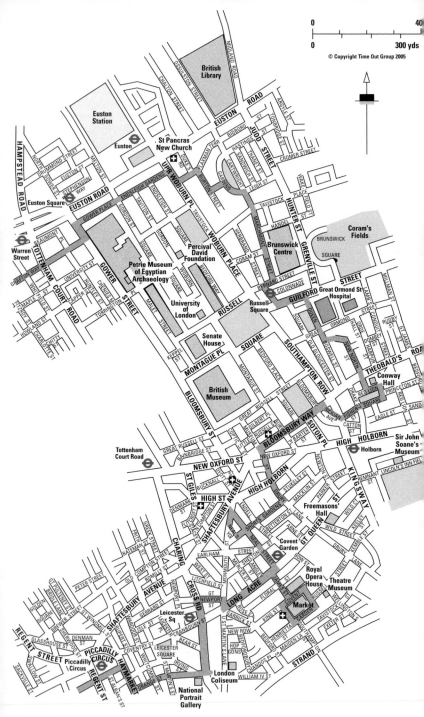

Mind, body, spirit, soul

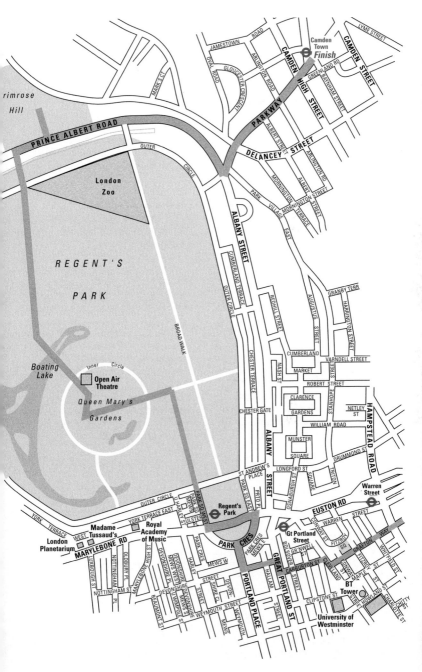

survives bodily death', it was no surprise that interest in the College soared after World War I, with the enthusiastic support of Sir Arthur Conan Doyle. The early days of other-worldly research – levitation, conversations with the dead, photographs of ghosts – have now given way to a contemporary emphasis on personal development. There's a wide variety of conventional courses and lectures covering personal growth, meditation, psychic development and trance, as well as 'channelled' lectures, where a spirit guide speaks through a human mouthpiece and one-to-one consultations with psychics, mediums and healers.

Follow the map to South Kensington tube – surely the only Underground station arcade where you can buy yourself an oriental rug. Continue past the station down Pelham Street, at the end of which you come out opposite Bibendum, a hugely expensive restaurant housed in the gloriously art deco Michelin House.

Turn left into the conspicuous consumerism of Brompton Road, eventually passing on your left the Roman Catholic Brompton Oratory, and behind it another church, the Holy Trinity. It's worth a quick peek inside the former. It was begun by Herbert Gribble in 1880, but much of its Baroque marble interior is authentic Italian and considerably older. Renowned for its emphasis on ritual and its high-profile congregations, it has been affectionately nicknamed the 'Ecclesiastical Department of the [adjacent] Victoria & Albert Museum'. The Oratory was also allegedly used until recently by KGB agents as a pick-up point for information.

The Holy Trinity church, known as 'HTB', is well-known as the centre of the Alpha Project, an evangelical Christianity course with a phenomenal conversion rate.

Turn right down Beauchamp Place and continue as it runs into Pont Street, past St Columba's Church (Church of Scotland). Walk on along Chesham Place and into Belgrave Square. At No. 33, past the embassies of Finland and Spain, stands another venerable occult institution, the Spiritualist Association of Great Britain. Here you can attend demonstrations of psychic art and clairvoyance, consult a medium or see a healer to find out if you are under 'psychic attack'. There is a café and a small, musty chapel, where messages have been left for loved ones who have 'passed to Spirit'. (I once attended a psychic art demonstration here, where a woman produced deft caricatures of the spirits apparently crowding round her. 'Don't all speak at once!' she snapped at them. 'I can only do one at a time!' Later she told us that one of the spirits she was drawing was reprimanding her for making his chin too big…)

Turn right out of the Spiritualist Association and follow the map to Vauxhall Bridge Road. At No.264 stands the Padre Pio Bookshop, devoted to the Italian Franciscan monk who was canonised in 2002. Padre Pio is said to have borne the stigmata (the wounds of the Crucifixion), and has been associated with a long list of miracles and supernatural good works, including apparently the trick of bilocation – appearing in two places at once. The shop contains a life-size statue of the man, plus a vast array of Catholic devotional objects from rosaries and veils to Virgin Mary plastic water bottles and high-kitsch 3-D postcards of Christ on the cross. Padre Pio's fingerless mitten is available for inspection, too.

Continue down Vauxhall Bridge, left into Rochester Row and right down Rochester Street to the Horticultural Halls, home to the Mind Body Spirit Festival in late May. Something of a cross between a trade fair and an Arab souk, this New Age jamboree offers stalls, demos, lectures and workshops on everything from gong therapy to dowsing, Tibetan singing bowls to sacred clowning, allergy testing to aura photography. All human life is here – probably a few other entities, too.

Follow the map to St James's Park. The oldest of the royal parks, it was set aside for hunting by Henry VIII. Along with the park's celebrity pelicans, descendants of a pair presented by Russia to Charles II, there's a wide selection of bird life and a truly Hitchcockian ordeal in store for anyone trying to feed them. Standing on the bridge over the lake, you are in the very heart of 'state' London, with a fine view of Buckingham Palace to your left and the jumbled façades of Horse Guard's Parade and Whitehall to your right. In the world, as it were, but not of it.

Once over the bridge, cut diagonally right across the park and go out opposite the Institute of Contemporary Arts (ICA) on the other side of The Mall. Housed in Carlton House Terrace, built by Regency architect John Nash, the ICA has celebrated over 50 years as a forum for exploring new directions in art – 'a laboratory rather than a museum,' in the words of Sir Herbert Read, 'where a new vision, a new consciousness is being evolved.' Its 1948 exhibition '40 Years of Modern Art', for instance, was the first assessment in this country of the Modernist movement; and it now hosts the annual Beck's Futures exhibition for UK-based emerging artistic talent. There's a good bookshop and, for a small day-membership fee, you can enjoy the late bar.

Climb the steps by the ICA and up into Waterloo Place, passing the (Grand Ol') Duke of York's column and the

Athenaeum gentleman's club on your left. (The almost identical building it faces is now the Institute of Directors.) Turn left along Pall Mall, then cross over and turn right into St James's Square. Here on Norfolk House on the right is a plaque marking Eisenhower's war efforts, and another, in the north-east corner, signals the spot where WPC Yvonne Fletcher was killed during the 1984 Libyan Embassy siege. Continue out of the square, up Duke of York Street, to emerge at the back of St James's, Piccadilly. This fine Christopher Wren church hosts an arts and crafts market (on the Piccadilly side), a Caffè Nero, free lunchtime concerts and a drop-in counselling service located in a bright green caravan. It's the postal address of the neo-Christian 'Creation Spirituality' movement – a spirituality premised on the essential goodness of creation which re-interprets 'original sin' as 'original blessing'. And it's home to Alternatives, a platform for 'exploring new ideas about consciousness and the sacred dimension of life from a non-dogmatic point of view'. Monday evening talks cover subjects such as Keys to Inner Freedom and Irresistible Self-Belief, and there are also weekend workshops. Speakers have included Paulo Coelho, Mark Rylance, Uri Geller and Deepak Chopra.

Follow the map to Charing Cross Road. On the way you'll pass the Hand &

Racquet pub, a favourite of Tony Hancock and his writers Galton and Simpson, which gets a mention in several of their *Half Hours*.

Turn left into Charing Cross Road. A little way up, cross over and pop down Cecil Court. This little bibliophile nirvana features Watkins Books, specialists in occultism, Eastern spirituality, alternative health and personal development. Watkins has the distinction of being founded (in 1897) as the direct result of a remark made by the occultist and adventurer Madame Blavatsky, who had been heard to complain that there was nowhere in London to buy books on mysticism and metaphysics. It was Blavatsky who founded the Theosophical Society in 1875 – later attracting such luminaries as WB Yeats, Thomas Edison and Vasily Kandinsky – and who did so much to introduce Eastern spirituality to the West. Wandering round Watkins, with its sections on Sufism, Divination and Ufology, you have the feeling that the key to all human knowledge is here. And hopefully they've got it second-hand.

Turn right down Great Newport Street, passing an outpost of the venerable veggie chain Cranks on the right. Cross St Martin's Lane and head along Long Acre.

If you fancy a break or a detour, turn right when you reach Covent Garden tube and walk down James Street for a wander around Covent Garden piazza, originally designed by Inigo Jones for the 17th-century aristocracy and now home to touristy market stalls, street entertainers (the likes of Eddie Izzard once performed here), the London Transport Museum (closed Aug 2005-late 2006) and the Royal Opera House. Also of interest is Jones's original church, St Paul's, known as the 'actors' church' and still a popular setting for memorial services for writers and performers.

Back at the tube, turn left into Neal Street and an area where hip meets hippie. In 1974 the wholesale fruit and vegetable market centred on the piazza was closed down and relocated. The whole area was threatened with conversion into office blocks, but the developers were kept at bay by a series of demonstrations and mass squats. Something of that spirit still lingers in these streets, now mixed in with a trendier, clubby vibe.

Among the converted Victorian warehouses of Neal Street, Food for Thought has been ladling out delicious veggie fare since 1971. (According to the *Vegetarian London* guide, Covent Garden has 'the greatest concentration of cruelty-free eating places in Britain'.)

Just off Neal Street, in Shorts Gardens, a little alleyway lined with travellers, skateboarders and backpackers takes you into Neal's Yard itself, a little island of alternative life that has retained a distinct community feel. Here you'll find some fine veggie cafés, a salad bar, Neal's Yard Remedies (where you can buy fresh organic herbs and homoeopathic remedies), an organic bakery and a therapy parlour.

Out through the other end of Neal's Yard and a right into Monmouth Street brings us to Mysteries, a New Age bookshop offering tarot, palm reading and healing. The room at the back, dedicated to tapes and videos, contains a Sacred Space or Fortunate Blessings Corner replete with fountain, Buddha, wind chimes, plants and crystals. Check out the notice board, too, with its astral messages, New Age-related flyers and offers of didgeridoo lessons.

Natural History Museum

Turn right out of Mysteries and back into Neal Street, where the Astrology Shop guarantees you a personal horoscope in five minutes. Then it's left into Shorts Gardens, past Inner Space, a 'meditation and self-development centre' and left along Drury Lane, crossing High Holborn and New Oxford Street. Bear right into Bloomsbury Way, past the Hawksmoor church of St George's.

Continue up Bloomsbury Way past the Swedenborg Society bookshop, then turn right through Sicilian Avenue. Cross over Southampton Row, go down Fisher Street and come out into Red Lion Square. We've come here to see Conway Hall, tucked away in the far corner, and run by the humanist South Place Ethical Society. It has a proud history as a platform for free speech. Sometimes known as 'the home of lost causes', or more charitably as 'Speakers' Corner with a roof', the venue is a truly broad church, opening its doors to a bewildering plurality of causes, from paganists to Scottish nationalists, humanist memorial services (with disco after) to Filipino Valentine's Day dances. There's always something going down here, not least the Sunday concerts (October to April), a regular event since 1887.

Back in Red Lion Square, cut down Old North Street and cross Theobalds Road into New North Street directly opposite. Turn left into Boswell Court and right into Queen Square. Here, on Great Ormond Street, stands the freshly refurbished Royal London Homoeopathic Hospital.

Homoeopathic remedies are said to work according to the principle of 'like cures like': a substance that produces certain symptoms in a healthy person will heal similar symptoms in an ill person. Remedies are infinitesimally dilute. Patients are referred by their GP to the hospital, a NHS Trust since 1993 and thought to be the only publicly funded complementary hospital in Europe. Other therapies, such as nutritional medicine, osteopathy and acupuncture are also used, in tandem with conventional medicine.

The Royals have long favoured homoeopathy, ever since Queen Adelaide, wife of William IV, took remedies in 1835. The hospital got its 'royal' prefix from George VI, who once named a racehorse after a remedy (Hypericum). Today's patron is the Queen, who takes remedies with her on her travels and has a homoeopathic doctor among her staff.

Another big fan of complementary therapies is Prince Charles, who has instituted a Foundation of Integrated Medicine to help reconcile differences between orthodox and alternative approaches. Certainly there is more official acceptance than ever before, with six NHS homoeopathic hospitals, universities opening departments of complementary medicine, and an estimated 40 per cent of GP partnerships in England providing some form of complementary treatment.

If you're feeling peckish, there are a couple of interesting places to eat around Queen Square – a wholefood café at the Mary Ward adult learning centre and a 'world food' café in the October Gallery around the corner.

Walk the length of Queen Square, where George III was once privately treated for his 'madness', and follow the map to the pavement parade of Woburn Walk. (The extensively stocked Alara Wholefoods at 58 Marchmont Street is good on organic and vegan fare, including wines, and has a great lunchtime takeaway selection.)

Turn right out of Woburn Walk into Upper Woburn Place. (St Pancras church on the corner here has free lunchtime recitals on Thursdays.) Cross over and turn left down Endsleigh Gardens and head on as it becomes Gower Place and passes University College, the first university to accept women students on an equal footing. Cross Gower Street and continue into Grafton Way virtually opposite, which will take you past University College Hospital. Cross Tottenham Court Road and follow the map to Portland Place.

The Hale Clinic

Turning right out of Portland Place we reach the elegant sweep of Regency terraces that is Park Crescent, originally planned by John Nash as part of a grand entrance to Regent's Park. The Hale Clinic, at No.7, is London's best-known complementary medicine centre, with around 80 practitioners (including 12 GPs). Officially opened in 1987 by the Prince of Wales, it was a haunt of his first wife, who was rumoured to come here for colonic irrigation. Other famous clients have included Linda McCartney, Richard Gere, Arnie and Fergie. The huge range of therapies on offer in the warren of treatment rooms include: ear acupuncture, lymphatic drainage, neuro-linguistic programming, ayurveda… Or you can pop in and browse around the separately owned bookshop and education centre downstairs.

Turn left out of Park Crescent, past Regent's Park tube. Cross busy Marylebone Road into Park Square West opposite and onto Regent's Park proper, an unfinished John Nash project on more land bagged for hunting by Henry VIII. Making your way northwards through London's cleanest green lung (according to a recent public survey), there's a reasonable cafeteria within the Inner Circle, which also houses the Open Air Theatre. To the west stands the spectacular profile of London Central Mosque, built in 1978. The coffin of Diana's companion, Dodi Al Fayed, was brought here for prayers in the hours following the fatal Paris crash, after which it processed southwards to a cemetery in Woking.

Follow the signs to London Zoo. The former wolves' enclosure on the Broadwalk side has been a feature of the zoo since it opened in 1829. Bram Stoker studied them while researching the transformation scenes for his novel *Dracula*; Richard E Grant regaled them with a drunken Hamlet soliloquy in the cult movie *Withnail and I*; and Ted Hughes found comfort in their howling after the suicide of his wife Sylvia Plath (see *Birthday Letters*). Sadly, the wolves have long since moved to a new home.

Beyond the zoo, head on north to Primrose Hill, crossing the Outer Circle, the footbridge over the Grand Union Canal and finally Prince Albert Road. The top of this grassy extension to Regent's Park affords a fine view back across the zoo over central London and beyond. It's sometimes used by UFO-spotters, and Druids used to hold a ceremony here at the summer solstice and some equinoxes. Returning to the bottom of Primrose Hill, turn left along Prince Albert Road and left again at the big junction down Parkway, at the bottom of which lies Camden Town tube.

The more psychoanalytically minded may prefer to catch a 31 or 46 bus round to Finchley Road to visit the Freud Museum, where the big man spent his last years, initially as an exile from Nazi Germany. His original couch is here, brought from Vienna, and there's a good bookshop, too. And if you fancy a spot of therapy yourself, you're heading in the right direction: up towards Hampstead, and the bulging waiting rooms of NW3…

Eating & drinking

Bibendum

Michelin House, 81 Fulham Road, SW3 6RD (7581 5817/www.bibendum.co.uk). **Open** *Oyster bar* noon-10.30pm Mon-Sat; noon-10pm Sun. *Restaurant* noon-2.30pm, 7-11.30pm Mon-Fri; 12.30-3pm, 7-11.30pm Sat; 12.30-3pm, 7-10.30pm Sun. Expensive modern European fare in a handsomely restored setting. The oyster bar is a less costly, more casual option.

Food for Thought

31 Neal Street, WC2H 9PR (7836 0239). **Open** noon-8.30pm Mon-Sat; noon-5pm Sun. Generous, filling and unpretentious vegetarian nosh.

Hand & Racquet

48 Whitcomb Street, WC2H 7DS (7930 5905). **Open** 11am-11pm Mon-Sat.

Garden Café

Queen Mary's Gardens, Inner Circle, Regent's Park, NW1 4NU (7935 5729). **Open** 10am-5pm Mon-Fri; 8am-5pm Sat, Sun.

Mary Ward Centre Café

42 Queen Square, WC1N 3AQ (7831 7711/ www.marywardcentre.ac.uk). **Open** 9.30am-8pm Mon-Fri; 11am-4pm Sat. Vegetarian.

Galleries, museums & theatres

Freud Museum

20 Maresfield Gardens, NW3 5SX (7435 2002/ www.freud.org.uk). **Open** noon-5pm Wed-Sun. **Admission** £5; £2 concessions.

ICA Gallery

The Mall, SW1Y 5AH (7930 3647/www.ica.org.uk). **Open** *Exhibitions* noon-7.30pm daily. **Admission** £1.50; £1 concessions Mon-Fri; £2.50, £1.50 concessions Sat, Sun.

London's Transport Museum

Covent Garden Piazza, WC2E 7BB (7379 6344/ www.ltmuseum.co.uk). **Open** 10am-6pm Mon-Thur, Sat, Sun; 11am-6pm Fri. **Admission** £5.95; £4.50 concessions; free under-16s when accompanied by an adult. Note that the museum is closed until November 2006 for refurbishment.

London Zoo

Regent's Park, NW1 4RY (7722 3333/www.london zoo.co.uk). **Open** *Nov-Feb* 10am-4pm daily. *Mar-Oct* 10am-5.30pm daily. **Admission** £14; £10.75 concessions.

Natural History Museum

Cromwell Road, SW7 5BD (7942 5011/www.nhm. ac.uk). **Open** 10am-5.50pm Mon-Sat; 11am-5.50pm Sun. **Admission** free; charge for special exhibitions.

October Gallery

24 Old Gloucester Street, WC1N 3AL (7242 7367/ www.octobergallery.co.uk). **Open** 12.30-5.30pm Tue-Sat. *Café* 12.30am-2.30pm Tue-Fri.

Regent's Park Open Air Theatre

Regent's Park, NW1 (0870 060 1811).

Mind & body

Alara Wholefoods

58-60 Marchmont Street, WC1N 1AB (7837 1172). **Open** 9am-6pm Mon-Wed, Fri; 9am-7pm Thur; 10am-6pm Sat.

Alternatives

St James's Church, 197 Piccadilly, W1J 9LL (7287 6711/www.alternatives.org.uk). **Open** depends on event, phone or check website for details.

The Hale Clinic

7 Park Crescent, W1B 1PF (0870 167 6667/ www.haleclinic.com). **Open** 8.30am-8.30pm Mon-Fri; 9am-5pm Sat.

Horticultural Halls

80 Vincent Square, SW1T 2PE (7828 4125/www. horticultural-halls.co.uk). Mind Body Spirit Festival (Spring)/Healing Arts Festival (November). For details call 7371 9191 or see www.mindbodyspirit.co.uk.

Inner Space

Brahma Kumaris Information Centre, 36 Shorts Gardens, WC2H 9AB (7836 6688/www.inner space.org.uk). **Open** 10.30am-6pm Mon-Thur, Sat; 10.30am-5pm Fri.

Mysteries

9-11 Monmouth Street, WC2H 9DA (7240 3688/ www.mysteries.co.uk). **Open** 10am-7pm Mon-Fri; 10am-6pm Sat; noon-5pm Sun.

Queens Health Shop

64 Gloucester Road, SW7 4QT (7584 4815). **Open** 9am-7pm Mon-Fri; 9am-5.30pm Sat.

Royal Homeopathic Hospital

60 Great Ormond Street, WC1N 3HR (7837 8833/ www.uclh.org).

Swedenborg Society

Swedenborg House, 20-21 Bloomsbury Way, WC1A 2TH (7405 7986/www.swedenborg.org.uk). **Open** 9.30am-5pm Mon-Fri.

Watkins Books

19 Cecil Court, WC2N 4EZ (7836 2182/www. watkinsbooks.com). **Open** 11am-7pm Mon-Sat.

Parks & palaces

Kensington Gardens

W8 (7298 2117/www.royalparks.gov.uk). **Open** dawn-dusk daily.

Kensington Palace

Kensington Gardens, W8 4PX (7937 9561/www.hrp org.uk). **Open** *Apr-Oct* 10am-5pm daily. *Nov-Mar* 10am-4pm daily. Palace is open for tours of the State Apartments.

Regent's Park

Prince Albert Road, NW1 (7486 7905/www.royal parks.gov.uk). **Open** dawn-30min before dusk daily.

St James's Park

The Mall, SW1 (7930 1793/www.royalparks.gov.uk). **Open** dawn-dusk daily.

Shopping

The Astrology Shop

78 Neal Street, WC2H 9PA (7813 3051/www. londonastrology.com). **Open** 11am-7pm Mon-Sat; noon-6pm Sun.

Spirit & soul

Brompton Oratory

Thurloe Place, Brompton Road, SW7 2RP (7808 0900). **Services** 6pm Sat (first mass of Sunday); 7am, 8am, 9am,10am (family), 11am (Latin), 12.30pm 4.30pm, 7pm Sun; 7am, 10am, 12.30pm, 6pm (Latin) Mon-Fri; 7am, 8.30am, 10am Sat.

College of Psychic Studies

16 Queensberry Place, SW7 2EB (7589 3292/ www.collegeofpsychicstudies.co.uk). **Open** 10.30am-7.30pm Mon-Fri; 9.15am-2.15pm Sat.

Conway Hall

25 Red Lion Square, WC1R 4RL (7242 8037). **Open** *office* 2pm-6pm daily. Ring for appointments or details.

Holy Trinity, Brompton

Brompton Road, SW7 1JA (7581 8255/www.htb. org.uk). **Open** 9.30am-5.30pm Mon, Wed-Fri; 10.30am-5.30pm Tue.

London Central Mosque

146 Park Road, NW8 7RG (7724 3363). **Open** 3.30am-5.30am, 8.30am-11pm daily; office 10.30am-4.30pm daily.

Kensington Gardens

Padre Pio Bookshop

264 Vauxhall Bridge Road, SW1V 1BB (7834 5363).
Open 9.45am-6pm Mon-Sat.

St Columba's Church

Pont Street, SW1X 0BD (7584 2321/www.
stcolumbas.org.uk). **Open** 10am-1pm, 2-4.30pm
Mon-Fri; for services on Sunday (phone for times).

St George's, Bloomsbury

Bloomsbury Way, WC1A 2HR (7405 3044/www.
stgeorgesbloomsbury.org.uk). **Open** 9.30am-5.30pm
Mon-Fri; 9.30am-1pm Sat, Sun.

St James's, Piccadilly

197 Piccadilly, W1J 9LL (7734 4511/www.st-james-
piccadilly.org). **Open** 8.30am-9pm Mon; 8am-7pm
Tue-Sun.

St Pancras New Church

Upper Woburn Place, NW1 2BA (7388 1461/
www.stpancraschurch.org). **Open** 11am-2pm Thur;
9.30-11am Sat. *Services* phone for details.

St Paul's, Covent Garden

Bedford Street, WC2E 9ED (7836 5221/
www.actorschurch.org). **Open** 8.30am-4.30pm
Mon-Fri; 9.30am-1pm Sun. *Services* phone for details.
Built by Inigo Jones, this church has been here since
1633. The churchyard is a restful spot in a busy part
of London.

Spiritualist Association
of Great Britain

33 Belgrave Square, SW1X 8QB (7235 3351/
www.spiritualistassociation.org.uk). **Open** noon-7pm
Mon-Fri; 11am-4.30pm Sat; 3-6pm Sun.

In the money

Irma Kurtz

Answering all those difficult questions about the streets and shops of Knightsbridge.

Start: Knightsbridge tube, Brompton Road exit
Finish: Knightsbridge tube
Distance: 8 miles/12.5km
Time: 4 hours
Getting there and back: Piccadilly line to or from Knightsbridge
Note: best to go when the shops are open…

My best friend, Ian, describes the act of walking as falling forward with intent. And that is precisely the way I have walked the great cities of this planet: falling into them as into love, with the intent of making magic (and occasionally thereafter with the intent of getting out alive). Strictly speaking, what I do is not precisely walking, or strolling, or even ambling: I meander in loops and circles, big and small, mainly these days around London, the wonderful city I fell in love with more than 40 years ago and continue to fall into, and love.

Mind you, mine is a street-market, bombed-out church, reclaimed plague-pit kind of attraction; I generally steer clear of areas where new money goes to grow old. I can count on one fist, for instance, the number of times in the past 20 years I have had the need or inclination to clamber out of the underground at Knightsbridge. Thus, learning in the course of a long walk to be charmed by too-too-debby Knightsbridge and its air-kissing neighbours – South Kensington and Belgravia – came as an entertaining revelation, like learning one's long-time darling has a hitherto unsuspected talent for yodelling.

I dragged myself free of the flow of hysterically driven shoppers being drawn out of Knightsbridge underground witlessly towards Harrods – never a destination of my heart – and turned right out of the Brompton Road exit, right again onto Sloane Street, and then once again behind the tube into quiet old Basil Street. If the unlikely day comes when I need to stay in a Knightsbridge hotel and I have around £200 a night to spend (that'll be the night!), the Basil Street Hotel will be my choice. Decorated with the glow and patina of a grand country house, and still serving a real Afternoon Tea, it is infinitely more alluring than big hotels in the neighbourhood, once grand but these days Disneyfied to purvey upstart dollar ostentation, not the genuine Olde English, bred-in-the-bone snobbery of the privately owned Basil Street Hotel.

Having entered Harrods humbly via the back door and made a pilgrimage through the food halls, tiled magnificently early in the century, I headed for the open air, away from the reek of burning yen and euro. Here I saw that the posh purlieus of my memory were changing. No planetary force will bring a market down and despoil a landscape for ever as effectively as that very El Niño of our high streets, McDonald's, and one of them was raging in the Brompton Road, a few yards away from one of Harrods' front doors.

In spite of flash names in nouveau couture on shop fronts, the area has a new down-at-mouth air, if not quite at heel. In Beauchamp Place, once bright and fashionable, a couple of disconsolate paparazzi slouched mournfully. Having lost the beautiful princess who favoured

San Lorenzo, they can expect no act classier than Naomi Campbell, or one of that ilk, to come out swinging and run her car.

San Lorenzo has long been a watering hole for the arrived and the arriving and the arrivistes. Once upon a time, when the world was young, I, too, used to lunch there, sometimes with a friend who was married to one of a brand new pop group called 'The Rolling Stones'. Or something. However, it was San Lorenzo's less fashionable neighbour, a little place called 132, that teased a memory submerged somewhere in London's great lunching decade, the 1960s. I stood thoughtfully for a minute on the pavement outside, struggling to recollect it, until something told me what or who was better forgotten and why I was better off forgetting.

Back on the Brompton Road, the only local pub I remember fondly (or at all), the Bunch of Grapes, holds out in oaken pride at the corner of Yeoman's Row. But it was too early for drink, and besides, the inner woman was already yammering for spiritual ease: a church stop, not a pit stop, is what she needed, there among the flesh pots of Knightsbridge. So it's over the road, past pretty Brompton Square, and straight to the door of the London Oratory of St Philip Neri – the Brompton Oratory.

O! Chill my zealous heart! The first thing I see is a sign under the portico warning: 'Begging in the church and forecourt is not permitted....'

Thus, as tourist, not supplicant, dutifully, not hopefully, I entered to admire respectfully, not reverentially, the baroque fixtures, contained in a building based by the architect, good old Herbert Gribble, on the church of Chiesa Nuova in Rome. According to a friend who is deeply into matters of espionage, in the late 1970s the KGB used one of the pillars flanking the main altar as a dead letter drop. Cheeky beggars!

I left impressed, not blessed.

Cheek to jowl with the exotic Oratory, the competition runs Holy Trinity, Brompton along strictly Anglican lines. The place was full of bustling women and bearded men setting up for a feast; trestle tables covered in white cloths replacing pews, and children rushing around, pushing wheeled toys into noisy collisions.

I beseeched a plump young matron near the door: 'Can you help me?'

Her earnest blue eyes welled with joy, she sketched a gesture of welcome, and I all but heard her say, 'At last! I've got one!' Alas, all I needed were directions to the Russian Orthodox Church, which I knew was somewhere nearby. She hadn't a clue where.

Walking through the pleasantly untidy garden behind Brompton Oratory is to enjoy luxurious silence such as few cities

Harrods – the grandest of them all.

on earth can offer. London surprises consistently with pockets of silence like this. Once upon a time the charming mews houses at the bottom of the garden looked out over Kensington Village, and though the view is gone, they still have the enviable serenity of homes on high places. Left into Ennismore Gardens, the shady square itself for keyholders only, and I am thrilled by the sighting of a rare turquoise Bentley with matching beige chauffeur and upholstery.

Towards the top of the wide street and there, set back from it, is the Russian Orthodox Church, serving a parish in London since 1741, on this location since 1956. Over the threshold, the smell of old incense seems to fill the upper spaces with mist; there are no pews, this Orthodoxy prays on its feet. A hooded figure, sexless and ageless, is lighting a candle before a cluster of icons. Icons hang everywhere – some ordinary, some mysterious, a few

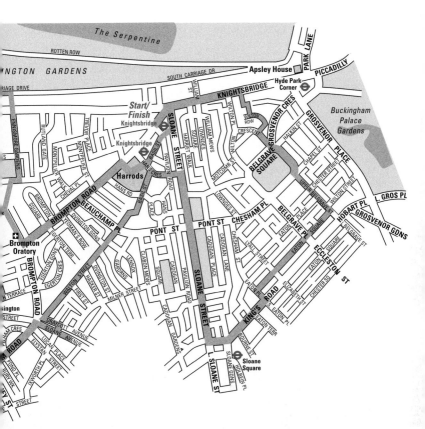

orgeous nearly beyond belief. At the altar,
front of a superb icon screen, it isn't
ng before the inner woman finds herself
stored and refreshed, ready to hit the
ad again and head for Hyde Park.
Falling forward intentionally on grass
soothing after pavements. Had I bought
takeaway, say, from Harrods Food Hall,
d have picnicked in the park near the
rtatious ghosts of Rotten Row. But
hadn't, so I didn't. Nor did I threaten
st-iconic calm with a visit to the avant-
arde Serpentine Gallery, only a few
undred yards away, in case something
nbearably contemporary and gruesome
as being exhibited there. Instead, I
ossed at Coalbrookdale Gate, paid

respects to the Prince Albert Memorial,
then, over to the Albert Hall, which, being
circular, insists upon being walked all
the way around under its running frieze,
from the Royal College of Art and the
Royal College of Music, to the mansion
blocks of Kensington Gore; some of them,
I hear, equipped with wine cellars. A fine
title for a thriller: Kensington Gore. Or
an exhibition at the Serpentine Gallery.

The Albert Hall, to paraphrase Sir
Thomas Beecham, is useful for a hundred
things: music is not one of them. Its
notorious echo was toned down in the
1960s; nevertheless, it always seems to
me a venue for 'musical events', rather
than pure sound. The annual series of

Promenade Concerts was moved here in 1941 when its old home was bombed, and anyone who still believes London to be staid and hidebound ought to attend the last night of the Proms and see what a raucous bunch of iconoclasts the natives can be.

Heading back, this time down Exhibition Road, past the golden blade of the Mormon temple that stabs the sky aggressively, the street was as ever packed with tourists and tour buses, self-important and not at all pedestrian-friendly. I gave the Science, Natural History and Victoria and Albert Museums a miss, as each constitutes a walk in itself. Mind you, museum restaurants are good places for shy people to lunch – there is no shame in solitude for culture vultures. Museums are also good, I seem to remember, for picking up European men. But I'm too bold to need a museum lunch, too old for a Continental catch.

So it was over the Brompton Road for a moody perambulation around Thurloe Square. Not long before I'd come across The Weeping and the Laughter, the autobiography of Viva King, erstwhile London lady of fashion, who used to live in one of the elegant houses on the square. Standing there in the bookshop, I had checked the index shamelessly: Noel Coward, yes, Augustus John, certainly, Peggy Guggenheim, you bet your boots, and naturally, Norman Douglas. But no listing of the awkward, awed American girl, swept along once or twice in the entourage of a Cambridge queen to Viva's salon. Viva had fallen for a young tough and was allowing him to ruin her in so classic a manner, even now I feel I never actually met the great hostess of Thurloe Square: I read her in a French novel.

Out of Thurloe Square, approaching South Kensington station, I gaze through the window of the Café Daquise at the happy carnivores chomping on Pork Knuckle Golanka and other substantial Polish fodder I never had the chance to taste in my meat-eating youth, and now in my fibrous, grazing years probably never shall. Even the potato pancakes being served look somehow meaty, not for us in the alfalfa of our dotage.

Londoners know their town by compass points, born New Yorkers like me think up, down, mid; Londoners tell urban distances in miles, I will continue to think in blocks. For about a mile (20 blocks) due west (downtown) the Old Brompton Road, unlike the younger one, serves a residential area, providing video shops, estate agents, off-licences and other necessities of workaday London life, until, just past the Coleherne pub – a really useful rendezvous for boys in leather – it offers the final service. When I was pregnant, I used to walk the cemeteries, looking for inspiration. And it was here, 26 years ago, in Brompton Cemetery, that I found a middle name for my little Londoner. He will never speak to me again if I say more than that it is Biblical.

The 'Great Circle' of catacombs and imposing mausolea allows death and sex to conjoin in shady privacy; an alliance unforeseen back in 1840 by the cemetery's designer, the appropriately named Benjamin Baud. It remains one of London's gay cruising grounds; poignant situated outside its Fulham Road exit is the Kobler Centre, attached to the Chelsea and Westminster Hospital and devoted to the treatment of HIV and AIDS.

Every traveller owes it to whimsy to take a turning sometimes for no real reason. So I turn off the seething Fulham Road into Hollywood Road just for its name. After an energising stop at the Hollywood Arms, a shop sign caught my eye: 'Swann's Way', it said, and its advertised speciality, Austrian womenswear, was so recherché, I decided it deserved a look. What passes for a stroke of luck in a smaller town takes on a supernatural gloss in London's vastness: you would have thought me

Beauchamp Place – the fashionistas may have moved on, but it still exudes style.

had to see me leap about when the shop's co-owner turned out to be an old friend, Holly Berry, now Lady Rumbold, with whom I'd lost touch going on for 100 years ago.

En route once more. A tingling perfume in the air I had come across before in Palm Springs, Martha's Vineyard, Monte Carlo; it is the smell of money growing on trees. That was no mother pushing a pram my way, I promise you; it had to be a virgin nanny or au pair. And the man in overalls painting the gate before one of the white mansions fell about laughing when I asked in passing: 'Your own place?' These two crescents around a central garden compose the Boltons, one of the most exclusive residential areas in any city.

'Ten million to buy,' said a handyman, taking a break in the garden, behind the Boltons' very own church, St Mary's, 'and then around 30 million more for squash courts, swimming pools and that. Most of 'em are English. But see that big white house over there? Belongs to a German who owns all the iron in the world.'

'Does that,' I asked, 'make him a magnet?'

At one end of the crescents, Bousfield Primary School, built on a site where Beatrix Potter used to live, looked clunky and jerry-built in all that 19th-century

splendour despite having won design awards in the 1950s: a bit like me, in fact. London's profusion of mews and lesser alleys affords stretches of traffic-free meandering – a right turn from the Old Brompton Road took me into the narrow footpath of Thistle Grove, just such a quiet anachronism, past walled gardens and cottages where householders polished brass doorknockers, all the way back to the Fulham Road without encountering a car. At the corner of Old Church Street stands what was once the Queen's Elm pub, named for the tree under which Elizabeth I sheltered from a sudden shower: for more than three centuries a licensed premises; the pub where Laurie Lee used to drink with cronies; also incidentally where yours truly began and pretty much ended one of her more spectacularly ill-advised love affairs. Vestiges of the old place remain, but it has been tarted up inside. I averted my eyes.

The Fulham Road from here is good for window-shopping: jolly fake jewellery makes Butler & Wilson into a fairyland grotto, and many shops sell designer household goods, all ending in a crescendo of taste in the Michelin Building, which sits like a gigantic art deco teapot at the top of Sloane Avenue. Appropriately, Sir

Brompton Oratory

JOHN·HENRY
CARDINAL·NEWMAN
1801 – 1890

Terence Conran, the man who more than 40 years ago yanked London's style into the 20th century, has a bailiwick here, the Conran Shop and Bibendum, with his kind of minimalist chic in food and houseware.

With a sinking sensation in my wallet I try to avert my eyes from the nucleus of designers' shops at the top of Sloane Avenue. Where does it come from? The feeling that a piece of velvet not much bigger than the posh label stitched into its lining can change one's life forever? Will power, I bid you farewell as I try and fail to hurry past alluring windows full of overpriced rags that whisper: 'Buy me! You cannot live without me!'

I used to bus my son to a posh school in this area from the far less salubrious part of London where we were living. Walton Street hasn't changed, twee antique shops and tweer houses, except that sushi is the new pizza. No doubt dreadful deeds have occurred behind these smug doors – murders, rapes, incest, treachery – but so well kept are secrets on middle-class London streets like this that my big-city antennae relax as they never do on the more flamboyantly rich streets of Belgravia, say, or Mayfair. The distance back again past Harrods, whence all roads lead in SW7, and over to Sloane Street is a pleasant stroll. Sloane Street itself sparkles with yet more names of upper-middle fashion: Versace, Dior, Vuitton. If I recollect correctly, the residential block, Knightsbridge Court, is where John Lennon's dentist used to practise: perhaps still does.

My first flat in London was in Chelsea only a few blocks from Sloane Square, back when it was a villagey neighbourhood. Then, I woke up one morning to find that our local butcher, greengrocer and chemist overnight had turned into stores selling pixie-boots and mini-skirts; Chelsea had begun to swing. To be honest, the innovative Royal Court Theatre, built where once stood a Dissenters' chapel on the south side of Sloane Square, is about the only mature eason to come here. Sedately, I turned my back on the King's Road and headed instead to Belgravia.

Call me curmudgeonly, but I am not crazy about Belgravia. Perhaps I would have preferred it back in the 18th century when the area was leafy by day, and feared by night for violent thieving. Now, it is glacial and remote and phoney, bespeaking crimes, if any, of a high-financial nature. And one incredibly inept crime of high passion in Eaton Row, where Lord Lucan murdered the nanny, mistaking her, presumably, for his wife. Whether the missing earl is on the run or dead by his own hand, he remains to this day an icon for T-shirt manufacturers all over the world. Granted, my low opinion of Belgravia is coloured because back in the days when journalism required me to interview celebrities, the most vain and arrogant and downright stupid movie stars were, mostly, found in rented flats around the area. The best part of Belgravia, as far as I am concerned, is the way I leave it, via tiny Wilton Row, behind the looming Lanesborough Hotel – once St George's Hospital – where is to be found the Grenadier pub, one of the prettiest in London, originally officers' mess for the Duke of Wellington, and haunted they say, though only in September, by the ghost of a card-cheating bounder.

After a pick-me-up it was through Old Barrack Yard back into Knightsbridge, where it all began. Many years ago when I was new in London, I was riding on the top of a rush-hour bus past this very spot. It was the first day of a tardy spring. Hanging in the branches of a tree at Hyde Park Corner at just about my eye level I saw a furled umbrella and a bowler hat; other items of apparel were scattered on the grass, and dancing in the thin sunlight was a man as naked as the day he was born. I looked around at the other passengers; nobody seemed in the least surprised. There you have it: the moment I fell intentionally in love with London.

Eating & drinking

Bibendum
Michelin House, 81 Fulham Road, SW3 6RD (7581 5817/www.bibendum.co.uk). **Open** *Oyster bar* noon-10.30pm Mon-Sat; noon-10pm Sun. *Restaurant* **Lunch served** noon-2.30pm Mon-Fri; 12.30-3pm Sat, Sun. **Dinner served** 7-11.30pm Mon-Sat; 7-10.30pm Sun. Expensive modern European fare in a handsomely restored setting. The oyster bar is a less costly, more casual option.

Bunch of Grapes
207 Brompton Road, SW3 1LA (7589 4944). **Open** 11am-11pm Mon-Sat; noon-10.30pm Sun. Perfect Victorian interior and standard English pub food.

The Coleherne
261 Old Brompton Road, SW5 9JA (7244 5951). **Open** noon-11pm Mon-Sat; noon-10.30pm Sun.

Daquise
20 Thurloe Street, SW7 2LP (7589 6117). **Open** 11.30am-11pm daily. Blinis, chlodnik, zrazy and, of course, borscht in this old Polish favourite.

The Grenadier
18 Wilton Row, SW1X 7NR (7235 3074). **Open** noon-11pm Mon-Sat; noon-10.30pm Sun. Good beer, fine traditional British cooking and a cosy feel – with a few glamorous fans, too.

Le Metro
28 Basil Street, SW3 1AS (7591 1213). **Breakfast served** 7.30am-noon Mon-Sat; 8.30am-noon Sun. **Lunch served** noon-3pm, **dinner served** 6-10pm, Mon-Sat. French basement café-bar, good for a quick bite, with lots of wines by the glass.

San Lorenzo
22 Beauchamp Place, SW3 1NH (7584 1074). **Lunch served** 12.30-3pm, **dinner served** 7.30-11.30pm Mon-Sat. Open since 1963, this large restaurant has a reputation as a celebrity hangout. The menu is heavy on Italian classics. Children are made welcome.

Hotels

Basil Street Hotel
8 Basil Street, SW3 1AH (7581 3311/ www.thebasil.com).

The Lanesborough Hotel
1 Lanesborough Place, Hyde Park Corner, SW1X 7TA (7259 5599/www.lanesborough.com).

Information

Royal College of Art
Kensington Gore, SW7 2EU (7590 4444/www.rca. ac.uk). **Open** 9.30am-5.30pm Mon-Fri.

Royal College of Music
Prince Consort Road, SW7 2BS (7589 3643/
www.rcm.ac.uk). **Open** varies. Stages at least one
lunchtime chamber music concert every Mon-Thur
during term time, with occasional evening events.

Museums & galleries

Albert Memorial
Kensington Gardens, SW7. The stunning memorial
to Queen Victoria's husband.

Natural History Museum
Cromwell Road, SW7 5BD (7942 5011/www.nhm.
ac.uk). **Open** 10am-5.50pm Mon-Sat; 11am-5.50pm
Sun. **Admission** free; charge for special exhibitions.

Science Museum
Exhibition Road, SW7 2DD (7942 4454/
www.sciencemuseum.org.uk). **Open** 10am-5.45pm
daily. **Admission** free. **Exhibitions** prices vary.

Serpentine Gallery
Kensington Gardens (nr Albert Memorial), W2 3XA
(7402 6075/www.serpentinegallery.org). **Open**
10am-6pm daily. *Tours* 3pm Sat. **Admission** free.

Victoria & Albert Museum
Cromwell Road, SW7 2RL (7938 8500/www.vam.
ac.uk). **Open** 10am-5.45pm Mon, Tue, Thur-Sun;
10am-10pm Wed, last Fri of mth. **Tours** daily; phone
for details. **Admission** free. *Exhibitions* prices vary.

Shopping

Butler & Wilson
189 Fulham Road, SW3 6JN (7352 3045/
www.butlerandwilson.co.uk). **Open** 10am-6pm Mon,
Tue, Thur-Sat; 10am-7pm Wed; noon-6pm Sun.

Christian Dior
31 Sloane Street, SW1X 9NR (7235 1357). **Open**
10am-6.30pm Mon, Tue, Thur-Sat; 10am-7pm Wed;
noon-5pm Sun.

Conran Shop
81 Fulham Road, SW3 6RD (7589 7401/www.
conran.com). **Open** 10am-6pm Mon, Tue, Fri; 10am-
7pm Wed, Thur; 10am-6.30pm Sat; noon-6pm Sun.

Harrods
87-135 Brompton Road, SW1X 7XL (7730 1234/
www.harrods.com). **Open** 10am-7pm Mon-Sat.

Kenzo Homme
70 Sloane Avenue, SW3 3DD (7225 1960/
www.kenzonet.com). **Open** 10am-6.30pm Mon,
Tue, Thur-Sat; 10am-7pm Wed; noon-5pm Sun.

Louis Vuitton
198-199 Sloane Street, SW1X 9QX (7399 4050/
www.vuitton.com). **Open** 10am-6.30pm Mon, Tue,
Thur-Sat; 10am-7pm Wed.

Smallbone of Devizes
220 Brompton Road, SW3 2BB (7581 9989/
www.smallbone.co.uk). **Open** 9am-5.30pm
Mon-Fri; 10am-5pm Sat.

Swann's Way
55 Hollywood Road, SW10 9HX (7351 7907).
Open 10.30am-6.30pm Mon, Tue, Thur, Fri;
10.30am-7pm Wed; 11am-5pm Sat.

Versace
183-184 Sloane Street, SW1X 9QP (7259 5700).
Open 10am-6pm Mon-Sat.

Theatres

Royal Albert Hall
Kensington Gore, SW7 2AP (7589 3203/box office
7589 8212/www.royalalberthall.com). **Open** *Box*
office 9am-9pm daily.

Royal Court Theatre
(English Stage Company)
Sloane Square, SW1W 8AS (7565 5000/
www.royalcourttheatre.com). **Open** *Box office*
10am-8pm Mon-Sat.

Worship

Brompton Cemetery
The Chapel Office (opposite Tesco Garage),
Fulham Road, SW10 9UG (7352 1201).
Open 7am-5.30pm daily.

Oratory Catholic Church
Thurloe Place, Brompton Road, SW7 2RP
(7808 0900/www.bromptonoratory.com). **Open**
7am-8pm daily. *Services* 7am, 10am, 12.30pm,
6pm Mon-Sat; 7am, 8am, 9am, 10am, 11am,
12.30pm, 4.30pm, 7pm Sun. **Admission** free;
donations appreciated.

Church of Jesus Christ of the
Latter Day Saints
64-68 Exhibition Road, SW7 2PA (7584 7553/
www.lds.org). **Open** *The Mission Office* 10am-5pm
Mon-Fri. *The Family History Centre* 10am-5pm Mon,
Sat; 10am-9pm Tue, Thur; 10am-7pm Wed, Fri.
Sometimes open Sun; phone to check.

Holy Trinity, Brompton
Brompton Road, SW7 1JA (7581 8255/www.htb.
org.uk). **Open** *Services* 8am, 9.30am (family),
11.30am (family), 5pm, 7pm Sun.

Russian Orthodox Church
67 Ennismore Gardens, SW7 1NH (7584 0096/
www.cathedral.sourozh.org). **Open** *Vigil* 5.30pm
Sat. *Divine Liturgy* 10.30am Sun.

St Mary's Church
The Boltons, SW10 9TB (7835 1440). **Open**
7.45am-6.30pm daily, but phone to confirm.

Victorian Gothic splendour at the **Albert Memorial**.

West side story

Joan Smith

18th-century hideaways from 20th-century carriageways – a Hogarthian haven.

Start: Hogarth roundabout, W4
Finish: Hogarth's House, Hogarth Lane, Great West Road, W4
Distance: 2 miles/3km
Time: 1.5 hours
Getting there: District or Piccadilly lines to Turnham Green, then E3 bus or 15-minute walk; 190 bus.
Getting back: reverse of above or 45-minute walk along river to Hammersmith tube.
Note: Chiswick House and Gardens are ideal for picnics and family days out, and so the walk could take up the whole day. The suggested route back along the riverfront to Hammersmith passes several pubs and is highly recommended. Chiswick Eyot is only accessible at low tide.

The Hogarth roundabout on the A4 in west London, one of the city's busiest exit routes, is not an obvious place to begin a walk. Most people associate it with traffic noise, car fumes, dog shit and smelly underpasses, the kind of place you might hurry to escape from on your way home from nearby Chiswick High Road. A testimony to our obsession with the car, it has been a desolate urban landscape ever since the six-lane highway was bulldozed through the Victorian terraces that used to slope gently down to the river. These days, it is a permanently congested route for cars, coaches and lorries heading towards the commuter towns strung out along the M4: Slough, Reading and Swindon. Thousands of drivers pass the roundabout every day

without realising they are only yards from the opening scene of Thackeray's *Vanity Fair*, where Becky Sharp scornfully tosses a copy of Dr Johnson's Dictionary out of the coach taking her from Miss Pinkerton' academy for young ladies on Chiswick Mall to a new life in the heart of London. Not that Becky liked Chiswick, which was hardly a fashionable address for a penniless young woman with her sights set on a good marriage and the glittering social round that preceded the Battle of Waterloo. 'So much for the Dixonary,' she exclaims as her coach bowls along the river, adding, like a character from a modern soap opera, 'and, thank God, I'm out of Chiswick.'

My feelings about this part of west London are quite the opposite, even though the immediate environment has deteriorated since Becky's day. As a small child, I lived a bit further west in the old Rothschild mansion in Gunnersbury Park where my father was a gardener. When I bought a house in Chiswick three years ago, after years of living in other parts of London and then in Oxfordshire, it was like coming home. Place names like Hammersmith are evocative of my childhood and, although most of the shops have changed hands, I now do my shopping where my mother did hers on Chiswick High Road in the 1950s. I don't remember coming down to the river as a child, but the first time I visited Chiswick Mall, shortly after I moved back to London, I immediately remembered the connection with *Vanity Fair*. I quickly spotted the courtyard of Chiswick Square where the Dictionary is supposed to have landed, standing back from Burlington Lane and next to he George & Devonshire pub. It's a little Georgian square overlooked by Boston House, built in 1740, at the back, and by older houses, built in 1680, on either side. To be honest, the geography doesn't seem quite right but there's a plaque on one of the walls citing the book-throwing incident, and the precise location doesn't really matter. The point is that when you get to know the area, you realise that no matter how unprepossessing it looks – and its appearance is not helped by the ghastly single-lane flyover that provides eastbound traffic with a short cut to Chiswick and Hammersmith – the Hogarth roundabout is the hub of some

of the loveliest (and most literary) places in West London. And they emphatically cannot be discovered by car.

After a short detour to Becky's courtyard, I usually turn south-east past the pub into Church Street, which bears an uncanny resemblance to a village high street somewhere in the Home Counties. For people like me, who loathe the country except in tiny doses, this is a perfect example of how easily its best features – double-fronted houses covered in wisteria and Virginia creeper, seeming to belong to a more leisured age – can be incorporated into an urban landscape. There's even a nautical-looking house with a ship-shaped

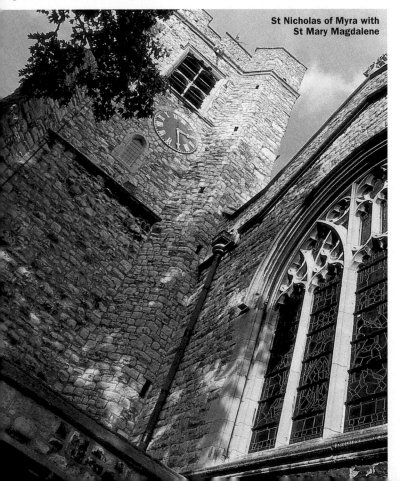

St Nicholas of Myra with St Mary Magdalene

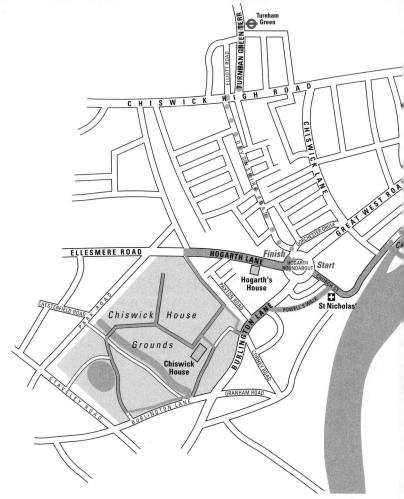

weathervane attached to its roof, as though it's been transported from some distant bluff overlooking the English Channel, a reminder of the days when a ferry carried passengers from the riverbank at the bottom of Church Street to Mortlake on the other side. But townies can take comfort from the reassuring presence of the Lamb brewery, rearing up behind some of the finest houses, filling the entire area with the aroma of hops when the wind is in the right direction. Its location was determined long ago, I assume, by the proximity of the Thames – not such an alarming prospect as it might once have been, for Church Street winds down to a section of the river

where fastidious wading birds such as herons testify to the cleanliness of the water. Down here, turning east on to Chiswick Mall, where the houses are divided from their lush waterside gardens by a tarmac road, you sometimes see cars half-submerged as ducks, Canada geese and the occasional swan paddle serenely by. Most of the front doors are flanked by grooves for wooden barriers that keep the water at bay, at least in theory, but there are compensations for the ever-present danger of floods. The gardens are as fertile as a river delta, bursting in the spring with lilac and wisteria, and at low tide you can walk across the riverbed to Chiswick Eyot,

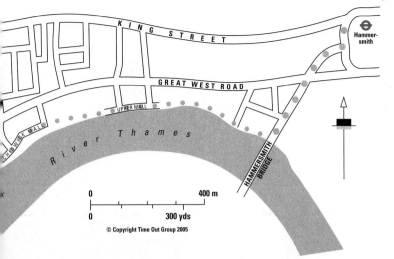

Hammer-
smith

UPPER MALL

CHISWICK MALL

River Thames

KING STREET

GREAT WEST ROAD

HAMMERSMITH BRIDGE

0   400 m

0   300 yds

© Copyright Time Out Group 2005

the long narrow island whose gnarled bushes and stunted trees are home to a flourishing colony of birds. The riverbed, last time I walked across, was gravelly and firm, but it's worth taking a few careful steps before striking out for the island. It's a curious sensation, stepping on to the broad wet sand, and unnerving if you've seen how quickly the tide can turn.

Back on dry land, looking in the other direction – west past Church Street and towards Chiswick Bridge – a bland modern development fronts the water, leaving only a featureless pavement walk to which pedestrians are allowed access during daylight hours. It makes sense to retrace your steps a little way into Church Street and turn left through the gate of St Nicholas's Church, which stands on a high bluff that used – before the new development – to overlook the river. The substantial monument on your left, a tall stone tomb surmounted with an urn and surrounded by black railings, is where William Hogarth is buried, dominating a scene that might have come straight out of Gray's *Elegy in a Country Churchyard*. The artist can have had no idea, when he moved to Chiswick at the height of his fame, that he would one day give his name to, of all modern monstrosities, a roundabout. Hogarth bought a house in

Chiswick during a heatwave in 1749, seeking a refuge from the airless inner city and the squalor that fascinated and repelled him. *Gin Lane*, the allegorical print that famously displays the corruption of city life, was published two years later. Shuttling backwards and forwards between Chiswick and the city, often by boat, Hogarth spent the next 15 years of his life here with his family, expiring suddenly in 1764 from a ruptured artery. The tomb was erected seven years later and his widow, Jane, asked the celebrated actor David Garrick to write a suitable epitaph. The verses he came up with, etched into the stone and beginning 'Farewell, great painter of mankind', are hardly inspired, but then neither is the tomb itself. A jumbled design that includes a mask, a laurel wreath, a palette, a pencil and a book entitled *Analysis of Beauty* prompted the artist's biographer, Jenny Uglow, to describe its design and erection as 'comically unHogarthian'. But artists cannot be held accountable for the memorials erected after their deaths, or indeed the company they keep post-mortem. Hogarth shares St Nicholas's churchyard with the American artist James Abbot McNeill Whistler, who was interred here after his death in 1903 and whose sensibility could hardly be more at odds with that of his predecessor. On the far side of the porch, where a narrow, high-walled lane leads out of the churchyard, the burial ground is scattered with a series of tapering stone tombs, many of them in a state of disrepair, which look like Egyptian sarcophagi. Their presence is unexpected in this very English churchyard and is in complete contrast to the elaborate burial vault in which a recessed panel records the virtues of Lucy de Loutherbourg, 'who closed a long life of active benevolence and utility with the resignation, fortitude and hopes of a Christian on the 29th September 1828 in the 83rd year of her age'. Every time I pass this substantial, six-foot-high memorial, I cannot help hoping Lucy's piety has been exaggerated in the old tradition of *de mortuis nil nisi bonum.* I doubt it, though. Throughout recorded history, women have led dull, worthy lives in the service of other people, which is why I'm so grateful to Thackeray for inventing the waspish, self-centred Becky Sharp.

Continuing along the lane, which is called Powell's Walk and not to be recommended to women on their own, you eventually find yourself back on Burlington Lane and an unavoidable stretch of noisy traffic. Turn left and continue past St Mary's Convent. On the other side of the road, behind a high wall, lies the unrivalled Palladian splendour of Chiswick House, one of my favourite places in London. It was built in the 1720s by Lord Burlington, to his own design, as a venue for concerts and parties, or so I was once told by one of the English Heritage guides who show people round the interior. In fact, Burlington began work on the house when the west wing of his Jacobean mansion (long demolished) was damaged by fire. Based on Palladio's Villa Capra, near Vicenza, the new house was connected by a link-building to the old one, which meant that Burlington did not have to worry about cramming in facilities that already existed in the earlier structure. Instead, he concentrated on making it

Hogarth's tomb

beautiful, designed around a circular first-floor room with a sublime dome, and with ceilings in the ornate rooms opening off it painted by William Kent. Recently restored, the house is an architectural jewel and defies Lord Hervey's dismissive (and possibly envious) claim at the time it was built that it was 'too small to live in and too large to hang on a watch chain'. It has a marvellous subterranean cellar in herringbone brick, while the ground floor consists of small rooms and passages at odd angles to each other; there are statues of Cicero and Roman emperors, and a sudden glimpse of a fabulous metal sphinx, resting on a waist-high plinth like a large cat that has decided to sit down and rest, casually ignoring the view through a nearby window of Kent's Italianate formal garden.

Although the main gates offer an unrivalled view of the house at the end of

Hogarth House

luxurious pink and white blooms whose petals resemble raspberry ripple ice-cream. This is only the beginning of months of colour for, as the camellias fall to the floor in bruised heaps, the wisteria on the outside of the building comes into flower, its pale blue and mauve bracts draping themselves over the glass. Then there are the hydrangeas, lace-capped and frothy at the height of summer, overlooking flowerbeds laid out in geometric patterns under a tall monkey puzzle tree.

The grounds of Chiswick House take perhaps three quarters of an hour to explore fully – the sunken pond, whose summer house becomes a stage for outdoor opera productions on summer evenings; the lake, with its humpbacked stone bridge; the 18th-century waterfall, now restored to full working order; the yew hedges, which Kent designed to create a series of dramatic vistas of the park and house.

On the far side of the gardens, a gate leads out on to the Great West Road and the short walk, heading east towards Hammersmith, to the tall thin house where Hogarth used to live. When you turn into the triangular garden, with its ancient mulberry tree, it is like stepping back into Hogarth's time; the house is protected from traffic noise by its high garden wall, and none of the windows in the main part of the house has a view of the road. The front elevation is dominated by a first-floor bay window, an oddly Italian detail for such an English house, which overhangs the modest front door. Inside, the rooms are pretty but small, hung with Hogarth's prints and his famous portrait, painted in 1750 – the year after he bought the house – of six of the family's servants. It is impossible to look at their serene faces, the women in bonnets and the men's hair neatly parted, without wondering how they all got on in such cramped quarters, even after Hogarth added a new kitchen and a third storey,

a wide courtyard, I usually enter the grounds by a narrow side gate off Burlington Lane. Turning right, I follow the path round to the wonderful 19th-century camellia house, an airy iron and glass structure with steps down to an enclosed garden. The camellia house is wide and low, with a central atrium flanked by two long wings that become, between February and April, a blaze of creamy whites, reds and pinks. Camellias are tremendously sexy flowers, especially the double varieties whose exuberant petals and phallic stamens suggest a carelessly hermaphrodite excess; the original of Dumas's *dame aux camélias,* a courtesan who is supposed to have worn red or white blooms to signal the state of her menstrual cycle, would have been spoiled for choice here. Some of the bushes are ancient, dating back to the 1820s, and they include with a staircase leading to attic rooms above. Perhaps the peace that still characterises the garden somehow managed to insinuate itself into the building, which still looks and feels like a Georgian country house in spite of everything modern urban development has been able to throw at it. From the ghastly A4, as lorries and coaches rumble past towards the roundabout that bears Hogarth's name, its survival seems like a small miracle. But that is to ignore the resilience of a part of London where so much of the 18th and 19th centuries has been preserved intact, if only you have the time and energy to set out on foot in search of it.

Tidal information

Thames Barrier Visitors' Centre, 1 Unity Way, SE18 5NJ (8305 4188/www.environment-agency.gov.uk).

Eating & drinking

Blue Anchor
13 Lower Mall, W6 9DJ (8748 5774). **Open** 11am-11pm Mon-Sat; noon-10.30pm Sun. Upstairs dining or riverside promenade for Thames views.

Burlington's Café
Chiswick House, off Burlington Lane, W4 2RP (8742 7336). **Open** *Oct-Mar* 10am-4pm Wed-Sun. *Apr-Sept* 10am-5pm daily.

Dove
19 Upper Mall, W6 9TA (8748 5405). **Open** 11am-11pm Mon-Sat; noon-10.30pm Sun. The smallest bar in the UK, a riverside terrace and much history.

ish Hoek

Elliott Road, W4 1PE (8742 0766). **Lunch erved** noon-2.30pm Tue-Sun. **Dinner served** -10.30pm Tue-Sun. Enthusiastic exponents of South frican fish dishes, including delights such as snoek, umpnose and kabeljou.

eorge & Devonshire

Burlington Lane, W4 2QE (8994 1859). **Open** 1.30am-11pm Mon-Sat; noon-10.30pm Sun. Food erved lunchtime only.

ld Ship

5 Upper Mall, W6 9TD (8748 2593/www.oldship 6.co.uk). **Open** 9am-11pm Mon-Sat; 9am-10.30pm un. A good family pub with food, ground-floor rrace and a garden.

a Trompette

-7 Devonshire Road, W4 2EU (8747 1836). **unch served** noon-2.30pm Mon-Sat; noon-3pm

Sun. **Dinner served** 6.30-10pm Mon-Sat; 7-9.30pm Sun. Excellent value for fine French food in a smart and unpretentious setting. One of the nicest restaurants in the area.

Church & houses

Chiswick House & Gardens

Burlington Lane, W4 2RP (8995 0508/www.english-heritage.org.uk). **Open** *Apr-Oct* 10am-5pm Wed-Fri, Sun; 10am-2pm Sat. Closed Nov-Mar.

Hogarth's House

Hogarth Lane, Great West Road, W4 2QN). **Open** *Apr-Oct* 1-5pm Tue-Fri; 1-6pm Sat, Sun. *Nov, Dec, Feb, Mar* 1-4pm Tue-Fri; 1-5pm Sat, Sun. **Admission** free.

St Nicholas of Myra with St Mary Magdalene

Church Street, W4 (8995 4717/www.chiswickparish church.org). **Open** 10am-noon Thur; 2.30-5pm Sun.

Chiswick House

Do you remember Derek Marlowe?

Nicholas Royle

On the trail of the late novelist, author of *A Dandy in Aspic*, *Do You Remember England?* and *Echoes of Celandine*.

> **Start:** Pimlico tube
> **Finish:** Ravenscourt Park tube
> **Distance:** 12.5 miles/20km
> **Time:** 8 hours
> **Getting there:** Victoria line to Pimlico
> **Getting back:** District line from Ravenscourt Park
> **Note:** no previous knowledge of Marlowe's work required. For the peckish as well as the bookish.

In his day, he would have needed no introduction. These days, to some people, he still needs none, but it's symptomatic of publishing in the 21st century that this piece is obliged to begin by introducing its subject to a potential new readership. Derek Marlowe was born, in Perivale, Middlesex, on 21 May 1938 and died in November 1996 in Los Angeles, having published nine novels and written numerous TV and film scripts. With his first novel, *A Dandy in Aspic*, Marlowe established himself as a classy prose stylist who held the reader in thrall to his equally generous gift for narrative. This winning combination was never to desert him throughout his career and his work consistently received acclaim at the same time as delighting readers, so it's a shame that all nine of his books are now out of print. But given the astonishing amount of trash that does get published these days in the

mad dash to find the 'next' Louis de Bernières or Helen Fielding, it's hardly surprising that Marlowe's novels can only be found in second-hand bookshops.

All that may change: a couple of publishers are looking at getting one or two Marlowes back on the shelves and, meanwhile, you can read the opening chapters of what would have been Marlowe's tenth novel, had he had chance to finish it, in *Neonlit: The Time Out Book of New Writing* (Quartet, 1998). There's even a possibility that his 1972 novel, *Do You Remember England?*, will be filmed.

One of Marlowe's favourite words was 'enthusiasm'; his novels are peppered with references to his characters' *enthusiasms*. My overriding personal enthusiasm, since I saw the film of *A Dandy in Aspic* in 1978 and subsequently read the book, has been for the work of Derek Marlowe.

Let me lead you on a trek, from Pimlico through Mayfair, to west London, that

Do you remember Derek Marlowe?

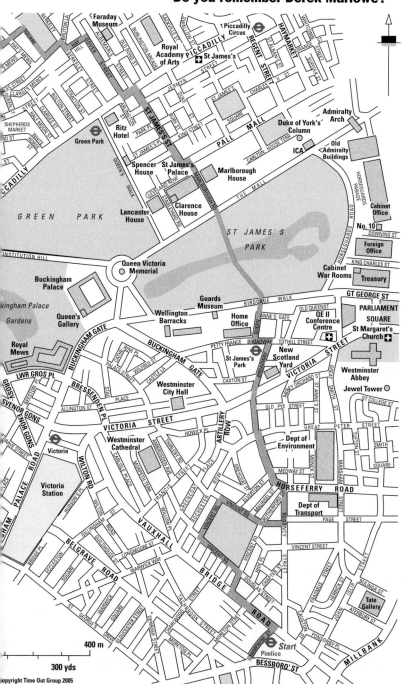

will not always take the shortest route between A and B. It will take you past many of the most splendid sights of London and some of the more mundane. Punctuating the walk are the various addresses Marlowe occupied in London, the houses and flats, family homes and otherwise, where he wrote his novels. The route does not follow the chronology of his movements; to do so would result in a walk *even more* eccentric than the one you are invited to do.

We start in Pimlico. But not before a quick jaunt via the Victoria and Northern lines to Tufnell Park. If, on the basis that it is outside London, we discount 17 Elton Avenue, Greenford, Middlesex, where Derek lived as a boy, Marlowe's first London address is actually 107 Fortess Road, NW5. Marlowe lived here in 1960, in his last year as a student at Queen Mary College, University of London. He shared with a boy from college – as he wrote in a letter to his

sister Alda and her husband Peter – and they paid 30 shillings each to share the three-roomed, furnished flat. 'My room has a little attic window with print curtains,' he wrote, 'and over my bed is a Modigliani and books.' Alda and Peter were then living in Copenhagen. 'Maybe one day,' he signed off, 'your little brother will be successful, then he can fly over to see you whenever he wants.' Within six years *A Dandy in Aspic* (1966) had become a bestseller and was made into a film for which Marlowe wrote the screenplay. But it's another Marlowe title that I slip through the letter box of 107 Fortess Road today along with a note explaining the nature of the project on which I am engaged. It strikes me as fitting, somehow, that there should be at least one copy of one of Marlowe's novels in each of the addresses where he lived.

Let's start with a flourish by giving away a UK first edition of the sinister

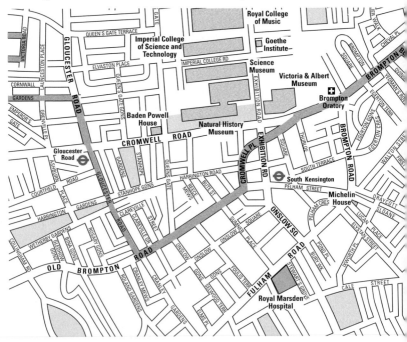

Do you remember Derek Marlowe?

1975 novel *Nightshade* (slightly soiled but in good condition with dustjacket – I'm indebted to writer Gareth Evans for tracking down and donating this copy).

Through the letter box it goes, landing with a thud on the mat where its creator wiped his feet 45 years ago, with not the slightest idea in his head at that point that he would one day write a novel about the unravelling of an English marriage on the voodoo island of Haiti. This act releases us from north London – all of Marlowe's London postcodes would henceforth commence with an S or a W – and we can jump back on the tube.

Leave Pimlico station by turning left out of the Rampayne Street exit and head for Vauxhall Bridge Road. On the opposite side slumps Random House. Long before Jonathan Cape was bought by Random House, which in turn was gobbled up by German giant Bertelsmann, that fine imprint published five of Marlowe's novels, *The Memoirs of a Venus Lackey* (1968), *A Single Summer With LB* (1969), *Echoes of Celandine* (1970), *Do You Remember England?* (1972) and *Somebody's Sister* (1974).

How nice it is to imagine Vintage – Random House's stylish paperback imprint – acquiring the rights to publish new editions.

Walk away from the river towards Victoria and turn right into Osbert Street leading to Vincent Square and its lush playing fields where the grey-flanelled Westminster School boys practising in the nets have changed little since Marlowe's day. In the autumn of 1964 at the age of 26, Marlowe moved into

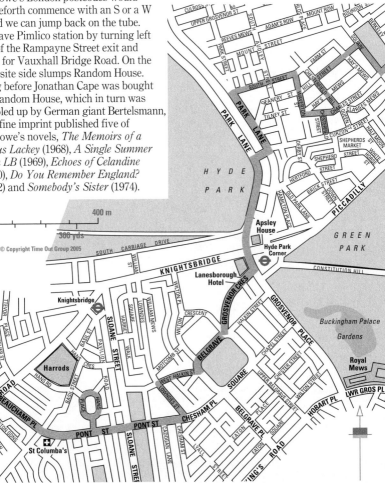

10 Vincent Square Mansions with Piers Paul Read and Tom Stoppard. Earlier that year at a school for writers in West Berlin, Marlowe and Stoppard (who, as we will see, already knew each other from Blenheim Crescent) had met Read. The three aspiring writers each got on with their own work, as well as making regular sorties into Berlin – West and East. 'Derek, of course,' recalls Read, 'had a beautiful girlfriend called Barbara: I do not think there was any moment in his life when there were not beautiful women at his beck and call.'

On his return from Berlin, Marlowe decided to write a spy thriller. With his experience as a playwright (his first play, *The Scarecrow*, won the Foyle Award for Best New Play of 1961), this represented a change of direction which Stoppard and Read tried to talk him out of. *A Dandy in Aspic*, which Marlowe wrote while staying with Alda and Peter in Kent, took just six weeks to polish off. 'I was always emptying the ashtrays,' recalls Alda.

Alexander Eberlin (played by Laurence Harvey in the film), a Russian spy working

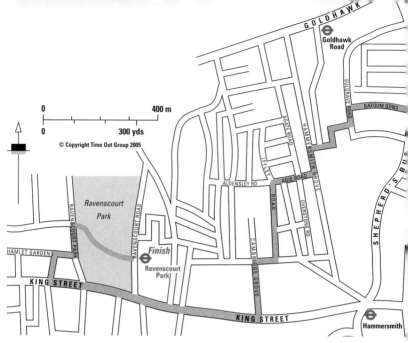

© Copyright Time Out Group 2005

for the British, is ordered to hunt down a Russian by the name of Krasnevin – himself. The plot becomes a gallimaufry of twists and turns and Marlowe's prose seduces even the most casual reader.

Follow the south-west side of the square to Walcott Street, where you'll find Vincent Square Mansions. The unknown occupiers of No.10 receive my only copy of NEL's film tie-in paperback edition of *A Dandy in Aspic*, leaving me with the UK first edition (Gollancz hardback, yellow dj).

Follow the square round to the opposite corner and turn into Fynes Street. Hit Regency Street and there on the corner of Regency and Page Streets is the excellent Regency Café, much favoured by cabbies and builders. Turn right out of the café and walk up to Horseferry Road. Turn left.

Mayfair beckons. Take pedestrianised Strutton Ground, home to a busy market, then cross Victoria Street and head up Broadway, past New Scotland Yard. Go left by the tube then right down Queen Anne's Gate, past the Home Office; go down to Birdcage Walk and cross into St James's Park. The shortest route follows the path across the lake

(Buckingham Palace on your left, Horse Guards to your right) to the Mall.

Follow the map to Berkeley Square, where at No.50 you'll find Maggs Bros, antiquarian booksellers; it doesn't have much past 1950, so no chance of hitting upon a Marlowe first edition. The way now becomes convoluted, so use the map to get to Chesterfield Street. Somerset Maugham (1874-1965) lived at No.6, Beau Brummell (1778-1840) at No.4. Brummell, the original dandy, was a hero of Marlowe's, whose own flamboyant dress-sense was expressed 1960s-style in velvet suits, white jeans, fancy shirts. Eberlin could afford to dress in bespoke suits thanks to his working for both the Russians and the British. Marlowe locates Eberlin's British bosses at 4 Chesterfield Street as a homage to Brummell, who crops up later in Marlowe's work in the erudite *A Single Summer With LB*.

Opposite Brummell's house is Bahama House and on Charles Street you'll find the Embassy of Myanmar (Burma in Eberlin's day); throughout this walk we'll pass dozens of embassies. The success of *A Dandy in Aspic*, a tale of international intrigue, meant that henceforth wherever in London Marlowe chose to live he would invariably pass a clutch of embassies on his way to buy a newspaper (*The Times* – he'd polish off the crossword in half an hour) or a pack of panatellas.

Eberlin's own rooms are at 24 South Street, a featureless four-storey affair of unclear function but kitted out with a security camera as a warning to the curious. Turn left at Park Lane. Head past the hotels (Dorchester, Hilton) to the subway. Cross and look left to see Byron perched on an island hedged in by signs and chevrons. Another of Marlowe's heroes, Byron was the subject of *A Single Summer With LB*. Marlowe based his story of the summer of 1816 on fact. The acknowledgements include a nod to Ken Russell, whose film of that summer's events, *Gothic*, would not be made for another 17 years. *A Single Summer With LB*, while required reading for those interested in Byron, is one for Marlowe completists.

At Hyde Park Corner, admire the great bulk of the former St George's Hospital (now the Lanesborough Hotel – why not have a drink in the Library or an early lunch at neighbouring Pizza on the Park?). Take Grosvenor Crescent to Belgrave Square, home to several embassies. Head for Pont Street via West Halkin Street and Lowndes Street, and make a detour to Hans Place (Jane Austen stayed on the site of No.23 with her brother Henry in 1814-15). From Pont Street, turn into Beauchamp Place, a chic shoppers' paradise with a smart Pizza Express at No.7.

Where Brompton Road veers left you'll see the Brompton Oratory on your right. Although Marlowe had spent the last years of his life in Los Angeles working in film and TV, he had grown tired of being a small cog in a big machine and planned to return to London where he would complete a new novel (working title *Black and White*) and spend more time with his son Ben. But Marlowe developed leukaemia and, in the course

of his treatment, tragically suffered a brain haemorrhage and died on 13 November 1996. Cremated in LA, his ashes were brought back to the UK by Alda and buried in his father's grave near Hastings. There was a memorial service in March 1997 at the Little Oratory; Piers Paul Read delivered the eulogy.

Carrying on down Thurloe Place, past the V&A (where Eberlin keeps a collection of Sèvres porcelain in a vault), past 30 Thurloe Place (once home to one of the best and longest-running literary magazines, the late Alan Ross's *London Magazine*) and you're in the heart of South Ken, with its myriad shops, cafés and restaurants. Head down Old Brompton Road, perhaps popping into Waterstone's at No.99. Were Marlowe's novels in print, he would have merited inclusion in the *Waterstone's Guide to Crime Fiction*, if only for his 1974 novel *Somebody's Sister*, a brilliant and complex San Francisco-set detective story.

Turn right up Gloucester Road. It's worth visiting the Gloucester Road Bookshop at No.123, a wonderful second-hand emporium with long opening hours, which might be able to offer something by Marlowe. Our next location is a short hop across Cromwell Road. As far as attractive routes are concerned, we are suddenly spoilt for choice (Kynance Mews is picturesque, lilac and wisteria blossoms tumbling down the walls, ceanothus brushing your legs), but let's opt for a left turn into Cornwall Gardens. At the end go right and check the wall on your right for a blue plaque in honour of the novelist Ivy Compton-Burnett (1884-1969) resident at 5 Braemar Mansions from 1934 until the end of her life. Go right again and look for an alleyway on the left side of Cornwall Gardens leading to Stanford Road. Stop when you reach Eldon Road and gaze straight down to the house facing you from the east side of Victoria Road. This is 71 Victoria Road, where Marlowe lived with his wife Sukie for four years.

Bought in 1968 for £37,000 with some of the proceeds from *A Dandy in Aspic*, it's a large house and must have been quite a change from flat-sharing. It may not be too fanciful to imagine Marlowe constructing a scene from *Do You Remember England?* while sitting at one of the top-floor windows gazing down Eldon Road at the sunset, given the pervading atmosphere of romantic melancholy in that novel. *Somebody's Sister* was probably also written here, but it's a battered US first edition of *Do You Remember England?* that I slip through the letter box of 71 Victoria Road today.

If the current occupiers decide the invitation to place this book on their shelves is made by an obsessive whose enthusiasms should not be indulged, I will at least have tried, for what it might be worth, to string up a karmic net, a psychogeographical web woven out of Marlowe's lines of dialogue, his lists of descriptive minutiae. The plot-lines of energy exist already, laid down by the man himself as he progressed from one home to another in his gradual move west.

From Victoria Road, Derek and Sukie – and Ben, born in Queen Charlotte's Hospital, Hammersmith, on 16 August 1969 – moved to the country. Marlowe

achieved what appears to have been his dream of the country life, a rural idyll in which he could play the bucolic dandy for his own – and his guests' – amusement. Foscombe was a large Gloucestershire manor house superbly situated on a hill with commanding views (in *The Rich Boy From Chicago* Freddie and Cissie buy 'a house in Gloucestershire on the peak of a hill with a view of eight counties, two of which contained some of their land'). Friends invited to stay would find themselves breakfasting on peaches and champagne. (For a glimpse of Marlowe's idyll, visit Gloucestershire and find the village of Ashleworth, where any local will direct you to Foscombe. A public footpath will take you to within sight of the house and afford you sufficient insight to understand what led Marlowe to dedicate the first of the two books he wrote there – *Nightshade* and *The Rich Boy From Chicago* – to it.)

In 1976 the Marlowes moved from Foscombe to Froxfield, Wiltshire, where they stayed until 1979, when, their marriage at an end, they moved back, separately, to London. Sukie and Ben went south of the river to Stockwell while Derek remained in west London, choosing a flat that was exactly the same distance from Victoria Road as Victoria Road had

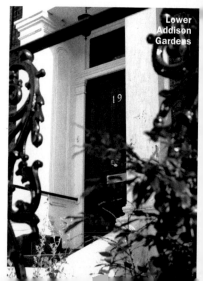

been from Holland Park Road (which we will come to later). And the same distance from Holland Park Road as it was from Victoria Road. Without wishing to confuse the reader, the three consecutive loci (if you ignore the six-year stint in the country) form an equilateral triangle. This may be utterly devoid of any significance, but it makes a pretty pattern on the map.

Walk up Victoria Road and turn left into Cottesmore Gardens ending up back at Stanford Road, where you turn right.

Head north up Kensington Court Place and you will spot a blue plaque in honour of TS Eliot at Nos.1-14 Kensington Court Gardens. Go left into Thackeray Street, up the side of Kensington Square into Young Street: Thackeray (1811-63) lived at No.16. Turn right into Ken High Street and left just before the Royal Garden Hotel into Palace Green, leading to Kensington Palace Gardens. Although this is a private road and closed to motor vehicles driven by you or I, it is open to pedestrians who are free to stroll past a whole string of embassies, as well as Kensington Palace. At the top we go left into Notting Hill Gate and left again into Palace Gardens Terrace. On our left in a few yards is the tiny Notting Hill Books (no Marlowes on my visit), then at No.122 is the Ark, an upmarket Italian restaurant whose premises once housed a French bistro (also called the Ark) that was a favourite with Marlowe. The flat the novelist took when he moved back to west London after the split from Sukie is a moment's walk away at 4C Strathmore Gardens. Resident here from 1979-83, Marlowe was concentrating on screenwriting. His last completed book was *Nancy Astor*, strictly speaking a novelisation of his own television script but, since the book described itself as a novel and Marlowe wrote both the script and the book, we'll consider it a novel. The current residents of 4C Strathmore Gardens can make their own minds up – they get a copy of Penguin's TV tie-in edition. Since it was published in 1982, it's possible he either wrote part of it here or at least checked the proofs.

Our next destination takes us to the heart of Notting Hill and back to 1964. Head back up Palace Gardens Terrace (Wyndham Lewis, 1882-1957, lived at No.61) and left into Notting Hill Gate. Turn right into Pembridge Road. On the right is Book & Comic Exchange, a very good source of second-hand fiction. Pembridge Road curves to the right, leading into Pembridge Villas. There are different routes from here to Blenheim Crescent, so there's no reason at all why we shouldn't jink up to Talbot Road via Courtnell Street and pay our respects to Nicolas Roeg, a resident of the street and one of the UK's greatest film directors. It's nice to know that as you walk up Courtnell Street you are literally following in the footsteps of the man who made *Walkabout*, *Bad Timing* and *Two Deaths*. If you want a link with Marlowe, it's pretty tenuous, but there is one: Paul Mayersberg, the screenwriter on Roeg's *The Man Who Fell to Earth* and *Eureka*, also adapted Marlowe's *Echoes of Celandine*, filmed by Stuart Cooper as *The Disappearance*, with Donald Sutherland (the star of Roeg's masterpiece, *Don't Look Now*). Pure conjecture, but I would think it likely that Roeg is familiar with Marlowe's work: the two favour a method of building a scene by accumulating visual information, offering alternative viewpoints and loading apparently incidental details with enormous, almost occult, significance.

Heading west along Talbot Road brings us to Powis Square and the house (top left corner) where James Fox goes to ground with Mick Jagger in *Performance*, directed by Roeg and Donald Cammell (in fact the interiors were filmed in Belgravia). Follow the west side of the square and go right. Turn right into Portobello Road and in a moment you come upon the Electric Cinema, one of London's finest, which reopened in 2001. It was here that *The Disappearance* got a short run in 1977.

Before venturing west of Ladbroke Grove, it's worth having a look at the stretches of Blenheim Crescent and Elgin Crescent that lie to the Grove's east side. In this tiny, villagey neighbourhood you will find a brace of bookshops – the Travel Bookshop and Books For Cooks. Eventually we burst forth across the Grove and saunter down the right side of Blenheim Crescent to stop outside No.48. Marlowe rented a bedsitter here in 1964; Stoppard, who also lived in the building, recalls that Marlowe lived on either the ground or lower ground floor. The house has seen some changes since the 1960s and the bottom two floors are now a self-contained maisonette, No.48A. Its occupants get a copy of *The Memoirs of a Venus Lackey* (Panther paperback, slightly soiled) with apologies for the tacky cover (nude girl on beach). It turns out that the owner of No.48A (she has kindly left me a message by the time I get home) is in the best possible position to know that you shouldn't judge a book by its cover, for she is the novelist Emma Tennant. An old acquaintance of Marlowe's, she is surprised to learn that he once lived in the space where she is now.

Blenheim Crescent curves gently. Cross Clarendon Road and duck into Portland Road, following it all the way down to Holland Park Avenue, keeping to the left side, and you pass the home of Marlowe's former flat-mate Piers Paul Read.

The trees lining Holland Park Avenue form a partial canopy that creates an almost submarine luminescence. Shortly before Holland Park roundabout you will pass the Kensington Hilton, where Marlowe suggested he and I meet for drinks in the bar on one of his flying visits to London in 1995, by which time we were in sporadic contact as I had published a couple of his short stories. He was always under pressure on these trips and, sadly, our appointment slipped his mind. Upset, he promised to treat me to dinner at my favourite restaurant on his next trip. But illness prevented any further visits and so we never did meet.

Pass the Hilton and cross Holland Road at the lights, turning right for a few yards until, looking to your right, the parallax view of the giant blue, syringe-like water tower (actually a barometer) and the two blocks of flats behind it resolves itself and the three line up, with the blue needle sandwiched. Now turn into Hansard Mews. To your right in the cutting below is a railway line that carries freight services and Eurostar trains returning to depot. Ahead, through the trees, catch sight of an incongruous, pretty mews. Follow Hansard Mews to its end and turn left into Lower Addison Gardens. Cross Holland Road a second time and come to a halt outside 19 Lower Addison Gardens. Marlowe had a flat on one of the upper floors, probably the top floor, between 1983-85, after leaving Strathmore Gardens. He wrote no books here, already making regular visits to the US. In *The Rich Boy From Chicago* Henry Bax's background is based loosely on Marlowe's own, and so, since it can't be ignored that we are standing no more than a hundred yards from the entrance to Cardinal Vaughan Memorial School, on Holland Villas Road, which Marlowe attended, it's with a copy of that novel (Penguin, inelegant cover illustration) that I hit the current occupiers of the top flat at No.19.

A winding route now takes us back to 1965 and Marlowe's whereabouts between Vincent Square Mansions and Victoria Road. The top flat at 8 Holland Park Road is the third point of the triangle formed by Victoria Road and Strathmore Gardens and we reach it by a tree-lined, zig-zag route down Holland Villas Road, Addison Crescent and Addison Road, then left into either Oakwood Lane or Oakwood Court (the former's private status prompts the thrill I get from interloping in the exclusive domains of the well-off), followed by Abbotsbury Road, Ilchester Place, Melbury Road, Holland Park Road.

Since it's possible that Marlowe wrote *Echoes of Celandine* here, I slip a copy (hardback, first, no dj – I'm not made of ney) into the communal hallway and mb back down the steps to Holland rk Road, looking up at the top of the ilding in case a curtain should twitch, vindow scrape open and a handsome ofile (thick, wavy brown hair, panatella) p out. One begins to suspect, in these changed surroundings, that time is less gid than one has been led to believe. Wander into Leighton House, yards wn the road, and lose any remaining nse of the present in the lulling Arab ill, with its restful blue tiles, soft tinkle running water, creaking boards.

The last lap. Turn right at the bottom Holland Park Road into Strangways errace (another private road; another easant water feature), then left into nat's left of Melbury, skip across eacherous Addison and nip into Napier. ne hulking great hangar in long shot ead of you is Olympia Exhibition entre. Between you and it lie Holland oad and the same railway we saw earlier Shepherd's Bush. Use the pedestrian ccess to Kensington (Olympia) station follow the sign to Kensington, Addison oad station and take the footbridge over e line; skirt the exhibition hall and find ythe Road. You'll know you're going e right way by the vast, crenellated lifice on your left. Built a century ago, ythe House is home to the National rt Archive. Trimmed with barbed wire id sentry boxes, it puts you more in ind of something out of *A Dandy in spic*. Beyond lies Blythe Road Restaurant nd, further on, Daddy's, an Iranian staurant which occupies premises rmerly occupied by Wilson's, an extremely ne Scottish restaurant. The ex-proprietor, ng-pipe playing Bob Wilson, was a ousin by marriage of Marlowe's, and the staurant was where family and friends ncluding the actor Nicholas Ball) gathered or a wake after the writer's death.

Cut across Shepherd's Bush Road and it-run down to King Street, pausing for efreshment in the Stonemason's Arms on ambridge Grove. Hit King Street and go

west – it's what Marlowe did. It's a straight line on the map from Strathmore Gardens to Lower Addison Gardens to his last home in London, our final destination, 80 Hamlet Gardens, W6. You protract that line in a westerly direction and you'll find it ends up as near as dammit in LA.

King Street throws up a very good Thai restaurant, Sabai Sabai, at Nos.270-272. Pass the entrance to Ravenscourt Park and turn right into Hamlet Gardens. Go to the end and turn left. Where the peeling green paintwork gives way to the fresher white, you'll see Marlowe's block. He lived at the top, in No.80, from 1985-90. Ken Russell's *Gothic* was released in 1987, a good enough reason to give the current owners a copy of *A Single Summer With LB* (Penguin, slightly worn) with a supplementary *Darklands 2* (Egerton Press, mint), featuring an exquisite short story, 'Digits', that Marlowe wrote either here or at 1505 Blue Jay Way, Los Angeles, his next and last address. (A kind letter arrives from the new owners of No.80. They know about Marlowe and are grateful for his miles of bookshelves.)

Double-back to Ravenscourt Park (road named after the park) and turn left; in 100 yards you reach a gate. It's a pleasant park with swings, slides, paddling pool, sand pit, open spaces, dog exercise areas, tea shop, duck pond,

Derek Marlowe

aromatic garden and occasional sightings of another major figure in British fiction, a contemporary of Marlowe's who is still very much with us thankfully – JG Ballard.

Now that the walk is at its end, your options are several. Quickest escape is via the District line at Ravenscourt Park. You might prefer to recline in the park's verdant pastures or head back to the river. The Thames is little more than a quarter of a mile away (the same distance separated the river from our starting point in Pimlico): relax with a drink on the terrace of the Dove and contemplate the fluid trajectories of Marlowe's career, assessing the degree of immortality conferred upon him by that which he has left behind, a unique body of work that richly deserves to be back in print.

Thanks to Viviane Barbour, Gareth Evans, Lee Harwood, Michael & Victoria Hastings, Michael Horovitz, Ben Marlowe, Piers Paul Read, Tom Stoppard, Emma Tennant, Alda Watson.

Eating & drinking

The Ark
122 Palace Gardens Terrace, W8 4RT (7229 4034 www.thearkrestaurant.co.uk). **Open** 6.30-11pm Mor 12.30-3pm, 6.30-11pm Tue-Sat; 12.30-3pm Sun. Cute Italian restaurant, ideal for brunch.

Blythe Road Restaurant
71 Blythe Road, W14 0HP (7371 3635). **Open** 6-10.30pm Mon-Sat. Chinese cuisine.

Dove
19 Upper Mall, W6 9TA (8748 5405). **Open** 11a 11pm Mon-Sat; noon-10.30pm Sun. Has the smalle bar in the UK, and also offers a riverside terrace, distinguished history and popular Sunday lunches

Library
Lanesborough Hotel, Hyde Park Corner, SW1X 7T (7259 5599/www.lanesborough.com). **Open** 11am-1am Mon-Sat; 11am-11pm Sun. Vodka martinis are a speciality at the bar, as are three-course teas in the afternoons.

Daddy's
236 Blythe Road, W14 0HJ (7602 1211). **Open** 11am-11pm daily. Iranian and Middle Eastern food.

Pizza on the Park
11 Knightsbridge, SW1X 7LY (7235 5273/ www.pizzaonthepark.com). **Open** noon-midnight daily. Splendid setting for jazz nights, not so wonderful for food.

Regency Café
17-19 Regency Street, SW1P 4BY (7821 6596). **Open** 7am-2.30pm, 4-7.30pm Mon-Fri; 7am-noon Sa

Sabai Sabai
270 King Street, W6 0SP (8748 7363). **Open** noon-2.30pm, 6-11.15pm Mon-Fri; 6-11.15pm Sat; 6-10.30pm Sun. Thai food.

Stonemason's Arms
54 Cambridge Grove, W6 0LA (8748 1397). **Open** noon-11pm Mon-Sat; noon-10.30pm Sun.

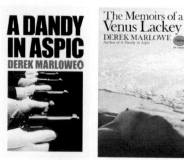

hurch pews, artwork for sale and excellent food with a southern hemisphere twist) can be found a this quirky pub.

Film

Bad Timing (Nicolas Roeg, 1980, GB)

A Dandy in Aspic (Anthony Mann, 1968, GB)

Don't Look Now (Nicolas Roeg, 1973, GB/It)

The Disappearance (Stuart Cooper, 1977, GB/Can)

Gothic (Ken Russell, 1986, GB)

The Man Who Fell to Earth (Nicolas Roeg, 1976, US)

Performance (Nicolas Roeg, 1970, GB)

Two Deaths (Nicolas Roeg, 1994, GB)

Walkabout (Nicolas Roeg, 1970, Aust)

Literature

All by Derek Marlowe:

A Dandy in Aspic

The Memoirs of a Venus Lackey

A Single Summer With LB

Echoes of Celandine

Do You Remember England?

Somebody's Sister

Nightshade

The Rich Boy From Chicago

Nancy Astor

Sweet Nothing short story in *Darklands*

Digits short story in *Darklands 2*

Regrettably none of the above is in print.

Black & White opening chapters of unfinished novel in *Neonlit: The Time Out Book of New Writing* (Quartet).

Other

Brompton Oratory
Thurloe Place, Brompton Road, SW7 2RP (7808 0900/www.bromptonoratory.com). **Open** 7am-8pm daily. *Services* 7am, 10am, 12.30pm, 6pm Mon-Sat; 7am, 8am, 9am, 10am, 11am, 12.30pm, 4.30pm, 7pm Sun. **Admission** free; donations appreciated.

Leighton House
12 Holland Park Road, W14 8LZ (7602 3316/www. rbkc.gov.uk/leightonhousemuseum). **Open** 11am-5.30pm Mon, Wed-Sun. **Admission** £3; £1 concessions.

Victoria & Albert Museum
Cromwell Road, SW7 2RL (7938 8500/www.vam. ac.uk). **Open** 10am-5.45pm Mon, Tue, Thur-Sun; 10am-10pm Wed, last Fri of mth. **Tours** daily; phone for details. **Admission** free. *Exhibitions* prices vary.

Shopping

Book & Comic Exchange
14 Pembridge Road, W11 3HL (7229 8420). **Open** 10am-8pm daily.

Books For Cooks
4 Blenheim Crescent, W11 1NN (7221 1992/ www.booksforcooks.com). **Open** 10am-6pm Tue-Sat.

Gloucester Road Bookshop
123 Gloucester Road, SW7 4TE (7370 3503). **Open** 9.30am-10.30pm Mon-Fri; 10.30am-6.30pm Sat, Sun.

Maggs Bros
50 Berkeley Square, W1J 5BA (7493 7160/ www.maggs.com). **Open** 9.30am-5pm Mon-Fri.

Notting Hill Books
132 Palace Gardens Terrace, W8 4RT (7727 5988). **Open** 10.30am-6pm Mon-Wed, Fri, Sat; 10.30am-1pm Thur.

Travel Bookshop
13 Blenheim Crescent, W11 2EE (7229 5260/ www.thetravelbookshop.co.uk). **Open** 10am-6pm Mon-Sat; 11am-4pm Sun.

Waterstone's
99 Old Brompton Road, SW7 3LE (7581 8522/ www.waterstones.co.uk). **Open** 9.30am-8pm Mon-Fri; 9.30am-7.30pm Sat; noon-6pm Sun.

The triumph of the bourgeoisie

Philip Ziegler

Grand designs and new money in old Holland Park.

Start: 8 Addison Road, W14
Finish: Albert Memorial, Kensington Gardens, SW7
Distance: 4 miles/6km
Time: 2.5 hours
Getting there: Central line to Holland Park, then 10-minute walk
Getting back: 10-minute walk to High Street Kensington (District or Circle lines); 9, 10 or 52 bus
Note: check opening times of Leighton House and Kensington Palace.

Two great houses and their surrounding parks dominate Kensington between the High Street and Notting Hill. The first, Holland House, is now a gutted ruin; the second, Kensington Palace, is half museum, half lodging house for fringe members of the royal family. In the 19th century the high tide of a rampant bourgeoisie lapped around the edges of their territories. The surprise is not that today they are so much diminished but that they survive at all.

To get the full flavour of what this walk is about it is worth starting a few hundred yards to the west of Holland Park and standing in front of No.8 Addison Road, about halfway between Holland Avenue and the High Street. This is the house that Halsey Ricardo designed for the great shopkeeper Sir Ernest Debenham. Ricardo preached the doctrine of 'structural polychromy', and few structures can

have been more polychrome than this one. It is an Italianate slab, with Florentine pilasters piercing bands of glazed bricks in lurid green and blue. The interior is still more extravagant; a plethora of purple, blue and turquoise De Morgan tiles, sometimes plain, sometimes in exuberant swirls of peacocks and art nouveau foliage. Some find the house splendid; it reminds me of those melodramatic iced cakes once found in the nastier teashops. Whichever you feel, it cannot be ignored. It is a triumphant affirmation of energetic, to-hell-with-you self-confidence; Sir Ernest wanted it this way – and if people didn't like it, so much the worse for them.

Other stately villas can be seen in Addison Road as one moves south towards the High Street – notably Nos.13 and 16 to the left and, if only for its Fort Knox-style defences, No.69 to the right – but nothing with the effrontery of Palazzo Debenham. Further on lies Lewis Vulliamy's Tudor-Gothic St Barnabas Church of 1827-29 – fashionable in its time, but the depressingly drab grey brick dampens one's spirits, and a feverish attempt to tart it up with bright blue woodwork only accentuates the gloom.

Turn left shortly after St Barnabas into Melbury Road. Here is the territory that Britain's more prosperous 19th-century artists made their own; the emphasis being on the prosperity rather than the artistry, since by and large they were a mediocre crew. To the right, Nos.2-4 are a pair of houses built for the sculptor Thomas Thorneycroft to designs by his (slightly)

Holland Park

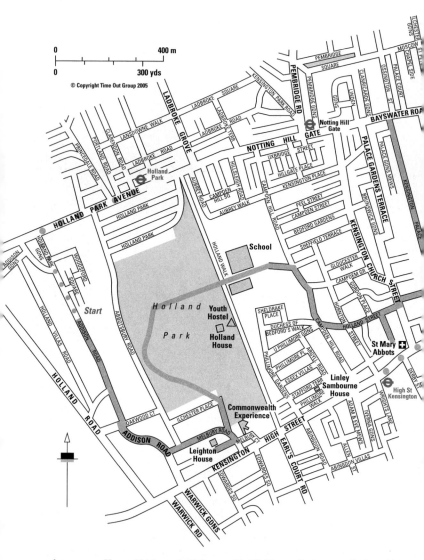

more famous son Hamo. No.8 was built by Norman Shaw for the academician Marcus Stone; the studios are so conspicuous that it looks like Kensington's answer to Hardwick Hall, more glass than wall.

No.29, Tower House, was designed by William Burges for his own occupation. The staircase turret that gives the house its name was an afterthought, but the building breathes the spirit of 13th-

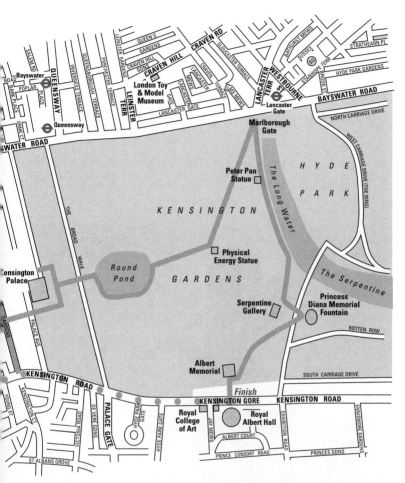

century Gothic. The interior was even
more fantastical; it went to rack and
ruin in the 1960s but is now handsomely
restored. Next to it, No.31 is by Norman
Shaw again; this time for the portrait
painter Luke Fildes. The house 'is getting
on famously and looks stunning', wrote
Fildes proudly in 1876. 'It is a long way
the most superior house of the whole lot;
I consider it knocks Stone's to bits!' It
is somewhat lumpen, perhaps, but a
decent, God-fearing piece of work.
Many grandees came here to be painted,
including Edward VII, who thought the

studio one of the finest rooms in London.

Our route turns sharply left into
Holland Park, but it is worth first
following Melbury Road round to the
right (Holman Hunt died at No.18) and
then walking a hundred yards or so up
Holland Park Road. No.10 was built for
another fashionable portrait painter,
James Shannon. Buried within the house,
which itself lurks behind hostile walls
and gates, is the original homestead
of Holland Farm. Then comes Leighton
House, open to the public and well worth
a visit. Lord Leighton was a bigger fish

than any of his neighbours, a highly successful president of the Royal Academy, a fine draughtsman and a painter of sound second-eleven status. The somewhat bleak exterior of his house gives no hint of the wonders within.

There is wall upon wall of paintings – many by Leighton, some of them quite good, but it is the extravagantly tiled Damascene walls, in particular the Arab Hall, that grab attention. The domed hall is extraordinarily successful, an explosion

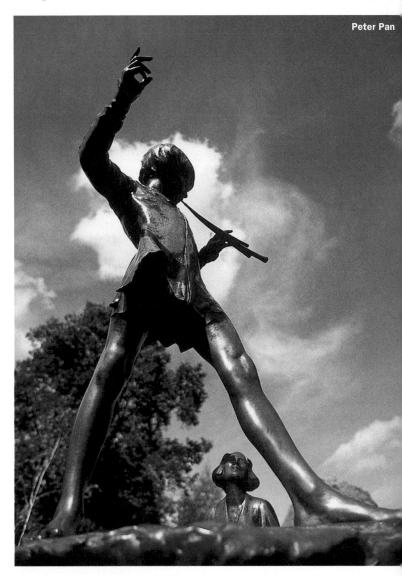

Peter Pan

of brightly coloured plaques that could be garish but fuse together in exhilarating harmony. In the centre a marble fountain plays; the pool it forms sometimes proves dangerously attractive to admirers of the glittering dome above.

To Lady Holland in 1876 these 'dreadful houses' seemed an impertinent intrusion on her aristocratic seclusion. To enter Holland Park, go back to Melbury Road, turn left but then almost immediately bear right into Ilchester Place. From the gate, the ruins of the house lie straight ahead. This great Jacobean mansion survived unscathed until bombs destroyed the greater part of it in 1941. Its finest hours came under an earlier Lady Holland, Elizabeth, former wife of the dissolute Sir Godfrey Webster. As a divorcee Lady Holland was unacceptable in the grand London houses, so she made grand London come to her – or its male half at any rate. The company was more Whig than anything else, but politics, or religion for that matter, mattered little – to be brilliant and good company was all that counted. Macaulay and Melbourne, Talleyrand and Brougham, Byron and Thomas Moore, Sydney Smith and Samuel Rogers time and again braved the long and uncomfortable journey, the indifferent food, the crowded table, the bossiness of their hostess, in quest of the liveliest conversation and the best company in London. The tidily sterilised ruins leave little room for ghosts but by night some inkling of what the house once was can still be gathered.

Walk straight ahead, leaving the ruins to your right. The formal gardens, sternly symmetrical but planted with more sensitivity than is usual in municipal undertakings, run away to the left towards the orangery.

Carry on another hundred yards or so, past the pigeons and grazing peacocks, to the Kyoto Garden. This Japanese garden, with its stream and waterfall, miniature bridges, pools set with lilies and amiably sluggish carp, seemed a little ill at ease

when first installed in 1991, but it has since become subtly anglicised and is a pleasant place to pause to read a book, or just to pause. Leave it by the other gate, continue around its perimeter keeping right, and you will discover the third Lord Holland, husband of Elizabeth, seated comfortably in a padded chair surveying the ruins of his house. He betrays no dismay at the sight; on the contrary, his benign and sage features make it obvious why he was so much loved and respected.

Walk on, bearing right at the edge of the park, and in 60 yards or so a path leads you out, across Holland Walk, into the midst of Holland Park Comprehensive School. The school's architects took some pride in keeping elevations low and preserving as many trees as possible, but the result is still bleak enough to chill any potential pupil. Once it was the standard bearer for comprehensive schooling, the choice of any idealistic parent of progressive views; then the law of the jungle prevailed. Now, like so many comprehensives, it provides an admirable service for those who are tough and motivated but can be hard on the less well equipped.

Imperceptibly the path widens into Campden Hill. The stately homes of Kensington, which occupied the site of the school and Queen Elizabeth College further on, have for the most part vanished, but where Campden Hill joins Campden Hill Road there is a more recent creation. No.1 Campden Hill is a massive red brick mansion designed by Henry Martineau Fletcher in 1914. It could have been by Lutyens in one of his less ambitious moods. It was acquired by the South African High Commission after World War II and was until recently called 'High Veld', though anything less veld-like than surrounding Kensington would be hard to find.

Turning right down Campden Hill Road, Observatory Gardens lies to your left. This high-spirited crescent was built on the site of James South's observatory, its dome designed by Isambard Kingdom Brunel. The replacement is riotously over the top, a florid extravaganza designed to entertain and notably succeeding. It could hardly be more different in spirit from Kensington Town Hall, which lies massively to the right after you have turned left into Holland Street. Nothing could be less frivolous than this powerful, austere brick structure, but it is neither oppressive nor depressing and is a source of legitimate pride to its creators.

After the Town Hall, Holland Street becomes a pleasantly unpretentious lane of the kind that can be found in most cathedral cities – the cathedral here being Gilbert Scott's gigantic St Mary Abbots. The body of the church is correct but charmless Early English; the spire, 250 feet high and so among the ten highest in the kingdom, is awe-inspiring. If in need of a rest, duck down Kensington Church Walk to the right of Holland Street. A friendly and secluded garden nestles beside St Mary's and there is nearly always a bench vacant for the footsore.

Back into Holland Street, you cross Kensington Church Street and push on. York House Place becomes a footpath and leads, past one of the most expensive recent developments in London to the right, into Kensington Palace Gardens, or Palace Green, as the southern end of the road is known. Here one is in the heartland of bourgeois affluence, a series of sumptuous mansions, in a few cases designed to accommodate the aristocracy, more often intended for upwardly mobile members of the business and professional classes. Today it has become primarily an enclave for the grander, or anyway the richer, of foreign embassies. The avenue was originally laid out in the 1840s, mainly on the site of the former kitchen gardens of Kensington Palace. The Commissioners of Woods and Forests, who were responsible for the development, insisted that each building should cost at least £3,000; the amount was substantial for the time, but most of the purchasers spent far more.

There are a couple of buildings worth attention to the right. No.1 Palace Green, almost on Kensington High Street, was built by Philip Webb for the future Earl of Carlisle. There was a fearful row between the progressive aristocrat, who backed his brash young architect, and the First Commissioner, Charles Gore, who believed that architecture had stopped with Nash. Gore thought Webb's plans 'perfectly hideous… far inferior to any on the estate; too much brick, too steep a roof, against every classical tradition'. There was some compromise, but the result is far more Webb than Gore: an impressively assertive building though a little cramped, as if hunching its shoulders preparatory to forcing its way through a narrow gap. Next door, at No.2, now the Israeli Embassy and thus anxiously policed, lived the novelist Thackeray. It was said the design was his own; certainly he took a keen interest, but Frederick Hering was the architect. Thackeray called it 'the reddest house in all the town', but today No.1 seems decidedly redder.

The real fun begins towards Notting Hill Gate, after Palace Green ends and the pleasure palaces confront each other across the tree-lined avenue. All are worth a look, but note in particular No.11, built for a rich Spanish merchant, with a ballroom added by Smirke in 1873, a château-like roof, and the interior sumptuously reconstructed for the Duke of Marlborough in the 1930s. It now houses the French ambassador. No.12 was designed in the office of Charles Barry and is a more modest first cousin to the Italianate clubs he built in Pall Mall – the Travellers and the Reform. The cotton merchant for whom it was created, Alexander Collie, went spectacularly bankrupt for £2 million in 1875. No.13 was the first to fall prey to a foreign ambassador, the Russian, in 1930. He must have felt out of place in such opulently capitalistic surroundings but announced that he intended to entertain five nights out of seven: 'a pleasant

Albert Memorial

prospect for Rothschild who lives just opposite,' wrote a neighbour sourly. The Rothschild mansion – Nos.18 and 19 – was sold in 2004 for £70 million, a world-record price for a private residence. Most exotic of all, though, is No.24, where Vulliamy – in a very different mood to when he built St Barnabas, Addison Road – decided the spirit of the Brighton Pavilion would successfully translate to Kensington and built this splendidly eclectic anglo-Moresque extravaganza.

If, instead of turning left or right when emerging from York House Place you push more or less straight on towards Kensington Palace, you enter the park and soon find yourself outside the heavily gilded gates that guard the statue of King William III and the south front of the palace that Christopher Wren rebuilt for

him. The gates are the grandest thing about it; the palace is substantial enough but unassumingly domestic compared with its near contemporaries, the Schönbrunn and Versailles.

Follow the Palace round to the left. As you enter the Palace grounds, on your left lies the elegant sunken garden of 1725, beautifully maintained and tranquil even at the busiest of times. Beyond is the entry into the Palace: Wren's splendid staircase, an enfilade of panelled state rooms with pompous flourishes added by William Kent, some minor pictures – all worth a visit but not a memorable experience. The Orangery to the north of the Palace – by Wren, Hawksmoor or Vanbrugh, or all may have had a hand in it – was built originally for banquets and still provides palatable tea and buns.

Kensington Gardens, to the east of the Palace, were laid out in the early 18th century and have been more or less open to the public ever since. Here, before the war, the nannies of Kensington wheeled their charges: the prams massive and, with luck, crested; the uniforms starched and formidable; the pecking order immutable. Now it is harassed mothers or au pairs in jeans, but the spirit of bourgeois gentility still hangs over the park. Princess Louise's statue of her mother, Queen Victoria, sits outside the east front of the Palace, looking across the Broad Walk to the Round Pond, where elderly gentlemen play with model yachts.

A few hundred yards beyond the Round Pond rears Watts's spirited statue, *Physical Energy*, a formidable horse and rider rampant that doubles, in Southern Africa, as a memorial for Cecil Rhodes. From there one can see how high-rise buildings threaten the precarious rusticity of the Gardens: Basil Spence's Knightsbridge Barracks to the south, the Hilton Hotel on Park Lane to the east, various blotchy monsterpieces along Bayswater. Most offensive of all are the roofs of the

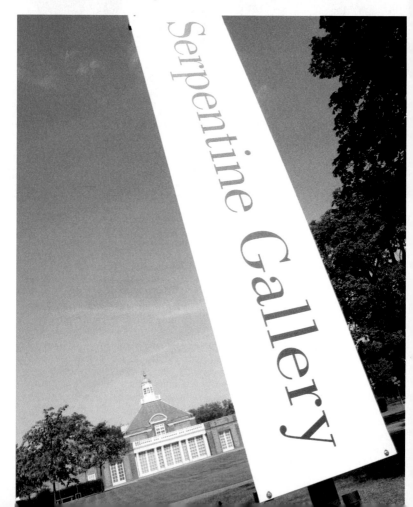

apartment block off York House Place, which mar the incomparable vista of St Mary Abbots and the Palace. It would have been worse if the Prince of Wales had not intervened and almost single-handedly thwarted the ambitions of the developers to push their penthouse flats still further into the stratosphere.

Another 400 yards or so beyond *Physical Energy*, in the north-eastern corner of the park, the Italianate Fountain Garden brings the Serpentine to a resounding close. Between there and Bayswater, Wren's brick and wood-panelled 'Alcove' that once controlled the entrance to the Palace sits in slightly self-conscious exile. Walking south from the fountains along the bank of the Serpentine one comes to George Frampton's statue of Peter Pan – it is insufferably twee, but the rabbits that encrust its base are still a source of delight to innumerable small children. The line of posts across the Serpentine in front of the statue shows that birds are better than nannies when it comes to preserving their pecking order. Cormorants have first claim on posts 12 to 17, except if a heron arrives, when all give way. On past Queen Caroline's handsomely proportioned summer house, designed by Kent, one comes to the Serpentine Gallery, a 1930s tea pavilion that has become the venue for some of London's most fashionably avant-garde exhibitions. At the time of writing it housed the work of a Japanese artist who makes sculptural installations from found and discarded material.

A deviation to the left will take you to the bizarrely moat-like Princess Diana Memorial Fountain – which has suffered immeasurable teething problems since its opening in July 2004 – before you curve back to the west to leave Kensington Gardens at the Albert Memorial. This is the gateway to the Albert Hall, Imperial College, the great museums. In that area, perhaps, even more than the rich streets through which we have just passed, lies the true triumph of the bourgeoisie. But that is another story and another walk.

Eating & drinking

Belvedere
Holland House, off Abbotsbury Road, W8 6LU (7602 1238). **Lunch served** noon-2.30pm Mon-Sat; noon-3pm Sun. **Dinner served** 6-11pm Mon-Sat. Extravagant French fare in a classy setting.

Elephant & Castle
40 Holland Street, W8 4LT (7368 0901). **Open** 11am-11pm Mon-Sat; noon-10.30pm Sun. Food served.

Holland Park Café
Holland Park, W8 6LU (7602 6156). **Open** 10am-30min before park closing time (dusk) daily.

Kandy Tea Room
4 Holland Street, W8 4LT (7937 3001). **Open** noon-5pm Wed-Fri; noon-6pm Sat, Sun.

The Orangery
Kensington Palace, Kensington Gardens, W8 3UY (7376 0239). **Open** *Oct-Easter* 10am-5pm daily. *Easter-Sept* 10am-6pm daily. Cakes and light meals.

Churches

St Barnabas Church
23 Addison Road, W14 8LH (7471 7000/www.stbk. org.uk). **Open** *Office* 10am-1pm, 2-5pm Mon-Fri. *Services* 9am, 10.30am, 7pm Sun; or by arrangement.

St Mary Abbots
corner of Kensington Church Street & Kensington High Street, W8 4LA (7937 5136/www.stmary abbotschurch.org). **Open** 7.10am-5.50pm Mon-Sat; 7.10am-8.15pm Sun. 28 services per week.

Houses, museums & parks

Holland Park
W11 (7602 9483/www.rbkc.gov.uk). **Open** dawn-dusk daily.

Kensington Gardens
W8 (7298 2100/www.royalparks.gov.uk). **Open** dawn-dusk daily.

Kensington Palace
W8 4PX (7937 9561/www.hrp.org.uk). **Open** *Mar-Oct* 10am-6pm daily. *Nov-Feb* 10am-5pm daily. Last admission 1hr before closing. **Admission** £11; £8.30 concessions; £7.20 5-15s; free under-5s; £32 family.

Leighton House
12 Holland Park Road, W14 8LZ (7602 3316/www. rbkc.gov.uk/leightonhousemuseum). **Open** 11am-5.30pm Mon, Wed-Sun. **Admission** £3; £1 concessions.

Serpentine Gallery
Kensington Gardens, nr Albert Memorial, W2 3XA (7402 6075/www.serpentinegallery.org). **Open** 10am-6pm daily. *Tours* 3pm Sat. **Admission** free.

Heaven on earth

Lucinda Lambton

Beneath the dramatic sarcophagi, obelisks and mausolea of Kensal Green lie some of the most colourful characters of the Victorian era.

> **Start and finish:** Kensal Green Cemetery entrance
> **Distance:** 1.5 miles/2km
> **Time:** 1 hour
> **Getting there:** Bakerloo line to Kensal Green, then 10-minute walk to cemetery entrance
> **Getting back:** reverse of above
> **Note:** check opening and closing times of the cemetery. Most graves are by the pathway, unless described as 'set in'. Could lead on to Margaret Drabble's walk (*see p220*).

Nothing could be more enlivening than a walk through Kensal Green Cemetery, London's first great necropolis, founded in 1832. Whatever your passion, it can be pursued within these walls. Surrounded by the scrunching cityscape of Harrow Road, you suddenly come upon it – a vast tract of arcadia. It is a place that makes your spirits – like those of the remarkable company that lie about you – reach for the skies.

A high wall and a classical gateway are but meagre clues to what lies beyond; pass under the arch and you are straightaway engulfed by glory. Where else in London can you find yourself surrounded by rampaging woodland, as well as by rural vistas as far as the eye can see, all enhanced by mausolea, monuments and memorials of every conceivable architectural style? Not only are the monuments rich and rare but the company they celebrate are startling in their singularity: Thackeray and Trollope lie here, as does Sir Charles Locock, who delivered all Queen Victoria's children.

Blondin the tightrope walker is buried at Kensal Green, as is WH Smith – with a marble book atop his grave. Charles and Fanny Kemble, father and daughter thespian stars, are here, as is John Smith, harpist to Queen Victoria. Elevated company whose bones lie beneath your feet.

Having entered through the Doric gateway, you turn right and, after staggering somewhat at the sight before your eyes, take a few steps and turn left on to the track 'South Avenue'. Follow the curve round and there, among the bulgingly mature chestnut, ash, plane, holly and beech, far over to the right, is a Gothic spire to Feargus O'Connor (1794-1855), the charismatic Chartist leader 'calculated to inspire the masses with awe'. A fiery radical who blazed through life, he was largely responsible for the Chartist movement. He died insane and a crowd of 50,000 came to his funeral at Kensal Green.

Look beyond the spire, to the left, where stands a Gothic canopy – under which two angels lurk – over the remains of George Augustus Frederick Percy Sydney Smythe, seventh Viscount Strangford (1818-57), believed to be the last person to have fought a duel in England, when, in 1852, he exchanged shots with his political rival in Canterbury. Described by Disraeli as 'a man of brilliant gifts, of dazzling wit, of infinite culture, and of fascinating manners', he was thought to be the model for the hero of *Coningsby*. He died aged 40, worn out by dissipation, brandy and water, and a delicate chest. 'Poor George,' lamented Lord Lyttleton at the time, 'he was a splendid failure'.

Facing Smythe there stands a stone cross to Philip Hardwick (1792-1870), architect of the Euston Arch so shamefully destroyed in 1962.

Back on the path and on you stroll, convinced by now that you are in the depth of the country, despite certain knowledge that the vast Sainsbury's 'module' and the Harrow Road are but yards away.

Your next goal is the white stone slab surrounded by railings in memory of William Makepeace Thackeray (1811-63) on the right. Author of (among others) *Vanity Fair* and *Barry Lyndon*, Thackeray, according to Mrs Thomas Carlyle, 'beat Dickens out of the world'. Dwell for a moment on his funeral, which took place here in 1863. Dickens was one of the chief mourners (having quarrelled for years, they had shaken hands only days before), as were the painters Millais and Frith. John Leech, the great cartoonist, was at the graveside, some six feet away from where he himself was to be buried the following year. George Cruikshank the caricaturist was also there, as were Browning and Anthony Trollope (whose bones you will be standing over before long). According to a contemporary account, there were occasional melancholy interruptions of weeping but 'more obtrusive were the cracks of sportsmen's rifles from the neighbouring fields, causing the horses to champ their bits in noisy restlessness'. It must have been a mighty coffin as Thackeray was over six feet three inches tall and his vast head housed a brain weighing 58 ounces. 'One of the greatest brains that England ever knew… its fiery fervour, its superb indignation against hypocrisy, pretension and deceit… is now hushed in the terrible serenity of death.' Its 'fiery fervour' had no doubt been ignited by his experience when, as a terrified six-year-old, he had been sent to see Napoleon on St Helena. The ex-Emperor, he was told, was 'eating three sheep a day and as many little children as he could catch'.

To the right and one plot further on, beneath a marble ledger whose inscription is sadly worn, lies his friend from schooldays to death, the famed cartoonist John Leech, 'the pictorial pillar of *Punch*', for which he drew some 3,000 illustrations. Described as a man of 'singularly handsome presence', his delight was to record life 'of a mirth-provoking kind'. Thanks, though, to ceaseless work wearing out his nervous system, he was to perish when only 47, due, according to Mark Lemon – an ex-editor of *Punch* – to 'the continual visitation of street bands and organ grinders'.

A step or two further, behind three rounded tombstones to the right, is the gabled ledger to Andrew Pears (died 1845). Founder of the Pears Soap and Perfume Company, he forced it to the fore in the late 19th century.

With the path becoming ever more rural in its roughness and the trees ever more enveloping with their size, you turn right just before a pink obelisk, on to a tiny grass path. Before this ends, on your right is the block of marble to Isambard Kingdom Brunel (1806-1859) along with his father Sir Marc Isambard Brunel (1769-1849). Brunel senior designed the

William Makepeace Thackeray

Thames Tunnel, while his son was of course responsible for the triumphant design of bridges, steamships and railways. The Great Western, passing hard by the cemetery, is in thundering earshot of his final resting place today.

Left, beneath a pink ledger, lies Sir Henry Hawkins (Baron Brampton, 1817-1907), Counsel for the defence of Arthur Orton, the notorious 'Tichborne Claimant', whose foible it was to ensure that his court had no fresh air and was as hot as it was possible to bear. He earned the soubriquet of 'Hanging Hawkins'.

Into Central Avenue and left. Here indeed is the Kingdom of Heaven on Earth, with vast trees shading lofty spires and striking temples. Obelisks soar, columns and caryatids support canopies, stone flames leap and angels fly.

Tear yourself away from the temptation to glide through these glories and look left on a Gothic sarcophagus – designed by William Burges – to Captain Charles Spencer Ricketts (1804-60), who joined the navy when he was only seven years old and served under Nelson.

Now hurl yourself into the celestial spheres of the Central Avenue, where your first stop should be on the left at the memorial to Major-General Sir William Casement (1780-1844), with four life-size 'telamones' dressed as servants of the British Raj, supporting a canopy over his military impedimenta. After serving in India for 47 years and six months he was about to return home, 'crowned', according to a contemporary report 'with well-merited honours and distinctions… when he was swayed by a sense of duty to defer his departure – a step which exposed him to the fatal attack which terminated his valuable life at Cossipore in 1844.' In death as in life, Casement is surrounded by luminaries of the Raj, with scores of them buried at Kensal Green.

On your right is a canopy resembling a four-poster bed which shelters William Mulready RA (1786-1863). With his face carved from his death mask, he lies on a

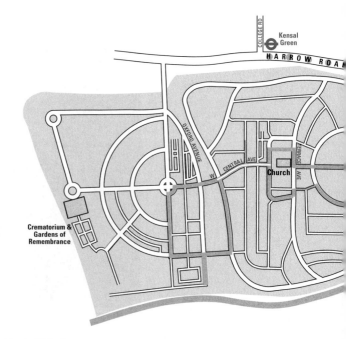

woven' stone mat of straw, laid on to a fringed bier, beneath which are carved scenes and implements of the artist's life. The son of an Irish maker of leather breeches, he was to design the first one-penny pre-paid envelope as well as becoming an artist and prolific illustrator. His works for children included *The Butterfly's Ball* and *The Lobster's Voyage to the Brazils* as well as *The Cullen Woman*. The monument was designed by Godfrey Sykes.

Next on your right is the most delicate of all monuments – to Mary Eleanor Gibson, who died in 1872. Angels fly forth from a richly carved and multi-corinthian columned canopy. It was designed by John Gibson, whose other architectural exercises await you on your walk.

Immediately to the left of the path you see the sombrely soaring obelisk to Sir Richard Mayne (1796-1868), the first joint commissioner of the Metropolitan Police (he second, Sir Charles Rowan, is in the

catacombs). Together they organised the training of men in duties hitherto unknown.

Further ahead, on the left, looms the vast memorial to Edmund Molyneux (1798-1864). Sadly truncated, with its fancy finialed spire removed, it is nevertheless alarmingly substantial. It was designed by John Gibson (whose remains are but a leap away) and commemorates the life of a solicitor who was Consul for Georgia.

On you step to see, right, the worryingly weathering red flame-topped cenotaph to Frederick Albert Winsor (1763-1830), he who brought gas lighting to Britain – as well as to Paris (he is in fact buried at Père Lachaise). In 1807, he lit up part of Pall Mall, to the sneering scorn of all. Even Sir Walter Scott weighed into the fray: gas was 'offensive, dangerous, expensive and unmanageable… he must be a madman who proposed to light London with smoke'. The memorial is emblazoned with such suitable sayings as 'At Evening Time there shall be Light'.

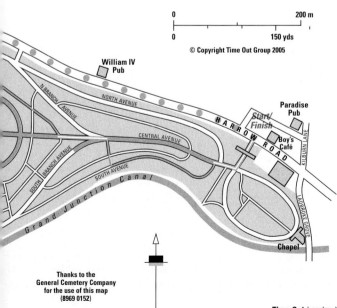

Thanks to the
General Cemetery Company
for the use of this map
(8969 0152)

Set in left, terrific and towering, is the polychrome Gothic mausoleum to John Gibson (1817-92), the architect who helped Barry with the drawings for the rebuilding of the Houses of Parliament.

Back on Central Avenue and on your left lies the elegantly lumpen sarcophagus to John Cam Hobhouse (Baron Broughton de Gyfford, 1786-1869), Lord Byron's best man and the poet's most intimate friend – the fourth canto of *Childe Harold* was dedicated to him. Member of Parliament and minister in Whig cabinets, he was imprisoned in Newgate for breach of parliamentary privilege in 1819. It was he who invented the term 'His Majesty's Opposition' for the anti-ministerial side of the House.

Now for a treat on your left. The Egyptian mausoleum to Andrew Ducrow (1793-1842), a showman of dazzling appearance and ability who, while dressed as a Roman statue or a Chinaman, would ride or drive as many as nine horses at once. He was famed, too, for 'Poses Plastique Equestre', striking attitudes as Zephyr or Mercury or otherwise a 'Yorkshire Foxhunter' while controlling horses at the gallop. 'The creatures were but the air on which he flew,' wrote one enraptured critic. 'What Godlike grace in that volant motion, fresh from Olympus, ere new lighted on some Heaven kissing hill.' There were elegant variations, when the curtain would rise to reveal Ducrow, in skin-tight marbled attire, motionless atop a plinth. Gradually his poses would change, from one antique statue to another. He died in 1842, a few days after his favourite horse John Lump. His hat and gloves – of stone – lie to the right of his extravagant mausoleum. This was a building of 'ponderous coxcombry', growled *The Builder* in 1836, after Ducrow had had it designed for his wife the year before. Dreadful scenes took place at her burial, with the showman, on finding the ground full of water, calling the priest 'a swindling old humbug' and marching off with the cemetery keys.

This fantastical building cost £3,000 – th equivalent of about £150,000 today.

Opposite is the temple-topped monument – sheltering the figure of Queen Hygea – to John St John Long (1798-1834), a 'quack doctor' who claimed to have hit upon new cures for consumption, rheumatism and other ailments by applying corrosive liniments and friction. Three of his patients died and he himself succumbed to consumption – aged only 37 – having steadfastly refused to take his own medicine. His epitaph is revealing: 'It is the fate of most men to have many enemies and few friends… John St John Long… Without comment.' The memoria – designed within St John Long's lifetime – was by Robert Sievier, who also lies within these walls.

On up the avenue, right, under a cross carved with vines (to the left of the seven pink obelisk), lies Frederick Salmon (178 1868), founder of St Mark's Hospital in 1835, originally 'The Infirmary for the Poor Afflicted with Fistula and other Diseases of the Rectum'. Salmon operated on Dickens for fistula.

Left is a triumph of chaste classicism with the extra and delightful detail of a carved tree within its pediment. It is the mausoleum to Captain George Aikman VC, a hero of the Indian Mutiny, who, with only 100 men, routed the 700-strong enemy at Amethi.

Right, classicism at its most severe wit the mausoleum to Dr George Birkbeck (1776-1841), founder of Birkbeck College, as well as being one of the founders of University College London. He also established the first mechanics institute in Britain.

Next plot but one on the right is the wrecked and ruined pink granite stump of a memorial, to the top-of-his-tree cartoonist, illustrator and ardent abolitionist George Cruikshank (1792-1878), who is in fact buried in St Paul's Cathedral. A social and political cartoon by the time he was 20 – with such barbs at Napoleon as 'little Boney gone to pot' – his fame grew great. He illustrated everything from Dickens to Grimm's fairy tales, although, according to Cruikshank himself, 'the great event of his artistic life' was to produce an unforgeable one pound note. The horror of seeing women forgers hanging from the gallows at Newgate had spurred him to action. His bust by Behnes (whose remains lie nearby) was stolen. A marble copy survives in Dickens's house in Doughty Street.

When you step into the next circle, look back to your right and relish the row of seven fine memorials that represent every architectural style. Although 'the Battle of the Styles' was raging while the cemetery was built, the results at Kensal Green were of happy contrast rather than conflict.

On the second half of the right curve into the circle sits the black pedestal to Hugh Falconer (1808-65), who established the tea industry in India. An ardent palaeontologist as well as a botanist, he returned from India with no fewer than five tons of fossil bones.

Onwards towards the chapel and to the right is the sarcophagus to Catherine Hayes Bushnell (1825-61), a soprano of whom it was said 'nature moulded and art polished to charm the world with music'. The cemetery guide of the day wrote that we must not feel sad 'when we look at all that is left to remind us of one who had the power to entrance and sway us with her sweet warbling… let us be gladdened with the thought that her soul, so full of divine melody, has gone to the realms where heavenly music echoes through the mansions of the just, and angels tune their harps to sing the praises of the creator.'

Step out of the sombre shadows of Centre Avenue, to be overawed by the Anglican Mortuary Chapel – the classical diadem of this bejewelled beauty of a cemetery – designed by JW Griffith and William Chadwick. To your left, raised on high, is the elegant marble sarcophagus – greyhound-like with its slender legs – to Princess Sophia (1777-1848), one of

George III's 15 offspring. Having had a child by an 'ugly old devil' of a courtier called William Garth, she had a desolate life and was to die totally blind aged 72.

To the right, beneath grey granite slabs, lies her brother, the Duke of Sussex (1773-1843). Augustus Frederick was a political progressive who supported parliamentary reforms galore, as well as being a genuine eccentric with artistic, scientific and intellectual interests. His house, alive with the sound of dozens of chiming clocks and singing birds, was jam-packed with over 50,000 books, including 1,000 Bibles. Great bronze chains were once festooned between the bollards surrounding the tomb. Sadly, they are no more, gone the same way as so many details that once graced Kensal Green, either stolen, vandalised or destroyed. The Duke, by choosing to be buried here – thanks to the fudging of William IV's funeral at Windsor – gave eminent respectability to the cemetery.

Step through the colonnade of the chapel and sense a most magical magnet beneath your feet, drawing you downward to those who lie in the catacombs below. Think, for example, of George Polgreen Bridgtower, a mulatto violinist to whom Beethoven dedicated the Kreutzer Sonata. Then there is Sir William Beatty, Nelson's surgeon at Trafalgar, who lies a stone's throw from Thomas Wakley, the medical reformer who founded *The Lancet*. Augusta Leigh – Byron's half-sister – lies nearby. There they all are, in rotting coffins, studded with gilt-headed nails, and resplendent with red, purple and brown velvet. Row upon row of fancifully formed plaques, their rust glistening like jewels, revealing the names of every occupant.

Above ground, glance to your right before you step on to the path and you will see through a stone doorway Georgina Clementson, whose father designed Trafalgar Square. She died when only 34.

On down Centre Avenue and first right on to a grassy path. 18 or so plots down on the left is the cross to Wilkie Collins

(1824-89), author of *The Woman in White*, *The Moonstone*, as well as *No Name* and *Armadale*, to name but four of his miraculously mysterious creations. He is buried with his mistress – the inspiration for *The Woman in White*.

Return to the main path and diagonally opposite you see the memorial to Blondin the tightrope walker. Emile Blondin (1824-97) walked over Niagara Falls on his 1,000-foot rope in 1859. He was then to walk it blindfold, then on stilts and yet again with his manager on his back. That same poor fellow was then pushed over in a wheelbarrow. Blondin's final flourish was to stop halfway along this perilous progress, set down a stove and cook and eat an omelette.

Take the next grass path to the left and 27 plots along on the right is the pink granite ledger to Anthony Trollope (1815-82), author of the likes of *The Barchester Chronicles* and *The Way We Live Now*. Having left school barely able to write, he became a clerk at the Post Office, where he worked in tandem with writing for the rest of his life. Here then lies the man who, as well as writing *The Eustace Diamonds*, also invented the postbox.

Back on to the main avenue, turn left and see before you on your right the magnificent mausoleum to the Duke of Cambridge (1819-1904), grandson of George III. He lies within these tapering Egyptian walls with his morganatic wife Sarah Fairbrother, the dancer and actress who specialised in 'breeches roles'. In contravention of the Royal Marriages Act they were 'married' and she became Mrs Fitzgeorge.

On you march, taking the fourth left (at the wooded 'roundabout'), and just before a path to the right, look in ten or so plots to the left, where – joy of joys – you will see a stone armchair. It honours Henry Russell (1812-1900), singer and composer – and a pupil of Rossini – whose music included 'Life on the Ocean Wave', 'There's a Good Time Coming, Boys' and of course 'The Old Arm Chair'. He

performed throughout America, and it is said, most surprisingly, that he had an enormous influence enticing immigration to the West. He composed some 800 songs in his 88 years.

Turn left at the bottom of the path and 15 plots along on your left is a cross to George Grossmith (1847-1912), author – along with his brother Weedon – of *The Diary of a Nobody*. He was also a singer – responsible for 'creating' a quantity of Gilbert and Sullivan's roles, such as the Major-General in *The Pirates of Penzance* and Bunthorne in *Patience*. With 'the agility and droll dignity of his small frame' – according to a critic – he was KoKo in the *Mikado*, as well as the Lord Chancellor in *Iolanthe*. An extra and joyful discovery: he wrote 'See me Dance the Polka'.

Take your first turning right to the most poignant memorial of all. Go further than you would think and there on the left behind a bush is a tiny cross – with letters by Eric Gill – to Marigold Churchill (1918-21), Winston and Clementine's daughter, who died of meningitis when only two and a half years old. Always known as 'Duckadilly', she was born four days after Armistice Day. A year after her death Churchill's grief, when writing to his wife, was still raw: 'I pass through again those sad scenes last year when we lost our dear Duckadilly. Poor lamb, it is a gaping wound whenever one touches it and removes the bandages and plasters of everyday life.' There was once a bench opposite the grave where he would come and sadly sit.

Back up the path and turn right where you will face a hill, amid seemingly endless space and with a lone poplar on the horizon. Glance to your right and down on the left is an open marble book atop a pink chest tomb. It is to WH Smith (1792-1865), whose mother founded the great chain of stores that still bear his name.

Retrace your steps and continue up towards Central Avenue, and then right on the avenue to return to the chapel.

...ke of **Cambridge**, grandson of George III.

...ght again before the chapel and from
...re you see London beneath you,
...ddenly and surreally part of your
...chly rural surroundings.

Follow the path round and on your left,
...dden by trees and bushes, is the largest
...ot in the cemetery, to the fifth Duke
...Portland (1800-79). William John
...avendish-Bentinck-Scott is underground
...death as he was in life when, between
...54-79, he burrowed and built a network
...underground chambers, as well as
...nnels and pigsties, stables and even
...eenhouses, at Welbeck Abbey in
...ottinghamshire. A man of startlingly
...clusive habits, he would seldom venture
...rth from his rooms, which were served
...ith particularly peculiar arrangements.
...ne, the 'perpetual chicken', was that a
...wl should be forever roasting on a spit,
... that whenever the Duke felt peckish,
...could be dispatched at speed along an
...nderground railway from the kitchen to

his rooms. He built a colossal underground
ballroom, although sadly no guest was
ever to prance on its floor.

A few yards on, at the end of the track,
turn and look left at an especially pleasing
mausoleum – one of the few left at Kensal
Green with their original doors. Opposite
is a grass path. Turn down it and first on
your left is a bulging and smooth-as-silk
slate boulder to Erich Fried (1921-88),
Austrian poet and translator. This is one
of the few, but now, thank God, growing
collection of good modern memorials.

Continue down the grass path and,
at the end, look left at the extraordinary
confection of a sarcophagus to William
Holland (1779-1856), of the famed Holland
and Holland furniture makers whose pieces
enriched houses – including Balmoral and
Osborne – throughout the land.

Once on this small curved path you are
in the Circle. Turn right and look back.
Here, slicing through your senses, you see
the full horror of the descent of funereal
art today. Stare straight ahead and your
every artistic sensibility is satisfied. Look
down about your feet, and every one is
dashed. As with architecture, so, too,
with this miniature branch of structural
design, the blighting blank modernist
block of the 1950s, '60s, '70s and '80s
reigned supreme. But here the similarity
ends. The great improvements that have
swept through the architectural world in
the last ten years have been missed by
the monumental mason.

Walking through today's cemeteries
and graveyards is like being in the
most brutalist of developments, with
one hideous difference: they are still
being built, hand over fist, with the same
blinkered fervour of the post-war years.
Great tracts of consecrated land continue
to fall victim to what can only be
described as a grotesque modernistic
world in miniature. Rules and regulations
as to the size, height and material of
memorials have resulted in the grimmest
uniformity. Democracy in life has become
a dictatorship in death, with every one of

Kensal Green Cemetery is characterised by architectural variety.

s forced to suffer a Ceaucescu-like
egimentation of marble and stone blocks,
ding roughshod over our remains. Even
he most aesthetically aware now have to
nd their days under a banal block on the
andscape. The graveyards of the past
ere intended as morally uplifting oases,
eflecting the tastes, the dreams and the
deals of the age. What in Heaven's name
o today's sterile stumps, relieved only by
risly green marble chippings, reflect of
ur dreams today? The tide is starting to
urn, however, and signs of this longed-for
hange can now be seen, with a handful of
maginatively carved and lettered modern
nemorials at Kensal Green. Let us do all
hat we can to support today's craftsmen
f the churchyard and cemetery.

There is one beacon shining hope
nto their midst. Harriet Frazer, with her
rganisation Memorials by Artists, has
stablished a nationwide service to put
he bereaved in touch with craftsmen
uited to their needs. Thanks to her,
here are now some hundreds of modern
nemorials beautifying Britain today.

Continue along the grass path walking
way from the chapel, and to your right
ou will see the urned pedestal to John
iston (1776-1864), George IV's favourite
omedian, whose face, according to
azlitt, was always 'bathed in jests'.

Further on, left, a pink plinth to Joseph
ocke (1805-60), a great builder of railways
said to be of the same rank as Stephenson
nd Brunel. He was given the Legion of
onour by both Louis-Philippe and
apoleon III.

At the next crossroads you will find
ree great mausolea, each on a corner.
nmediately on your left, however, is the
ddly sweeping urn-topped obelisk to Dr
hn Elliotson (1791-1868), the first to use a
ethoscope in Britain and apparently one
the first 19th-century physicians to 'wear'
beard. He was largely responsible for
unding University College Hospital and
as an ardent mesmerist who convinced
th Thackeray and Dickens of his powers.
hackeray dedicated *Pendennis* to him.

Opposite, to the left of the coroneted
mausoleum, is Dr John Bright's empty
plot (1789-1858). His ledger stone was
destroyed by a bomb in World War II.
Physician Extraordinary to Queen
Victoria, he made many medical
discoveries. One, an ailment of the
liver, was of course 'Bright's Disease'.

Step south and on the left corner is the
mausoleum to Sir John Dean Paul (died
1852), who was responsible for buying
the land for Kensal Green Cemetery,
thereby giving the dead, as well as the
living, such repose in the place today.

A tiny and tempting detour is to walk
south (right) 22 plots and look left to the
gabled ledger over the body (although
not the head, which is in Lincoln's Inn
Fields) of Charles Babbage (1791-1871),
who first thought of 'calculating
numerical tables by machinery' in
1812. Between 1820-22 he devised his
'analytical engine' – with perforated
cards – and so invented the computer.

Retrace your steps and turn right at the
mausolea and proceed around the Circle.
Behind an ivy-clad mausoleum and set
in four to the left you see the curious
memorial to Thomas de la Rue (1793-1866),
founder of the great printing firm. Playing
cards were his forte and it was he who
first patented iridescent film on paper. To
discover a 'first' in any field is exhilarating.
In the Elysian fields of Kensal Green there
are almost as many such discoverers as
there are blades of grass.

On your right and barely visible
beneath two shifted stone slabs, lies
William Behens (1795-1864), the sculptor.
His art was ranked high but his habits
so low that his respectable brother was
forced to change his name. His busts of
both Cruikshank and Thomas Hood at
Kensal Green have been destroyed by
vandals as you can see with the next
stop (left), where the likeness of Thomas
Hood (1798-1845) was once proudly on
display. Beneath the pink pedestal lies
the humorous and whimsical poet who
most famously plunged into pathos with
his 'Song of the Shirt':

'Stitch stitch stitch
In poverty hunger and dirt
And still with a voice of dolorous pitch
She sung the song of the shirt.'

Hood was beset by misfortune, and at one point mortgaged his brain with the publishers for cash. 'The tragic necessity laid upon him of jesting for a livelihood while in the very grasp of death,' wrote a contemporary, 'imparts painful interest to his biography.'

Opposite stands an obelisk to Michael William Balfe (1808-70), baritone and composer admired and befriended by both Cherubini and Rossini. His own opera *The Bohemian Girl* is famed to this day, as is his setting of 'Come into the Garden, Maud'.

Six plots on to the right is the stern urn to John Claudius Loudon (1783-1843), for years my hero, with his tomes on architecture, art, horticulture and agriculture. He was one of the first to lay out public parks and squares and furthermore designed the wrought-iron glazing bar that enabled conservatories to burst forth with such bulging forms as can be seen at Kew.

Four plots on and on the left lies Sarah Lane (1822-99), the actress of whom it was written that 'the pantomime fairy that she displayed at Christmas was less important than the everyday fairy she played amongst the homes of the poor'.

Look diagonally right to a thick unadorned column over Francis Freeling (1764-1836), reformer of the Post Office, who, according to the Duke of Wellington, made Britain's the best in the world. Thomas Hood so admired Freeling that he named his daughter after him – 'Frances Freeling Hood' – surname and all.

Across Centre Avenue and along on the right towards the end of the path, set in and framed by ivy, is the chest tomb to 'The Great Deliverer of his Country', Sir Charles Locock (1799-1875), 'accoucheur' to Queen Victoria, who brought all her children into the world, while introducing her to chloroform. Not only that, he also delivered the Kaiser.

Retrace your steps by one plot and take a tiny path into the trees to the left. Straight ahead and rearing up in the distance you will see the giant form of 'Hope' over the remains of Alexis Benoit Soyer (1809-58). Inventor of 'fast food' in that, with his 'magic stove' and other methods, he worked dietary miracles in the Irish potato famine as well as reorganising the cooking for the entire army in the Crimean War. Soyer was originally a swell chef par excellence, for princes and grandees galore. His great triumph was at the Reform Club – breakfast for 2,000 at Queen Victoria's coronation.

Admire it from afar and go on along the small path to the right and before the pink obelisk on the left lies Soomar Goodeve Chuckerbutty (1826-74), one of the first Indians to be made a doctor under Western teaching.

At the kink in the path turn left on to another and six from the end look left, se in, to the ordinary headstone of Dr James Barry (1795-1865), concealing the most extraordinary life of all. For 'James' Barr was a woman, who spent her entire life a a man in the army, entering as a hospital assistant and scaling the ranks to becom a surgeon – with all the pre-anaesthetic horrors – then rising to Inspector Genera Lord Albermarle described 'him' as 'the most wayward of men; in appearance a beardless lad… there was a certain effeminacy about his manner which he was always striving to overcome. His style of conversation was greatly superio to that one usually heard at the mess tab in those days.' Remarkably, he was often accused of breaches of discipline. He had a quarrelsome temper and even fought a duel when stationed at the Cape. It was said that the servant who waited on him for years had not the slightest suspicion of his true sex.

Join the tarmac path ahead, turn right and after 40 yards on the right – one of the most pleasing of architectural details within these walls – is a supremely solid

dimented canopy, with a Graeco-
yptian head at each corner. It
nmemorates John Gordon (1802-40),
andowner in the West Indies.
All but spent with elevated exhaustion,
u stagger into Centre Avenue once again.
the left, after 40 yards, another sculptural
ity: a massive marble pedestal writhing
th a quantity of curls and curves. It
nmemorates Frank McClean (1837-
04), astronomer, who built the Cape of
od Hope telescope. Also buried is his
her, John Robinson McClean (1813-73),
civil engineer who worked on Paris for
poleon III as well as for the Viceroy of
ypt on the Suez Canal.
Delight in the bronze palm leaves
o plots on to the left and drink in
lamenting beauty on the Michaelis
nument on the same side. Two rows
diagonally right, is the grave of Rose
Clercq (1845-99), the actress who played
first Lady Bracknell in *The Importance
Being Ernest*. She mourned at Wilkie
llins's funeral within these walls. Salute,
b, the size of the obelisk on your left to
eph Richardson (1790-1855), 'Inventor
the Instruments of the Rock Roll, Bell
d Steel Band', and last but by no means
st (never has this saying been more
thfully said) halt before the mausoleum
your left. It honours Imre Kiralfy (1845-
19), designer of the White City Stadium
the Olympic Games in 1908.
fear you have pondered over a mere
ction of those who lie within these
lls. Raise a cheer to a few more
fore you go. To Major Charles Clopton
ingfield, who invented lawn tennis.
Sir Carl William Siemens, who laid
first Atlantic cable. To Edward
tor Seaton, whom we have to thank
compulsory vaccination. To Thomas
ncock, inventor of vulcanised rubber.
Sir John Ross, discoverer of the North
gnetic Pole. To Leigh Hunt, the first to
cover and publish Shelley and Keats.
Richard Boyle, who laid the Japanese
lways. To William Whiteley, founder of
department store where you could buy

anything 'from a pin to an elephant'.
Finally and deafeningly, it's hurrah
and huzzah to Sydney Smith, whose wit,
with such cracks as 'there are three sexes:
men, women and clergymen', must still
be resounding in the cemetery to this day.
What a gathering and a half. Look back
at the cemetery from afar, at the great
swathe of countryside cutting through
the chimneys – by day, green; by night,
jet black – and ponder on the people who
lie within its walls. I have never been in
any doubt that there is a perpetual party
going on – a glorious and glittering party
of 19th-century luminaries – for, if there
is life after death, you could find no more
vibrant a collection of characters than
those gathered together at Kensal Green.

Eating & drinking

Boy's Café
615 Harrow Road, W10 4RA (8969 9132). **Open**
11.30am-3pm, 5.30-11pm Mon-Sat; noon-3pm, 5-10pm
Sun. Thai food.

Paradise by Way of Kensal Green
19 Kilburn Lane, W10 4AE (8969 0098). **Open**
12.30-11pm Mon-Sat; noon-10.30pm Sun. Gastropub.

William IV
*786 Harrow Road, NW10 5JX (8969 5944/
www.william-iv.co.uk).* **Open** noon-11pm Mon-Thur;
noon-midnight Fri, Sat; noon-10.30pm Sun. Well-kept
real ales, good wines and a Mediterranean menu.

Information

Friends of Kensal Green Cemetery
*c/o Sam Bull, Flat 1, Cranfield Court, Homer Street,
W1H 4NB (7402 2749).* Tours of the cemetery: 2pm
every Sunday – *see below*.

General Cemetery Company
Harrow Road, W10 4RA (8969 0152).

Kensal Green Cemetery
*Harrow Road, W10 4RA (8969 0152/www.kensal
green.co.uk).* **Open** *Apr-Sept* 9am-5.30pm daily. *Oct-
Mar* 9am-4.30pm daily. *Tours* 2pm Sun; *tours incl
catacombs* 2pm 1st & 3rd Sun of mth (bring a torch).
Admission free. *Tours* £5 donation; £4 concessions.

Memorials by Artists
*Snape Priory, Snape, Saxmundham, Suffolk IP17
1SA (01728 688934/www.memorialsbyartists.co.uk).*

Contributors

Dan Cruickshank is the author of *London: the Art of Georgian Building* and *Life in the Georgian City*, and editor of the 20th edition of *The Sir Banister Fletcher History of Architecture*. He is also a regular presenter on BBC2, including the series *Around the World in Eighty Treasures*, and was visiting professor of architecture at the University of Sheffield.

Margaret Drabble writes both fiction and non-fiction. She has published 16 novels, most recently *The Red Queen* (2004). She has also written biographies of *Arnold Bennett* (1974) and *Angus Wilson* (1995). She edited *The Oxford Companion to English Literature*, of which the sixth edition appeared in 2000. She lives in London and West Somerset.

Dan Fielder is editor-in-chief of Sticky Content, a web writing and editing company. Clients include Heinz, Legal & General, Dare Digital and the Natural History Museum. He is a columnist for the *Sunday Express*, and has written for Radio 4's *Dead Ringers*.

William Forrester is a lecturer, tour guide and broadcaster. He has lectured for the National Portrait Gallery and the National Trust, and leads tours around London and the south-east. He has written and presented programmes for Central and Thames TV, as well as Radio 4. A wheelchair user himself, he has published *Access in London*, a guide to the capital for wheelchair users.

Margaret Forster is a writer of fiction and non-fiction. She has written more than 16 novels, including *Georgy Girl* (1965), *Have the Men Had Enough?* (1989), *Lady's Maid* (1990) and *Is There Anything You Want?* (2005). Her non-fiction includes *William Makepeace Thackeray: Memoirs of a Victorian Gentleman* (1978), *Elizabeth Barrett Browning* (1988), *Daphne du Maurier* (1993), *Hidden Lives* (1995), *Good Wives? Mary, Fanny, Jennie and me 1845-2001* (2001) and *Rich Desserts and Captain's Thin: A Family and Their Times, 1831-1931* (2004). She lives by Hampstead Heath and in Loweswater in Cumbria.

Darcus Howe is a writer and broadcaster. Presenter of Channel 4's cult programmes *The Devil's Advocate* and *The White Tribe*, he is also a *New Statesman* columnist and a regular contributor to the *Observer*. He lives in Brixton.

Robin Hunt may currently be in Budapest working on The Novel. Previously he lived in London and New York.

Robin James works in the House of Commons, currently as Clerk of the Home Affairs Select Committee. He lives in Hackney.

Liz Jensen is the author of five novels, most recently *War Crimes for the Home* and *The Ninth Life of Louis Drax*. She lives in Wimbledon.

Rick Jones is a freelance writer and teacher of modern languages. He was a *Time Out* columnist and music critic for the *Evening Standard*.

Kate Kellaway is a staff writer for the *Observer*. She has four children and lives in north London.

Irma Kurtz is an American-born freelance writer for national newspapers and magazines. She is the agony aunt for *Cosmopolitan* magazine and the author of several books, including *The Great American Bus Ride* and *Then Again: Travels in Search of my Younger Self*. She has lived in London for more than 30 years and currently lives in Soho.

Lucinda Lambton is a photographer, writer and broadcaster. The history of the lavatory and architecture for animals – with both books and films – are among her more obscure areas of expertise. *The A-Z of Britain* is just one series in the 51 programmes she has made for the BBC; she has made another 22 for ITV. With *Old New World*, she found her Old World roots in the New, and also proved that America is now more traditional than Europe. Her most recent film examined Jamaica's architectural heritage. She was elected Honorary Fellow of the Royal Institute of British Architects in 1997.

James Miller was born in London in 1976. He is currently writing a novel and completing a PhD in American Literature. His work has appeared in a number of anthologies. He lives in central London where he spends his time drinking coffee and pacing the streets.

Kim Newman's short stories have been collected in *The Original Dr Shade* and *Famous Monsters*; his novels include *The Night Mayor, Bad Dreams, The Quorum, Life's Lottery* and no Dracula. His non-fiction includes *Nightmare vies* and *Millennium Movies*. Born in Brixton, now lives in north London.

aham Norton is a brown-eyed fair-haired hman, standing a good five foot ten high. He ploys these attributes as a stand-up comedian Edinburgh Festivals and on nationwide tours, the has made countless TV and radio earances. He has won four British comedy ards and is probably best known as the host he BAFTA award-winning Channel 4 show *Graham Norton*.

omas Pakenham divides his time ween London and Ireland. He is the author *The Boer War* (1979), *The Scramble for ica* (1991), *Meetings with Remarkable es* (1996), *Remarkable Trees of the World* 03) and *Remarkable Baobab* (2004). His *untains of Rasselas* (1959) was re-issued 998.

ter Paphides spends most of his waking rs traversing the muddy ha-ha that divides enthood and journalism. His work can mostly found in *The Times*, *Observer Music Monthly*, jo and *Junior*. He has two daughters – Dora r) and Eavie (two) – both of whom agree that stern popular culture peaked with the 1973 ase of *Hocus Pocus* by Focus.

atibha Parmar is a filmmaker whose ny films have been shown on television and nternational film festivals. She has lived in don since 1967 and considers it her home.

n Richards is the author of five novels, latest of which – *The Mermaid and the inks* – was chosen for Richard and Judy's mmer reading list. He also writes for TV ere his credits include the BBC drama oks and Channel Four's *No Angels*.

Ruth Richardson is a historian, ter, broadcaster and a passionate Londoner. book *Death, Dissection & the Destitute* 01 Phoenix/Chicago University Press) s the story of corpses for dissection in context of British funerary culture, from Renaissance to the present day. She has lished many articles in medical and torical journals and has lectured in versities and medical schools in the , Europe, USA and Canada. She also adcasts for BBC Radio.

onne Roberts is an award-winning rnalist who has worked in television and vspapers since the 1970s. She is the author several books, including two novels, one of ich has recently been adapted for television. latest novel, *Shake!*, set in the 1960s, was lished in June 2005. A non-fiction work,

Open Heart Surgery, a year in the life of a relationship, is published by Short Books in 2006. She lives in south London with her family.

Jon Ronson is a writer and documentary filmmaker. He writes a column for the *Guardian* and has written the bestselling *Them: Adventures With Extremists* and *The Men Who Stare At Goats*. His documentaries include *Secret Rulers of the World* and *Tottenham Ayatollah*.

Martin Rowson's work appears regularly in, among other places, the *Guardian*, the *Times*, the *Scotsman*, the *Mirror*, the *Independent on Sunday* and *Tribune*. His books include cartoon versions of *The Wasteland* and *Tristram Shandy*. In 2001 he was appointed Cartoonist Laureate for London by Ken Livingstone, in return for one pint of beer per annum. He lives with his wife and two children in Lewisham.

Nicholas Royle was born in Manchester in 1963. He is the author of five novels – *Counterparts*, *Saxophone Dreams*, *The Matter of the Heart*, *The Director's Cut* and *Antwerp* – in addition to more than 100 short stories. He has edited 12 anthologies including *A Book of Two Halves*, *The Time Out Book of New York Short Stories* and *Dreams Never End*. He lives in Manchester with his wife and two children.

Joan Smith was born in west London. She is the author of five novels and several volumes of non-fiction, including *Misogynies* and *Moralities*. She is a newspaper columnist and critic, and writes regularly for *Tribune*. She chaired the PEN Writers in Prison Committee from 2000 to 2004.

Janet Street-Porter edited the *Independent on Sunday* for two years until July 2001, and is currently Editor at Large. She created a variety of television formats for young people, from *Network 7* for Channel Four to the *Rough Guide* series for the BBC. She set up *Live TV* in 1994, and has since presented several walking series for BBC television. She is Vice President of the Ramblers Association.

John Vidal is the environment editor of the *Guardian* and the author of *McLibel*. He has been Environment Journalist of the Year three times.

Philip Ziegler After 15 years in the Foreign Service, he became a publisher and worked with Collins until commissioned to write the official biography of Lord Mountbatten. Other biographies include those of Lord Melbourne, Edward VIII and Harold Wilson. He has also written *The Black Death*, *London at War*, *Soldiers: Fighting Men's Lives 1901-2001* and, most recently, *Rupert Hart-Davis: Man of Letters*.

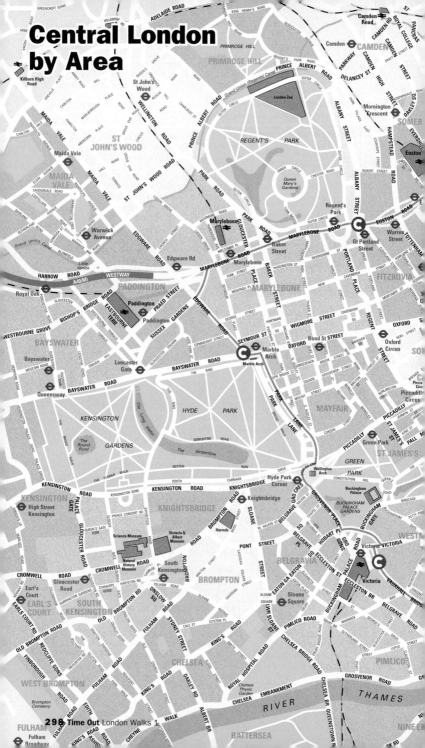

Central London
by Area

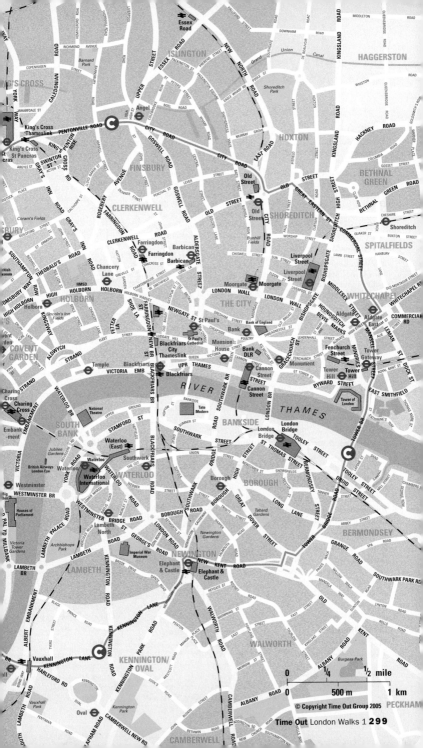

Walks for...

Architecture
Dan Cruickshank – the City's buildings explored. **Robin James** – Westminster's palace and cathedral. **Lucinda Lambton** – a celebration of funereal designs. **James Miller** – London's changing face. **Janet Street-Porter** – Clerkenwell's conversion. **Philip Ziegler** – Holland Park's 19th-century piles.

Art
William Forrester (*p58*) – tours of the National and Portrait galleries, and the British Museum. **William Forrester** (*p168*) – accessing the South Bank galleries. **Joan Smith** – Chiswick House and Hogarth's home. **Philip Ziegler** – Leighton House and the Serpentine Gallery.

Booklovers
Dan Fielder – reading matter to cleanse the soul. **Nicholas Royle** – Derek Marlowe's novels delivered across the city. **Janet Street-Porter** – second-hand delights of Clerkenwell.

Cemeteries & graveyards
Irma Kurtz – cruise by Brompton cemetery. **Lucinda Lambton** – the great and the good of Kensal Green. **Peter Paphides** – full Marx to Highgate. **Ruth Richardson** – bodysnatchers' hunting grounds. **Joan Smith** – Hogarth entombed.

Eating & drinking
Graham Norton – gay bars and clubs of Soho. **Pratibha Parmar** – enjoy the world's cuisines in Shoreditch. **Janet Street-Porter** – from pie and mash to self-service oriental.

Film & theatre
William Forrester (*p58*) – the curtain raised on the West End. **Kim Newman** – the horror flicks set in Soho. **Nicholas Royle** – location spotting for Nicolas Roeg's films.

Gardens & parks
Margaret Drabble – edging through Wormwood Scrubs. **Margaret Forster** – a circuit of the Heath. **Darcus Howe** – the highs of Brockwell Park. **Robin Hunt** – a dream residence in Regent's Park. **Kate Kellaway** – Parliament Hill and Boudicea's grave. **Robin James** – respite from intrigue in St James's. **Liz Jensen** – wombling on Wimbledon Common. **Rick Jones** – amble through woods and parkland. **Thomas Pakenham** – meetings with trees in Richmond and Kew. **Peter Paphides** – wild Hampstead Heath and tame Waterlow Park. **Yvonne Roberts** – Clapham and Wandsworth commons compared. **Jon Ronson** – quaint Mount Street Gardens. **Martin Rowson** – dramatic views from Hilly Fields. **Joan Smith** – Chiswick gardens for tea. **John Vidal** – parklands fronting the Thames, ending at Hampton Court. **Philip Ziegler** – a Japanese retreat and Kensington Gardens.

History
Dan Cruickshank – building the Square Mile. **Robin James** – nation-building at Westminster. **Lucinda Lambton** – past lives remembered. **Ruth Richardson** – medicine through time. **Joan Smith** – 18th-century Chiswick. **Philip Ziegler** – 19th-century Holland Park.

Nightime
Graham Norton – neon lights of Piccadilly and Soho. **Kim Newman** – the dark alleys and backstreets of horror film locations. **William Forrester** (*p168*) – the night lights of the South Bank.

Parents with children
Margaret Forster – ponds and kites on Hampstead Heath. **Robin Hunt** – play in the park by the zoo. **Liz Jensen** – water and windmills. **Rick Jones** – endless greenery and woodland. **Kate Kellaway** – childhood memories in Hampstead. **Lucinda Lambton** – leaping among the gravestones. **Thomas Pakenham** – hide and seek in the Isabella Plantation. **Peter Paphides** – tree-climbing, a cemetery and a tea room. **Martin Rowson** – short and sweet. **Joan Smith** – family picnic in Chiswick House grounds.

Shopping
Irma Kurtz – from Harrods to the Conran Shop. **Graham Norton** – spend the pink pound in Soho. **Jon Ronson** – some Mayfair stores and Shepherd's Market.

Religion
Dan Cruickshank – countless City churches. **Dan Fielder** – spiritual homes of all sorts. **Darcus Howe** – Brixton celebrates the sabbath. **Liz Jensen** – the Buddhist temple of Wimbledon. **Irma Kurtz** – Roman Catholic, Russian Orthodox and Anglican. **Ben Richards** – churches and mosques of the East End.

River & canals
Margaret Drabble – canalside by Kensal Green cemetery. **William Forrester** (*p168*) – exploring the South Bank. **Robin Hunt** – Regent's Canal by the zoo. **James Miller** – historic Bankside from London Bridge. **Thomas Pakenham** – a riverside walk from Richmond to Kew. **Pratibha Parmar** – a canalside link from Hoxton to Islington. **Ben Richards** – finish in a historic riverside pub. **Joan Smith** – riverside pubs line the route to Hammersmith. **John Vidal** – riverside along the Thames Path.

Woods
Margaret Forster – Caen wood on Hampstead Heath. **Rick Jones** – Lesnes Abbey and Oxleas woods. **Thomas Pakenham** – ancient oaks in Richmond Park.